Making Good Citizens

Making Good Citizens

Education and Civil Society

Edited by
Diane Ravitch and
Joseph P. Viteritti

Yale University Press

New Haven & London

Designed by Rebecca Gibb.
Set in Adobe Garamond type by The Composing Room of Michigan, Inc.
Printed in the United States of America by Vail-Ballou Press, Binghamton, New York.

Library of Congress Cataloging-in-Publication Data

Making good citizens : education and civil society / edited by Diane Ravitch and
    Joseph P. Viteritti.
        p.   cm.
    Includes bibliographical references and index.
    ISBN 0-300-08878-7 (cloth : alk. paper)
    1. Citizenship—Study and teaching—United States.   2. Civics—Study and
teaching—United States.   3. Education—Aims and objectives—United States.
I. Ravitch, Diane.   II. Viteritti, Joseph P., 1946—   .
    LC1091 .M28   2001
    370.11′5—dc21

                                                                2001000692

A catalogue record for this book is available from the British Library.

10   9   8   7   6   5   4   3   2   1

Contents

Acknowledgments

This symposium was conceived with the cooperation and support of the Smith Richardson Foundation, and with additional funding from the Lynde and Harry Bradley Foundation. The book is one of a series published under the auspices of the Program on Education and Civil Society at New York University, sponsored by the John M. Olin Foundation with additional support from the Achelis and Bodman Foundations. The views expressed in the chapters are solely attributable to their authors.

Once again we are grateful for the opportunity to work with an excellent staff of professionals at Yale University Press. We owe special thanks to John Covell, who supported the project with great enthusiasm, Susan Arellano, for seeing it through to completion, and Dan Heaton for his extraordinary skills as a manuscript editor. We also want to thank our research assistant Kevin Kosar and administrative assistant Joyce Kong for their help in the preparation of the manuscript.

Introduction

Diane Ravitch and Joseph P. Viteritti

The last decade of the twentieth century will be remembered by scholars of civic education as a time when research and social commentary converged to call into question the condition of American democracy. Robert Putnam's striking metaphor of "bowling alone" resonated with many as an accurate description of the problematic state of our civic life. Putnam claimed that Americans had become less inclined to join the voluntary associations that for generations had served as the backbone of their communities and expressions of their common ideals.[1] In a provocative essay published in 1995, he laid out a disturbing array of empirical evidence showing that membership was down in such long-established volunteer organizations as Parent-Teacher Associations, the Boy Scouts, and the Red Cross, as well as fraternal societies like the Lions, the Elks, the Jaycees, and the Masons, and women's groups such as the League of Women Voters and the Federation of Women's Clubs.[2]

The apparent civic disengagement of large numbers of Americans was especially startling in a country that Tocqueville once described as a nation of joiners.[3] Civil society—that noncommercial aspect of community life that exists somewhere between the individual and government—is an essential part of the American formula for democracy. It is inside the clubs, churches, and neighborhood associations composing civil society where people develop the skills and attitudes required for cooperative social action, characteristics that build trust, reciprocity, generosity, and public spirit.[4] These same local organizations also serve as an important buffer between our private lives and government authority, a middle ground that is indispensable in a free society.[5]

To be sure, Putnam's thesis evoked some strong dissents. The late Everett Carl Ladd was one of the most outspoken critics of the decline thesis. Roper Center data cited in his book showed that although PTA membership was down, parents were forming and joining new organizations within their school districts that were not tied to professional interests and teachers' unions. In the eyes of many parents, the national PTA appears to have lost its grassroots base as a voice for parents and is frequently perceived as a representative of the interests of professionals rather than children. Although many of the old-line civic associations are losing membership, other groups like environmental organizations and soccer leagues are experiencing growth.[6] Some surveys indicate that the same people who are reluctant to join established organizations on a long-term basis are apt to volunteer a few hours a week at a local charity or community group. Over the past decade the nature of civic involvement has undergone significant changes, Ladd argued, but it is not necessarily on the decline.

Sociologist Robert Wuthnow maintains that in a highly mobile contemporary society, neighborhoods and places of residence are not the enclaves that they used to be. Community is defined less by geography and more in terms of a commonality of interests among like-minded people whose membership in organizations is temporary and fluid.[7] The porous organizations to which they belong, or pass through, are often brought together in response to specific needs that allow individuals to participate in projects with definite objectives attainable over a relatively short period of time, such as a food drive during the holiday season or a campaign to launch a new playground. Indeed, the activities that take place in such settings represent an important kind of civic involvement, but it is questionable whether the "loose connections" they engender among people constitute a viable substitute for the bedrock community associations of yesteryear.

The political scientist Theda Skocpol insists that a civic life characterized by locally rooted membership organizations like the American Legion and the Elks has gone the way of the once-popular television program *Leave It to*

Beaver.[8] These localized groups, she says, have been replaced by such large nationally based advocacy organizations as the National Right to Life Committee and the National Abortion Rights Action League, which are hierarchic in structure and run by professional managers who are more oriented to the prime-time airways than the community forum. Skocpol laments that these staff-heavy organizations—preoccupied with lobbying, research, and media projects—provide few opportunities for membership activity. It appears that the most significant contribution most members make to the overall goals of the association is financial. Writing a check has replaced the regularized face-to-face political activity that once characterized local community life.

The replacement of localized membership associations dedicated to the general betterment of face-to-face communities by a new assortment of national interest groups focused on the promotion of a particularized political agenda is exactly what other observers have in mind when they say that Americans have lost their sense of common purpose. In a widely read book that appeared several years ago, Michael Sandel decries an impoverished vision of citizenship that afflicts Americans of all political persuasions, with conservatives distrusting government and liberals skeptical of the search for common values. He describes the United States as a procedural republic, absent a public philosophy, that does no more than mediate individual and group differences.[9] The legal scholar Mary Ann Glendon agrees; she portrays a political culture in which people are more absorbed in securing their own rights and claims against the state than wondering what they might do to contribute toward its overall good.[10]

On a more positive note, Francis Fukuyama assures us that the moral and communal corrosion America suffered during the final decades of the last century—what he calls "The Great Disruption"—was a temporary condition that will inevitably be reversed.[11] While accounting for multiple signs of social dissolution in the recent past—increased crime, a weakening family structure, decreasing trust—Fukuyama ultimately puts his faith in the sociability of human nature, which he believes compels people to create norms that bind us together and allow us to live and work with each other cooperatively.

Whether civil society in America is in the process of degeneration or regeneration, whether the values that serve as the foundation for democratic governance have been lost forever or are undergoing a healthy readjustment to changing conditions, there are sure signs about the present situation that cannot be ignored or denied. Over the past forty years Americans have become more cynical about politics and less likely to participate in elections. Increasingly they do not have confidence that their representatives in office will act responsibly and "do the right thing." When asked, most Americans say that they perceive politicians as puppets of powerful interests rather than high-minded leaders devoted to a worthy cause.[12] Political activism, manifested recently through the initiative, referendum, and other forms of direct popular action, has been antigovernment in spirit, launched either to revolt against taxes, impose term limits on incumbents, or break the hold of political fund donors. And even these forms of direct democracy have been greatly influenced by powerful organized interests.[13] No doubt the impeachment crisis of the Clinton years and the disputed presidential election of 2000 will contribute to additional public cynicism about our political leaders and institutions.

By the middle of the last decade, two national panels were established to study how Americans could revitalize civil society. The National Commission on Civic Renewal was a bipartisan effort cochaired by William Bennett and Senator Sam Nunn; its executive director was the political theorist and former Clinton adviser William Galston.[14] The Council on Civil Society, still in operation after delivering its final report, is chaired by Jean Bethke Elshtain of the University of Chicago.[15] The analyses, recommendations, and even membership of the two panels overlapped. Both expressed deep concern about the quality of our civic life, with the NCCR addressing itself to issues of civic renewal through the revitalization of community institutions, and the CCS focusing on moral renewal and the development of fundamental beliefs that make democracy possible.[16]

THE ROLE OF EDUCATION

It should come as no surprise that there has been an outpouring of literature on the subject of civil society and its relation to America's democratic aspirations. Among the many publications on this topic that have appeared in recent years, several chronicle a range of civic activities observable in distinct communal settings.[17] Others discuss the issue within a moral domain, some of them carrying reminders that, with the sprouting up of antisocial groups like private militia, not all collective social action leads to desirable outcomes.[18] Still others, marking civil society's importance as a subject of scholarly inquiry, trace the evolution of the concept as an intellectual and historical phenomenon.[19] But with a few notable exceptions, the subject is seldom treated in relation to education.

Among the few studies that have considered education and civil society, each assumes a different point of emphasis, all of which are considered in this book.

Building on an extensive body of prior research, Norman Nie and his colleagues provide an empirical analysis of the relation between educational achievement and civic participation.[20] In a historical and philosophical study of the common school, Stephen Macedo makes a case for public schools as wellsprings of civic virtue in a diverse society but also supports private school choice as a way to provide better opportunities for inner-city children in failing public schools.[21] Approaching the subject from the perspective of law and political theory, Rosemary Salomone argues that the traditional common school model has become obsolete in an increasingly pluralistic society where people have diverse values.[22] Marion Orr and Wilbur Rich have written case studies explaining how and why the accumulation of black social capital in urban communities has not been converted into meaningful school reform.[23] Two earlier works demonstrated the limited efficacy of civic education in American schools.[24]

Ever since the late nineteenth century, Americans have relied upon government schools as a principal purveyor of deeply cherished democratic values. For many generations of immigrants, the common school was the primary teacher of patriotism and civic values. Many came to see the common school as the guarantor of the nation's promise of democracy and freedom. At the end of the twentieth century, however, there was widespread concern about whether the schools were continuing to fulfill that role.[25] For a variety of reasons, the public schools seemed to have relinquished their historic role as agencies of civic assimilation. Instead, they were actively fostering policies that encouraged students to identify with their race or their ethnic or cultural origins rather than with the overarching civic ideals of the American community.[26]

In the 1980s and 1990s many public schools embraced diversity as their mission at the cost of civic assimilation. In doing so they taught children to identify with their own ancestral heritage rather than a common stock of American ideals. The rise of multiculturalism as an ideology directly conflicted with the public school's once-prized mission of civic assimilation. As the public schools shifted from being the central agency for promoting civic understanding to being an agency for sponsoring racial, ethnic, and cultural identity, faith in the public school ideal weakened. Because Americans have typically believed that their public schools played a key role in building the moral foundation for a robust democracy, there were inevitably questions about whether the schools' faltering commitment to civic assimilation was in some way connected to the decline of our civic spirit.

Proponents of civics education have rightly complained that the teaching of civics has not had a secure place in the schools, whether public or private. A national assessment of students' knowledge of civics and government released by the U.S. Department of Education in 1999 showed that most American youths have a weak grasp of the principles that underlie the U.S. Constitution and lack a basic understanding of how government works.[27] A little more than 20 percent of the students in each of the grades that took the test (fourth, eighth, and twelfth) scored at the "proficient" level. These results indicated that our schools—both public and nonpublic—are not preparing young people with the civic knowledge needed to function as informed citizens.

Nor have schools done a very effective job of instilling or nourishing the values that form a disposition toward responsible citizenship. Educators have avoided taking up controversial moral questions in the classroom for fear that they will offend the sensibilities of one group or another, or trespass into areas of discussion that are wholly private prerogatives. This reluctance echoes the recently fashionable idea in higher education that everything is relative, simply a matter of taste or preference, and that truth is a social construct, existing only in the eye of the beholder. Such attitudes teach young people that there are no universal standards of right and wrong, leaving them unequipped to contend with important ethical questions that are at the center of responsible civic discourse. Debates over abortion, capital punishment, welfare reform, and the United States' global responsibility as a superpower are not just political contests set off by opposing forces, they are at bottom highly nuanced discussions that require knowledge and involve crucial moral considerations, so as to engage in principled debates.

A spate of books in the 1980s, such as Powell, Farrar, and Cohen's *The Shopping Mall High School* and Gerald Grant's *The World We Created at Hamilton High,* suggested that something in the very politics of education was hollowing out the soul of the common school.[28] Such critics as Theodore Sizer and Deborah Meier noted a fundamental absence of animating purpose in the comprehensive public school that attempted to be all things to all students. Others complained of bureaucratic inertia, of institutions overwhelmed by an abundance of disconnected programs targeting discrete groups of students.

In the 1990s disquiet over the condition of public education encouraged policy makers to search for alternatives to the traditional common school model of education.[29] By the year 2000, thirty-six states and the District of Columbia had passed charter school laws, which permit the creation of public schools that are independent of local school districts. In addition, Wisconsin, Ohio, and Florida passed voucher laws that allow certain children (low-income children in Milwaukee and Cleveland, children in persistently low-performing schools in Florida) to attend nonpublic schools at public expense. These voucher laws have been the subject of intense litigation in both the federal and state courts, on grounds that they violate constitutional requirements for the separation of church and state. In addition to these public programs, more than seventy-five thousand low-income students across the nation have received private scholarships to attend nonpublic schools, with funds raised by such groups as the Children's Scholarship Fund and Children First America.

These charter and voucher programs have been vigorously attacked by critics who charge that they undermine the vital role that traditional public schools have historically played in melding a diverse population into a common citizenry. They maintain that such initiatives are divisive, encouraging communities to split off into racial and religious enclaves, thereby threatening our sense of common purpose and, in extreme cases, breeding intolerance and further isolating minority children. These assertions raise significant questions about how communities form and about the role that distinct groups play in establishing the foundation for a vibrant civil society. They run directly counter to the claims of those who believe that such self-contained localized groups of like-minded people actually facilitate civic life in a free society.[30]

The constitutional and civic arguments made against school vouchers pose a dilemma: on the one hand there has been a strong tradition of church-state separation in this country; on the other, faith-based communities remain the most stable forms of civic association at a time when others are in decline.[31] This is one of the central problems that undergird contemporary discussions of civil society and its relation to education.

EDUCATION AND CIVIL SOCIETY

This book brings together a group of distinguished scholars to examine how schooling has contributed to the present condition of civil society in America and, more important, how education might improve that condition. The authors come from a wide variety of fields. Some are educational researchers by profession, others have devoted their careers to aspects of politics, government, society, or law that are germane to the issues we have set out to address. Our objective was not just to engage education scholars in a discussion on civil society but also to involve scholars from other disciplines in thinking about education.

The topics covered in this book encompass the following issues:

The Present Condition. Are Americans becoming disengaged from public life? Have we lost our moral compass? Are we losing our capacity to live together in vibrant and productive communities?

The Relation Between Education and Democracy. What role does education play in promoting a healthy democracy? What assertions have classical and modern political theorists made to this effect? Are their claims supported by empirical research from the United States or other nations?

Educating for Democracy. Have public schools done an adequate job preparing young people to become productive citizens? Have schools conveyed the knowledge, skills and disposition needed to bolster civic life? Have schools shied away from the important ethical concerns that define us as a people? Has the curriculum struck a proper balance between the rights and obligations of citizenship?

The Common School: Past, Present, and Future. Has the common school lived up to its promise to form a single populace from a diverse people? Has it demonstrated a capacity to accommodate citizens with a plurality of values? Is it possible to renew the promise of public education?

The Impact of School Choice. Will the growth of new forms of schooling, especially charter schools and vouchers, have a divisive effect on civic life? Will school choice enhance democracy or weaken it?

The Place of Religion in Education. Is the American civic culture inhospitable to religion? How might public schools incorporate the study of various religions into their curricula without offending First Amendment principles of separation?

Religion and Civil Society. What role do religious institutions play in fostering a robust civil society? How did the Framers of the Constitution view the connection between education, religion, and civic life? Are their perspectives relevant today?

International Perspectives. How does the American common school culture differ from the beliefs found in other free nations? What might we learn from other nations as we think about ways to make education more conducive to a robust democracy?

The essays in this collection fall, not very discretely, into three general categories: politics, values, and religion. They draw on a variety of disciplines, including history, political science, psychology, philosophy, and law. Some contributors focus more on education, while others dwell more specifically on civil society; but all engage the issues in concert, and the outcome makes for an informative and spirited exchange. Some of the authors are concerned with developing the capacity of public schools to advance a civic agenda; others maintain that it is necessary to reach beyond the common school model and rethink the way education is provided; and still others are focused on the way schools and communities interact to cultivate an aptitude for democracy.

The first four chapters of the book provide a foundation that explains the connection between education and civic involvement. Diane Ravitch reviews the work of some of America's leading thinkers in education—Noah Webster and Thomas Jefferson, Horace Mann and John Dewey—reminding us that each had a vision of schooling based upon his view of a preferred social order. It is Robert Hutchins, however, whom she finds most instructive. Hutchins's ideal of democratic self-rule required that every person receive an education that a ruler would have, a liberal education that gives young people the skills, knowledge, habits, ideals, and values to continue to educate themselves throughout life.

Norman Nie and D. Sunshine Hillygus use data from the National Center for Education Statistics to examine how a variety of educational variables are linked to forms of political participation, community service, and civic consciousness. This material, drawn from the 1994 follow-up to the "Baccalaureate and Beyond" longitudinal survey, includes extensive information on scholastic achievement, school quality, and curriculum. It shows verbal ability, measured as scores on the Scholastic Aptitude Test, to be the most reliable predictor of civic involvement.

Robert Putnam reports on a fifty-state survey that correlates community-based social capital with student achievement. Viewing the dynamic from the opposite direction of Ravitch and Nye and Hillygus, he finds that effective social networks at the community level have a positive impact on the academic performance of schools.

Gerald Grant picks up on Putnam's theme, looking closely at a diverse urban neighborhood to analyze how the disastrous leakage of different forms of social capital in the latter twentieth century affected the lives of children. He argues that this loss was as much the result of misbegotten social policy as it was of the ordinary desires of middle-class Americans to live out the suburban dream. Drawing on both ethnographic and census data, he goes on to describe the community-building efforts that have brought some hope to residents, although he is not optimistic about the eventual outcome without major changes in social policy for children. Taken together, the four chapters seem to suggest that the relation between schools and communities is reciprocal, with each capable of affecting the success of the other.

The next five chapters deal broadly with the topic of values. William Damon, drawing on personal interviews with adolescents, describes how young people have grown disillusioned with civic life and have withdrawn from social connections outside of their immediate friends and families. Damon believes that the problem of disengagement among youths is both cognitive and motivational. He suggests that young people need belief systems that capture both their hearts and their minds, and he explains how schools can communicate messages about democracy, patriotism, and spirituality that engage students' imagination.

Warren Nord develops a "common ground" approach to moral education designed to handle moral disagreement. His plan builds on consensus where there is agreement and gives an important role to liberal education—as informed, fair, critical conversation about moral issues and the nature of morality itself—when there is disagreement. He argues that an adequate account of moral education must take seriously "deep justifications" of morality that include religious traditions not typically included in public school curricula.

Nathan Glazer explores the role that culture plays in education, as school populations become more diverse. Glazer maintains that the kind of social consensus that allowed the common school to thrive no longer exists. He contends that public schools should rely more on persuasion and less on compulsion as agents for defining a public morality, and explains why families whose personal values are different have demanded choices beyond the public school. Acknowledging the potential for further fragmentation that choice holds, he raises concerns that ethnic communities with distinct levels of social capital may have more or less to gain from such educational fragmentation.

Mark Holmes examines the disjunction between a public school monopoly and a pluralist society in terms of education for moral citizenship. Notable is the tension he finds as individualism supplants community. Drawing on the experiences of Canada and England, Holmes argues that there is a role for society and parents in the development of school choices but that citizenship is a necessary quality of all schools.

The legal scholar Rosemary Salomone reviews the landmark *Yoder* and *Mozert* cases as a context for examining the curricular challenges brought by religious groups and exploring what education for democratic citizenship means in a society that values pluralism and freedom of conscience along with civic understanding and commitment. She makes the case that perhaps we can balance these seemingly conflicting ends more effectively through a concept of education based on common learning rather than common schooling.

The next four chapters focus on the topic of religion. Jack Rakove begins with a historical perspective, asking how the Framers of the United States Constitution envisioned the relation between religion, education, and civic life; and he provides an interpretation of how their vision informs, shapes, and limits the relation among these spheres in a contemporary context. Rakove gives careful consideration to the influential contributions of Thomas Jefferson and James Madison. Recognizing the difficulty of applying eighteenth-century thinking to the changed circumstances of the twenty-first, Rakove argues that the Founders left us with a uniquely American understanding of civic life that prescribes a rather strict separation between church and state.

Jean Bethke Elshtain offers us a different historical perspective by concentrating on the observations of Tocqueville. Citing recent empirical studies, she emphasizes the continuing relevance of his insight concerning how religious associations promote the civic involvement of their members. She argues that the determination of ardent secularists to drive a wedge between religion and public life is doomed, because faith and politics—and hence civic education—have been intermingled throughout American history and always will be.

Alan Wolfe responds to those who fear that activists associated with the religious right support a political and educational agenda that undermines the basic principles of American democracy. Wolfe observes that even the most fervent religious movements tend to moderate over time, and he counsels that American democracy "softens" religious purism far more than strict religious movements "harden" American democracy. He warns against a paradoxical political position which holds that in order to achieve the pluralist goal of respect for all, we must insist on the nonpluralist means of having everyone subscribe to the same point of view.

Charles Glenn contrasts the American notion of separation between church and state with the nearly universal practice in modern democracies of providing public support for children to attend religious schools of their choice. Glenn looks closely at the experiences of Germany, France, and the Netherlands. He contends that these differing European models of education represent a more desirable approach to the realization of religious freedom than that of the American common school, less inclined to breed conflict and more likely to promote a sense of community. He concludes by outlining several lessons that can be taken from the European model and adapted to the American scene.

In the last chapter Joseph Viteritti considers how a limited program of school vouchers for the poor might alleviate the interrelated problems of educational inequality and social inequality. He explains that there is no hope of redressing what Gunnar Myrdal called the great dilemma of American democracy without eliminating the racial gap in learning. Acknowledging the risks involved with implementing choice and the limited information available from prior experiments, Viteritti argues that a targeted voucher program could enhance both the educational opportunity and civic vitality of disadvantaged communities.

NOTES

1. For an elaboration on the theme see Robert D. Putnam, *Bowling Alone: The Collapse and Renewal of American Community* (New York: Simon and Schuster, 2000).
2. Robert D. Putnam, "Bowling Alone: America's Declining Social Capital," *Journal of Democracy* 6 (1995). See also Robert D. Putnam, "Turning In, Turning Out: The Strange Disappearance of Social Capital in America," *PS: Political Science and Politics* 28 (1995).
3. See also Arthur M. Schlesinger, "Biography of a Nation of Joiners," *American Historical Review* 50 (1944); Murray Hausknecht, *The Joiners: A Sociological Description of Voluntary Association Membership in the United States* (New York: Bedminster, 1962).
4. See generally James S. Coleman, "Social Capital and the Creation of Human Capital," *American Journal of Sociology* 94 (1988); Francis Fukuyama, *Trust: The Social Virtues and the Creation of Prosperity* (New York: Free Press, 1995); Robert D. Putnam, *Making Democracy Work: Civic Traditions in Modern Italy* (Princeton: Princeton University Press, 1993).
5. Peter L. Berger and Richard John Neuhaus, *To Empower People* (Washington, D.C.: AEI Press, 1977).
6. Everett Carl Ladd, *The Ladd Report* (New York: Free Press, 1999), pp. 25–90. See also Sidney Verba, Kay Lehman Schlozman, and Henry E. Brady, *Voice and Equality: Civic Voluntarism in American Politics* (Cambridge: Harvard University Press, 1998).
7. Robert Wuthnow, *Loose Connections: Joining Together in America's Fragmented Communities* (Cambridge: Harvard University Press, 1998), pp. 9–82, 203–27.
8. Theda Skocpol, "Advocates Without Members: The Recent Transformation of American Civil Life," in Theda Skocpol and Morris P. Fiorina, eds., *Civic Engagement in American Democracy* (Washington, D.C.: Brookings Institution Press, 1999), p. 461.
9. Michael Sandel, *Democracy's Discontent: America in Search of a Public Philosophy* (Cambridge: Harvard University Press, 1996).
10. Mary Ann Glendon, *Rights Talk: The Impoverishment of Political Discourse* (New York: Free Press, 1991). See also Lawrence M. Mead, *Beyond Entitlement: The Social Obligations of Citizenship* (New York: Basic, 1986).
11. Francis Fukuyama, *The Great Disruption: Human Nature and the Reconstruction of Social Order* (New York: Free Press, 1999).
12. See Joseph S. Nye, Philip D. Zelikow, and David C. King, eds., *Why People Don't Trust*

Government (Cambridge: Harvard University Press, 1997); E. J. Dionne, *Why Americans Hate Politics* (New York: Simon and Schuster, 1996). But also see Wendy M. Rahn, John Brehm, and Neil Carlson, "National Elections as Institutions for Generating Social Capital," in Skocpol and Fiorina, *Civic Engagement in American Democracy.*

13. For conflicting perspectives on the role of interest groups in initiative and referenda campaigns, see David Broder, *Democracy Derailed: Initiative Campaigns and the Power of Money* (New York: Harcourt, 2000); Elisabeth Gerber, *The Populist Paradox: Interest Group Influence and the Promise of Direct Legislation* (Princeton: Princeton University Press, 2000).

14. See National Commission on Civic Renewal, *A Nation of Spectators: How Civic Engagement Weakens America and What We Can Do About It* (University of Maryland, 1998). See also the collection edited by the panel's research director, Robert K. Fullinwider, *Civil Society, Democracy, and Civic Renewal* (Lanham, Md.: Rowman and Littlefield, 1999).

15. Council on Civil Society, *A Call to Civil Society: Why Democracy Needs Moral Truths* (New York, 1998). The themes of this report are also developed in Jean Bethke Elshtain, *Democracy on Trial* (New York: Basic, 1995); Mary Ann Glendon and David Blakenhorn, eds., *Seedbeds of Virtue: Sources of Competence, Character, and Citizenship in American Society* (New York: Madison, 1995).

16. See Linda C. McClain and James E. Fleming, eds., "Symposium on Legal and Constitutional Implications of the Calls to Revive Civil Society," *Chicago-Kent Law Review* 75 (2000), comparing the two reports and their implications.

17. E. J. Dionne, ed., *Community Works: The Revival of Civil Society in America* (Washington, D.C.: Brookings Institution Press, 1998); Don E. Eberly, *America's Promise: Civil Society and the Renewal of American Culture* (Lanham, Md.: Rowman and Littlefield, 1998).

18. Peter Berkowitz, *Virtue and the Making of Modern Liberalism* (Princeton: Princeton University Press, 1999); Nancy L. Rosenblum, *Membership and Morals: The Personal Uses of Pluralism* (Princeton: Princeton University Press, 1999); Elliot Sober and David Sloan Wilson, *Unto Others: The Evolution and Psychology of Unselfish Behavior* (Cambridge: Harvard University Press, 1998); Margaret Levi, "Social Capital and Unsocial Capital," *Politics and Society* 24 (March 1996); Sheri Berman, "Civil Society and Political Institutionalization," *American Behavioral Scientist* 40 (1997).

19. John Ehrenberg, *Civil Society: The Critical History of an Idea* (New York: New York University Press, 1999); Brian O'Connell, *Civil Society: The Underpinnings of American Democracy* (Hanover, N.H.: University Press of New England, 1999); Michael Schudson, *The Good Citizen: A History of American Civic Life* (New York: Free Press, 1999).

20. Norman Nie, Jane Junn, and Kenneth Stehlik-Berry, *Education and Democratic Citizenship in America* (Chicago: University of Chicago Press, 1997).

21. Stephen Macedo, *Diversity and Distrust: Civic Education in a Multicultural Society* (Cambridge: Harvard University Press, 2000). See also Amy Gutmann, *Democratic Education* (Princeton: Princeton University Press, 1999, rev.).

22. Rosemary C. Salomone, *Models of Schooling: Conscience, Community, and Common Education* (New Haven: Yale University Press, 2000).

23. Marion Orr, *Black Social Capital: The Politics of School Reform in Baltimore, 1986–1998*

(Lawrence: University Press of Kansas, 1999); Wilber C. Rich, *Black Mayors and School Politics: The Failure of Reform in Detroit, Gary, and Newark* (New York: Garland, 1996).

24. Michael X. Delli Carpini and Scott Keeter, *What Americans Know About Politics and Why It Matters* (New Haven: Yale University Press, 1996); Richard G. Niemi and Jane Junn, *Civic Education: What Makes Students Learn?* (New Haven: Yale University Press, 1998).

25. See Diane Ravitch, *Left Back: A Century of Failed School Reforms* (New York: Simon and Schuster, 2000).

26. See Nathan Glazer, *We Are All Multiculturalists Now* (Cambridge: Harvard University Press, 1997).

27. David J. Hoff, "Beyond Basics, Civics Eludes U.S. Students," *Education Week,* November 24, 1999.

28. Aurthur J. Powell, Eleanor Farrar, and David Cohen, *The Shopping Mall High School: Winners and Losers in the Educational Marketplace* (New York: Houghton Mifflin, 1985); Gerald Grant, *The World We Created at Hamiliton High* (Cambridge: Harvard University Press, 1988).

29. See Diane Ravitch and Joseph P. Viteritti, eds., *New Schools for a New Century: The Redesign of Urban Education* (New Haven: Yale University Press, 1998).

30. Michael S. Joyce and William A. Schambra, "A New Civic Life," in Michael Novak, ed., *To Empower People: From State to Civil Society* (Washington, D.C.: AEI Press, 1996); Alan Ehrenhalt, *The Lost City: Discovering the Forgotten Virtues of Community in the Chicago of the 1950s* (New York: Basic, 1996).

31. Joseph P. Viteritti, *Choosing Equality: School Choice, the Constitution, and Civil Society* (Washington, D.C.: Brookings Institution Press, 1999); Warren A. Nord, *Religion and American Education: Rethinking a National Dilemma* (Chapel Hill: University of North Carolina Press, 1995); Charles Leslie Glenn, *The Ambiguous Embrace* (Princeton: Princeton University Press, 2000).

Chapter 1 Education and Democracy

Diane Ravitch

Writing in 1787, Noah Webster said that the subject of education was "trite" and that it had already been "exhausted by the ablest writers, both among the ancients and moderns." He doubted that he had anything to add to the speculations of those who had preceded him, but add he did to that "exhausted" subject, and at great length.[1] What attracted his attention and has continued to capture the attention of countless writers and thinkers since then was the prospect that education could shape tender minds, and even more important, that education could be consciously employed to shape society.

Throughout our national history, educators, public officials, pressure groups, and concerned citizens have struggled for the power to decide what children in school should learn and how they should be taught. Sometimes they struggled because they were sincerely interested in improving education, but often the combatants in education politics have had a singular, overarching goal: they have fought for their vision of schooling because it embodied their ideology and their goals for the future of society.

From the earliest days of our nation, educational theorists have contended that their ideas—and only their ideas—were best suited for future citizens in a democracy. In the throes of a debate about education, it is always best to scrutinize carefully the differing definitions of both education and democracy, and the likely fit between them. Of one thing we can be reliably sure: those who have a vision of schooling usually have a vision, too, of a particular kind of social order.

Noah Webster was the first educator who saw the potential in schooling and textbooks as instruments to create a new American society. Although there were no public schools in the post-Revolution era, Webster was certainly a founding father of American public education; he clearly saw the value to the state in using the schools and textbooks to promote a strong sense of national identity. The education of youth, he advised, was more consequential to the state than making laws or preaching the gospel. He believed that the new nation needed, above all, a common language; he advanced the cause of cultural nationalism by writing schoolbooks and a dictionary of the American language, with its own distinctive American pronunciations. Webster's famous blue-backed speller sold in the tens of millions; designed as a vehicle of a common language, it taught many Americans how to spell and speak, how to overcome the regionalisms that divided members of the new nation. Always attentive to his royalties, Webster was also the father of copyright law in America. Form the child, Webster urged, and you will ultimately form the nation, its government, and the character of its civil society. As a relentless booster of popular education, Webster contributed mightily to the American experiment in democracy, even though he became a bitter foe of democratic rule and universal suffrage as he grew older.

While Webster was writing textbooks for the nation's rudimentary schools, his contemporary, Thomas Jefferson, submitted legislation in 1779 to create a public school system in Virginia; his proposals were not passed. Jefferson believed that those in power were likely to succumb to the temptation to become tyrants and that the best safeguard against tyranny was mass education. Jefferson wrote, "I know of no safe depository of the ultimate powers of the society but the people themselves; and if we think them not enlightened enough to exercise their control with a wholesome discretion, the remedy is not to take it from them, but to inform their discretion by education."[2] He was especially keen for young people to study history, because if they knew the experience of other ages, they would be "enabled to know ambition under all its shapes, and prompt to exert their natural powers to defeat its purposes."[3] The success of democratic government, he believed, depended on an informed public, which could protect its rights against those who might usurp them. Jefferson described the schools and their curriculum not as instruments of organized social control but as mechanisms by which citizens could arm themselves with literacy and knowledge and defend themselves against the predictable incursions of a powerful government.

Clearly, Webster and Jefferson held quite different views about the role of education in a democratic society. Webster wanted to educate youth to determine the future character of the state; Jefferson wanted to educate youth so that the people could protect their freedoms against the potential intrusions of the state. Over time, the shadow of these two theoretical positions grew larger. In the first half of the twentieth century, education theorists were drawn to Webster's idea that the schools could be used as a tool for social engineering, and that individual needs must be subordinated to large social goals. Policy makers were drawn to Webster's views, to the possibility that they could engage in social planning by shaping education policy; parents, religious groups, and other actors in civil society were far likelier to prefer Jefferson's pluralistic views, which recognized that individuals and groups in a democratic society must remain free to make their own choices, not serve as instruments for someone else's social plans.

If Webster and Jefferson appear to be at different ends of the ideological spectrum in their views about the relation of schooling to democracy, Horace Mann was an intermediate figure who tried to harmonize both individual purposes and social goals but inevitably was closer to Webster than Jefferson. Like Webster, Mann believed that the training of the schoolroom would eventually ripen into the "institutions and fortunes" of the state.[4] In 1837 Mann became secretary of the Massachusetts state board of education, where for twelve years he argued that popular education was integrally connected to freedom and democratic government. The schools, he maintained, must distribute intelligence broadly throughout the population. Mann understood the value of investing in human capital. As people gained knowledge, he argued, they would gain the power to develop their talents and to advance the frontiers of science, commerce, law, and the arts. As knowledge was more equally diffused, the entire society and economy would grow. Intellectual education, he said, would remove the causes of poverty and spread abundance.

Mann today is best known as the father of the American common school—that is, the idea that the state should maintain free public schools in every community, to which all children are sent to learn together, presumably obliterating differences of class and social condition. Less well known is Mann's acknowledgment that parents who were dissatisfied with the quality of their local public schools were "bound by the highest obligations, to provide surer and better means for the education of their children."[5]

Only recently has there been close attention to the antidemocratic aspects of Mann's views or to the passionate anti-Catholicism of the common school movement.[6] Mann's nonsectarianism, we now recognize, was nondenominational Protestantism. He did not object to the Bible in the schools, or to other religious practices, so long as they did not advance a specific religion. Those who did not wish to have the principles of nondenominational Protestantism inculcated in their children by the state objected to Mann's common school. Other prominent leaders of the common school movement, some of whom were state superintendents in the Midwest and South, were outright anti-Catholic bigots, associated with the Know-Nothing Party. Critics of the common school movement claimed that it was not democratic to compel parents to send their children to schools that rejected their parents' values, and that democracy implied not centralization but a greater diversity of educational agencies.

In spite of its critics, the common school movement was propelled by a great sense of moral and political rectitude, as well as by the popularity of nativism and anti-Catholicism, and it scored victories in state after state in the mid-nineteenth century. By the end of the nineteenth century, the United States had a popular public school system, with free, nearly universal elementary education and with high schools available to a steadily increasing percentage of young people.

At the opening of the twentieth century, it was generally accepted that public education should be provided by the state at public expense and that the purposes of democracy were served best by offering a common academic education to children for as long as they were willing and able to stay in school. Mann's idea that intellectual education was the foundation of democratic education seemed firmly established; most youngsters, for example, studied a foreign language, even when they were not required to do so, and Latin was a staple of the high school curriculum in big cities, small towns, and even rural areas.

The early years of the twentieth century, however, saw a redefinition of the relation between education and democracy. A new class of educational experts, associated with the newly created schools of pedagogy, advocated a sociological analysis of education. Working in tandem with social workers, progressive school reformers decreed that the highest goal for a democratic school system was social efficiency.

Although schooling in the nineteenth century had been characterized by a great deal of organizational diversity, the advocates of public schooling in the early years of the twentieth century insisted that there must be a bright line between public and private schooling. Leaders of the new pedagogical profession identified professionalism with the extension of the power of the state in public schooling. Ellwood P. Cubberley of Stanford University, the leading historian of education for many years, taught generations of teachers and administrators that government control of schooling was a sure indicator of a nation's democratic character. He treated disparagingly the various forms of nonpublic and quasi-public schooling that had characterized American education in the nineteenth century. In his textbooks about education, Cubberley asserted that a nation's educational progress could be measured by the extent to which control of its schools had passed from church to state, from private to public, and from laymen to professionals. The most highly evolved nations, he suggested, were those in which there was "state control of the whole range of education, to enable the State to promote intellectual and moral and social progress along lines useful to the State." Like Noah Webster, Cubberley envisaged the school system as an engine of social control, an agency that could plan social progress, and assign children to their future roles.[7] In Cubberley's model a democratic school system was one in which the state, acting through its expert professional staff, exercised complete control over the schools.

Progressive reformers in the early decades of the twentieth century supported industrial education as the very best means to achieve social efficiency. In 1906 the Massachusetts Commission on Industrial and Technical Education recommended industrial and vocational education in the public schools, as well as industrial schools that were completely separate from the regular school system. The experts said that industrial education would benefit children, who would be ready for work; employers, who would have a ready supply of trained labor; and the nation, which would enjoy prosperity. The commission concluded that the vast majority of children needed training for jobs, not a liberal education.

In the same year, the National Society for the Promotion of Industrial Education was formed to lobby for the cause. So popular was industrial education that one educator likened its spread to a "mental epidemic," not unlike religious revivals or Klondike gold fever. A historian wrote later of this period that "bankers, businessmen, industrialists, philanthropists, social workers, educators, all jumped on the bandwagon. Few movements in the history of American education have taken so sudden and so powerful a hold on the minds of school reformers."[8]

Advocates of industrial education insisted that it was wasteful to expose most children to an academic education. They believed that schools should train students for the work that they would eventually do as adults. Because most children would grow up to become farmers, laborers, industrial workers, and housewives, they said, schools should train them for these roles. In the first two decades of the century, the industrial-education movement lobbied successfully at the state and federal levels to get vocational programs into the curriculum and to ensure that students were "guided" into practical programs as early as the seventh or eighth grade. So successful was the movement that advocates persuaded the U.S. Congress to pass the first major piece of federal legislation for the schools, the Smith-Hughes Act of 1917 for vocational and industrial education.

The most important triumph for the industrial-education movement was the general acceptance of curricular differentiation in junior high schools and high schools. School reformers insisted that the academic curriculum was not appropriate for all children, because most children—especially the children of immigrants and of African Americans—lacked the intellectual capacity to study subjects like algebra and chemistry.

In a democracy, the school reformers said, students should get the curriculum that was suited to the needs of society, in line with their own individual capacities. To meet this goal, many districts offered several different curricula, intended to train workers for agriculture, business, clerical jobs, domestic service, industrial work, and household management. The standard academic curriculum, once considered appropriate for anyone who advanced to high school, was redefined as the college-preparatory curriculum, suitable only for the small minority of students who intended to go to college.

This was an important and even dramatic change of goals in American education. Progressive reformers rejected the once-traditional idea that all students should get an intellectual education to prepare them for citizenship in a democratic society. The reformers claimed that this notion was not only antiquated but antidemocratic. They insisted that a democratic society needed men and women who were equipped for their future vocational roles; the mission of the public schools in a democratic society, they said, was to train students to perform their expected roles. In that way, society would function efficiently, and the schools would not waste resources by overeducating young people who were likely to become barbers, clerks, laundresses, or farmers.

It was just about the time that the industrial education movement was reaching its apogee that the eminent philosopher John Dewey published his landmark book *Democracy and Education* in 1916. Dewey was quite critical of the zeal for industrial education that was then popular. He pointed out that any effort to train youngsters for a specific occupation was bound to be self-defeating, because as new industries emerged and old ones disappeared, individuals who had been trained for a specific trade would be left behind with obsolete skills. He saw too that industrial and vocational education was likely to represent an acceptance of the status quo, merely perpetuating existing inequities in society.

Dewey's warnings about the likely negative consequences of industrial and vocational education had little effect; indeed, they were ignored, probably because the movement was so far advanced that it could not be stopped or even slowed. For most reformers, industrial and vocational education seemed like natural alternatives to the academic curriculum, which they viewed as elitist and sterile, as did Dewey.

Dewey's views about the meaning of democracy and the nature of education, however, became part of the common wisdom among education reformers, and they continue to influence educational thought today. Dewey wrote that "a democracy is more than a form of government; it is primarily a mode of associated living, of conjoint communicated experience."[9] As he defined it, the more individuals participate in shared interests, the more that they must refer their actions to those of others, the more numerous and more varied are their contacts with others who are different from themselves, the more democratic is society. The widening of interests, Dewey said, was the result of the development of travel, commerce, manufacture, and new means of communication. These changes produced exchanges that inevitably must break down the barriers of class, race, and nationality. In Dewey's conception of democracy, then, the particularities of neighborhood, region, religion, ethnicity, race, and other distinctive features of communal life are isolating factors, all of which may be expected to dissolve as individuals interact and share their concerns.

Dewey's conception of democracy was essentially antipluralist. His views stand in sharp contrast to those of the philosopher Horace Kallen, who praised cultural pluralism in a much-discussed article in 1915.[10] Kallen reacted against the coercive assimilationist policies of his era, preferring instead that public policy should encourage distinctive cultural groups; he called for "a democracy of nationalities." He wanted America to become a nation of nations and suggested the metaphor of an orchestra composed of many different groups, each playing its own instrument. Dewey, however, did not admire groups that had interests of their own, suggesting that they became too selfish, too devoted to protecting their own interests. He was fearful of "the antisocial spirit" of any group that had "interests 'of its own' which shut it out from full interaction with other groups." Such a spirit, he worried, promoted "isolation and exclusiveness," which tended to preserve past customs rather than stimulating the sort of exchanges that broke down selfishness and traditional customs.

Educators could quite reasonably conclude after reading Dewey that any schools serving a particular group—such as parochial schools or single-sex schools—were undemocratic because of their isolating effects. Dewey's definition of democracy, on the other hand, was quite supportive of the comprehensive school, the large school that incorporates all kinds of programs and curricula under one roof. Because these views gained currency when many cities were undertaking school construction programs in the 1920s, they lent support to the creation of larger schools with multiple programs.

But what should schools do to advance democratic society, aside from trying to bring everyone under a single administrative umbrella? What should their educational program be? This was far more difficult for the conscientious educator to discern, for it was easier to understand what Dewey was against rather than what he favored. Certainly his view of democracy implied that individuals should join in shared activities to the greatest extent possible. Beyond that, his followers understood that life is growth, education is growth, and growth is its own justification. Dewey believed that students should engage in "orderly and ordered activity," but he was eclectic or at least "catholic" with a small *c* about what they should study.[11]

He wrote, for example, that it was absurd for educators to try to establish what they believed to be the proper objects of education, just as it would be absurd for the farmer "to set up an ideal of farming irrespective of conditions." Whether farmers or educators, both were responsible for carrying out certain activities from minute to minute and hour to hour rather than accepting aims imposed from without by external authority. Dewey claimed that "education as such has no aims."[12]

Yet the comparison between education and farming was odd, even bizarre, and it showed the weakness of Dewey's argument and its tendency to confuse educators about the relation between their methods and their purposes. Farmers must know in advance what they intend to grow; if they wish to be successful, they must pay heed to agricultural science. They must plan ahead, based on their goals, and use the methods likeliest to advance those goals. When their crops come in, they must carefully measure their results to know which seeds and methods were most productive. Any farmer who did not know what crop he wanted to grow, under what conditions it was likely to grow, and which methods were most successful, would surely be a poor farmer. And certainly farming has clear aims; no one says that people farm to improve their personality or to get exercise or to commune with nature. They farm to grow crops; if they don't achieve this aim, they won't achieve any of the others and they won't even be farmers. Why then must education be without aims?

Ultimately, Dewey believed that anything might be studied in ways that made it valuable, especially if students understood its social significance. He wrote that it was not possible "to establish a hierarchy of values among studies. It is futile to attempt to arrange them in an order, beginning with one having least worth and going on to that of maximum value. . . . Since education is not a means to living, but is identical with the operation of living a life which is fruitful and inherently significant, the only ultimate value which can be set up is just the process of living itself."[13] This view led Dewey to conclude that there was no reason to favor a course in zoology over a course in laundry work; he said that either could be narrow and confining, and either could be a source of understanding and illumination about social relationships. This was true in theory, but in practice the children who were studying zoology were learning about the principles of science, while the children in the laundry work course were learning to wash and press clothes.[14]

Because he believed that no subject was of intrinsic value, Dewey's ideas undercut the academic curriculum at the very moment that it was under attack by advocates of industrial education, vocational education, and social efficiency. If everything that might be studied was of equal value, whether zoology or laundry work, whether geometry or sewing, then why struggle to preserve equal access to algebra, chemistry, foreign language, and other subjects? This may not have been Dewey's intention, but it was in fact what happened in the 1920s and 1930s.

The work of creating new curriculum tracks and assigning students to them was facilitated by the invention of the group intelligence test during World War I. At that time, the nation's most prominent educational psychologists offered their services to the military; they devised group tests that made it possible to quickly determine which recruits were officer material and which were not. The tests were successfully used to assign nearly two million men.

When the war was over, the psychologists turned their skills to developing group IQ tests for the schools. By the early 1920s, intelligence testing was a regular feature in American public education. Progressive educators hailed the new IQ tests, which created a scientific basis for curricular differentiation. The test developers assured the public that intelligence was innate and fixed; the aura of scientific certainty with which the testers advanced their work persuaded teachers and principals that the tests were a reliable scientific tool that would enable them to guide their students into the proper curriculum. No longer would these decisions be based on guesswork. The tests allowed the schools to decide quickly which students should be in the college track, which should be directed to technical careers, and which should be firmly guided into a curriculum track that would equip them for nothing more than unskilled labor.

All of this was considered a socially efficient approach to the problem of mass education in a democratic society. Educators believed that they were using the most scientific tools to achieve the most democratic results: an education fitted to the needs of each individual and the needs of society. The best minds in education recommended curricular differentiation based on IQ testing; all the best, most progressive districts followed their recommendations.

There were not many dissenters, but there were a few. William Chandler Bagley of Teachers College spoke out vigorously against both curricular differentiation and IQ testing. He saw them as decidedly undemocratic, and he argued during the 1920s and 1930s for a common academic curriculum and higher standards for all students. Bagley endured professional opprobrium for his contrarian views. Isaac Kandel, an internationally renowned scholar who was also at Teachers College, complained in 1934 that the lower schools had adopted social promotion as the norm and that the high schools had reduced their standards to the lowest kind of pabulum.[15] Under these intellectually debilitating conditions, Kandel noted, the high school seemed to have embraced the cult of mediocrity.

Unlike Dewey, Bagley and Kandel believed that schools in a democratic society must improve the intelligence of their pupils through the systematic study of certain subjects. They did not agree that the purpose of education is more education, and that education is relative only to itself. Both were sharply critical of the reformers who wanted to abolish subject matter or reduce standards to the vanishing point. They agreed with Dewey that a democratic society needs a certain fund of common values and ideas so that it can function as a community of shared purpose; but they did not believe this fund of shared values would arise without instruction and purpose.

Another dissenter from the educational ideology that had become commonplace by midcentury was Robert Hutchins. Hutchins, the president of the University of Chicago, achieved a large popular following in the late 1930s because of his eloquent advocacy of the great books. During the next two decades, Hutchins was one of the most prominent critics of American education.

Hutchins identified four ideas that were responsible for the emptiness of education.[16] First was the doctrine of adjustment, the idea that the purpose of education is to adjust or adapt young people to fit into their society. This was wrong, he said, because society and the economy change with such rapidity that the student would be educated for the past, not the future. Vocational training was a particularly pertinent example, which not only failed to educate young people but even failed to prepare them for the work that was its focus.

The second misguided idea, according to Hutchins, was the doctrine of immediate needs, the idea that students should study only what interests them at the moment. This, Hutchins insisted, had produced an ad hoc curriculum of miscellaneous courses, a reliance on marketing and sales techniques to find needs and fill them, and, once again, a withdrawal from the responsibility to educate young people. This doctrine of immediate needs, he said, had disintegrated the curriculum of both the schools and the universities, as they vainly sought to offer courses on every imaginable need and want.

The third of these misleading doctrines he called the doctrine of social reform. This was the idea that educators could use the schools to promote social reform. The problem here, said Hutchins, was that the only reforms that a school can espouse are the ones that the public already wants to do. It can't be the leading edge of an unpopular reform, so it must reflect society rather than change society. Worse, he warned, if the schools are seen as vehicles for reforms, they may be converted into battlegrounds for competing political programs and become vehicles for dubious agendas.

The fourth of the wrong doctrines, which he found most abhorrent, was the doctrine of no doctrine at all. This is the curriculumless curriculum, the school that meets all needs, the program of infinite variety, lacking any ideals, any sense of good and bad, or better and worse. This doctrine guarantees that there can be no common intellectual life, no basis for communication among Americans about anything aside from sports and other entertainments.

What underlies all these doctrines, Hutchins asserted, was the belief that everybody has a right to an education but that not everyone is capable of being educated. The tension between these two beliefs produces an adulterated education of low quality.

Hutchins believed that the true doctrine of education requires us to recognize that we improve society by educating the individuals who compose it. Education, he wrote, deals with the development of the intellectual powers of people. In a democracy, where the government is based on self-rule, every person is a ruler, and all need the education that rulers should have. They should have, in other words, a liberal education, because that is the education appropriate to free men. A liberal education is one that gives young people the skills, knowledge, habits, ideals, and values to continue to educate themselves for the rest of their lives. Everyone, whether a bank president or a ditch-digger, must be educated, Hutchins asserted.

"The liberally educated man," he wrote, "must know how to read, write, and figure. He must know and understand the ideas that have animated mankind. He must comprehend the tradition in which he lives." Citizens in a democracy must be educated to exercise their intelligence, to think and discuss, to debate and reflect. "Perhaps the greatest idea that America has given the world," said Hutchins, "is the idea of education for all. The world is entitled to know whether this idea means that everybody can be educated, or only that everybody must go to school."[17]

From Noah Webster to Thomas Jefferson to Horace Mann to John Dewey to Robert Hutchins, American education has been offered many definitions of the ways in which education and democracy are connected, the ways in which one might promote the other. Well ahead of his time, Webster understood that education could be used to shape society. Jefferson saw education as a valuable means to preserve one's freedom and rights against the depredations of the powerful. Mann believed that education would allow people to develop their talents and to develop the national economy at the same time. Dewey envisioned education as a lever to reform society by expanding the contacts among different people and reducing the exclusiveness of groups. Hutchins insisted that education would improve democratic society by improving individuals and teaching them to use their minds well.

My own estimation of these thinkers reflects, unsurprisingly, my own values and beliefs. In Webster, one sees the beginnings of an ideology that saw students as instruments who could be formed to serve the purposes of the state. This is the root of social engineering. One sees this ideology in full flower with the rise of the industrial-education movement, whose proponents discussed among themselves what to do with other people's children, who would receive an education that the planners would not accept for their own children. Jefferson continues to appeal to those who are unwilling to surrender their fate to social planners and other wielders of governmental and corporate power. He recognized that education should foster the critical intelligence of the citizenry, so that each person might understand and defend his or her rights.

Mann articulates an appealing concept of education as a mechanism for social and economic development, based on intellectual development. But Mann's philosophy is recalled today mainly for his advocacy of centralized governmental power in education; Mann's followers passed laws in the states to reduce the power of local school boards, to expand state bureaucracies, and to create a sharp differentiation between public and nonpublic schools that did not exist before 1850, a distinction that does not exist in American higher education.

Dewey was the most influential of all of these thinkers because he was an icon for educators throughout the twentieth century. But he left problems in his wake, caused in no small part by the obscurity of his prose. His view of democracy as associated life, involving everyone in sharing purposes with everyone else, suggests a sort of homogenization of cultural life that looked very distant in 1916 but no longer does. Worse, his identification of education with the process of living and being and experiencing created no end of confusion. If education is growth, and the purpose of growth is more growth, if education has no end outside itself, how are teachers to set priorities? How are they to establish reasonably coherent curricula and programs? For a handful of gifted and brilliant teachers, the Deweyan prescription of no prescription works; for most, it remains a problem or perhaps an irrelevance.

Hutchins's analysis, it seems to me, was right, but his proposed remedy— teaching the great books—was wildly impractical, as even he occasionally admitted. Nonetheless, he understood better than anyone else that the education of citizens must be a first priority for the schools of a democracy. He understood that a democracy's goal must be not just universal enrollment but universal education. He understood, at a time when others were content with the mediocre intellectual caliber of the schools, that the schools were far from meeting their responsibility for universal education. Democratic education, he knew, meant that everyone must be educated as if they were children of the most advantaged members of society. He wanted everyone to have a liberal education and to be able to communicate through reading, writing, and speaking. He wanted these things not because it was his preference but because he understood that a democracy depends on the intelligence and resourcefulness and character of its citizens. These, he knew, could not be left to chance.

Now, at the opening of the twenty-first century, we must attend to the strengthening of civil society, humane culture, and our democratic institutions. Already we see a cheapening and coarsening of popular culture, as commercial interests pursue the widest possible audience for the crassest possible entertainments. Unless the schools provide our children with a vision of human possibility that enlightens and empowers them with knowledge and taste, they will simply play their role in someone else's marketing schemes. Unless they understand deeply the sources of our democracy, they will take it for granted and fail to exercise their rights and responsibilities. The schools must teach youngsters about our history, our civic institutions, and our Constitution. More, they must give students the intellectual tools to comprehend science, mathematics, language, the arts, literature, and history. There are many reasons to believe that these important goals are not being achieved, or are not being achieved for enough children. Democratic habits and values must be taught and communicated through the daily life of our society, our legal institutions, our press, our religious life, our private associations, and the many other agencies that allow citizens to interact with each other and to have a sense of efficacy. The best protection for a democratic society is well-educated citizens.

NOTES

1. Noah Webster, "Education," *American Magazine,* December 1787, p. 23.
2. Gordon C. Lee, "Learning and Liberty: The Jeffersonian Tradition in Education," in Lawrence A. Cremin, ed., *Crusade Against Ignorance: Thomas Jefferson on Education* (New York: Teachers College Press, 1961), p. 17.
3. Thomas Jefferson, "A Bill for the More General Diffusion of Knowledge," in Cremin, *Crusade Against Ignorance,* p. 883.
4. Horace Mann, Twelfth Annual Report to the Massachusetts State Board of Education, in Lawrence A. Cremin, ed., *The Republic and the School: Horace Mann on the Education of Free Men* (New York: Teachers College Press, 1957), p. 80.
5. Horace Mann, First Annual Report to the Massachusetts State Board of Education, in Cremin, *The Republic and the School,* p. 33.
6. See Lloyd P. Jorgenson, *The State and the Non-Public School, 1825–1925* (Columbia: University of Missouri Press, 1987).
7. Ellwood P. Cubberley, *The History of Education* (Boston: Houghton Mifflin, 1920), pp. 578, 673; also, Ellwood P. Cubberley, *Public Education in the United States* (Boston: Houghton Mifflin, 1919), pp. 120–21.
8. Sol Cohen, "The Industrial Education Movement, 1906–17," *American Quarterly,* Spring 1968, p. 96.
9. John Dewey, *Democracy and Education* (New York: Macmillan, 1916), p. 101.
10. Horace M. Kallen, "Democracy Versus the Melting Pot: A Study of American Nationality," *The Nation,* February 1915.

11. Dewey, *Democracy and Education,* p. 119.

12. Ibid., p. 125.

13. Ibid., p. 281.

14. John Dewey, *The Way Out of Educational Confusion* (Cambridge: Harvard University Press, 1931), p. 21.

15. Diane Ravitch, *Left Back: A Century of Failed School Reforms* (New York: Simon and Schuster, 2000), chapter 8.

16. Robert M. Hutchins, *The Democratic Dilemma* (Uppsala, Sweden: Almqvist and Wiksells, 1951).

17. Ibid., pp. 29, 51.

Chapter 2 Education and Democratic Citizenship

Norman Nie and D. Sunshine Hillygus

More than a half-century of empirical research on mass political behavior points to the consistent and overwhelming influence of education on myriad facets of democratic citizenship. Amount of formal education is almost without exception the strongest factor in explaining what citizens do in politics and how they think about politics. Philip Converse once referred to educational attainment as the universal solvent of political behavior.[1] Yet we know precious little about what goes on inside the educational process that has such a profound effect on so many aspects of democratic citizenship. The overwhelming number of studies (and there are literally thousands of them) about education's relationship to one or more civic values or behaviors focus on the quantity of education rather than its content.[2] Even the most sophisticated of the education models are variants of "the more, the more" or "the more, the better" hypothesis—more education correlates with more participation, more voting, more political skills, more political knowledge, and so on.[3]

The specific content of higher education, alternative educational experiences, or differences in what the student brings to his or her college education or accomplishes during it have rarely been examined in relation to important aspects of democratic citizenship. Richard Niemi and Jane Junn have conducted an in-depth analysis of the effects of structural and individual characteristics of secondary education on the political knowledge of high school seniors, but there is no thorough examination of the specific role of higher education in the development of democratic citizenship.[4] For the first time, empirical data are now available that allow us to explore some of these issues. The Baccalaureate and Beyond (B&B) study sponsored by the National Center for Education Statistics, limited though it may be for this task, will enable us to peek inside the "black box" of a college education.[5] Given the absence of previous research about the relationship between specific college education effects and democratic engagement, values, and so forth, this chapter is primarily an exploratory empirical analysis. With the mixture of survey data and data from student records, we can now begin to ask some meaningful questions about the intricate relationship between education and democratic citizenship: What role does curriculum play in fostering civic-minded and politically active citizens? How do such factors as academic grades, scholastic aptitude, and achievement influence patterns of political engagement and civic values? And does the quality of the academic institution attended shape the political orientations of its recent graduates?

Although this chapter focuses on the relationship between college education and democratic citizenship—while the book generally emphasizes elementary and secondary education—the two are clearly intertwined. We conclude, in fact, that the skills acquired earlier in the educational process (or perhaps even before that) may ultimately be more important than postsecondary experiences in shaping future levels of political and civic engagement.

We employ data from the 1993–94 Baccalaureate and Beyond Longitudinal Follow-up Study, a survey of college graduates who received a bachelor's degree during the 1992–93 academic year.[6] From a final sample of 10,800 college graduates, we selected those who attended four-year accredited institutions and who took the Scholastic Aptitude Test (SAT) before college matriculation, resulting in a subsample of 3,100 recent graduates. Because separate verbal and math scores were available only for the students who took the SAT, we selected this specific subset so that we could explore the relationship between these indexes of aptitude and our measures of democratic behaviors and attitudes. Descriptively, the vast majority of our sample is in their twenties, with more than two-thirds between the ages of twenty-two and twenty-five and more than 95 percent between twenty-one and twenty-nine, so they are of the same generation. As graduates of four-year universities where SATs are required, they were among the better high school students. Sociologically, they are more homogeneous with regard to race and parental education than either the general population or the average college graduate.[7] They are more likely to be from better-educated families and less likely to be nonwhite. Only 5 percent are black and 4 percent Hispanic. Nonetheless, the Baccalaureate and Beyond Longitudinal Study is particularly promising because the same respondents will be followed every four years for a total of twelve years so that this analysis can be replicated as these recent graduates advance through adulthood.

THE INDEPENDENT VARIABLES

The notion that formal educational attainment is the primary mechanism behind citizen engagement and a desire for public influence is largely uncontested.[8] The contribution of this chapter is to identify the specific elements of a college education that are important. In that pursuit, we examine the impact of ten variables about students and their college experience on various citizenship variables. The B&B study has collected rich data on individual curricula, achievement, and aptitudes, in addition to information on institutional quality. Much of this information was compiled from student school records rather than student recall, increasing the validity of the measures. For each of the 3,100 recent graduates in our sample, we have details regarding how many and what kind of courses they took—whether humanities, social sciences, science/ engineering, education, or business. For each of these fields, we have the actual number of credit hours taken. We also know their cumulative grade point average (GPA)—perhaps the best single measure of performance over a college career. And we know something about their proficiencies with words and math as gauged by math and verbal SAT scores.[9] Finally, we have a measure of the quality of each of the universities they attended, and whether that institution is public or private. These data represent a gold mine of knowledge about both the student and the college environment, allowing us to identify the specific effects of these different educational attributes on six measures of democratic citizenship.

THE DEPENDENT VARIABLES

In addition to detailed information about student achievement and aptitude, institutional quality, and individual curricula, the B&B data set contains several measures of civic and political engagement, though the set of political behavior and orientations available in the B&B survey are anything but perfect for our purposes. Ideally, we would also have measures of democratic orientations, tolerance, and other features of democratic citizenship. However, as with any secondary analysis, we take what we can get. And what we do have is thorough information on voting turnout, four measures of participation beyond the vote, a measure of civic voluntarism, and a propensity for political discussion and persuasion. Finally, we have measures that we think tap the underlying values of desire for public influence in contrast to private financial gain. We detail the operationalization and measurement of each of these dependent variables individually.

Political Participation

In assessing the specific effects of a college education on these various characteristics of democratic citizenship, we turn first to the fundamental dependent variable of political participation. Participation in politics is at the foundation of democratic citizenship because it is a principal mechanism by which citizens pursue and protect their political interests. Political participation takes many forms, from writing a check to a favorite candidate, to working on an election campaign, to petitioning a local official for increased neighborhood police protection.

Because all these activities are interrelated, we have combined into a single scale of political participation the activities of campaign volunteering, attending a political rally or meeting, contributing money to a political campaign, and writing a letter to a public official. Thus individuals who have participated in only one activity receive a lower participation score than those involved in many political activities. This overall political participation scale was created using an appropriate dimensional methodology for dichotomous data, and then transformed to range from 0 to 100 so that we can talk about the percentile of political participation. Appendix A compares our sample's participation in the individual political activities with the general population of college graduates and college graduates of the same age (using National Election Survey data). The exact technique for constructing the political participation scale from these individual activities is described in Appendix B.

Presidential Vote

Although citizens are more likely to vote than to engage in any other political activity, voting in national elections differs substantially from other participatory acts and will thus be considered separately in this analysis. Voting can be considered political engagement insofar as it enables citizens to express their general preference for one leader or party over another, but it can convey little information about the context of specific interests. It is a political activity that requires much less time, effort, and information than the more difficult acts of political participation included in our political engagement scale. Citizens often vote out of a sense of civic duty, and this notion of responsibility may be one cause of the consistently exaggerated turnout rates in every voting survey. Through validation studies, it is known that some 10–15 percent of respondents indicate that they voted when they in fact did not. Because the B&B survey offered two questions asking whether the respondent voted in the 1992 presidential election, we were able to cross-validate these variables to get a more accurate assessment of turnout—but the reported rates assuredly remain inflated. The percentage of B&B respondents who affirmed in response to two separate questions that they voted in the 1992 presidential election is still probably high at 72 percent, yet compares quite closely to the 69 percent turnout rate of college-educated cohorts (of equivalent age group) reported by the National Election Studies.

Community Service

Though nonpolitical in nature, participation in community service is another fundamental aspect of American pluralist society. In this chapter we therefore examine the impact of our education variables on participation in nonpolitical, voluntary activities. This tradition of giving time and energy to community causes and charities that lie somewhere between the family and the state has been cited as a unique and sustaining feature of American democracy.[10] Within our sample, 23 percent report that they currently volunteer at least two hours per week, and 69 percent report that they have participated in community service at some time (excluding work-related and court-ordered community service). We test our model of educational attributes on the total reported community service hours in the past two years.

A wide body of literature has established the link between nonpolitical civic participation and explicitly political participation. Conover and Searing, for example, identify public service as part of the citizenship profile of a "good citizen" in a democracy.[11] Verba, Scholzman, and Brady find that nonpolitical settings offer the opportunity to learn, maintain, and improve such civic skills as communication and organization capacities.[12] Volunteer activity plays an important role in democratic citizenship both because it develops civic skills and because it is instrumental in establishing the social and political networks so important to political activity. Citizens who organize a book drive or coordinate volunteers for a soup kitchen are likely to be more effective when they get involved in the political world. Also, community-service participation is generally an interpersonal activity, often taking place either within an organizational setting (volunteering at a women's shelter, for example) or through organizational membership (a reading club hosting a book drive, for instance). Associating with fellow citizens organized around any interest, political or otherwise, increases the probability of contact with government and politics while forming the networks that act to create further engagement with others in society. It should be remembered that even garden club members may be pulled into politics because the government controls what seeds they can grow, what fertilizers they can and can't use—and if they are not vigilant, the government may even tarmac over their garden.

Political Persuasion

The B&B survey asks, "In the last 12 months, did you talk to any people and try to show them why they should vote for one of the parties or candidates?" Although political discussion does not fit the classic definition of political participation—an attempt to influence government policy or the selection of government leaders who make that policy—it is nonetheless an important characteristic of democratic citizenship. Political persuasion indicates both an individual's level of political interest and his or her degree of political engagement. Political persuasion represents the attempt not only to defend one's interests and preferences but also to get someone else to share and pursue those same interests. Since the seminal work of Campbell, Converse, Miller, and Stokes, political-persuasion variables have often been included in analyses of political participation as a fundamental indicator of political engagement.[13] Within the B&B sample, 23 percent of respondents report that they have engaged in this political activity. This percentage is quite a bit smaller than that reported by both the general population of college graduates (41 percent) and the same age cohort of college graduates (41 percent), but these differences can easily be attributed to survey timing. The NES sampling is conducted just before and immediately following a national election, which inevitably increases the likelihood that an individual has engaged in political discussion. The B&B survey, on the other hand, was not conducted in conjunction with any election, nor was a presidential election within the one-year time frame established by the question.

Public vs. Private Regard

Although the data set does not allow for a thorough examination of democratic values, attitudes, and opinions, we can scrutinize education's varied and complex impact on two fundamentally contrasting values underlying political behavior—a general notion of the public vs. private regard. Respondents to the B&B survey were presented with several contrasting values and asked whether each was important to them. One value was whether they thought it was important to have an influence on America's political structure. Another was whether it was important to be well off financially. Following the classic distinction by Wilson and Banfield, we use our college-education variables to see how they affect these public vs. private values.[14] Within our sample, 39 percent of respondents indicated that it is important to them to influence the political structure, and 63 percent reported that it is important to them to be well off financially.[15]

Given the oft-emphasized role of self-interest in political activity, we might expect that the educational effects behind these two values are not fundamentally distinct. After all, scholars often argue that economic interests motivate political action, attitudes, and opinions. So those interested in influencing the political structure would do so on behalf of their own economic interest, and those for whom financial success is important should also recognize the relationship between politics and economics, and participate accordingly. Yet we in fact find that quite different processes are at work in explaining education's impact on these contrasting values.

A NOTE ON METHODOLOGY AND DATA PRESENTATION

Before we present our findings, a short word on methodology and data presentation is necessary. We are dealing in this chapter with a sample from a highly censored population: a sample in which most of the traditional variables used to explain measures of citizen activity and orientation are constants. For example, all B&B respondents are college graduates, so that educational attainment, the so-called "universal solvent" of political behavior, has no variation. Life cycle and birth cohort, two other powerhouse explanatory variables of political phenomena, are also constant. Moreover, because the respondents are so young, large differences in life circumstances predicated on differential income or occupational prominence have not had time to develop. The effects we seek and expect to find are therefore going to be relatively small. For instance, even if we conjecture that the value of a Harvard degree will ultimately increase political engagement, or that GPA, as a measurement of motivation, is ultimately predictive of career achievement, there may have been insufficient time for these factors to generate the important sociological distinctions they may portend. With a median age of twenty-four in our sample, the sociological clock has not yet had time to magnify such distinctions.

Ours is therefore a search not for large R^2s or big coefficients but for patterns of statistically significant relationships. In other words, we are not attempting to fully explain civic and political participation; rather, we are exploring the varied effects of education on such engagement. In all of our models the other usual demographic variables, such as race and ethnicity, gender, marital status, continued graduate training, and parental education, are also always included so that we can be as certain as possible that we have a fully and correctly specified model.

Given that we have six variables indexing citizen behaviors and orientations, and ten measures of educational characteristics, we have a real data presentation dilemma. Exacerbating this presentational problem is the fact that some of our dependent variables are continuous (political participation and community service) while others are dichotomous (voting, political persuasion, public regard vs. private regard). All our findings are based on OLS regression results in the case of the continuous variables and Logit regression results in the case of the dichotomous ones. Although we have two parallel techniques appropriate for the scale of measurement, it is difficult to directly compare the magnitudes of the coefficients between them. In the body of the essay, therefore, we rely upon a combination of line graphs and symbol tables to summarize the main findings from the models. The line graphs plot the effect of a given educational variable (controlling for all other variables in the fully specified model) on one of the citizenship variables. The symbol tables are organized by major blocks of the independent educational variables and summarize the relationship of each of the component variables across the characteristics of democratic citizenship. We signify a statistically significant positive relationship by a plus sign, the lack of a significant relationship by a zero, and a negative relationship by a minus sign. Particularly strong relationships are highlighted by a double-plus or double-minus. The actual coefficients, standard errors, and so on can be found in Appendix C. We believe that these presentation techniques will render this large matrix of complex relationships more comprehensible.

FINDINGS

Aptitude, Proficiency, Performance, and Citizenship

Are more capable and better-performing college graduates more politically active? Are they more likely to vote and/or to participate in political discussions? Do they contribute more to community service? And are they more likely to give more regard to public or private issues? Most interesting of all given recent debates—is there any evidence at all that basic intelligence itself has a relationship to our measures of citizenship? Table 2.1 presents findings that get us one step closer to finding the answers to these questions.

Grades

In examining the effect of cumulative grade point average (GPA) and test scores on the six measures of democratic citizenship, it is clear, first and foremost, that GPA plays no role in political participation, voting, or hours of community service. Whatever combination of ability and effort goes into its production, cumulative GPA—clearly the best overall measure of undergraduate academic performance—shows almost no relationship with the different measures of civic behavior or orientation (as indicated by zeros in the table). The sole exception is that those with poorer grades are slightly more likely to be more concerned about achieving wealth and financial success than those with higher grades. At the same time, GPA is not correlated with the belief that it is important to have an effect on society's political structure. There appears to be no relationship between GPA and political participation, voting, activity in community service, political persuasion, or feeling that it is important to have an effect on politics and the political structure. Whatever motivates an individual to succeed as a student does not appear to also inspire him or her to excel as a citizen—there is simply not a correlation between GPA and political engagement. It is possible, of course, that relationships may emerge later in life, but it is hard in this instance to construct a plausible scenario.

College Entrance Test Scores

Table 2.1 also reports the findings concerning the effect of SAT scores on the dependent variables. SAT college-entrance tests are typically taken in the summer before, or the early fall of, the senior year of high school and are meant to be a gauge of scholastic aptitude in vocabulary, reading comprehension, and quantitative reasoning. The degree to which the SAT measures innate abilities, family

Table 2.1. The Effect of Achievement and Ability

	Participation scale	Vote in presidential election	Political persuasion	Community service participation	Importance of political influence	Importance of financial success
Grade point average	o	o	o	o	o	−
SAT verbal score	++	++	++	+	o	−
SAT math score	−	o	−	o	−	o

Note: Tables report the sign of the effect of the independent variables, controlling for gender, marital status, race, parent's education, and continuing student status, school ranking, and curriculum.

and/or cultural background, or the amount of hard work by the student has been the source of heated debate. This debate centers on whether IQ and aptitude tests measure genetic cognitive proficiency or reflect schooling, socioeconomic background, or individual motivation.[16] We have no intention of entering this debate, and we simply assume that the verbal portion of the SAT measures verbal aptitude and that the math section measures quantitative aptitude—whatever the source of that ability.

If overall intellectual ability is some combination of mathematical and verbal capacities, then more intelligence does not appear to increase political engagement, civic participation, or public mindedness.[17] Given the opposing effects of math and verbal SAT scores on several measures of democratic citizenship, we find no evidence for a general intelligence factor (the much-debated G) exerting an influence on our measures of political engagement and public orientation. These fascinating findings regarding test scores are both subtle and complex. Quantitative aptitude, measured as SAT math scores, has no impact—or, in some instances, actually a negative impact—across the set of citizenship variables. In three cases—overall participation, political persuasion, and desire to influence the political structure—these negative relationships are even statistically significant. In other words, higher SAT math scores correlate with lower levels of participation. The effect of verbal aptitude is exactly the opposite.

The most striking findings in table 2.1 relate to the strong positive relationship between verbal SAT scores and political participation, voting turnout, political persuasion, and civic voluntarism. The effect of verbal aptitude is particularly powerful given that we have controlled for the prominent cultural and background explanations for variations in aptitude exams, among other things,

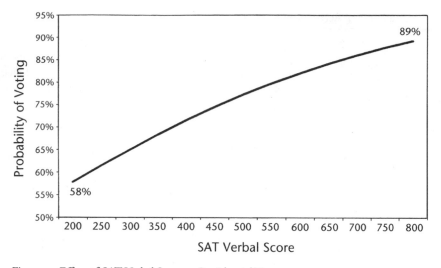

Figure 2.1 Effect of SAT Verbal Score on Presidential Vote

by including parental education and race/ethnicity in the analysis. Let us look more closely, for example, at the relationship between verbal SAT scores and the dependent variables of civic voluntarism and voting. Figures 2.1 and 2.2 illustrate the substantive impact of verbal proficiency on these dependent variables.

Figure 2.1 displays the strength of the relationship between SAT verbal score and probability of turning out in the 1992 presidential election. Holding all other variables at their means (and indicator variables set to zero), the probability of turning out to vote along the range of verbal scores moves from under 60 percent to almost 90 percent. Although we should be leery of Logit point estimations at the extremes, figure 2.1 demonstrates the profound influence of verbal ability on turnout for the entire scale of possible verbal scores. In a sample with no variation in education and age—two of the most important predictors of turnout—a difference of more than 30 percent between the lowest and highest scores is quite dramatic.

The findings are parallel for civic voluntarism. As can be seen in figure 2.2, individuals with the lowest SAT verbal scores report that they gave little more than an hour to community service in the past two years, while those at the other end of the verbal aptitude continuum donated more than twelve hours. Table 2.1 indicates that verbal aptitude similarly has a statistically significant positive impact on political participation and political persuasion. The fact that the SAT is taken at least a year before college matriculation and survives with such strength through more than four years of college training—in which cur-

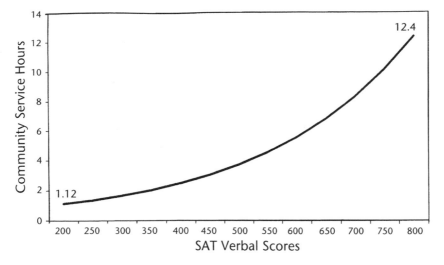

Figure 2.2 Effect of SAT Verbal Score on Community Service

riculum itself is often selected based on these proficiencies—makes these findings that much more remarkable. Verbal aptitude clearly has a significant effect on all our measures of civic and political engagement.

Math aptitude, on the other hand, has a statistically significant and substantively meaningful, albeit smaller, *negative* relationship with the overall citizen participation scale and political discussion and has no statistically significant positive or negative relationship to any of the other measures of citizenship. We might have expected that those with exceptional quantitative skills would also have exceptional analytical and problem-solving abilities—skills quite essential to political activity. And, in fact, verbal and math scores are correlated quite highly (.65). But even if one could build a strong hypothesis for why quantitative reasoning improves political skills, the data clearly reject any such relationship. Controlling for all else, including verbal aptitude, those who score better on the math section of the SAT actually perform fewer participatory acts than do others. Among those with the lowest math scores, political participation averages around the 55th percentile, while those with highest scores decline to the 40th percentile. What do these patterns mean, and how important are they?

We believe they are profoundly important. It is probably of little surprise that verbal ability is important in determining an individual's level of participation. Politics, after all, is a game of language, persuasion, and oral and written communication. To write a letter to a public official, an individual must feel comfortable in finding the words and forming the sentences to express his or her opinion. To engage in political persuasion an individual must have the verbal acuity to communicate his or her position. Social scientists and political philosophers have long emphasized the relationship between politics and language. Murray Edelman, who has written extensively on the importance of language in politics, maintained that "language is an integral facet of the political scene: not simply an instrument for describing events but itself a part of events, shaping their meaning and helping to shape the political roles officials and the general public play."[18] Most recent empirical studies that explore this relationship rely on a basic ten-word vocabulary test and have never viewed verbal ability alongside and/or controlling for quantitative reasoning.[19]

We are unaware of any studies that have considered the relationship between political engagement and verbal aptitude so thoroughly or have done so in the context of other fundamental educational characteristics. Holding all else constant, those who excel in verbal abilities are more likely to vote, to engage in more difficult acts of participation, to attempt to persuade others to their own political convictions, and to become more involved in community service than those with less verbal aptitude. Verbal proficiency shows the strongest relationship of all the many educational variables we examine and is pervasive across the measures of political engagement and persuasion. These findings suggest that it is this kind of aptitude, not overall intelligence itself, that matters. Aptitude for quantitative reasoning plays either no role or perhaps even a small negative one in an individual's level of political engagement and community service. And math aptitude similarly appears to have a negative impact on desire to influence society's political structure. All else held constant, young college graduates with greater quantitative proficiency are more likely to avoid things political.

The findings are clear for the B&B recent graduates—those with strong verbal skills are drawn to things social and political and those who have weaker verbal aptitude are more likely to avoid these areas of life. Conversely, those with strong math aptitude are less likely to participate in the civic and political sphere. The implications of these surprising findings are quite profound.

Quality of School

Another important variation in educational experience concerns the institution of higher learning that was attended by the student. Institutional quality varies widely, and if we accept that this can affect career preparedness and opportunity, then it certainly seems plausible that it can also affect political preparedness and opportunity. A degree from Central State University is simply not equivalent to a degree from an Ivy League university. Such variation likely manifests itself through both intrinsic skill building and social-network position.[20]

Traditionally, the best education, as determined by the labor and academic market, is provided by the institutions richest in resources. So institutions with greater resources—amply funded libraries, distinguished faculty, computer facilities, and so on—should create better citizens by imparting superior political knowledge. The student body of a university is also often included as an institutional resource, so being among the "best and the brightest" is a circumstance that might provide social incentives for participation. If your friends are discussing politics, you are more likely to discuss politics yourself. Several studies have identified the fundamental role that social networks play in shaping an individual's political engagement.[21] Thus we have created a measure of school quality, an eight-tier ranking based on the *U.S. News and World Report* rankings, with the worst schools included in tier one and the best schools in tier eight.[22] By this same logic, we have included in our explanatory model an indicator variable for whether an institution is public or private.

The results with respect to institutional quality fall mostly into the category of null findings, but they are nonetheless revealing. As shown in table 2.2, school ranking quite consistently has no independent effect on any measure of political engagement. The only exceptions are that students from higher-quality schools are slightly more likely to personally feel that it is important to influence the political structure and are slightly more likely to turn out to vote. Similarly, whether an individual attended a public or private university makes no difference in future political behavior, though again, it has a significant positive effect on whether an individual desires public influence. Thus despite theoretical reasons to hypothesize otherwise, institutional quality does not have a pervasive impact on the political engagement of recent graduates. It is certainly plausible that the effect of an elite education has simply not had time to take effect. In other words, as these recent graduates age, as they settle in to their communities, and as some decide to get involved in politics themselves, perhaps the importance of an elite education and the social networks it creates will be magnified. But at this period in their life cycle, the effects of institutional quality are simply not apparent.

As an aside, we also examined the role of private high school attendance in political engagement for similar "quality of institution" reasons. We find, again, that a private high school—or the characteristics of those individuals selecting to attend a private high school—has negligible effects on most measures

Table 2.2. The Effect of Institutional Quality

	Participation scale	Vote in presidential election	Political persuasion	Community service participation	Importance of political influence	Importance of financial success
School ranking	o	+	o	o	+	o
Private institution	o	o	o	o	+	o

Note: Tables report the sign of the effect of the independent variables, controlling for gender, marital status, race, parent's education, and continuing student status, GPA, SAT scores, and curriculum.

of civic and political behavior. The only exception is that individuals who attended a private high school are more likely to find it important to influence the political system, but they are no more likely to actually vote, participate, discuss politics, or donate time to community service.

THE EFFECTS OF COLLEGE CURRICULUM

Already our findings have illustrated the complex and varied impact of college education on democratic citizenship. It appears that what students bring to college is more important than where they went to college and how they did while there. The question that naturally arises is whether what they studied in college matters. In other words, does the college curriculum selected affect future levels of political engagement? Students typically enter college with roughly the same curricular background—a certain number of math, science, English, and foreign language credits are required for college admittance. There is little room for emphasis in a particular subject area while in high school; it is only in college that an individual is able to concentrate study on a specific area of interest. It could certainly be argued that curriculum should have no influence on future political participation. Individual interests and proficiencies, after all, often determine the curriculum that an individual selects. Indeed, several scholars find no relationship between civics courses and political knowledge and socialization in secondary schools.[23] We find, however, that the type of curriculum studied—whether social science, business, science/engineering, or education—seems to directly affect education's impact on political engagement. These results bolster Niemi and Junn's findings that a civic education in high school has a positive impact on political knowledge among high school students.[24]

We analyze the effect of curriculum by first estimating the effect of social science, science/engineering, education, humanities, and business credits (ten credit units) on our measures of political engagement. The clearest pattern in table 2.3 is the ubiquitous role that a social science curriculum plays on every political behavior and orientation we measure, even controlling for GPA, SAT scores, quality of school, marital status, continuing student status, gender, parental education, and race/ethnicity. With regard to the multi-item index of citizen participation and hours committed to community service, the relationships are particularly strong. But number of social science credits also has a statistically significant effect on voting turnout and desire to have an influence on the nation's political structure. B&B graduates who majored in social science were found two years later to be among the most active, engaged, and public-regarding citizens, compared with those who majored in any other field.

The pattern for business school majors is just the opposite. An increase in the number of business courses is correlated with a statistically significant decrease in political participation, voting turnout, hours of community service, and perceived importance of influencing the political structure. Although the negative coefficients for political and community engagement are not as strong as the positive ones for social science credits, they are all statistically significant. And when it comes to influencing the public sphere vs. attaining private wealth, business school majors show very strong proclivities to avoid the public and embrace the attainment of wealth. That business majors should embrace the attainment of wealth is hardly astonishing; that they should so eschew all that is political and communal, however, is a bit surprising. After all, politicians are often business leaders themselves.

The pattern for graduates who majored in science and engineering, though not as pervasively apolitical, is similar to the findings for business majors. Students who concentrated their studies in biology, chemistry, physics, engineering, and similar fields appear less likely to participate politically or to want to influence the community's political structure. To be apt and heavily engaged in the study of the physical and/or biological world seems to correlate with less interest and engagement in the civic and/or political. Finally, the impact of curricular patterns for the humanities and education, perhaps surprisingly, is less clear.

In a book written primarily by education scholars, we would be remiss not to emphasize these findings regarding education curriculum. Unfortunately, we do not have encouraging conclusions regarding the influence of education courses on civic and political engagement. An education curriculum does seem to encourage the value of public influence, but this is the only significant positive relationship. Those with more education credits are, in fact, less likely to

Table 2.3. The Effect of College Curriculum

	Participation scale	Vote in presidential election	Political persuasion	Community service participation	Importance of political influence	Importance of financial success
Science/engineering credits	−	o	−	o	−	o
Social science credits	+ +	+	+ +	+ +	+	o
Humanities credits	o	o	o	o	o	−
Business credits	−	−	−	−	−	+ +
Education credits	o	−	o	o	+	−

Note. Tables report the sign of the effect of the independent variables, controlling for gender, marital status, race, parent's education, continuing student status, GPA, SAT scores, and school ranking.

vote in a presidential election. And an education curriculum seems to have no effect on overall political participation, political discussion, or community service. It is quite interesting that the individuals given the responsibility of providing a civic education for the nation's children do not appear among the civic-minded themselves.

Figure 2.3 gives us a better handle on quantifying these curricular effects on citizen behavior. Again, it is important to remember that we are dealing with relationships within a sample homogeneous with regard to age and education, and that we are concurrently controlling for a wide range of variables ranging from demography to verbal and math aptitude and quality of college. Nevertheless, the curricular relationships remain substantial. Controlling for all other factors, graduates who took few or no social science courses averaged in the 46th percentile on our political participation scale, while social science majors near the maximum ranked nearly ten points higher at the 55th percentile. Slightly smaller reverse patterns exist for science and business courses. As the number of credit hours in these fields of study increase, percentile rank on the participation scale declines by six points—from the 50th percentile to the 44th. Holding all else equal, B&B graduates who majored in business or science/engineering reported that they participated less in politics than did the average graduate in the class and much less than their counterparts who spent their classroom hours in the social sciences. Humanities and education credits were included for comparison but do not have a statistically significant relationship.

A parallel pattern holds true for turnout in the 1992 presidential election. An increase from the lowest to the highest number of social science credits

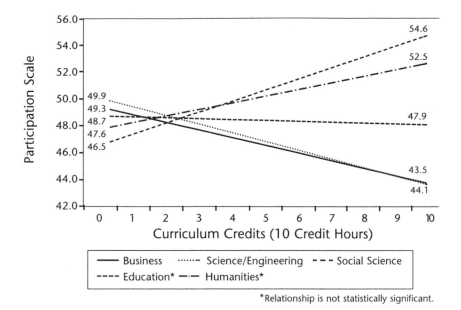

Figure 2.3 Effect of Curriculum on Participation Scores

increases the probability of voting from 73 percent to 84 percent, while an increase over the range of business credits decreases the probability of voting from 78 percent to 59 percent, and an increase over the range of education credits decreases the probability of voting from 77 percent to 65 percent.

The relationship of a social science curriculum to civic voluntarism is just as dramatic. As can be seen in figure 2.4, those with the fewest social science credits donated less than 2.5 hours to community service in the past two years, while those at the other end of the spectrum contributed more than four times as much. Clearly social science curriculum correlates with interest in things civic and political. More interestingly, increased humanities and education training—both quite verbal curricula—do not lead to increased political engagement or desire for public influence. This finding leads us to believe that in addition to self-selection, the content of social science curriculum may perhaps encourage people to become more publicly aware and politically engaged.

APTITUDE, CURRICULUM, AND CITIZENSHIP: REINFORCING EFFECTS

This study has two prominent positive findings. First, higher levels of verbal aptitude correlate with higher levels of political participation, higher rates of

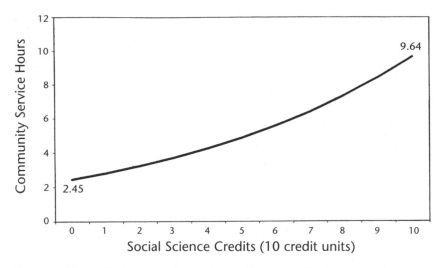

Figure 2.4 Effect of Social Science Curriculum on Community Service

voting turnout, more civic voluntarism, and a heightened sense of public vs. private regard when we hold constant family background, demographics, and college performance and experiences. Second, among the most prominent fields of study available at modern colleges and universities, only a social science curriculum is positively related with the types of citizen behavior just adumbrated. Here, too, the effects on political behavior persist when we control for other powerful predictors of participation, including verbal aptitude. Thus verbal aptitude and a social science curriculum each seem to have an independent direct influence on political engagement and behavior.

This is one of the rare instances with microsurvey data in which the direction of causality is of little doubt. Individuals typically take the SAT college entrance exams at seventeen or eighteen years of age. B&B survey collected political behavior data on these students after they had completed their college degree, some five to six years later. Newtonian understandings of causation would seem quite sufficient here. Likewise, the cumulating of social science credits occurs well before responses to the survey items measuring political behavior.

However, establishing direction of causation helps little in untangling the meaning of causation. We find that verbal aptitude increases participation, persuasion, and civic voluntarism irrespective of the number of social science courses taken, and, likewise, social science has a positive effect on political engagement when we control verbal proficiency. At the same time, verbal aptitude has a significant effect on the college curriculum selected (see table 2.4).

Table 2.4. The Effect of SAT on College Curriculum (standardized coefficients)

	Social science credit hours	Humanities credit hours	Education credit hours	Business credit hours	Science/ engineering credit hours
SAT verbal score	.208*	.275*	−.093*	−.175*	−.1*
(100-point units)	(7.9)	(10.6)	(−3.6)	(−6.6)	(−3.9)
SAT math score	−.199*	−.117*	−.081*	.148*	.332*
(100-point units)	(−7.3)	(−6.4)	(−3.0)	(5.4)	(12.6)

Notes: T-statistics in parentheses. These regressions control for gender, marital status, race, parent's education, continuing student status, GPA, SAT scores, and school ranking. *Indicates significance at $p < .01$.

An individual is perhaps more likely to be drawn to and succeed in areas in which he or she already excels. So the high school students with exceptional verbal skills are likely to choose college curricula in which their skills can be utilized (for example, social science and humanities courses). As such, a social science curriculum may reinforce political interest by taking those who are already interested in things social and political and intensifying interest and concern over a several-year course of study. And the democratic benefits from a social science curriculum serve not only to increase political activity among the biology, engineering, and computer science majors but also to strengthen the mechanisms inducing political behavior for the already politically minded.

Table 2.4 displays the relationship between verbal and math SAT scores and choice of curriculum. The results follow expected patterns. Controlling for background, demographic, and quality of institution variables, we find that individuals with stronger verbal aptitude take more social science and humanities credits and fewer science/engineering courses. It is of little surprise to find that students select a major that aligns with their precollegiate proficiencies. It is surprising, however, that while there is a strong relationship between verbal aptitude and both social science and humanities courses, there is no relationship between a humanities curriculum and democratic citizenship—only the social sciences have led students to increased civic and political participation.

As we can see in the path diagram in figure 2.5, the correlation between the number of courses taken in the humanities and our main measure of political participation is zero—there is no relationship.[25] At the same time, the correlation between credit hours in the social sciences and political participation is quite strong. This diagram again underscores the powerful relationship be-

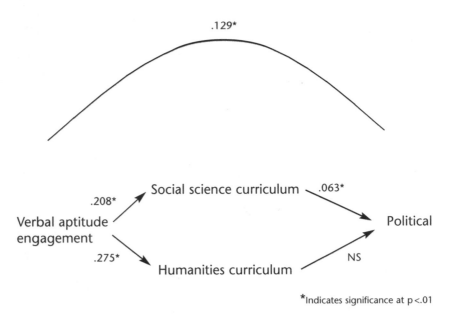

*Indicates significance at p <.01

Figure 2.5 Path Analysis with Standardized Coefficients

tween verbal aptitude and political engagement. An individual's verbal skills before college entrance have two distinct effects on future civic and political activity: not only does verbal aptitude have a direct path to participation and engagement, but it also maintains an indirect path by leading students to major in the social sciences, where they are further stimulated to become politically active and engaged citizens. With the recent release of the next wave of B&B data (the 1997 follow-up), we can begin to study whether these findings are replicated when the students are in their late twenties.

And what of the larger implications of our findings? Our results clearly show the importance of extant proficiencies before college matriculation. Even accounting for other powerful predictors, the verbal skills that a student brings to his or her postsecondary education distinctly influence future political participation. Whether verbal SAT scores measure skills acquired in primary and/or secondary schools or innate verbal proficiency may not yet be finally determined, but our findings suggest that individuals with greater verbal aptitude are more politically active, civic-minded, and attuned to public affairs.

In the aggregate, SAT scores have shown some oscillations over time, trending downward for some years but recently rebounding. Other measures of verbal ability in the general population, such as the NORC word identification test, show virtually no movement in the past quarter of a century in spite of massive increases in educational attainment.[26] The reasons for these trends are not at all clear and are the source of much debate. Yet no matter which side of the nature-nurture debate one is on, most would agree that modifying underlying distributions of verbal aptitude in society can only be viewed as a difficult and long-term undertaking. Nevertheless, if there is any chance to affect those skills, our data suggest that it must come earlier in the educational process than postsecondary instruction. Thus greater emphasis on the development of verbal skills (reading and particularly writing) in elementary and secondary education should certainly be considered.

By contrast, protecting and improving the social science curriculum seems a much more manageable endeavor. And according to our findings, such a task would have a clear impact on increased civic voluntarism and political engagement among the citizenry. Just as Niemi and Junn found for secondary education, curriculum in college does indeed enhance democratic citizenship.[27] Our data clearly suggest that creating a more vibrant and attractive social science curriculum to attract more students will create a more participatory, engaged, and public-regarding citizenry (at least among young college graduates).[28] This connective seems particularly true for those types of social science courses most likely to attract those with exceptional verbal aptitude—that is, history, Western civilization, sociology, political science, macroeconomics, and the like. Moreover, given our finding that the individuals charged with teaching these topics are themselves less engaged, it appears that a greater emphasis on a social science curriculum by future educators would be especially beneficial.

Unfortunately, curriculum reform appears to be going in exactly the opposite direction. The types of social science courses we have alluded to are part of a liberal arts curriculum that seems on the wane at many institutions of higher education. This is in the largest degree due to pressures to become more "occupationally relevant." After all, we are told, this is what pays our salaries and keeps the doors open. The findings in this chapter, however, should offer our colleagues, college administrators, government leaders, and friends of democracy everywhere one more reason to resist such changes.

APPENDIX A: POLITICAL DESCRIPTIVES

Figure 2.6 compares the percentage of B&B respondents involved in various political activities with the general population of college graduates and college graduates of equivalent age group (both based on the 1982–92 National Election Studies (NES) data). The questions from the two surveys differ somewhat, but the general political activities of interest are equivalent (see questions below).

We certainly would expect that these recent graduates might be somewhat less active than the general population of college graduates. These recent graduates are likely not yet established in their careers, communities, or social networks. It is therefore of no surprise that only 5 percent of the B&B respondents have contributed to a political party or campaign, while 19 percent of the general population have done so. Interestingly, the B&B graduates are somewhat more likely to write to a public official (13 percent) than the general population (8 percent). And the percentages working on a political campaign and attending political meetings are quite similar—6 percent and 13 percent, respectively, for the B&B graduates, and 7 percent and 14 percent, respectively, for the general population. Reassuringly, the participation levels of the NES college graduates of similar age are quite similar to those of the B&B respondents. They differ by no more than five percentage points on any of the political activities except political discussion, which can likely be attributed to survey timing.

Survey Questions on Political Behavior

B&B Survey Questions

In the last 12 months, did you talk to any people and try to show them why they should vote for one of the parties or candidates?

[In the past 12 months,] did you give any money or other financial support to help the campaign for any political party or candidate?

During the past two years have you actively campaigned for any candidate for elected office? (IF YES, CLARIFY—Was that your own or someone else's campaign? IF SOMEONE ELSE'S—Was that paid or volunteer work?)

[In the past 12 months,] have you written a letter to any public official to express your opinion?

[In the last 12 months,] did you go to any political meetings, rallies, dinners, or things like that?

Now I'd like to ask you about any civic activities you might have taken part in the last year. Between July 1, 1993, and (June 30, 1994/CURRENT DATE), did you perform community service or volunteer work, other than court ordered?

National Election Studies Questions

During the campaign, did you talk to any people and try to show them why they should vote for or against one of the parties or candidates?

Did you go to any political meetings, rallies, speeches, dinners, or things like that in support of a particular candidate?

Did you do any [other] work for one of the parties or candidates?

During an election year people are often asked to make a contribution to support campaigns. Did you give money to an individual candidate running for public office? Did you give money to a political party during this election year?

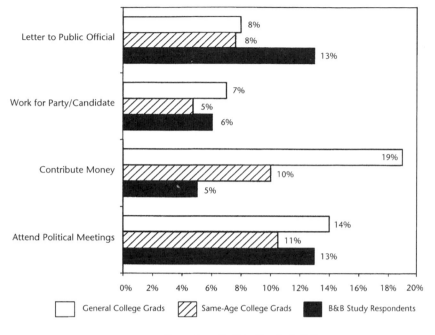

Percentage Participation in Activity

Figure 2.6 Participation Comparison of Study Respondents and General Population

Have you ever written a letter to any public officials giving them your opinion about something that should be done? [Question asked only 1964–76, so percentages reflect these years.]

APPENDIX B

Our political-engagement scale, ranging from 0–100, with 100 indicating the highest level of activity, is a summary of the following participatory acts: contributing money to a political campaign, working on a political campaign, writing a letter to a public official, attending a political meeting, and "other" political activities. These participatory acts are transformed into a participation scale using homogeneity analysis by means of alternating least squares, or HOMALS. For a more detailed account of this technique see Albert Gifi's *Nonlinear Multivariate Analysis.*[29] Briefly, homogeneity analysis can be viewed as a principal-components analysis of nominal data. This procedure simultaneously quantifies categorical variables while reducing the dimensionality of the data into a smaller set of uncorrelated components that represents most of the information found in the original variables. The object scores from this analysis were then converted to percentages to give the dependent variable a more tangible scale. The participation score has a mean of 48.9 and a standard deviation of 23.7.

APPENDIX C: REGRESSION COEFFICIENTS

	OLS: Political participation	OLS: Community service hours	Logit: Presidential vote	Logit: Political persuasion	Logit: Influencing politics	Logit: Financial wealth
Constant	45.75	−2.0	−.469	−1.35	.848	2.033
Female	−1.8	.268	.073	−.49**	−.168	−.215*
	(1.01)	(.139)	(.101)	(.103)	(.096)	(.098)
Hispanic	−1.15	.47	−.235	.465*	.233	.156
	(2.48)	(.35)	(.237)	(.229)	(.238)	(.258)
Asian	1.42	.19	−.461*	−.405	.111	.427
	(2.4)	(.319)	(.225)	(.277)	(.238)	(.257)
Black	1.99	2.17**	−.246	−.31	.325	.730**
	(2.2)	(.309)	(.201)	(.187)	(.201)	(.248)
Graduate school	1.45	.285**	−.103	.061**	.428**	.061
	(1.5)	(.21)	(.155)	(.014)	(.165)	(.014)
Married	5.22**	−.39	−.103**	.320	−.056	.036
	(1.9)	(.256)	(.205)	(.154)	(.177)	(.179)
GPA	−.02	.002	.000	−.001	−.001	−.002*
	(.011)	(.001)	(.001)	(.001)	(.001)	(.001)
Parent's education	.265	.052**	−.001	−.001	−.011	−.011
	(.139)	(.019)	(.014)	(.014)	(.013)	(.014)
Business credits	−.58*	−.12**	−.093**	−.028	−.103**	.245**
	(.294)	(.04)	(.028)	(.031)	(.028)	(.032)
Education credits	−.079	−.01	−.06*	−.020	.068*	−.108**
	(.376)	(.051)	(.035)	(.041)	(.034)	(.034)
Humanities credits	.488	.016	−.053	.032	−.029	−.054
	(.352)	(.049)	(.036)	(.035)	(.033)	(.033)
Science credits	−.645*	−.058	−.022	−.049**	−.08	−.019
	(.257)	(.035)	(.026)	(.027)	(.026)	(.025)
Social science credits	.808**	.137**	.061*	.096**	.063**	.026
	(.292)	(.04)	(.030)	(.029)	(.027)	(.027)
Private	−1.36	.227	.041	−.1442	.292*	−.038
	(1.2)	(.168)	(.125)	(.127)	(.116)	(.019)
SAT math scores	−.024**	0.00	.000	−.001*	−.001*	.000
	(.007)	(.001)	(.001)	(.0007)	(.001)	(.001)
SAT verbal scores	.031**	.004**	.003**	.002**	−.001	−.002*
	(.007)	(.001)	(.001)	(.0007)	(.001)	(.001)
School tier	.376	.023	.057*	.016	.084**	.029
	(.252)	(.034)	(.025)	(.026)	(.024)	(.024)
R^2/Nagelkerke R^2	.039	.073	.061	.052	.064	.114
N	2494	2375	2545	2504	2545	2285

Note: Standard errors in parentheses, *$p < .05$, **$p < .01$.

NOTES

The authors would like to thank Jane Junn for giving us the idea for this chapter, the National Center for Education Statistics for the gracious use of their data, and Lutz Erbring and Todd Shields for their useful comments and suggestions.

1. See Philip E. Converse, "Change in the American Electorate," in Angus Campbell and Philip E. Converse, eds., *The Human Meaning of Social Change* (New York: Russell Sage Foundation, 1972), p. 324.

2. See, for example, Angus Campbell, Philip E. Converse, Warren E. Miller, and Donald E. Stokes, *The American Voter* (New York: Wiley, 1960); Richard Brody, "The Puzzle of Participation in America," in Anthony King, ed., *The New American Political System* (Washington, D.C.: American Enterprise Institute, 1978); Norman H. Nie, Sidney Verba, and John Petrocik, *The Changing American Voter* (Cambridge: Harvard University Press, 1979); Steven J. Rosenstone and Raymond E. Wolfinger, *Who Votes?* (New Haven: Yale University Press, 1980); Steven J. Rosenstone and John Mark Hansen, *Mobilization, Participation, and Democracy in America* (New York: Macmillan, 1993); Sidney Verba, Kay Lehman Schlozman, Henry E. Brady, *Voice and Equality: Civic Voluntarism in American Politics* (Cambridge: Harvard University Press, 1995); Warren E. Miller and J. Merrill Shanks, *The New American Voter* (Cambridge: Harvard University Press, 1996).

3. There is, however, a serious debate as to whether education serves as a skill-building or sorting mechanism. See Norman H. Nie, Jane Junn, and Kenneth Stehlik-Barry, *Education and Democratic Citizenship in American* (Chicago: University of Chicago Press, 1996), and Verba, Schlozman, and Brady, *Voice and Equality*, for contrasting theories of education.

4. See Richard Niemi and Jane Junn, *Civic Education: What Makes Students Learn* (New Haven: Yale University Press, 1998).

5. This essay is based on the central, if implicit, premise that what citizens do and believe about politics plays a significant, if not easily determined, role for the maintenance of stable democratic governance.

6. See *Baccalaureate and Beyond Longitudinal Study: 1993/1994 Methodology Report* (Washington, D.C.: U.S. Department of Education, National Center for Education Statistics, 1996).

7. These differences can likely be attributed to both the regional differences between SAT and ACT takers and varying institutional requirements.

8. The authors of at least two studies, however, argue that intelligence causes both education and turnout, so that the perceived relation is actually spurious. See Robert C. Luskin, "Explaining Political Sophistication," *Political Behavior* 12 (1990), and Carol A. Cassel and Celia Lo, "Theories of Political Literacy," *Political Behavior* 19, no. 4 (1997).

9. For a comprehensive study of the SAT and its place in the educational system, see Nicholas Lemann, *The Big Test: The Secret History of the American Meritocracy* (New York: Farrar, Straus, and Giroux, 1999).

10. Tocqueville made this observation about American democracy in the mid-nineteenth century. See also Niel J. Smelser, *Theory of Collective Behavior* (New York: Free Press,

1962), or Hannah Arendt, *The Origins of Totalitarianism* (New York: Harcourt, Brace, 1973) for discussion on the importance of civic participation.

11. Pamela Johnston Conover and Donald D. Searing, "Citizenship, Socialization, and Democracy," in Ian Budge and David McKay, eds., *Developing Democracy* (London: Sage, 1994).

12. Verba, Schlozman, and Brady, *Voice and Equality*.

13. Campbell et al., *The American Voter*.

14. James Q. Wilson and Edward C. Banfield, "Public-Regardingness as a Value Premise in Voting Behavior," *American Political Science Review* 58 (1964).

15. The correlation between the two variables is .014, which is insignificant with either a one- or two-sided test.

16. For some of the literature on this debate see Christopher Jencks, *Inequality: A Reassessment of the Effect of Family and Schooling in America* (New York: Basic, 1972); N. J. Block and Gerald Dworking, "I.Q. Heritability and Inequality," part 1, *Philosophy and Public Affairs* 3 (1974): 331; Anne Anastasi, *Psychological Testing*, 4th ed. (New York: Macmillan, 1976); Stanley S. Gutterman, "IQ Tests in Research on Social Stratification: The Cross-Class Validity of the Tests as Measures of Scholastic Aptitude," *Sociology of Education* 52 (1979); Richard J. Herrnstein and Charles Murray, *The Bell Curve: Intelligence and Class Structure in American Life* (New York: Free Press, 1994); Claude S. Fischer, Michael Hout, Martin Sanchez Jankowski, Samuel R. Lucas, Ann Swindler, and Kim Voss, *Inequality by Design: Cracking the Bell Curve Myth* (Princeton: Princeton University Press, 1996).

17. If more intelligent people participated more, our findings would actually suggest that individuals with higher math scores are *less* intelligent than those with lower scores. This simply does not seem plausible.

18. Murray Edelman, *Political Language: Words That Succeed and Policies That Fail* (New York: Academic Press, 1977), p. 4. See also Murray Edelman, *Politics and Symbolic Action: Mass Arousal and Quiescence* (New York: Academic Press, 1971), and Murray Edelman, *The Symbolic Uses of Politics* (Urbana: University of Illinois Press, 1977).

19. See, for example, Verba, Schlozman, and Brady, *Voice and Equality*, and Nie, Junn, and Stehlik-Barry, *Education and Democratic Citizenship in America*.

20. Nie, Junn, and Stehlik-Barry, *Education and Democratic Citizenship in America,* present the hypothesis that education is important in democratic citizenship behavior because it plays a fundamental role in social-network positioning.

21. Verba, Schlozman, and Brady, *Voice and Equality;* Rosenstone and Hansen, *Mobilization, Participation, and Democracy in America;* and Nie, Junn, and Stehlik-Barry, *Education and Democratic Citizenship in America*.

22. There is certainly controversy surrounding these rankings. We collapse the individual rankings into rough tiers, so our ranking should hold up reasonably well.

23. See, for example, Paul Allen Beck, "The Role of Agents in Political Socialization," in Stanley Allen Renshon, ed., *Handbook of Political Socialization* (New York: Free Press, 1977), or Joseph Murphy, *The Educational Reform Movement of the 1980s* (Berkeley: McCutchan, 1990).

24. Niemi and Junn, *Civic Education,* chapters 6 and 7.

25. The model contains all previous controls, and the results hold for our other measures of democratic citizenship as well.
26. Moreover, our own research on these measures shows that the common-wisdom targets, such as declining school quality, excessive television viewing, and so on, do not stand up to empirical scrutiny.
27. Niemi and Junn, *Civic Education.*
28. These results hold when we control for numerous background characteristics.
29. Albert Gifi, *Nonlinear Multivariate Analysis* (New York: Wiley, 1990).

Chapter 3 Community-Based Social Capital and Educational Performance

Robert D. Putnam

The African proverb "It takes a village to raise a child" has become a cliché in current discussions about education in the United States. One interesting question that arises from this call for community engagement is whether some kinds of villages do a better job of raising and educating children than others.

Discussions of the effects of community characteristics on educational performance can usefully be framed in terms of "social capital." In the educational context the late James S. Coleman defined social capital as "the norms, the social networks, and the relationships between adults and children that are of value for the child's growing up."[1] The hypothesis is that social capital—social networks and the norms of reciprocity and trustworthiness that arise from them—fosters the effectiveness of institutional structures such as schools.[2] In this chapter I examine some new evidence in support of that hypothesis. I begin with a word or two about the central concept of social capital.

Social capital entered contemporary parlance in the wake of Coleman's seminal work on the role of social networks in education, but the idea was independently invented at least six times over the twentieth century. Interestingly, the earliest known coinage was in the context of the Progressive Era debate about educational reform. In 1916 L. J. Hanifan, the state supervisor of rural education in West Virginia, outlined virtually all the key elements in our contemporary conception, as part of an argument for what would now be called "community schools." For Hanifan, social capital referred to:

> good will, fellowship, sympathy, and social intercourse among the individuals and families who make up a social unit, the rural community, whose logical center is the school. . . . The individual is helpless socially, if left to himself. . . . If he comes into contact with his neighbor, and they with other neighbors, there will be an accumulation of social capital, which may immediately satisfy his social needs and which may bear a social potentiality sufficient to the substantial improvement of living conditions in the whole community. The community as a whole will benefit by the coöperation of all its parts, while the individual will find in his associations the advantages of the help, the sympathy, and the fellowship of his neighbors.[3]

Social networks have value: that is the central insight of social capital theory. Some of the benefits of social networks flow directly as "private goods" to participants in those networks. For example, research in many countries has shown the importance of informal social networks for job placement. On the other hand, as Hanifan clearly recognized, some of the consequences of social networks are "public goods," whose benefits flow to bystanders, not just to participants themselves. For example, local crime is lowered by dense networks of neighbors, thus benefiting even reclusive residents.[4]

Social networks can have powerful community effects for several interrelated reasons. Most fundamentally, networks of engagement are typically associated with a norm of generalized reciprocity: I'll do this for you now, without expecting anything immediately in return, because somewhere down the road someone else will do something for me. Communities or organizations in which this norm is followed can more efficiently restrain opportunism, facilitate cooperation, and lower transaction costs. Honesty, reciprocity, and trust are social emollients.

Networks are also valuable because they transmit information and propagate reputations. Honesty may be its own reward, but that reward is augmented if others know and act on your reputation for good faith. Networks also serve as examples of successful collaboration, thus serving as a cultural template for resolving new problems of collective action. Finally, dense networks of civic engagement may encourage altruism or at least mutual respect and concern among members of the networks. For all these reasons, communities of high social capital are often simply nicer places to live.

The "external" effects of social networks, however, are not always positive for all bystanders.[5] Social capital, like physical and human capital, can be used for socially unproductive purposes. To take a most obscene example, the Nazis relied on German social capital to seize and hold power, just as they relied on the German rail network (physical capital) and German chemical expertise (human capital) to carry out the Holocaust. Thus students of social capital need to examine empirically the consequences of social networks and to distinguish theoretically among various different forms of social capital.

The issue of whether and how social capital influences educational performance is given added urgency by new evidence that America's stocks of social capital have been unexpectedly and dramatically depleted during the past several decades, precisely the period in which such measures of "school performance" as test scores have declined. Most discussion of educational reform in recent years has assumed that poor educational outcomes are attributable to something that schools and educators must have done wrong. The evidence in this chapter, however, raises fundamental questions: Is it possible that the faltering educational performance of America's students over the past several decades may have been blamed, at least in part, on the wrong cause? To what extent do poor test scores, high dropout rates, and the like reflect not a schooling problem but a community problem?

TRENDS IN SOCIAL CAPITAL IN AMERICA

Historically, America has been blessed with unusually high levels of social capital. This fact, first emphasized by Tocqueville, is confirmed by contemporary social scientific evidence.[6] Over the last third of the twentieth century, however, many familiar forms of civic engagement and social connectedness declined.[7]

First, many types of communally oriented political participation have plummeted. As is well known, electoral turnout, both national and local, has declined by roughly 25 percent since the early 1960s, but it is not merely from the voting booth that Americans are increasingly AWOL. In fact, the decline of participation in less ritualistic forms of politics has been even steeper. The frequency with which Americans attended a public meeting on town or school affairs, or served as an officer or committee member of some local organization, or worked for a political party all declined by more than 40 percent between 1973 and 1994.

Nominal membership in organizations has declined very little over recent years. But that simple measure of social connectedness is increasingly inflated by "checkbook" membership in massive mailing-list organizations whose members never meet (and most of whom say that they do not regard themselves as members.) These organizations, like the American Association of Retired Persons (AARP) or the American Automobile Association (AAA), are politically and commercially important, but they do not really represent community-based social networks.

By contrast, membership rates in most major civic organizations that do have local chapters, from the PTA to the Lions Club to the League of Women Voters, fell by roughly half between the early 1960s and the late 1990s. Active engagement in local clubs and organizations of all sorts (not just old-fashioned "funny hat" organizations) fell by roughly half over the last third of the twentieth century. Although Americans remain an unusually religious people, our active involvement in religious organizations, as measured by church attendance, for example, fell between 25 percent and 50 percent over the same years. These estimates of organizational disengagement are entirely confirmed by daily time diaries kept by national samples of Americans in 1965, 1975, 1985, and 1995. Insofar as social networks are embodied in locally based organizations, over the last third of the twentieth century roughly half of the social capital stock of U.S. communities simply evaporated.

Many of our social connections, however, are reflected not in formal organizations but in informal leisure activities—having friends over for dinner, hanging out in bars, gossiping with neighbors, playing cards, in short, schmoozing. Several independent survey archives show that virtually all these forms of social capital have also badly eroded during the last several decades. Entertaining friends at home fell by about 30–40 percent, as did going out to bars and other night spots, or spending an evening with the neighbors, or playing cards, or playing a musical instrument. Despite the trendiness of health and fitness, participation in sports has fallen over this period, especially team sports. Those time-diary studies confirm that we spent less than two-thirds as much time on informal socializing at century's end than we did three decades earlier. Our use of leisure time has been substantially privatized, as we have shifted from doing to watching. Americans have silently withdrawn from social intercourse of all sorts, not just from formal organizational life.

Most measures of American generosity and altruism followed, with almost uncanny precision, the ups and downs of our civic involvement over the course of the twentieth century. As a fraction of our income, philanthropy of all sorts rose steadily from the 1920s to the 1960s, and then declined steadily thereafter. Evidence on volunteering tells a more complicated story, for over the past few decades aggregate volunteering was pumped up by a remarkable increase in volunteer activity among retired members of the World War II generation—what I term "the long civic generation"—but volunteering among Americans in the prime of life (especially the baby boomers) actually slumped. Despite loose talk to the contrary, there is no evidence that active involvement in other-regarding social movements, such as environmentalism, has risen in recent decades; indeed, the best evidence suggests the reverse.

Nor is this erosion of American social capital limited to community settings. A massive and widely discussed loosening of bonds within the family is reflected in higher divorce rates, more single-parent families, and a sharp increase in one-person households. (Rioux and Berla report that "only 7 percent of today's school-age children come from families that were typical in 1965—two-parent, single–wage earner families."[8]) Moreover, even among married couples the frequency of family dinners has declined by about one-third, as has the frequency with which parents take vacations with their children, or watch TV with them, or even simply "just sit and talk" with them.

Last but not least, social trust—not just trust in leaders and political institutions, but trust in "the generalized other"—has declined. The proportion of Americans saying that "most people can be trusted" (as opposed to "you can't be too careful") fell by two-fifths between 1960 (when 58 percent chose that alternative) and 1999 (when only 34 percent did). Distressingly, the erosion of social trust has been even sharper among high school students, for whom this measure was cut virtually in half between 1976 (46 percent trusting) and 1997 (24 percent trusting). I read this evidence not as a reflection of an epidemic of youthful paranoia. Rather, our children are telling us that in their experience people really aren't trustworthy. From the point of view of civic life, this erosion in honesty and social trust may be even more significant than any decline in organizational involvement. A world in which we distrust one another is a world in which social collaboration seems a bad gamble, a world in which democracy itself is less safe.

Strikingly, these various declines in social connectedness are evident in all corners of American society. The adverse trends in voting, joining, schmoozing, giving, trusting, and the like are down among both women and men, down on both coasts and in the heartland, down in central cities, in suburbs, and in small towns, down among the rich and among the poor, down among whites and down among African Americans, down among college graduates and down among high school dropouts. Social disengagement is an equal-opportunity affliction. The only exception to this uniform pattern is generational, for the erosion of civic involvement is least visible among Americans born in the first third of the twentieth century and raised before or during World War II (the long civic generation), and most marked among the baby boomers and their children. In fact, this generational arithmetic implies that the state of social capital in America is almost bound to get worse over the next several decades, for each year U.S. communities lose another cohort of the most civically engaged portion of their citizens.

The decline in various forms of social capital and civic engagement since the 1960s is not merely the latest installment of an ineluctable, secular degradation of social relations in modern society. Rather, the course of U.S. history has included both ebbs and flows in the creation of social capital.[9] The available evidence suggests, in fact, that social connectedness—associational membership, philanthropy, trust, even card playing and league bowling—rose for most of the first two-thirds of the twentieth century. I see certain hopeful parallels between trends in contemporary America and earlier periods of social distress that served as a prelude for subsequent epochs of intense social capital formation. Be that as it may, the more recent changes form a backdrop for my exploration here of how patterns of civic engagement and parental involvement in schools might affect educational outcomes. The central question addressed in this chapter is this: what are the likely educational consequences of the collapse of many forms of social connectedness and civic engagement over the past thirty years?

SOCIAL CAPITAL AND THE
EDUCATIONAL PROCESS

The concept of social capital, though now being applied to a wide range of phenomena, from economic development in India to crime rates in Sweden to breast cancer survival in the United States, originated in claims about the effects of social networks and norms in education on America. The empirical bases of those claims remain controversial, largely because of important methodological difficulties, including

- the difficulty of distinguishing between structural and compositional effects (Is it, for example, the networks of middle-class neighborhoods that really matter or merely the material resources of middle-class individuals?)
- the difficulty of distinguishing between selection and socialization effects (Is it the parents who send their kids to private schools or the community in which those schools are embedded, for example, that really matters?)
- the difficulty of documenting precise causal mechanisms (As yet, few studies have been designed to test alternative hypotheses about how social capital might influence educational processes.)

Nevertheless, there is good reason to suspect that many forms of social capital powerfully influence the educational process. These forms include the following:

The family. The literature documenting the effects of the family on the educational success of children is, of course, massive. There seems little doubt that different family forms embody different quantities and qualities of social capital, and that they have different consequences for children's socialization. While much here remains controversial, there is some evidence that the traditional nuclear family is a more successful agency of socialization than the less conventional forms of single-parent or blended families that have become more common throughout the West over the past generation. Recent research also suggests that teens who spend more time with their parents (regularly eating dinner with the family, for example) do better in school and suffer less from various forms of risk-prone conduct, such as the use of drugs and alcohol, violence, and suicidal behavior, even holding constant poverty, family structure, race, and other such factors.[10]

Parent-school engagement. A substantial body of literature has accumulated in recent years suggesting that educational outcomes are improved when families are directly engaged with schools. Anne Henderson, for example, has summarized a large number of studies tending to show that when parents are involved with their children's education, children do better in school and the schools they attend are better. Henderson and Berla, in their review of the research, assert that "the evidence is now beyond dispute. When schools work together with families to support learning, children tend to succeed not just in school, but throughout life. . . . When parents are involved in their children's education at home, their children do better in school. When parents are involved at school, their children go further in school, and the schools they go to are better."[11]

Social capital within schools. Attention has also been given to the possibility that schools themselves vary in terms of social capital in ways relevant to educational outcomes. For example, this is one way of interpreting the observation by Lee and Smith that schools organized in a "communal" way are more effective than "bureaucratic" schools.[12] Much of the research on "effective schools," "school-based management," and "school size effects" might also be reinterpreted in this way.

Community-based social capital. Other forms of social capital have also been linked to improved educational outcomes. These include youth organizations (as studied by Heath and McLaughlin), religious organizations, and other forms of civic engagement.[13] As recent analysts of differences in educational achievement across the American states argue (though without direct evidence), "social capital influences achievement through such things as peer effects, quality of communication and trust among families in communities, the safety of neighborhoods, and the presence of community institutions that support achievement."[14] However, I have found little empirically based analysis of possible effects of broader community connectedness on educational outcomes. The central hypothesis explored in this essay is that community-based social capital improves educational performance.

COMMUNITY-BASED SOCIAL CAPITAL AND EDUCATIONAL OUTCOMES

Recent research on social capital and educational outcomes suggests that learning may be influenced not only by what happens in school and at home, but also by social networks, norms, and trust in the wider community.[15] One initial test of this hypothesis is to examine correlations between educational outcomes and social capital at the aggregate level. In this essay I use the American states as my unit of analysis because abundant data are available at that level on educational performance, on various measures of social capital, and on other possible influences on educational performance.[16] It will be desirable in future research, of course, to carry this line of inquiry to more locally defined units of analysis, including eventually the individual school and neighborhood.

As is well known, educational outcomes differ markedly across the American states, as evidenced by test scores from the National Assessment of Educational Progress (NAEP), by Scholastic Achievement Test (SAT) scores, and by dropout rates.[17] In nationwide math tests in 1992, for example, only 13 percent of public school eighth graders in North Dakota and 14 percent of Iowans scored below the nominal midpoint, as compared to 50 percent of Louisianans and 55 percent of Mississippians. High school dropout rates in 1993–95 ranged from 3 to 4 percent in Connecticut, Iowa, and Maine to roughly four times that high in West Virginia, Louisiana, and Texas.[18] Could such contrasts be related, at least in part, to differences in community-based social capital?

States—and therefore the communities that constitute them—differ significantly in their levels of community-based social capital and civic engagement, as suggested by such simple indicators as organizational involvement, participation in public affairs, community volunteerism, informal socializing, and social trust. I have collected a baker's dozen of independent indicators of these features of community life. Some of these indicators measure involvement in civic organizations, some measure engagement in public affairs, some measure volunteerism, some measure informal socializing, and some measure social trust. I interpret these all as partial, imperfect indicators of an underlying latent variable—the density of community-based social networks—and evidence presented below tends to confirm this interpretation. My data are drawn from a variety of sources, including three independent national survey archives.

- General Social Survey: Nearly every year between 1972 and 1996 the National Opinion Research Corporation polled a national random sample of the adult population, totaling nearly seventy thousand cases over this period. From these surveys I derive state-level measures of two variables: social trust and group membership.[19]
- Roper reports: Roughly ten times per year between September 1973 and October 1994, the Roper survey organization polled a national random sample of approximately two thousand persons of voting age, yielding a survey archive of nearly four hundred thousand respondents over more than two decades.[20] From these data I have compiled state-level measures of the average frequency of participation in a range of civic and political activities during the preceding year, including "attend[ing] a public meeting on town or school affairs, "serv[ing] as an officer of some club or organization," and "serv[ing] on a committee for some local organization."
- DDB Life Style surveys: Every year since 1975 the DDB marketing firm has commissioned a national mail panel survey of roughly 3,500 respondents, including dozens of questions about economic, social, consumer, and personal behavior. Although these surveys are based on quota samples, within well-defined limits they provide reliable data, highly convergent with other well-known national surveys, including the General Social Survey and the Uni-

versity of Michigan's Survey of Consumer Sentiment.[21] From this archive, totaling more than eighty thousand cases, I have compiled state-level averages for attendance at club meetings, volunteer work and community projects, home entertaining and socializing with friends, and social trust.[22]

- In addition to these survey-based measures, I have also included in my analysis a measure of electoral turnout and a measure of the incidence of nonprofit organizations.[23]

These thirteen indicators of formal and informal community networks and social trust are in turn sufficiently intercorrelated that they appear to tap a single underlying dimension. For example, in a principal components factor analysis a single dominant factor accounts for 58 percent of the total shared variance. In other words, these thirteen indicators measure related but distinct facets of community-based social capital, and I have combined them into a single social capital index.[24]

As a measure of community-based social capital (networks and norms of reciprocity), any single indicator in this list is flawed. Voting turnout, for example, reflects not only civic responsibility but also electoral competitiveness, while each of our survey-based measures is affected by sampling error along with many other forms of "noise." Given the wide range of sources for these data, however, these errors are probably uncorrelated across the diverse measures. The *shared* variance in the measures—what is measured by the composite factor score—is precisely the underlying interstate difference in civic engagement and social connectedness. The factor score, in other words, is a purer measure of community-based social capital than is any of its individual components. Table 3.1 summarizes these thirteen indicators and their correlation with the summary index.

The variance among the states on the underlying measures is quite substantial, with ratios of roughly 3:1 between high- and low-ranking states. Average levels of social trust as expressed in the General Social Survey, for example, range from 17 percent in Mississippi to 67 percent in North Dakota. The average number of associational memberships per capita varies from 1.3 in Louisiana and North Carolina to 3.3 in North Dakota. Turnout in recent presidential elections has varied between 42 percent in South Carolina and 69 percent in Minnesota. The number of nonprofit organizations per one thousand residents ranges from 1.2 in Mississippi to 3.6 in Vermont. The average number of club meetings attended per year varies from four in Nevada to eleven in North and South Dakota. The reported frequency of volunteering varies from five times

Table 3.1. Components of Comprehensive Social Capital Index

	Correlation with index
Measures of community organizational life	
Served on committee of some local organization in last year	0.89
Served as officer of some club or organization in last year	0.84
Mean number of club meetings attended in last year	0.75
Mean number of group memberships	0.72
Measures of engagement in public affairs	
Turnout in presidential elections, 1988 and 1992	0.83
Attended public meeting on town or school affairs in last year	0.75
Measures of community volunteerism	
Number of nonprofit (501[c]3) organizations per 1,000 population, 1989	0.80
Mean number of times worked on community project in last year	0.63
Mean number of times did volunteer work in last year	0.63
Measures of informal sociability	
Agree that "I spend a lot of time visiting friends"	0.71
Mean number of times entertained at home in last year	0.67
Measures of social trust	
Agree that "Most people can be trusted"	0.88
Agree that "Most people are honest"	0.82

per year in Nevada, Mississippi, and Louisiana to twice that in Utah. The fraction of the population who report attending a public meeting on town or school affairs in the previous year ranges from 10 percent in Georgia and New York to 32 percent in New Hampshire.

The correlations in table 3.1 (and the underlying factor analysis) imply that these interstate differences go together. Places with dense associational networks tend to have frequent public meetings on local issues, places that have high electoral turnout tend to have high levels of social trust, places with lots of local clubs tend to support many nonprofit organizations, and so on. Figure 3.1, which maps my summary statewide measure of social capital, shows that, geographically speaking, the national social capital "barometric map" is fairly straightforward. The primary "high pressure" zone is centered over the headwaters of the Mississippi and Missouri Rivers and extends east and west along the Canadian border. The primary "low pressure" area is centered over the Mississippi delta and extends outward in rising concentric circles through the former Confederacy.[25] California and the mid-Atlantic states lie near the national average.[26]

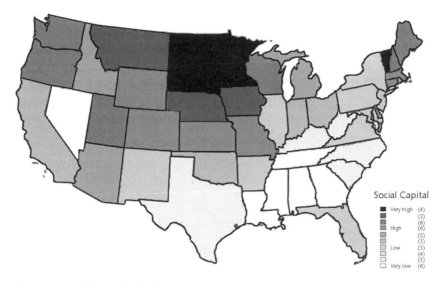

Figure 3.1 Social Capital in the American States
Reprinted from Robert D. Putnam, *Bowling Alone: The Collapse and Revival of American Community* (New York: Simon and Schuster, 2000). Used with permission.

This social capital index is strongly correlated with educational outcomes. States where citizens meet, join, vote, and trust in unusual measure boast consistently higher educational performance than states where citizens are less engaged with civic and community life. Somehow the former, as contrasted with the latter, seem to encourage relatively high achievement in both primary and secondary school. Figures 3.2–3.5 demonstrate a surprisingly consistent correlation between social capital and my diverse measures of educational performance.[27] More than half of all interstate variation in these three measures of educational outcomes appears linked to levels of social capital.[28]

Figure 3.5 pulls together all three measures of educational outcomes—elementary school scores on the NAEP, adjusted SAT scores, and high school dropout rates—into a single summary index of educational performance.[29] As the figure clearly demonstrates, nearly three-quarters of the total interstate variance in educational performance is directly explicable in terms of differences in community-based social capital.

But could these strong relations be spurious? States also differ along many other dimensions that might in principle confound this simple bivariate relationship—racial composition, affluence, economic inequality, adult educational levels, poverty rates, educational spending, teachers' salaries, class size,

Elementary School Achievement and Social Capital

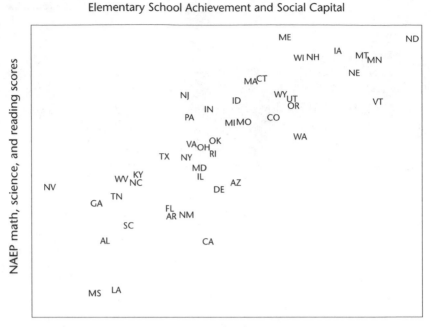

Figure 3.2 Elementary School Achievement and Social Capital

SAT Scores and Social Capital

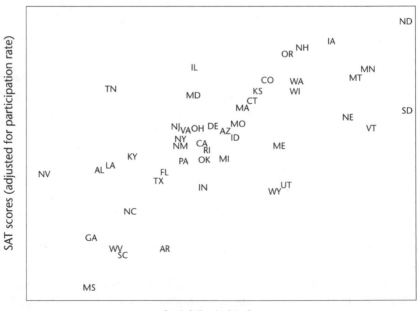

Figure 3.3 SAT Scores and Social Capital

High School Dropout Rates and Social Capital

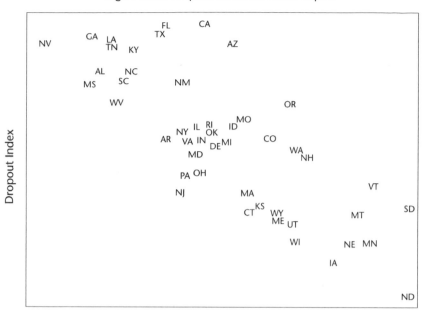

Figure 3.4 High School Dropout Rates and Social Capital

Educational Performance and Social Capital

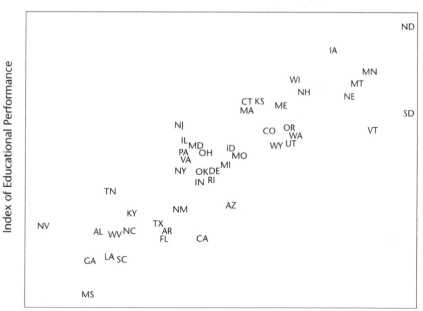

Figure 3.5 Educational Performance and Social Capital

family structure, religious affiliation, the size of the private school sector (which might "cream" better students from public schools), and so on.[30] In an effort to test the robustness of the presumed "social capital effect," I have conducted a reasonably comprehensive set of multiple regression analyses, including each of the factors just listed. Not surprisingly, several of these other factors have independent effects on educational outcomes, but controlling for all these other variables, in all cases community-based social capital remains by far the strongest single influence on educational outcomes. The best-fitting model in each case is presented in tables 3.2–3.4, along with an indication of what variables I have been able to exclude as having no statistically significant independent effect.

In the case of the NAEP elementary school test scores (table 3.2), the most powerful correlate of educational outcomes is social capital at the community level.[31] Statewide test scores are systematically higher where citizens are actively engaged in community affairs. Consistent with other studies, I also find that states with more racial minorities, lower per-capita income, more single-parent families, and larger classes tend to have lower test scores.[32] These correlations are plainly intelligible in terms of socioeconomic deprivation. Educational spending appears to have no direct effect, although additional analysis (not shown here) suggests that it has a modest indirect effect via its impact on class size.[33] Several other variables, such as the racial composition of a state and the educational levels of its adult citizens, also have indirect effects on the NAEP test scores via their covariance with social capital. The bottom line, however, is that with or without controls for a large number of other possible influences—including, most important, multiple measures of socioeconomic disadvantage—the most direct and pervasive factor affecting this measure of statewide educational performance is community-based social capital.

Table 3.3 shows that community-based social capital and state income levels are strong predictors of SAT scores, adjusted for participation rates.[34] Once these two variables are controlled, none of the other variables in the analysis has any direct effect on SAT scores.[35] As in the case of the NAEP test scores, SAT scores are indirectly associated with the racial composition of the state, the average educational levels among adults, and the incidence of poverty. However, all those factors become statistically insignificant when I control for social capital, implying that race, poverty, and education affect SAT scores only indirectly, via their impact on social capital. The absolute size of the "social capital effect" is large. For example, the size of the coefficients in table 3.3 implies that an increase in community social capital of one-half standard deviation (less than the

Table 3.2. Predicting Statewide NAEP 4th- and 8th-Grade Math, Science, and Reading Scores, 1990–96

Full model

Multiple R	.932	DF		Regression	12
R²	.869			Residual	33
Adjusted R²	.822				
Standard error	.338	F = 18.26		sig F = .000	

Variable	B	SE B	Beta	t	sig t
Community social capital, 1972–94	0.298	0.136	0.282	2.196	0.035
Single-parent rate, 1984–90	−0.070	0.030	−0.206	−2.284	0.029
Whites (%age of state population), 1990	0.020	0.011	0.228	1.793	0.082
Pupil-teacher ratio, 1988–90	−0.071	0.042	−0.206	−1.694	0.100
Population aged 25 with 4 years high school, 1990	0.020	0.020	0.148	1.051	0.301
Personal income per capita, 1990	0.000	0.000	0.135	0.767	0.449
Catholics as %age of state population, 1991	−0.007	0.006	−0.113	−1.073	0.291
Teachers' salaries, 1989*	0.000	0.000	0.060	0.565	0.576
Income inequality, 1990	−2.147	5.243	−0.059	−0.410	0.685
Educational spending per pupil, 1989–92*	0.000	0.000	0.056	0.401	0.691
Poverty rate, 1987–90	−0.007	0.039	−0.038	−0.181	0.858
Elem./secondary pupils in public schools (%), 1990	0.006	0.024	0.029	0.259	0.797
(Constant)	−1.299	2.852		−0.455	0.652

*Educational spending and teachers' salaries are adjusted for interstate differences in cost of living.

Reduced model

Multiple R	.924	DF		Regression	6
R²	.854			Residual	39
Adjusted R²	.831				
Standard error	.329	F = 24.717		sig F = .000	

Variable	B	SE B	Beta	t	sig t
Community social capital, 1972–94	0.445	0.094	0.421	4.711	0.00003
Whites (%age of state population), 1990	0.030	0.009	0.341	3.473	0.0013
Personal income per capita, 1990	0.00008	0.00002	0.291	3.729	0.0006
Single-parent rate, 1984–90	−0.057	0.024	−0.218	−2.381	0.022
Pupil-teacher ratio, 1988–90	−0.057	0.024	−0.166	−2.358	0.023
Catholics as %age of state population, 1991	−0.009	0.005	−0.154	−1.879	0.068
(Constant)	−1.541	1.146		−1.345	0.186

Table 3.3. Predicting Statewide SAT Scores (adjusted for participation rates), 1993

Full model

Multiple R	.820	DF		Regression	12	
R²	.673			Residual	33	
Adjusted R²	.554					
Standard error	18.17	F = 5.661		sig F = .000		

Variable	B	SE B	Beta	t	sig t
Community social capital, 1972–94	29.896	7.282	0.834	4.106	0.0002
Personal income per capita, 1990	0.006	0.002	0.643	2.315	0.027
Whites (%age of state population), 1990	1.293	0.600	0.443	2.155	0.039
Elem./secondary pupils in public schools (%), 1990	−2.237	1.265	−0.308	−1.768	0.086
Poverty rate, 1987–90	1.765	2.091	0.282	0.844	0.405
Educational spending per pupil, 1989–92*	−0.011	0.009	−0.278	−1.253	0.219
Population aged 25 with 4 years high school, 1990	−0.854	1.046	−0.181	−0.816	0.420
Single-parent rate, 1984–90	1.398	1.633	0.157	0.856	0.398
Catholics as %age of state population, 1991	−0.282	0.330	−0.143	−0.854	0.399
Pupil-teacher ratio, 1988–90	1.080	2.259	0.092	0.478	0.636
Income inequality, 1990	−4.685	281.19	−0.004	−0.017	0.987
Teachers' salaries, 1989*	0.000	0.002	−0.003	−0.017	0.987
(Constant)	28.261	152.96		0.185	0.855

*Educational spending and teachers' salaries are adjusted for interstate differences in cost of living.

Reduced model

Multiple R	.757	DF		Regression	2	
R²	.573			Residual	43	
Adjusted R²	.553					
Standard error	18.19	F = 28.834		sig F = .000		

Variable	B	SE B	Beta	t	sig t
Community social capital, 1972–94	23.061	3.595	0.643	6.414	0.0000001
Personal income per capita, 1990	0.0030	0.0009	0.332	3.309	0.0019
(Constant)	−56.063	17.180		−3.263	0.0022

difference between Massachusetts and Pennsylvania, for example, to take two states near the middle of the national distribution) is equivalent to an increase in statewide per-capita income of nearly $3,850 in terms of its effect on SAT scores. (By way of comparison, that is equivalent to the difference in per-capita income between Washington, the fifteenth-richest state in the union, and Tennessee, the fifteenth-poorest.) In short, with or without controls for all other

Table 3.4. Predicting Statewide High School Dropout Index, 1990–95

Full model

Multiple R	.882	DF		Regression 12		
R²	.778			Residual 33		
Adjusted R²	.697					
Standard error	.544	F = 13.005		sig F = .000		

Variable	B	SE B	Beta	t	sig t
Community social capital, 1972–94	−0.616	0.218	−0.473	−2.825	0.008
Single-parent rate, 1984–90	0.112	0.049	0.346	2.285	0.029
Income inequality, 1990	10.419	8.419	0.232	1.238	0.225
Pupil-teacher ratio, 1988–90	0.098	0.068	0.229	1.448	0.157
Whites (%age of state population), 1990	0.025	0.018	0.227	1.373	0.179
Population aged 25 with 4 years high school, 1990	−0.031	0.031	−0.180	−0.984	0.332
Elem./secondary pupils in public schools (%), 1990	0.036	0.038	0.135	0.937	0.355
Poverty rate, 1987–90	−0.023	0.063	−0.102	−0.369	0.714
Educational spending per pupil, 1989–92*	0.000	0.000	−0.072	−0.394	0.696
Catholics as %age of state population, 1991	0.003	0.010	0.040	0.288	0.775
Personal income per capita, 1990	0.000	0.000	0.021	0.093	0.926
Teachers' salaries, 1989*	0.000	0.000	0.012	0.087	0.931
(Constant)	−11.093	4.580		−2.422	0.021

*Educational spending and teachers' salaries are adjusted for interstate differences in cost of living.

Reduced model

Multiple R	.873	DF		Regression 5		
R²	.762			Residual 40		
Adjusted R²	.732					
Standard error	.512	F = 25.56		sig F = .000		

Variable	B	SE B	Beta	t	sig t
Community social capital, 1972–94	−0.758	0.153	−0.582	−4.949	0.00001
Income inequality, 1990	11.679	4.649	0.260	2.512	0.016
Pupil-teacher ratio, 1988–90	0.111	0.034	0.259	3.232	0.002
Single-parent rate, 1984–90	0.082	0.035	0.253	2.325	0.025
White population (%), 1990	0.025	0.014	0.227	1.809	0.078
(Constant)	−10.769	2.860		−3.766	0.0018

variables I tested, by far the best predictor of adjusted statewide SAT scores is the character of community connectedness in these states.

Finally, as table 3.4 reveals, high school dropout rates are best predicted by social capital at both the community and family levels. In addition, states with high pupil-teacher ratios and states with relatively unequal income distributions also appear to have high dropout rates.[36] Together these four variables account for roughly three-quarters of all interstate variation in dropout rates, and among the four, community-based social capital is clearly the most powerful single influence.

In short, my exploration of three distinct measures of educational outcomes strongly suggests that greater attention should be paid to the educational consequences of differing levels of community-based social capital. In fact, my analysis suggests that this factor is considerably more important than any other demographic, economic, or purely educational influence in accounting for interstate differences in educational outcomes. Race, income, family structure, class size, and socioeconomic inequality appear to have a significant impact on one or another of these three measures of state educational performance. However, community-based social capital is the only variable that is significantly related to all three measures of educational performance and is the single strongest influence on all three.

These striking findings in turn raise three important questions:

1. Methodology: Are these results robust and reliable?
2. Causes: What are the origins of interstate differences in levels of social capital?
3. Mechanisms: How, precisely, does community-level social capital influence educational outcomes?

Methodology

With the framework here outlined, the empirical results seem reasonably robust across different model specifications. However, a number of qualifications must be added.

- *Level of analysis.* The real effects of community-based social capital presumably operate at the local level, of which statewide measures are an imperfect reflection. My analysis has focused on interstate differences, primarily because systematic measures of social capital at the local level are not yet available. For example, my analysis shows that states with more two-parent families have high NAEP test scores and lower dropout rates, but I have not shown specifically that students from two-parent homes do better than students from other family backgrounds, for any such claim would entail the "ecological fallacy." (This fallacy refers to the risk of false inference about individual-level relations from aggregate-level data.) With respect to community-wide social capital (social trust, group membership, turnout, nonprofits, civic activism, and so on), it would be desirable to replicate the analysis at the local level.

It is sometimes assumed, as the authors of a recent RAND study note, that "measurements at lower levels of aggregation always dominate measurements at higher levels of aggregation." As these authors point out, however, there is no reason in general to assume that more aggregate estimates of correlations are always biased upward, unless the statistical model itself is misspecified by the omission of one or more relevant explanatory variables. Thus, they conclude, "there are no a priori reasons to prefer analysis at the state or individual level, since results should agree if the models are linear and well specified."[37]

In the present case my analyses have included virtually all the contextual variables that are commonly cited as relevant to statewide educational outcomes. Moreover, the very sharp interstate differences on these measures make clear that the average student (or the average school) in Mississippi operates within a very different civic context from that of the average student or school in Minnesota. My multiple regression analyses show that these different civic contexts are closely associated with contrasting educational outcomes.

- *Endogeneity and reciprocal causation.* It is certainly possible—indeed, it seems quite likely—that several of my independent variables (for example, poverty, race, income, and education) are themselves causally intercorrelated. The data and the methodological framework deployed here are not well adapted for exploring such linkages. On the other hand, my analyses suggest that the connection between social capital and educational outcomes is probably not spurious in any simple sense. Moreover, the way in which statewide adult educational level enters these equations suggests that at least a substantial fraction of the causation flows from social capital to educational outcomes and not the reverse: if social capital were only an effect of education and not also a cause, then controlling for social capital should not eliminate (as it does) the direct connection between adult educational levels and educational performance across the states.

- *Frail and missing data.* For a number of states data are unavailable for certain components of both independent and dependent variables in this analysis.

For example, data on the full complement of seven NAEP test scores are available for only twenty-seven states, and I have extended my analysis by including states for which one or another of those measures is missing. Moreover, some of my measures of trust and group membership for small states are of uncertain reliability.[38] In order to minimize the impact of missing cases and random error in particular variables, I have used indexes based on a number of quite independent indicators.

Causes

If social capital is so important, where do interstate differences in average levels of social capital come from? This important question is beyond the scope of this essay. Within my statistical framework, social capital is modestly correlated with race, poverty, and educational levels, though which is cause and which consequence in those linkages remains uncertain. In particular, given my principal results, it seems reasonable to conclude that statewide adult educational attainments are in part a consequence of differences in social capital.[39] Even so, all three variables together (race, poverty, and adult educational levels) account for less than half of the interstate variance in community-based social capital. Although social capital is clearly correlated with other forms of capital, it is not merely froth on the tide of socioeconomic forces.

I have also uncovered some hints that interstate differences in social capital have relatively deep historical roots. Based on descriptive accounts of state politics in the 1950s, Elazar categorized the political cultures of the American states in terms of the degree to which they evinced more or less civic norms, and Sharkansky quantified Elazar's measure.[40] As I show in figure 3.6, there is a striking correlation between the Elazar-based measure of state political culture in the 1950s and my measure of community social capital, based largely on data from the 1980s and 1990s. Moreover, in a multiple-regression context, including contemporary measures of poverty, race, educational levels, and income, the Elazar measure is the dominant predictor of contemporary levels of social capital. On the basis of historical analysis, Elazar attributed these differences to nineteenth-century immigration patterns, and indeed I find a very strong correlation (not shown here) between high statewide levels of social capital and the fraction of the population from Scandinavian backgrounds.

Conversely, it is hardly happenstance that the lowest levels of community-based social capital are found where social structures were historically slave based. The more virulent the system of slavery (and the more repressive the Jim

Political Culture (1950s) and Social Capital (1970s-1990s)

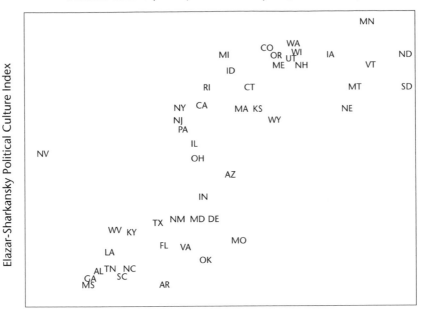

Social Capital Index

Figure 3.6 Political Culture (1950s) and Social Capital (1970s–1990s)

Crow system after Reconstruction) in the nineteenth century, the less civic the state today. Slavery was, in fact, a social system *designed* to destroy social capital among slaves and between slaves and freemen. Such historical patterns lead me to suspect that these interstate differences in patterns of civic engagement and social trust may be traced back at least into the 1950s and perhaps even into the nineteenth century, although quantitative evidence for those deeper roots is, as yet, lacking.

Mechanisms

States that are high in community-based social capital, as measured here, turn out to be much more congenial places in which to live by many different measures. Even holding constant many other factors that influence indexes of social well-being and institutional performance, such as economic affluence, racial composition, political party strength, urbanism, educational levels, and the like, community-based social capital is a strong and robust predictor of each of the following indicators of collective well-being and civic responsibility:

- Crime, as measured (for example) by the murder rate.
- Child welfare, as measured (for example) by infant mortality, teen pregnancy, and juvenile delinquency rates.
- Access to higher education, as measured by rates of participation in postsecondary education.
- Health, as measured (for example) by the mortality rate.
- Civic responsibility, as measured by IRS tax compliance, cooperation with the census, and voluntary contributions to public broadcasting.
- The effectiveness of state government, as measured by ratings of administrative efficiency and rates of public corruption.
- Tolerance, as measured by survey questions about race relations, civil liberties, and gender equality.[41]

The very sweep of this pattern of correlates of social capital is consistent with the basic thesis of social capital researchers that social capital helps overcome dilemmas of collective action and tends to encourage altruism and social solidarity. In a loose sense, communities of high social capital seem "nicer" places to live. But what might be the specific mechanisms by which community-based social capital improves educational performance?

James Coleman's introduction of the term *social capital* into the lexicon of educational research focused especially on "family-based" social capital, and he laid out a series of mechanisms by which closely linked families might foster educational performance. My results suggest that community-based social capital represents a public good that can also serve as a resource for child development and learning, but it is less clear just how community-based social capital might have educational effects. My best guess is that high levels of social capital foster both parental and wider community engagement with the education of children, broadly defined. In turn, that connection improves learning conditions and fosters appropriate student attitudes both in and out of school.

To some extent we can directly test these speculations about the causal mechanisms linking community-based social capital and educational performance with evidence from our statewide analyses. Some evidence for how social capital (both family-based and community-based) might affect school climate comes from a 1993–94 nationwide survey that asked teachers about a variety of possible problems in their own schools—student violence, weapons in the hands of students, student apathy, absenteeism, lack of parental involvement, and so on. Might these measures of school-related behavior of parents and students be associated with measures of community-based social capital?

Parental Support and Social Capital

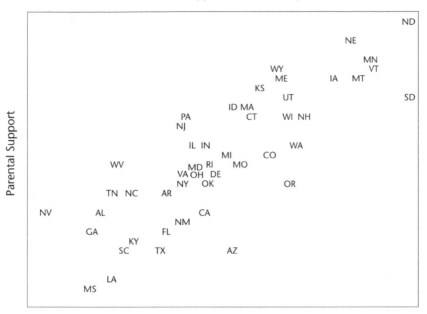

Figure 3.7 Parental Support and Social Capital

As an indicator of parental engagement with schools, I use the percentage of teachers who report that a lack of parental support is not a "serious problem" in their school. Four indicators of student behavior (weapons, physical violence, absenteeism, and apathy) were all highly intercorrelated, so they can plausibly be combined into a single index of student misconduct.[42]

As figures 3.7 and 3.8 make clear, both parental support and student [mis]behavior thus measured are strongly associated with community-based social capital. In other words, where civic engagement in community affairs is high, teachers report high levels of parental support and low levels of student misbehavior. To explore whether these correlations might be spurious, I employed multiple regression to predict both parental support and student misconduct, adding into the equations all the various social, economic, and educational factors considered earlier—race, poverty, family structure, religion, income level, income inequality, teacher salaries, class size, educational spending, statewide educational levels, and so on. Most of these variables turned out to have no direct link to parental and student behavior at the state level. The best-fitting

Table 3.5. Predicting Parental Support in School

Reduced model

Multiple R	.907	DF		Regression	4
R^2	.822			Residual	43
Adjusted R^2	.805				
Standard error	2.990	F = 49.61		sig F = .000	

Variable	B	SE B	Beta	t	sig t
Community social capital, 1972–94	3.787	0.786	0.438	4.818	0.00002
Single-parent rate, 1984–90	−0.790	0.190	−0.363	−4.157	0.00015
Educational spending per pupil, 1989–92*	0.0023	0.001	0.220	3.052	0.004
Income inequality, 1990	−58.218	26.897	−0.186	−2.164	0.036
(Constant)	108.250	11.839		9.144	0.00000

*Educational spending is adjusted for interstate differences in cost of living.

results are displayed in tables 3.5 and 3.6, and the central finding is clear and consistent. Students and parents are more productively engaged with the educational process in states with high levels of civic engagement and with many two-parent families. (As between these two forms of social capital, community-based social capital appears to matter more than family structure, although both are statistically significant.) The correlations between community and family structure, on the one hand, and student and parental engagement in schools, on the other hand, remain substantial even after taking into account other, more obvious economic, social, and educational factors.

Table 3.5 shows, in addition, that parental support is negatively related to income inequality and positively related to educational spending, while table 3.6 shows, in addition, that student misconduct is associated with larger classes and with a *higher* level of education among a state's adults. Even taking into account these secondary (and not entirely explicable) factors, however, more than half of all interstate variation in student misconduct and more than two-thirds of all interstate variation in parental support can be traced to community- and family-based social capital.

In short, teachers report high levels of parental support and low levels of student misconduct precisely in places blessed with high levels of community- and family-based social capital. This evidence suggests that the attitudes and behavior that parents and students bring to the educational process are even more deeply affected by the strength of community and family bonds than by the general socioeconomic or racial character of their communities.

Student Misconduct and Social Capital

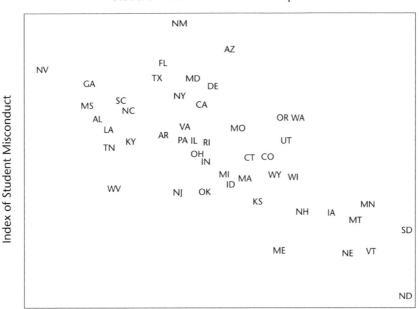

Figure 3.8 Student Misconduct and Social Capital

Another hint in my data about possible mechanisms linking social capital and schooling draws on an NAEP-based measure of children's television watching.[43] Statewide levels of social capital are strongly negatively correlated with levels of kids' TV watching. In Mississippi, Alabama, and Louisiana (near the bottom of my social capital rankings), 51–56 percent of all fourth graders report watching at least four hours of TV per day, compared with 29–35 percent of their counterparts in North Dakota, Wyoming, and Utah (near the top of the social capital ladder). Nor does this negative correlation between TV watching and community-based social capital appear to be the spurious consequence of socioeconomic deprivation. Controlling for race, poverty, income, inequality, family structure, and adult TV viewing, children (like their parents) watch less TV where social trust and civic engagement are high.[44] In turn, those are the same states with better educational outcomes. Of course, stronger evidence than this would be necessary to pull apart the multiple strands of influence among this nexus of variables, but these patterns suggest the possibility that community structure may influence educational outcomes in part through its

Table 3.6. Predicting Student Misconduct in School (weapons, violence, absenteeism, and apathy)

Reduced model

Multiple R	.815	DF		Regression	4
R^2	.664			Residual	43
Adjusted R^2	.633				
Standard error	.614	F = 21.25		sig F = .000	

Variable	B	SE B	Beta	t	sig t
Community social capital, 1972–94	−0.789	0.195	−0.612	−4.055	0.0002
Single-parent rate, 1984–90	0.108	0.036	0.333	3.000	0.004
Population aged 25 with 4 years high school, 1990	0.046	0.022	2.61	2.060	0.045
Pupil-teacher ratio, 1988–90	−0.100	0.041	0.226	−2.409	0.020
(Constant)	−7.620	1.817		−4.193	0.000

impact on the use of leisure time.[45] Where community bonds are strong and community life active, both children and adults spend fewer hours ensconced before the television.

Another possible mechanism linking community-based social capital and educational outcomes, suggested by Bryk and Schneider, might be that social capital in the wider community might encourage greater social capital within the schooling process itself.[46] However, my efforts to confirm this linkage empirically proved fruitless. For example, one potential index of school-based social capital draws on nationwide surveys that measured the degree to which teachers "cooperate with one another," "share beliefs about the school's mission," and report "clear goals and priorities" within their school.[47] These three indicators are themselves closely correlated—where teachers report a high level of intraschool cooperation, they also report a high level of shared, clear goals— so it is plausible to combine them into a single index of school-based social capital. In a bivariate context, that index is significantly (though modestly) correlated with academic performance. When community-based social capital is introduced into the equation, however, the "effects" of my measure of school-based social capital are entirely washed out. The statewide differences in educational performance that I have focused on are not attributable to differences in school-based social capital, at least as measured here. Other as-yet-undiscovered mechanisms may link community-based social capital and educational outcomes, through effects on school operations, for example. In conclusion, although my empirical analysis is preliminary, I believe that it warrants more focused attention on the ways in which the community context may affect the educational fate of children throughout the country.

CAUTIONARY CONCLUSIONS

Much effort will be needed both to test theories linking social capital and educational outcomes and to develop more effective "social capital–intensive" strategies for improving education in the United States. The design and implementation of reforms aimed at increasing the effectiveness of social capital in education will be complicated by a number of fundamental dilemmas of social capital formation. As a prolegomenon to any deeper exploration of the social capital approach to educational reform, I want to close by noting some of the tough moral issues that this approach raises.

- *Equity-efficiency trade-offs:* Discussion of reforms in this area needs to distinguish between efforts that create new social capital (that is, the creation of new networks, norms, and trust) and efforts that exploit existing social capital (that is, the channeling of existing networks, norms, and trust to support educational activities). Although most reformers think of themselves as engaged in the former task, much of their success may in fact derive from the latter. For example, the preliminary assessments of the important Chicago reform imply that successful sites are located in communities with higher prior levels of social capital.[48] The Alinsky-style work of the Texas Industrial Areas Foundation's "alliance schools" initiative relies heavily on the preexisting stocks of social capital embodied in religious congregations.[49] My work on interstate differences in social capital hints that educational outcomes may be influenced by community differences that have deep historical roots.

    Creating new social capital is undoubtedly more difficult than redirecting existing social capital. The latter strategy is thus probably more practicable, but it also tends to reinforce existing social inequities. In terms of social capital, like financial capital, the rich usually get richer. This was the assessment, for example, of the effects of the generally successful regional reform that I studied in Italy—all regions benefited from the decentralization, but areas in the north that were rich in social capital at the outset benefited more than their poorer counterparts in the south, so that the north-south gap actually increased.[50] The same pattern might be expected of strategies for educational reform that rely heavily on preexisting stocks of social capital.
- The controversial *link between government and social capital:* A lively debate

has begun about the linkage between government policy and social capital formation. Conservatives argue, in effect, that the decline in social capital in the United States is attributable primarily to the rise of the welfare state, which has had a "crowding out" effect on private connectedness. Government, it is said, has a kind of "reverse Midas touch," turning whatever social capital it touches to dross. Liberals, on the other hand, even those who are skeptical about centralized bureaucracy, believe that government can serve as partner and facilitator in the creation of social capital. One instructive example is the role of the Department of Agriculture's county agents and the hugely successful government-sponsored 4-H Clubs in fostering social connectedness in rural areas where physical circumstance impeded the formation of social capital. This broad debate cries out for more empirical research.

- *Inclusive vs. exclusive social capital.* Social capital (that is, networks and norms of reciprocity) comes in many different forms. One especially important distinction is that between "bonding social capital" (that is, networks that link us to people like ourselves), and "bridging social capital" (that is, networks that link us to people unlike ourselves). Both bridging and bonding social capital can have positive effects, but for a democratic society, bridging social capital is especially valuable, for it seems more likely to have positive externalities. Yet as a general rule, bridging social capital is harder to build than the bonding variety—"birds of a feather flock together."

  If we possessed a golden magic wand that could create more "bridging" social capital that crossed racial and other social cleavages, we would certainly use it. However, we are more likely to discover—although even this will not be simple—an aluminum magic wand that can create more social capital, but only of a nonbridging sort. The tough question that we shall then face is this: should we use the aluminum wand, if that is all we can find? Policies that aim at creating bridging social capital (like cross-district busing) might conceivably end up destroying bonding social capital (like neighborhood schools) without any compensating increase in bridging social capital. It is certainly not my purpose here to enter into the substantive controversies about the consequences, educational and social, of busing. Moreover, my observation is emphatically not meant to deflect the search for the golden magic wand, but only to point to a fundamental moral dilemma that is highlighted by the social capital lens. Advocates of a social capital approach need to be especially attentive to the balance between bridging and bonding social capital.

- *Class, status, power, and social capital.* Social and political participation depends on resources, as well as opportunities and motivations. Thus participation-based initiatives may magnify existing social disparities.[51] Moreover, organization always involves power. Changes in social capital are very likely to entail changes in the distribution of power. This prospect will surely complicate efforts to invest in social capital and will make them politically highly controversial. One hypothesis worth examining is the disconcerting idea that policies designed to foster new social capital may often encourage vertical, not horizontal structures. For example, massive efforts by the central Italian government over the past half-century to speed development in the Mezzogiorno (for example, through massive fiscal transfers) had the effect of strengthening long-standing vertical patterns of patron-client exploitation and dependence. Some retrospective reviews of the War on Poverty seem to substantiate an analogous interpretation.

In short, strengthening social capital is not an antiseptic, risk-free strategy for improving education. On the other hand, the evidence in this essay, as well as the long tradition in U.S. education of close connections between schools and communities, lends credence to the view that revitalizing American community life may be a prerequisite for revitalizing American education. Conversely, this evidence suggests that educational critics and would-be reformers should take seriously the possibility that—beyond the deeds or misdeeds of educators, the alleged foibles of those young people themselves, and even the details of curriculum and educational administration—a major culprit for the educational misadventures of American youth over the past several decades may be the civic lethargy and social disengagement of American citizens.

NOTES

1. James S. Coleman, *Equality and Achievement in Education* (Boulder, Colo.: Westview, 1996).
2. Ibid.; James S. Coleman, "Social Capital in the Creation of Human Capital," *American Journal of Sociology* (supplement) 94 (1994); James S. Coleman and Thomas Hoffer, *Public and Private High Schools: The Impact of Communities* (New York: Basic, 1987); Barbara Schneider and James S. Coleman, eds., *Parents, Their Children, and Schools* (Boulder, Colo.: Westview, 1993).
3. Lyda Judson Hanifan, "The Rural School Community Center," *Annals of the American Academy of Political and Social Science* 67 (1916). Ever the practical reformer, Hanifan was self-conscious about using the term *capital* to encourage hard-nosed businessmen and economists to recognize the productive importance of social assets. Having introduced the idea of social capital, he observes, "That there is a great lack of such social capital in some rural districts need not be retold in this chapter. The important question at this time is: How can these conditions be improved? The story which follows is an ac-

count of the way a West Virginia rural community in a single year actually developed social capital and then used this capital in the improvement of its recreational, intellectual,
moral, and economic conditions." His essay, which included a list of practical exercises
for community-based activists, was originally prepared in 1913 for West Virginia school-
teachers as "a handbook for community meetings at rural schoolhouses," and it was subsequently incorporated in L. J. Hanifan, *The Community Center* (Boston: Silver, Bur-
dett, 1920). I am grateful to Brad Clarke for first spotting this usage of the term *social
capital.*

4. See Robert D. Putnam, *Bowling Alone: The Collapse and Revival of American Community* (New York: Simon and Schuster, 2000), pp. 307–25, for brief overviews of research
supporting the generalizations in this paragraph.

5. That the consequences of social capital are not, by definition, always positive is now
widely acknowledged by most students of social capital, as summarized in Robert D.
Putnam, "The Prosperous Community: Social Capital and Public Life," *American
Prospect* 13 (1993), and Putnam, *Bowling Alone.* This recognition is an important difference between the conception outlined here and the "functional" definition of social
capital employed by Coleman and borrowed by Robert D. Putnam, *Making Democracy
Work: Civic Traditions in Modern Italy* (Princeton: Princeton University Press, 1993).

6. In the 1990–91 World Values survey, for example, Americans expressed more social trust
and claimed membership in more voluntary associations than most other nations surveyed.

7. This section of the essay draws on Putnam, *Bowling Alone,* which presents much of the
underlying evidence.

8. J. W. Rioux and N. Berla, *Innovations in Parent and Family Involvement* (Princeton: Eye
on Education, 1993), p. 363.

9. For statistical evidence on this point, see Gerald Gamm and Robert D. Putnam, "The
Growth of Voluntary Associations in America, 1840–1940," *Journal of Interdisciplinary
History* 29 (1998); for an extended discussion of trends in social capital in the Gilded Age
and Progressive Era, see Putnam, *Bowling Alone.*

10. *Teens and Their Parents in the 21st Century,* a report prepared by the Council of Economic Advisers (Washington, D.C.: Executive Office of the President, 2000).

11. A. T. Henderson and Nancy Berla, eds., *A New Generation of Evidence: The Family Is
Critical to Student Achievement* (Washington, D.C.: National Committee for Citizens in
Education, 1994), p. 1

12. Valerie E. Lee and J. B. Smith, "High School Restructuring and Student Achievement:
A New Study Finds Strong Links," *Issues in Restructuring Schools* 7 (1994).

13. See Shirley Brice Heath and Milbrey W. McLaughlin, eds., *Identity and Inner-City Youth*
(New York: Teachers College Press, 1993).

14. David W. Grissmer, Ann Flanagan, Jennifer Kawata, and Stephanie Williamson, *Improving Student Achievement: What NAEP State Test Scores Tell Us* (Santa Monica, Calif.:
RAND Corporation, 2000), pp. 17–18.

15. M. Delago, *The Puerto Rican Community and Natural Support Systems: Implications for
the Education of Children,* Center Report 10 (Baltimore: Center on Families, Communities, Schools, and Children's Learning, Johns Hopkins University, 1992); Heath and

McLaughlin, *Identity and Inner-City Youth;* Peter W. Cookson, *School Choice: The Struggle for the Soul of American Education* (New Haven: Yale University Press, 1994); Anthony S. Bryk and Sharon G. Rollow, "The Chicago Experiment: The Potential and Reality of Reform," *Equity and Choice* 9 (1993). In addition to these studies, the idea that social networks and the associated norms can influence educational outcomes is also suggested by the large literatures on "peer group effects," including James S. Coleman, *The Adolescent Society* (New York: Free Press, 1961); James S. Coleman, *Equality of Educational Opportunity* (Washington, D.C.: U.S. Government Printing Office, 1966); Coleman, "Social Capital in the Creation of Human Capital"; and James S. Coleman, Thomas Hoffer, Sally Kilgore, *High School Achievement: Public, Catholic, and Private Schools Compared* (New York: Basic, 1982); and on "neighborhood effects," as reviewed in Christopher Jencks and Susan E. Mayer, "The Social Consequences of Growing Up in a Poor Neighborhood: A Review," in Laurence E. Lynn Jr. and Michael G. H. McGeary, eds., *Inner City Poverty in the United States* (Washington, D.C.: National Academy Press); and J. L. Aber, "The Effects of Poor Neighborhoods on Children, Youth, and Families: Theory, Research, and Policy Implications," background memorandum prepared for the Social Science Research Council Policy Conference on Persistent Urban Poverty, November 9–10, 1993, Washington, D.C.

16. For a thorough methodological discussion of the use of statewide aggregate data to test propositions about influences on educational performance, see Grissmer, Flanagan, Kawata, and Williamson, *Improving Student Achievement.*

17. I have discovered state-level data from seven nationwide NAEP tests, as reported in National Center for Education Statistics, *Digest of Education Statistics, 1992* (Washington, D.C.: U.S. Government Printing Office, 1992); National Center for Education Statistics, *Digest of Education Statistics, 1995* (Washington, D.C.: U.S. Government Printing Office, 1995); National Center for Education Statistics, *NAEP 1996 Science Report Card for the Nation and the States* (Washington, D.C.: U.S. Government Printing Office, 1997; also available at http://www.ed.gov/NCES/naep/96report/97497.shtml); National Center for Education Statistics, *NAEP 1996 Mathematics Report Card for the Nation and the States* (Washington, D.C.: U.S. Government Printing Office, 1997; also available at http://www.ed.gov/NCES/pubs/ce/c9718d03.html). Average reading proficiency for public school fourth graders in 1994 (available for thirty-nine states), average science proficiency for public school eighth graders in 1996 (available for forty states), average math proficiency for public school fourth graders in 1992 (available for forty-one states) and 1996 (available for forty-three states), and average math proficiency for public school eighth graders in 1990 (available for thirty-seven states), 1992 (available for forty-one states), and 1996 (available for forty states). All of these measures are highly correlated, suggesting that interstate differences in elementary school achievement are highly reliable. The mean bivariate correlation among the five statewide math measures over seven years is $r = .94$; the five math measures have average correlations of $r = .95$ with the statewide science score and $r = .86$ with the statewide reading score, and the science and reading scores are correlated at $r = .94$. In order to maximize the number of cases while simplifying the reporting of my results, I have therefore combined these seven measures into a composite index of statewide NAEP achievement, based on the av-

erage standardized scores across all tests available for each state. This index is essentially identical to a principal components factor score based on the seven measures. In all, twenty-seven states have all seven test scores, eight states have six of the seven scores, three states have five and four scores respectively, five states have three scores each, and two states have only one score each. Two states have no scores at all available. The essential result I report, involving the primary importance of community-based social capital, is confirmed even when I limit my analysis to the forty-one states for which at least four of the seven NAEP scores are available.

Powell and Steelman have demonstrated that state SAT scores must be corrected for substantial interstate differences in SAT participation rates. My analysis therefore uses their participation-adjusted SAT scores. See Brian Powell and Lala Carr Steelman, "Bewitched, Bothered, and Bewildering: The Use and Misuse of State SAT and ACT Scores," *Harvard Educational Review* 66 (1996).

Six convergent (though not identical) measures of dropout rates are available: the percentage of "status dropouts," ages sixteen to nineteen, for 1990, as reported in National Center for Education Statistics, *Dropout Rates in the United States, 1991* (Washington, D.C.: U.S. Government Printing Office, 1992), p. 13; the percentage of those aged sixteen to nineteen in the 1990 census who were not in regular school and had not completed twelfth grade or a GED (as reported in the *Statistical Abstract of the United States* [Washington, D.C.: U.S. Census Bureau, 1995], p. 159); the percentage of those aged sixteen to nineteen in the U.S. Census Bureau Current Population Surveys of 1993–1995 who were not enrolled in school and had not completed high school or a GED, as reported in Annie E. Casey Foundation, *Kids Count* (Baltimore: Annie E. Casey Foundation, 1997); the "public high school graduation rate, 1989–1990," as reported in Victoria Van Son, *CQ's State Fact Finder* (Washington, D.C.: Congressional Quarterly, 1993), p. 106; and the high school completion rates for 1990–92 and for 1993–95, National Center for Education Statistics, *Digest of Education Statistics, 1997* (Washington, D.C.: U.S. Government Printing Office, 1997). In my analysis I combined these six measures into a single-factor score; in fact, all essential results reported here are confirmed in separate analyses of the six measures. I have also replicated the analyses presented here, using instead average high school completion rates for the decade 1991–1999 (National Center for Educational Statistics 2000) as the dependent variable.

18. I shall present evidence predicting each of these three measures of educational achievement separately. It is worth noting, however, that the three are themselves reasonably intercorrelated. My NAEP-based index of academic achievement is correlated $r = -.76$ with the composite dropout measure and $r = .62$ with the participation-adjusted SAT scores. The SAT measure is correlated $r = -.49$ with the dropout measure.

19. Since 1972 social trust has been repeatedly measured in the General Social Survey by responses to this question: "Generally speaking, would you say that most people can be trusted or that you can't be too careful in dealing with people?" Altogether 20,752 people have responded to this question over the past two decades. Aggregated at the state level, this question generates reasonably reliable measures of social trust for forty-six states. This GSS-based measure is correlated with a comparable measure based on this same question in the National Election Studies (1960–1992): $r = .65$. If I limit my

analysis to the thirty-two states with a minimum sample of one hundred respondents each for both the NES and the GSS measures, the reliability coefficient over three decades is r = .78.

Since 1974 associational membership has been repeatedly measured in the General Social Survey by responses to this question: "Now I would like to know something about the groups or organizations to which individuals belong. Here is a list of various organizations. Could you tell me whether or not you are a member of each type?" My measure is the average number of different types of groups (corrected for a recently discovered error in the GSS aggregation algorithm) to which respondents of a given state belong. Altogether 19,326 people have responded to this question over the past two decades. Aggregated at the state level, this question generates reasonably reliable measures of social trust for forty-six states. Of course, both this measure and the comparable measure of social trust are less reliable for very small states in which the total sample size is small. This measurement error has the effect of artificially attenuating correlations involving these measures and other variables, such as educational achievement.

20. The Roper polls have continued after December 1994, but the data are no longer available to academic researchers, and in any event the wording of the crucial questions changed significantly in January 1995, so that direct comparison with the earlier data is no longer possible. Data from the Roper archives were used in Steven J. Rosenstone and John M. Hansen, *Mobilization, Participation, and Democracy in America* (New York: Macmillan, 1993), and are described in more detail there and in Putnam, *Bowling Alone*. Reasonably reliable statewide averages for the Roper-based measures are available for forty-three states.

21. The DDB Life Style data underrepresent the very poor, the very mobile, and African Americans. For further details, see Putnam, *Bowling Alone*, pp. 420–24. Statewide scores for the DDB Life Style–based measures are available for all forty-eight states of the continental United States.

22. The specific questions, respectively, are "How often in the last year did you attend a club meeting?"; "How often in the last year did you do volunteer work?"; "How often in the last year did you work on a community project?"; "I spend a lot of time visiting friends" (agree-disagree); "How often in the last year did you entertain at home?"; and "Most people are honest" (agree-disagree). The wording of the last question differs slightly from the GSS measure of social trust, and the sampling frames and interview methods of the two surveys are quite different. Nevertheless, these two statewide measures of social trust are quite convergent (r = .79 for all available states; r = .85 for the thirty-eight states for which at least one hundred respondents are available in each survey).

23. My measure of turnout is simply the average percentage of the voting age population who voted in the presidential elections of 1988 and 1992, as reported in the *Statistical Abstract of the United States* (Washington, D.C: U.S. Census Bureau, 1994), 289. These data are available for all fifty states.

My measure of the incidence of nonprofit (501[c]3) organizations is simply the number of such organizations in each state in 1989 (as reported in the *Non-Profit Almanac* for 1992–93), divided by the state's population in 1990. (I thank Professor Thomas Rice for pointing me to these data.) These data are available for all fifty states. This measure is stable over time; the 1989 measure that I use is very strongly correlated (r = .89) with the same measure in 1992.

24. Of the seventy-eight possible bivariate correlations among these thirteen indicators, seventy-two are statistically significant in the proper direction at the .05 level or better and none are in the wrong direction. The mean intercorrelation across the seventy-eight is r = .54.

   The social capital index is simply the average of the standardized scores on the thirteen component measures. To maximize the number of cases, I computed this average even for those few cases in which data were missing on as many as five of the underlying thirteen indicators; this procedure enabled me to include all states except Alaska and Hawaii in my analysis. Effectively, this index is identical (r = .999) to the factor score on the first factor to emerge from a principal components factor analysis of the thirteen component variables. In other work, including Putnam, *Bowling Alone,* I have used alternative versions of this index that also include indicators of the mean number of civic and social organizations per capita as reported by the U.S. Commerce Department and the mean rate of volunteering calculated from the 1989 Current Population Survey. However, these alternative versions are, in fact, virtually identical to the version used here (r > .996).

25. The few exceptions from the surprisingly smooth gradients in figure 3.1 are intuitively explicable—Nevada is unusually low, whereas Mormon Utah is relatively high. A recent community-level survey of social capital nationwide suggests that levels of social capital in large, ethnically diverse cities, like Los Angeles and Boston, may be lower than the respective statewide levels.

26. One other plausible measure of social capital—church attendance—is empirically unrelated with the other indicators used here. The fraction of all respondents in the 1974–94 General Social Survey who report attending religious services at least "nearly every week" is essentially uncorrelated with my social capital index (r = −.06). Some states with high levels of religious observance (Alabama, for example) are low on my measure of community-based social capital, but other relatively religious states (Minnesota, for example) are high in social capital. Conversely, South Dakota is high on social capital but low on church attendance, while Hawaii is relatively low on both. Church attendance, as measured here, is also entirely uncorrelated with my various measures of educational performance. For all these reasons, I exclude church attendance from my analysis here.

27. Because the District of Columbia is an outlier on measures of educational performance and because it is in effect a single large urban school district, I exclude it from my statistical calculations throughout this essay.

28. My social capital index is highly correlated with each of the seven NAEP tests, taken separately: fourth-grade math, 1992: r = .81; fourth-grade math, 1996: r = .67; eighth-grade math, 1990: r = .90; eighth-grade math, 1992: r = .91; eighth-grade math, 1996: r = .88; fourth-grade reading, 1994: r = .68; eighth-grade science, 1996: r = .85.

29. This summary index of educational performance is essentially a factor score based on the only factor to emerge from a principal-components analysis of the three separate measures (NAEP scores, SAT scores, and dropout rates). The three are highly intercorre-

lated with one another and thus with the summary index: NAEP scores: r = .91; SAT scores: r = .82; dropout rates: r = −.86.

30. I explored several possible measures of statewide racial composition, including the percentages of African Americans, Hispanics, Asian Americans, and whites in the 1990 census. Across states, these measures are highly correlated with measures of the racial composition of 1991 public school enrollment (r = .99 for the three minority groups and r = .89 for whites). In the end, the most broadly and closely correlated of these measures with my three educational outcomes proved to be the percentage of whites in the state population, so I use that measure, in order to stack the deck against my social-capital hypothesis.

My measure of affluence is personal income per capita in 1990.

My measure of economic inequality is the Gini coefficient for statewide income inequality, as reported in I. Kawachi et al., "Social Capital, Income Inequality, and Mortality" *American Journal of Public Health* 87 (1997).

From a variety of possible measures of statewide adult educational levels, I chose the percentage of the population aged twenty-five and over in 1990 who had completed at least four years of high school, as reported in the *Digest of Educational Statistics, 1992*, p. 21. I chose this measure because it was more closely correlated with educational outcomes than alternative measures, such as the percentage of the adult population who had graduated from college or had completed fewer than two years of high school, and I wished to stack the deck in favor of explanations other than social capital. Analyses using these other indicators of adult educational levels (not shown here) fully confirm the conclusions reported in the text.

My measure of poverty rates is the mean percentage of the state population living below the poverty line as measured in the Current Population Survey of the Bureau of Labor Statistics over the four years 1987–90.

Figures for both teachers' salaries and per-pupil educational spending have been adjusted for interstate cost-of-living differences, following F. Howard Nelson, "An Interstate Cost-of-Living Index," *Educational Evaluation and Policy Analysis* 13 (1991), although I have also conducted parallel analyses using the unadjusted figures, as reported in Nelson, p. 109, and National Center for Education Statistics, *Digest of Education Statistics, 1995*, p. 165. The salary data are for 1989; my spending measure is based on the mean annual figure for the three years from 1989–90 to 1991–92.

My measure of class size is the mean pupil-teacher ratio 1988–90, as reported in *Digest of Education Statistics, 1995*, table 65.

Family structure is measured by the average percentage of "families with own children which are headed by a single parent"—that is, single-parent families—between 1984 and 1990, as measured in the monthly Current Population Survey of the Bureau of Labor Statistics, as cited in *Kids Count.*

Religious affiliation is measured by the portion of the population that is Catholic; Van Son, *CQ's State Fact Finder,* 228.

31. Tables 3.2–3.4 show only the full model (including all possible independent variables) and the reduced model (including only those variables that are statistically significant in

the full model). Not shown are results of intermediate analyses in which I sequentially added and deleted the less significant variables, looking for unexpected interactions. The regression analyses presented in this essay are based, conservatively, on exclusion of all cases with any missing data; analysis using pairwise deletion produces slightly different results for the secondary influences on school performance, such as class size and spending levels, but in every case confirms the primary importance of community social capital.

32. The reduced model in table 3.2 faintly suggests that states with more Catholics have lower NAEP test scores, but this anomalous finding does not reach statistical significance.

33. High per-pupil spending is positively associated with both small classes and high teachers' salaries, but class size and salaries are themselves strongly negatively correlated. This pattern implies that states are implicitly making a financial trade-off between class size and teachers' salaries. Furthermore, the pattern of correlations between these three variables and educational outcomes implies that increased spending is associated with improved outcomes if and only if it is used to reduce class size.

34. Powell and Steelman, "Bewitched, Bothered, and Bewildering."

35. Powell and Steelman report that adjusted SAT scores are associated with higher per-pupil spending, and I confirm that in a simple bivariate analysis. However, I find that that relation vanishes under controls for social capital. Because of complex interactions among race, poverty, family structure, and educational spending, race appears to have a significant effect in the "full" model, but once those ancillary and statistically insignificant factors are removed from the equation, the direct effect of race also becomes statistically insignificant. See Powell and Steelman, "Bewitched, Bothered, and Bewildering."

36. The reduced model in table 3.4 faintly suggests that states with more racial minorities have lower dropout rates, but this anomalous finding does not reach statistical significance.

37. Grissmer, Flanagan, Kawata, and Williamson, *Improving Student Achievement,* quotations at pp. 32 and 96.

38. For example, in the General Social Survey, Vermont displays surprisingly low levels of trust and group membership, but even when the GSS samples over two decades are combined, those estimates are based on only thirty-seven and thirteen cases, respectively.

39. For an important essay suggesting that interstate differences in educational institutions (such as the founding of high schools) are strongly affected by levels of social capital, see C. Goldin and L. Katz, "Human Capital and Social Capital: The Rise of Secondary Schooling in America, 1910 to 1940," *Journal of Interdisciplinary History* 29 (1998).

40. Daniel J. Elazar, *American Federalism: A View from the States* (New York: Crowell, 1966); Ira Sharkansky, "The Utility of Elazar's Political Culture," *Polity* 2 (1969).

41. See Putnam, *Bowling Alone,* section IV. Our measure of participation in higher education is drawn from *Measuring Up 2000: The State-by-State Report Card for Higher Education* (Washington, D.C.: National Center for Public Policy and Higher Education, 2000), p. 168. One measure of public corruption is drawn from Kenneth J. Meier and Thomas M. Holbrook, "'I Seen My Opportunities and I Took 'Em': Political Corruption in the American States," *Journal of Politics* 54 (1992).

42. These data are drawn from National Center for Education Statistics, *Schools and*

Staffing in the United States: A Statistical Profile, 1993–94 (Washington, D.C.: U.S. Government Printing Office, 1996), as reported in Education Week, *Quality Counts: A Report Card on the Condition of Public Education* (Washington, D.C.: Editorial Projects in Education, 1997). The index of student conduct (based on principal components factor analysis) is correlated with its component indicators as follows: percentage of secondary teachers who say student possession of weapons is a "moderate" or "serious" problem in their schools: r = .96; percentage of secondary teachers who say physical conflict among students is a "moderate" or "serious" problem in their schools: r = .90; percentage of teachers who report that student apathy is *not* a serious problem: r = .83; percentage of teachers who report that student absenteeism is *not* a "serious" problem: r = .81.

43. This measure is a composite index based on the percentage of eighth graders in 1990 and 1992 who reported watching six or more hours of television daily, of fourth graders in 1992 watching four or more hours daily, and of eighth graders in 1992 watching two hours or more daily. All these measures are highly intercorrelated (r = .83–.89), which implies that relative frequency of TV watching by children is a rather robust feature of state cultures. Children's TV watching, as measured here, is correlated r = .61 with single-parent families and *r* = −.82 with community-based social capital.

44. In a multiple regression framework, race and community-based social capital are roughly equivalent in their impact on children's television viewing. Together they account for 77 percent of interstate variance in children's TV watching. Statewide income, poverty, inequality, family structure, and adult television-viewing rates appear to have no independent effect. Within a similar multiple regression framework, statewide levels of adult TV watching (as measured in the GSS) are themselves best predicted by a combination of poverty and low community-based social capital, with other variables having no independent effect.

45. In this sense my work tends to converge with that of Heath and McLaughlin, *Identity and Inner-City Youth.*

46. Anthony S. Bryk and B. Schneider, "Social Trust: A Moral Resource for School Improvement," unpublished, 1996.

47. These data are drawn from *Schools and Staffing in the United States: A Statistical Profile, 1993–94*, as reported in Education Week, *Quality Counts.*

48. Bryk and Rollow, "Chicago Experiment," and Marilyn Gitell, "School Reform in New York and Chicago: Revisiting the Ecology of Local Games," *Urban Affairs Quarterly* 30 (1994).

49. Dennis Shirley, *Community Organizing for Urban School Reform* (Austin: University of Texas Press, 1997).

50. Putnam, *Making Democracy Work.*

51. On the other hand, we need to beware of stereotypes. Both in the broader public arena and in the educational arena, there is some evidence that, controlling for socioeconomic status, African Americans are more likely to participate than whites.

Chapter 4 Fluctuations of Social Capital in an Urban Neighborhood

Gerald Grant

We had come home from a vacation in New Hampshire and settled in with a good movie. Afterward, as I walked a few city blocks to return the video, I saw three wilding males in their mid-teens coming up the street. They were jumping up to break off overhanging branches, and one of them had a thick stick about a yard long that he was using to whack everything in sight. As they got to the small string of stores near the commercial district, the boy with the stick began swinging at a sign hanging by the auto repair shop. A few pieces of plastic fell to the sidewalk. A man about forty years old came out of a house and crossed the street just ahead of me. When he got close to the teenagers, they paused and looked at him intently. But they broke into smiles when he yelled, "Go for it, man!" His voice was slurred from drugs or alcohol. They happily resumed whacking away. Later, I saw that half the sign was in shreds. Unfortunately, this was not an isolated incident but part of a slowly escalating pattern of incivility and occasional violence among both whites and blacks—abusive language, rock-throwing attacks on gays, urinating on lawns, breaking bottles on sidewalks, and threats against those who complain about such behaviors.

I have lived in this Syracuse neighborhood, one of the most diverse census tracts in Onondaga County, for more than twenty years. I was born and grew up about a mile from here. I was not frightened for my own safety by what I saw, though some of my children who have moved away think I should be. I was angered and discouraged, however, and I began to rehearse again all the reasons why attempts to help save this neighborhood might be futile, as much as I loved it and wanted to enjoy the fruits of its genuine diversity. Like many of my neighbors who are committed to it, I saw its survival as a test of the aims of a democratic society. Could we not only live together but also thrive together? Although the neighborhood has maintained a diverse population for more than a generation, the outcome is not at all certain.

The Westcott area, as the neighborhood is known, takes its name from the main street where rail lines made it the city's first "trolleycar suburb" early in the twentieth century. Leading Syracuse merchants built distinguished residences on Allen Street. A prominent physician erected my seven-bedroom house there in 1921. Today a large housing project forms the northern border of the neighborhood. Many blocks suffer from urban blight, while others are undergoing renewal and gentrification. Yet the neighborhood retains the character of an urban village and has preserved much of what the "new urbanism" is trying to create. Breakfast at the Common Grounds Café includes easy conversation across the tables and across lines of race and class, young and old, gay and straight, artists, workers, lawyers, and professors.

In *The World We Created at Hamilton High*, I wrote about the high school that serves the Westcott area and, under a racial-balance plan, other parts of the city, including my old neighborhood.[1] In that book I attempted to tell the story of urban education in the post–World War II era through a sociologically informed history of one high school. My account conceptualized the transformations in "Hamilton High," which had opened in 1953, as a series of social revolutions that radically altered the network of authority relations within the school. It was the story from the inside out, as those transformations were experienced by students and teachers within the school.

In this essay I shift the point of view to examine what was happening in the neighborhoods as those transformations were unfolding in the school. I shall focus primarily on the Westcott neighborhood but also draw on changes in the Brighton neighborhood, where I lived until graduating from high school in 1955. The essay will incorporate a parallel history contrasting developments in the neighborhood and the school, with special attention to the causes of accretion or depletion of social capital, especially as it affects the lives and educational opportunities for children. By social capital I mean all the social networks and human relationships that sustain the lives of children and affect the maintenance of good norms. Or as James Coleman put it, "social capital is the set of resources that inhere in family relations and in community social organization and that are useful for the cognitive or social development of a child or young person."[2] Physical capital is created by makings changes in materials to form tools that facilitate production, and human capital is created by developing new skills and capabilities in persons so they can achieve new ends. Social capital is less tangible; it is created when the relations among persons change in ways that facilitate action. It "inheres in the structure of relations between persons and among persons." If a group of persons do things to develop a sense of trust among themselves, for example, their relations have changed. They have more social capital that they can "spend" to do things that groups that have not developed that trust are less able to do. This conceptual framework will guide my analysis of fluctuations of social capital in an urban neighborhood.

URBAN "RENEWAL"

At the end of World War II, Syracuse was still a boomtown with a mixed industrial base. Willis Carrier had founded what became the largest air conditioning company in the world on the west side of the city. Learbury clothing made suits for Brooks Brothers (you could buy them at the factory for half the price) and many other labels. Nettleton shoes, New Process gear (which made parts for General Motors cars), General Electric, Will and Baumer Candles, and the Solvay Process Company (later Allied Chemical) prospered here. Syracuse University quadrupled in size under the GI Bill.

It was a city with marked ethnic neighborhoods: Irish on Tipperary Hill, and Italians, Poles, and Germans clustered in heavily Catholic parishes on the north side. The city's Protestant manufacturing elites lived in the Sedgwick area off James Street on the east side or the Strathmore area overlooking downtown from the green hills of Onondaga Park. Many Jews still lived in what locals then unselfconsciously referred to as Jewtown, the old area of Jewish bakeries and kosher meat shops just southeast of downtown. It abutted the black settlement referred to as the Fifteenth Ward or, among white children, as Niggertown. Joyce Carol Oates, who was an undergraduate at Syracuse, captures both the sociological context and the ethnic politics of the city well in her novel *What I Lived For*.[3]

Many middle-class and professional Jewish families had moved east of the old Jewish neighborhood into the Westcott area and further into new homes being built on the hills of the city's east side. An Orthodox temple and Jewish community center had been built in Westcott, as well as a bakery with bagels and horn rolls, and a large funeral home that primarily served Jews. Even as New York's fair-employment legislation and expanding job opportunities encouraged growth of the African-American population, however, discriminatory housing practices confined most blacks to the Fifteenth Ward. African Americans moved into housing abandoned by Jews and fanned out slowly block by block. Through the 1950s, school boundary lines were gerrymandered and additions were built to primarily black public schools to ensure that most blacks stayed within slightly expanded contours of the old Fifteenth Ward.

Most of that ward was demolished in the 1960s with major infusions of state and federal urban renewal funds as part of a grand plan of what was then called "slum clearance," driven by notions of "urban cleansing." It was combined with major interstate highway construction that cut through and destroyed many old city neighborhoods, white as well as black. But only the black Fifteenth Ward was virtually bulldozed out of existence. The "renewal" was planned to include a major cultural complex of museums and parks adjacent to a new government center, including a futuristic city hall, designed by Paul Rudolph, that looked like an airport in a Third World country. Aside from the Everson Museum, a stunning building designed by I. M. Pei, most of the complex, including the grandiose city hall, was never built. What the city got was wider highways on concrete stilts, more parking lots and garages, and a few new high-rise apartments and commercial buildings.

There was money to tear things down and construct new highways. But not much to build things except for public housing. And that is what Syracuse, like many other cities, did. Some African Americans from the Fifteenth Ward moved into housing that was now being rapidly abandoned by whites, including my old neighborhood in the Brighton area. Many whites who left were motivated by racism. They also did not want to live next to ugly interstate highways that chopped up their back yards. All were affected by the American dream of new suburban housing on large lots financed with low federally insured mortgages giving the middle class major tax benefits. In his classic book of suburban migration, Kenneth Jackson estimated that the federal subsidy in the form of mortgage and tax benefits for the middle and upper middle class in an elite suburb was several times the subsidy to a welfare family in the inner city.[4]

The poorest blacks were moved into new public housing. One of the largest new public housing tracts, named Rolling Green Estates, stretched for several blocks along the northern border of the Westcott area. The 1950 census showed nine African Americans living in that census tract; in 1970 there were 1,444, most of them residents of Rolling Green Estates and most of them poor. The percentage of black residents rose from less than 1 percent to 40 percent in the same period. The percentage of owner-occupied housing dropped from 48 to 25 percent, reflecting wholesale middle-class white flight (more than half left) and conversion of single-family homes to multiple dwellings. The center of the Westcott neighborhood lies on the line between two census tracts. The southern tract showed more moderate change, with an increase from nearly zero to 9 percent African American and a drop from 67 percent to 55 percent owner-occupied housing by 1970.

Middle-class white flight continued and resulted in considerable depletion of the Westcott community social capital, which we shall examine in a moment. But let us look first at the cost to African Americans who were removed from the Fifteenth Ward. Options other than clearance and removal of blacks were never seriously considered. A combination of historic preservation, rehabilitation, and upgrading of existing housing with voluntary scattered-site relocation of black residents could have maintained the social networks of a real community with stores, churches, and neighborhood organizations while also increasing the possibility for residential racial integration. The old Fifteenth Ward was a community that, while segregated, offered jobs, informal mentoring, and networks of community support. All those social structures were destroyed along with the buildings that were leveled.

Secondly, the funneling of the poorest blacks into massive housing projects like Rolling Green Estates not only isolated them from other working-class and middle-class African Americans with whom they had lived in the Fifteenth Ward but also set them apart from middle-class whites in the new neighborhood. Rolling Green residents were concentrated in a dense concrete and brick zone five blocks long that was a grim contrast with the frame housing with back and front yards that characterized the rest of the Westcott neighborhood. A few storefront churches opened along the perimeter of Rolling Green Estates, but these hardly compensated for the massive loss of social support networks experienced by these poor black children—higher proportions of whom lived in single-parent households than was true of the old mixed-class black settlement that had been destroyed. It was a place that invited a sense of abandonment and despair.

When major desegregation of public schools began in the late 1960s, the adolescents from Rolling Green Estates began to enter the virtually all-white Hamilton High. Proponents assumed that racial integration would bring major advantages in ending racial isolation for both black and white students and would be particularly beneficial to African Americans, who would have access to an enriched curriculum taught by what was widely regarded as an elite teaching faculty.

Those hopes were realized for some African-American students, especially middle-class blacks who lived outside the housing projects. But disproportionate numbers of students from Rolling Green Estates were placed in a dead-end basic track, where they were taught a diluted curriculum. They entered a school with a virtually closed social system of white fraternities and sororities. They left predominantly black schools where they had felt successful in both academic and social realms to make their way in an environment where they were labeled as failures in the classroom and were often politely shunned in the hallways. They came together with whites only to learn how far behind they had been in de facto segregated elementary and junior high schools.

As the black presence at Hamilton High escalated, eventually accounting for more than 40 percent of the enrollment, riots broke out. In 1970, after a memorial service for Martin Luther King Jr., African-American students rampaged through the school, breaking equipment in a physics laboratory and tearing into the library, where they overturned tables, swept books off the shelves, smashed windows, and tore up floor tiles. School was closed ten times that year because of clashes of various kinds. The gap between "desegregation" and "integration" was evident to all. Opportunity for informal contact between black and white students was limited to those few minutes while students passed in the halls, during which faculty held their breath. Paid aides and a policeman were permanently stationed in the school. Hamilton, like other recently desegregated high schools in the city, went on "block sessions": classes were shortened and school ended at 1:00 P.M. so that students could be sent home for lunch rather than risk confrontations in the school cafeteria. Assemblies were canceled for more than a decade. There were no dances.

Consultants were brought to Hamilton High to open discussions between black and white students. White students, many of them children of liberal parents who favored integration in principle, vented their anger about lewd remarks blacks made in hallways and expressed fears that blacks were "ruining our school." African Americans detailed incidents of racism by teachers who they felt had given up on them and by fellow students who they felt had rebuffed them. The principal at that time summed up the discussions: "There was an awful lot of hate involved there . . . and there was some progress. It was brought about by whites and blacks alike being forced to say just who the hell are you and what are you doing? And who the hell are you with all your money? And who the hell are you trying to break up my school?"[5]

Many teachers felt they were failures, ill-equipped to teach the poorly prepared black students who entered their classrooms. The strategies they had previously employed no longer worked. They lacked the knowledge, the resourcefulness, the imagination, or the energy to teach these new, often angry black students. Some teachers, especially middle-aged white males, admitted their fears of black students and confessed their inability to establish the necessary order in their classrooms. They were ground down, exhausted, defeated, and confused. By fall 1971, almost three-quarters of the teachers who had taught at Hamilton High in 1966 had resigned, retired, or transferred.

If social capital lies in stable human relationships, we see its loss in several ways. The huge turnover of teachers (accompanied by rapid turnover of principals) weakened the ties and shared norms that had existed between parents and schools. This affected expectations about academic achievement and homework as well as standards of behavior. Younger replacement teachers, some of whom smoked marijuana with students at parties, were at odds with more traditional teachers who stayed on. The faculty, which had formerly eaten together in the teachers' lounge, now split into three lunch factions. Teachers were unsure whether colleagues would back them up if they challenged a disruptive student in the halls. In the span of a decade, nearly half the middle-class parents departed for suburbs. Some of those who remained chained the doors of the school one morning to express their feeling that the school was no longer a fit or safe place for their children to enter. Black and white parents did not meet, as they once had, to help plan school dances or social events, for these were canceled for years. Suspension of these events meant that parents had little opportunity to develop the trust and sense of common aims that are essential for the growth of social capital. It also severely deprived the students, who were denied opportunities to form relationships in clubs and extracurricular activities and to extend social networks and exercise leadership abilities in a way they had done in their former schools, whether predominantly white or predominantly black. Only recently have African-American analysts like Vanessa Siddle Walker focused on these kinds of losses suffered by black students whose schools were closed.[6]

Within the Westcott neighborhood, there were no full-scale riots. But tensions rose and violence increased on the streets in the 1970s. Large groups of black teenagers from Rolling Green Estates congregated angrily in front of a neighborhood market that employed no African Americans. Windows were broken and police were called. Soft-drink bottles were smashed on sidewalks by youths who sauntered by with boom boxes blaring from shoulder straps. Black boys nine or ten years old did "wheelies" on their bicycles, pirouetting in front of cars that had come to a corner stop sign, keeping drivers at bay for long minutes. Inside the cars, scared whites, like many teachers at Hamilton High, often did nothing except lock their doors.

By the end of the seventies, the withdrawal of social capital from Westcott was severe. Middle-class out-migration had continued, including teachers at Hamilton High who formerly lived in the city. The synagogue and Jewish community center closed, both moving to the suburbs. This withdrew not only services for youth but also the street presence of a strongly integrated community that helped anchor good norms throughout the neighborhood. As part of school consolidation that was the core of the city school district's desegregation plan, the only elementary school within the neighborhood was closed. There was no longer a school to serve as the nexus of community, which would have brought parents together across race and class lines within the neighborhood. Elementary school parent-teacher organizations are perhaps one of the most effective building blocks of social capital. Parents of young children have the highest attendance at school events; elementary schools draw parents into the school as volunteers and classroom helpers more than at any other level of schooling. Parents are most likely to engage in face-to-face interactions around grade school issues and to develop the trust that is essential for shared norms and common expectations.

At a time of greatly increased need for social support as a result of a major infusion of poor children, a significant number of whom were at risk because of inadequate prenatal care, drug or alcohol abuse, and family stress, social capital and other resources in the neighborhood were in sharp decline. The number of adult socializers fell in relation to the number of children needing socialization and support. In 1950, 10 percent of the population in the Rolling Green census tract was aged fourteen or younger, while 15 percent fell in the primary care-giving ages of twenty-five to forty-four. Twenty-three percent were under fourteen by 1980, but those in the care-giving group had risen to only 29 percent. This was a change in ratio from 1.5 caregivers for each child to roughly one to one.

The decrease in social capital was also affected by the deinstitutionalization movement. The exodus from the school and the Westcott area was followed by the arrival of mentally and physically disabled persons released on a massive scale from residential facilities in New York State. The number of Hamilton students classified as having some form of disability requiring special attention more than tripled from fewer than 30 to 102, including students classified as autistic who had never before attended public schools. Those seeking to open group homes knew that the liberal political tradition within the Westcott area would reduce the likelihood of neighborhood protests that could drastically slow placements for the disabled. Not until nearly a dozen group homes had been opened within the neighborhood did the first organized protest come, over the attempted establishment of a large halfway house for recovering alcoholics. Some of these homes housed teenagers who had been placed there by the courts because they had suffered child abuse or by parents who had filed petitions for "persons in need of supervision" because they felt they could no longer control or provide for them. A study of turnover of adult staff in these homes showed that the average staff member stayed less than one year. It was not a cushy job, and these teenagers, most of them white, were not always well supervised.

The plight of these teenagers further underscored the depletion of social capital in the neighborhood, particularly the loss of what Coleman described as "intergenerational closure." By this Coleman meant that children know each other's parents, and the parents are also in communication with other parents in the neighborhood. In communities where parents have such communication, expectations and obligations connect the adults, and each adult can "use his drawing account with other adults to help supervise and control" his or her children. They can use their mutual obligations to aid them in raising their own children and establish good norms that reinforce each other's sanctioning of the children. This means that aiding persons in trouble earns rewards, and breaking bottles on the sidewalk evokes strong sanctions. According to Coleman's estimate of the relative disadvantage in a community without such closure, those parents have only three-fifths as much power to control children as parents in communities with closure are able to exercise.[7]

Intergenerational closure was weakened not only by the loss of the elementary school and the synagogue, and the out-migration of many middle-class parents, but by the inclination of more who remained, both white and black, to send their children to private and parochial schools outside the neighborhood. This was rational behavior from their point of view, though it further depleted social capital within Westcott. They felt that they could obtain closure and gain back the interparental reinforcement of norms and expectations that they felt was endangered if not lost in their own neighborhood. A national study comparing public and private schools attributed lower dropout rates in Catholic schools not to religious practices or superior forms of teaching but to increased social capital formed by the strong community of support around the school.[8] An individual does not lose much by withdrawing and shifting loyalties to another group, in this case a private school. But the cumulative loss of those withdrawals within the neighborhood significantly weakens the social fabric. A new headmaster of one of the leading private schools, seeking more diversity, offered more scholarships to blacks and recruited an admired African-American social studies teacher from the junior high school that served the Westcott neighborhood. It helped draw more blacks to his school, as well as liberal whites whose parents wanted their children to attend a racially diverse school that they saw as having stronger norms and higher expectations than Hamilton High.

COMMUNITY ON THE REBOUND

Hamilton High had stabilized by the 1980s. Relations between black and white students had improved markedly. The days when parents had put chains on the doors were a distant memory unknown to most students who now attended the school. Unlike students who first desegregated the school, these students had gone to elementary and middle schools together. And unlike desegregation patterns in large cities, the ratios between black and white children had stabilized, and most schools remained racially balanced through the nineties. At Hamilton, 40 percent of the enrollment in 1999 was white, 42 percent African-American, 16 percent Asian or other, and 2 percent Hispanic. Black and white parents now worked together to develop the school's strategic plan and served together on the school's management team, including some black alumni. Two of the principals during the nineties were African Americans, and of six city school superintendents appointed since school desegregation had begun, three were black.

Although the difference in achievement scores between black and white children had increased in the early 1970s, by 1985 the gap had closed significantly. Both black and white SAT scores rose in that period, but the black mean rose 62 points compared with 13 points for whites. Conditions in the school were more conducive to learning, and African-American students were better prepared to take advanced sequences in math and science. Yet large gaps in achievement levels and dropout rates remained. The average 1999 pass rate for white students in Hamilton mathematics courses was 81 percent, for African Americans

54 percent, Latinos 68 percent, and other (primarily Asian Americans) 84 percent. The proportion of students from families in poverty grew in the 1990s, with nearly 40 percent eligible for free lunch. This was the measure New York State used to compare school performance on statewide Regents examinations. When measured against nearby suburban schools, Hamilton High appeared to be a poorly performing school. But those who looked carefully at score data that were now published in all newspapers saw that Hamilton did much better than schools with similar levels of poverty. For example, 54 percent of Hamilton students passed the 1998 Regents exam in English, compared with 35 percent in similar schools.

Within the Westcott neighborhood, white flight slowed dramatically. Although the percentage of black residents in the northern half of the neighborhood had increased to 55 percent in 1990, all but 5 percent of that increase had occurred by 1980. But poverty had steadily worsened, with 17 percent in poverty in 1970, 22 percent in 1980, and 47 percent in 1990, more than double the percentage in poverty in the city as a whole. In the southern census tract the percent black reached a peak of nearly 10 percent by 1970 but had fallen to 6 percent by 1990. This reflected a return to the neighborhood of some middle-class whites with children, as well as considerable gentrification and restoration of historic homes, much of it by gay and lesbian couples who were increasingly attracted to Westcott. In the early 1990s the rental market dropped sharply because of a major downsizing by nearby Syracuse University. The proportion of black and poor rose significantly on several blocks within the more middle-class southern half of the neighborhood as landlords turned to federally subsidized section 8 tenants to fill vacant apartments. The poverty rate climbed from 11 percent in 1970 to 27 percent in the 1990s. There were other signs of trouble and instability as well.

The continuing loss of jobs and population in the city affected every neighborhood. Population dropped from 216,038 in 1960 to 147,306 in 2000. Poverty deepened citywide from a rate of 14 percent in 1970 to 23 percent in 1990. Many of Syracuse's old industries, like Nettleton Shoes, had closed or moved south. Others, like Carrier Air Conditioning, had long since moved to suburban settings where land was cheap and tax breaks were offered. The percentage of city residents in poverty climbed sharply. The tax base eroded and the commercial life of the city dried up. Boarded up stores and dwellings proliferated. Street life atrophied out of fear of predators and because more residents used automobiles to travel to distant shopping centers. More angry dogs ran loose on streets.

One measure of social capital in a neighborhood is the number of gathering places where residents meet to talk and interact: shops, coffeehouses, libraries, taverns, bookstores. In my old Brighton neighborhood, the change was devastating. In 1950 there were 101 such work and gathering places in the six-block heart of the Brighton business district, but only 38 were left in 1989.[9] The loss was far less severe but nonetheless real in the Westcott neighborhood. One of the attractions of Westcott was precisely the urban-village appeal of shops and coffeehouses, movie theater and bookshops. One expected to meet friends on the way to the newsstand or to sit in the café after a movie. The center began to collapse in the 1980s. The dry cleaning shop, jewelry store and watch repair, local five-and-dime, Rite Aid drugstore, hardware store, one of two bookstores, and eventually the neighborhood supermarket all closed. The theater turned into a porn movie house. At one point almost half the two-block business district was vacant. Two new taverns and three pizza shops had opened up, but the area was dreary and poorly lighted at night.

At a point when it looked like the leakage of social capital would become a flood, things slowly began to improve. Increases in street crime and the conversion of a good neighborhood theater to a porn house might have been the turning point that led to the founding of the Westcott East Neighborhood Association in the mid-eighties. Members made plain from the beginning that this would not be just another neighborhood watch group, as important as those might be, but would engage in community development on a wide scale. Over the next decade it helped spin off other community efforts, such as a local teen center, arts and gardening projects, community murals, code enforcement, and block parties. State, city, and some federal funds were drawn to the neighborhood. Housing Visions and East Side Neighbors in Partnership made a significant impact on rehabilitation of housing on several blocks within the Westcott neighborhood, though most of their projects were beyond its boundaries. A neighborhood preservation association obtained funds from the university and the city to offer low-cost guaranteed mortgages to low-income persons who would agree to be live-in owners. In its first ten years, this program led to the conversion of more than three hundred rental dwellings, many of them poorly maintained, to good residential housing.

Formation of the Westcott Community Development Corporation helped to revivify the business district. By the end of the nineties, the business district had almost no vacancies. The movie theater had been successfully renovated and reopened under new ownership, drawing good crowds for first-run films. Several new eateries opened, serving Middle Eastern, Mexican, and Chinese food. A new art gallery and framing shop now occupy the old hardware store, a specialty-clothing store has been a success where the five-and-dime had been. Efforts to attract a supermarket to the neighborhood continue; a small grocery opened as part of a pizza-and-beer outlet; the old supermarket, vacant for nearly three years, was attractively transformed to serve as a day center for disabled adults.

Several efforts have been aimed at regenerating social capital for teenagers, though no one would have used that language to describe their efforts. The Westcott Community Center began to offer programs for teenagers and the elderly in a two-story brick building that had been a city fire engine station. The East Side Neighbors in Partnership undertook a major renovation of the long-vacant Jewish War Veterans Home, raising nearly a million dollars to convert it to a center for the arts, with special emphasis on programs for teenagers. The center, which lies midway between the Rolling Green Estates and the business district, will include small apartments for live-in artists whose rent will be paid by offering art and music instruction to neighborhood teens. Named ENACT— Eastside Neighborhood Arts, Culture, and Technology—the center will also include state-of-the-art video and recording equipment as part of a new community radio station. The Westcott East Neighborhood Association drew teenagers into mural projects that involved making and glazing hundreds of tiles.

Two projects symbolized the rebirth of the neighborhood to wider audiences within the metropolitan area. Continued investment in renovation and restoration of historic homes in the district led to a two-page spread in the Syracuse newspapers in 1999 heralding the first Westcott house tour, sponsored by the county preservation association. It sold out, drawing to the neighborhood hundreds of visitors, many of whom would have hesitated to walk around the area two decades earlier. The second was the creation of the Westcott Cultural Fair, celebrating the diversity of the neighborhood. It began on a small scale, then became an event that features dozens of musical groups, arts and crafts, varieties of ethnic foods, and information on community programs. It now opens with a community parade in which the mayor and city council members march along with many children from the Westcott community and mummers and dancers and bands. The daylong event draws more than five thousand residents and visitors.

Renewal of the Westcott neighborhood is real, and the loss of social capital has been partially reversed by the actions just described. And that is no small achievement. It may be that the gains Hamilton High has experienced in the development of human capital (with better academic outcomes than schools with similar levels of students in poverty) is partially explained by the growth of social capital in the neighborhood. But to end the story here would be to end with comforting but false assurances. More of the story needs to be told in order to reveal the full dimensions of the struggle to create a good neighborhood. For the outcomes are far from certain and the lives of children are in the balance.

COMMUNITY IN JEOPARDY

I want to turn now to a more fine-grained analysis of life in the Westcott neighborhood, especially as the children who live there experience it. This portrait emerges from twenty-three interviews with Westcott residents, more than half of whom were teenagers, completed in the summer and fall of 1999. Ten of the interviewees were white and nine were black. The remaining four were Puerto Rican, Native American, East Indian, and one teenager who described himself as "Blackinese," part African American and part Japanese.[10] The aim of the research was to analyze these teenagers' social networks and to discover how they negotiated the social world. Each teenager was seen as at the hub of a social network. Each relationship or bond the teen had with another person was conceptualized as a spoke in his or her wheel. We were particularly interested in what supportive relationships they had with adults—parents or guardians, mentors in youth organizations, coaches, a music teacher, ministers or church volunteers, or someone at work who took an interest in them. We found radically different networks for different teenagers within the same neighborhood.

Some have parents who are only occasionally present in their lives and virtually no other positive bonds with supportive adults. Yet they see Westcott as a supportive neighborhood. A few of them have moved to Westcott from other more crime-ridden and poverty-stricken parts of the city. They see it as a big change. One teen, Beppy, told us that people there are friendlier and laid back: "Nobody gets bent out of shape here. You feel safe here. . . . You can go outside at 5 in the morning and be safe from gunshots. . . . You walk around here and people have gardens and things." These are youths who are living mostly on their own. They are smoking dope, doing a little hustling, getting "toasted" in a nearby park where they spend a lot of time. "We're like brothers. We normally kick it, go out, go to parties, get drunk. We always watch each other. If we all end up going to a park and somebody gets drunk, you know, we always watch after them. We never let him leave our side if he wants to go and pick a fight. But we don't pick a fight. The fights always come to us." They may carry weapons on occasion. More often, like Beppy and his friends, they travel with a Doberman or other attack dog trained to do serious damage on command. Guns are carried for protection when they are thought to be needed. Beppy explains: "If they pull a gun on me, all right, I am not the kind of person that would get scared. . . . But if they put the gun away I am going back to my house and get my gun and just not show it to them."

The good life is getting high and hanging out, mixed with some "excitement" when things get draggy. This might be spraying some graffiti on a wall or stealing mail to get a credit card they could use or hitting on some girl. But Beppy insists he doesn't steal for the thrills. "Cause I don't get no thrill out of it. You know, unless I am getting paid, [then] I'll take it; if not, then I won't take it." Beppy says he has no goals in life other than to get a lot of money. When pressed, he mocks that his goal is to "die and come back a leopard." Then, more seriously, he adds that he likes music and wants to be "a singer, a rapper," a big recording star. He looks to no one for advice:

> INTERVIEWER: Is your mom the most influential person in your life?
> BEPPY: Most what?
> INTERVIEWER: Influential, a person that you rely on the most for advice?
> BEPPY: No.
> INTERVIEWER: Who is?
> BEPPY: Me.
> INTERVIEWER: You? So you are on your own.
> BEPPY: Yeap.

Several of them have jobs in fast-food joints and may cite someone at work that they could turn to for help. But other than an occasional employer, there may be no one holding these kids accountable, expecting them to work hard or to measure up to any ideals. Neither teachers nor cops are trusted; on the contrary, they are regarded as part of the opposition. To be seen as cooperating or being compliant with either diminishes one's respect on the street. Although they are likely to have siblings or "cousins" who have been imprisoned, most of these teenagers have not yet been locked up; still, they are into the life of the street and headed that way.

Within the same neighborhood are teenagers, both black and white, who have many positive bonds with adults: parents who set curfews and supervise homework, coaches who are demanding, teachers whom they trust and respect, and advisers at church and at work. TJ is an African-American male who had recently graduated from high school when we interviewed him. His parents had sent him to a parochial high school even though they are not Catholic. They feared that things would go badly for him if he remained in public school. TJ had begun to hang out with some boys who were veering toward the street life. He did well in his new school, after an initial struggle. The academic shift had been a wake-up call for him because he had been getting straight A's but got C's and C− grades at the new school. "It was a lot more work so I had to make higher expectations for myself." He started getting a few B's in his sophomore year and ended his senior year with mostly A's and B's and a college scholarship. He occasionally sees his old middle school friends, who are still in the neighborhood, but it's not the same as it was before: "Well, a lot of them are, you know, on the streets now. Selling drugs, maybe not selling drugs, but smoking weed or whatever and they are not really into school. They are not headed in the same direction as me and it's kinda sad; you look and you see the people I grew up with. We all had the same goals when we started. We kinda drifted away. . . . I do see them walking around and stuff. I will ask them what they are doing next year and they are like, 'I didn't even graduate, you know, I am just trying to get a job and stuff.'"

TJ believes that many of his old friends would like to go to college and feels sad that they are being left behind. He is quick to reassure us that they have as much academic ability as he does: "I just feel bad cause it seems like something they want to do. I mean it's not like they are stupid or anything. . . . We were all together and we all did well in school. I guess they just got involved in the wrong things."

We asked why he did not suffer his friends' fate. TJ did not hesitate: "My parents, they really wanted me to get an education. Education was always first. Always do your homework. They was always, I was just, I just always did it. It was just like second nature. I didn't want to fail at anything. I didn't want to let my parents down. It was like, you know, I had temptations, but I just knew it was something my parents wouldn't want me to get into." There was no sliding by: "My mom has always been on me to work every night. She comes home and asks if I have my work done. I'm like 'yeah,' and she says, 'Let me see it.' She will check over it. She taught me how to type, and my dad got me a computer."

Perhaps half the children in the neighborhood lie between the poles represented by Beppy and TJ. They have not yet adopted the street life Beppy lives, nor do they have the rich networks of support that have sustained TJ. Many of them live in the Rolling Green Estates or in subsidized apartments or homes in deteriorating areas of the neighborhood. There may be one parent at home who is working two jobs to make ends meet. Children on tricycles are unsuper-

vised on the street after dark. They miss medical checkups, and their health suf-
fers. Those in school will come home to empty apartments. Sometimes their
mother can make supper between jobs, and at other times the children have supper alone, watching television and eating food purchased from a fast-food joint.

Without more spokes in their wheels, few children in such circumstances are
going to make it. They will continue watching TV or will be tempted to pass a
joint rather than tackle math homework. Skipping school is easy. Girls are
more likely to get pregnant, especially in a culture where the old sanctions
against sexual activity no longer apply. Boys who want to achieve will be tested
by what Elijah Anderson has called the "code of the street."[11] Although they do
not want to cross the line into petty crime that Beppy's brothers consider standard stuff, they will adopt the swagger and low-hanging pants and trademark
boots or jogging shoes that the "brothers" display. This sends a signal: "Don't
mess with me. I deserve respect." But the lure of the street is powerful and the
brothers are cool. They will test you. To prove you are cool you will be expected
to go along with breaking some windows, then delivering some drugs. And
later you may not be able to resist when offered some crack cocaine: "Try this,
you can handle it." You learn to disguise achievement in school and to "code
switch"—that is, to shift linguistic gears and body language as you pass from
middle-class conformity with teachers into an oppositional stance with Beppy's
crowd; you move without thinking from attitudes of deference to postures of
defiance. But without other supports or voices to stay your slide, the attraction
of the brothers increases. You begin skipping school and falling behind in
math. You had hoped to go to college. Maybe you still will. But this way of becoming a man by becoming a brother—getting some cash and a car and the
"props" or respect that goes with it—might be okay for a while. You can go to
college later.

FOUNDATIONS OF COMMUNITY

What could make a difference in such a boy's life? What could turn a young girl
away from premature motherhood? Let us examine what families and community organizations could do to expand the supply of social capital, and ask what
changes in social policy are needed.

Family

No one would dispute that the primary source of moral and social capital lies in
the family, though there is much disagreement about how to strengthen family

structure for poor children, especially poor black children. Conservatives see laziness and weak moral character as the causes of most family poverty. Liberals tend to view the poor as victims of inequality and discrimination; any critique of family irresponsibility is labeled as racism or "blaming the victim." In the past decade the pendulum has swung toward the center, with broad support for "workfare" reforms and a return to concern for character education in public schools. One of the principal sources of the support for vouchers and charter schools, especially among the black poor, is that these forms of school choice are seen as a way to escape the moral neutrality and bureaucratic legalism typical of many large urban public schools.

This new moral center was evidenced in several ways in the Westcott neighborhood in the 1990s. A black principal of Hamilton High won strong support from parents when he instituted new codes of dress and behavior. Most parents stood behind him when some critics complained that too many students were being suspended. Teachers did not believe that he would be able to get students to take off their hats, but within a week the hats were gone in a school where they had become emblems of casual cool in the classroom. After explaining to each class of students why he felt the change was necessary to improve the climate of the school, the principal had been at the front door every morning politely but firmly telling students that they must remove their hats or have them confiscated.

In the Westcott neighborhood evidence of a new consensus emerged in a dispute in a block where several poor families, most of them black, had recently moved in with section 8 housing subsidies. They were not the first black residents; the block had been about one-fourth African American. Neighbors saw evidence of drug activity in two of the newly rented houses and complained of young children being unsupervised on the street late into the night, and music blaring at all hours. A resident of one house was arrested on crack cocaine charges. Neighbors charged that the landlord, who owned many rental properties in the neighborhood, would take any tenant, no matter what the tenant's previous record of uncivil behavior, under the guaranteed section 8 housing vouchers program, which produced a steady stream of income for him. The landlord accused the neighbors of being racists, and his accusations were reported in the Syracuse newspapers. But blacks in the same neighborhood spoke out against the landlord, including the editor of an African-American weekly. Section 8 subsidies for the two houses were subsequently denied, triggering a countersuit by the landlord. An investigation by the regional New York–New Jersey Housing and Urban Development office concluded that "both minorities and non-minorities interviewed" did not feel that race was an issue in the neighborhood complaints.[12]

The neighbors on that block were raising basic questions about care and supervision of children, and the old race card did not play. Both white scholars like Christopher Jencks and Susan Mayer and black intellectuals such as William Julius Wilson and Glenn Loury have since addressed these issues more directly in research about social capital.[13] Black ministers and some civil rights leaders are more willing to speak publicly about the need to strengthen the core of family responsibility and to urge parents to read to their children, turn off the television, and make a space in the kitchen where children can do homework. Although the erosion of such practices may be most severe among the poor, it affects many in the middle class as well, where both parents may be working long hours and may be unable to spend as much time with their children as they would like. Students from rich as well as poor families have high levels of drug and alcohol abuse. All families need help, though some need more than others. New structures of support are necessary.

Faith-based social reforms have gained new ground and should be seen as experiments worthy of public funding. An African-American woman who had converted to Islam developed a proposal to take over the management of Rolling Green Estates in the Westcott neighborhood. She had been a branch manager of a bank in New York City and came to Syracuse to work in real estate, becoming actively engaged in many inner-city reform efforts. She wanted to establish a mission or modern form of a settlement house within the housing project, run by a tenant council. She planned to offer classes in prenatal and postnatal care, organize child-care support groups, and open a food pantry with cooking classes geared toward a healthy diet, as well as make a place for religious services of all denominations within the project. Unfortunately, she was turned down on the grounds that she had no previous experience in managing a large housing project.

Community

The social capital that lies in neighborhood relations and is reflected by the organizational life of the community is precious. If the family is the womb, the neighborhood constitutes the placenta that nourishes the child. I sketched above the remarkable growth of community organizations in the Westcott neighborhood. These organizations created new jobs, reversed the decline of the neighborhood commercial district, rehabilitated housing, and initiated a variety of neighborhood community projects. In terms of their central functions, however, they did two things that helped to stay the downward slide of children at risk.

First, they began the work of reconstituting and strengthening good norms. This can happen only when people come together to talk about the common problems they face and decide to take action. They need to develop shared understandings in face-to-face relationships. Organizations grew. There was a community meeting one could attend almost any night of the week. Newsletters proliferated. This was not easy and not always peaceful. Heated arguments often broke out about poor policing or what to do about a proposed zoning change for a new super drugstore with a drive-in window that would sell beer as well as pharmaceuticals. Some persons left in a huff. But as is true of lively town meetings throughout New Hampshire, they discovered that agreements could be reached.

Policing was a critical issue. Neighbors compared stories about the decline of quality policing. Residents learned that others had stopped calling to complain about noise or suspected drug trafficking because they had in effect been told by the police officer who came only after many complaints, "It goes with the territory, doesn't it? Why do you live in a neighborhood like this?" Residents became fed up with a 911 system of high-tech policing that was oriented to rapid radio communications, with squad cars kept in reserve to respond to violent crimes. They complained about a triage that directed many neighborhood complaints to a tape recorder for later transcribing. And why were there no foot patrols? A community police officer began attending most meetings of the largest neighborhood group, the Westcott East Neighborhood Association, which has nearly two hundred dues-paying members. Over a period of several years police became more attentive to what Fred Siegel has called the "moral regulation of public space," though the sense of menace and disorder on Westcott Street never reached the level he described in New York.[14] Foot patrols were started on weekends under a private grant secured by the Westcott Community Development Center.

Surveillance combined with real sanctions is necessary to secure safe streets and underwrite good norms. And the change in street behavior is noticeable, although incidents of wilding like the one described at the beginning of the chapter are still not uncommon. Citizens know that urban streets have always been contested terrain, as Peter Baldwin reminds us in his study of attempted reforms of public space in Hartford in the nineteenth century.[15] They also know that one cannot rely solely on giving police a bigger stick. Westcott community organizations have learned to be proactive. For example, on another block where high turnover brought in many new section 8 tenants, a block party was held. More than sixty residents, about a third of them African American, came to enjoy ice cream sundaes. Everyone present was asked to answer two questions posted on large charts tacked to a porch railing: What do we like about Harvard Place? What would make Harvard Place a better place? They liked many things about their block. One child who had moved there from Rolling Green Estates liked being on a block with porches where people said hello when he walked by. To make it a better place, a nine-year-old black girl asked that people coming down the street "stop using so many curse words and stop breaking bottles on the sidewalk." A vote was taken to define the top three priorities for improving the block: taking down a burned-out house, planting more flowers, and painting a badly peeling house. Everyone also pledged to support the nine-year-old girl's plea. By the end of the year several neighborhood organizations cooperated to accomplish all three objectives of the poll.[16]

The second–most essential action neighborhood organizations can take to regenerate the supply of social capital is to bring people together across racial and generational lines to work on community improvement projects that are visible to all. It was important that the ice cream party went beyond talk to action, that more than a dozen black and white residents got on ladders to paint the dilapidated house, and that everyone saw flowers planted and new bike racks installed. The work establishes new relationships as neighbors lend each other tools and hold the ladder for one another.

Projects that cross generational lines, that put children in new relationships with adults, are critical to refreshing the supply of social capital. Several projects that brought the wisdom and resources of adults to children outside their own families are worth mention. One of the most successful involved hundreds of children and adults in making tiles for a community mural. Tables were set up in many public neighborhood settings. Adults and children sat side by side making tiles and cooperated in later stages of painting and glazing. In such settings teenagers became acquainted with adults who might later hire them to cut lawns or paint a garage, or who might write a letter of recommendation for them. Many of the adults who participated were retirees who had not previously found such a congenial setting for interacting with children from other parts of the neighborhood. Some of the most active members of the boards of neighborhood organizations are in their seventies. The most ambitious endeavor may be the East Side Neighborhood Arts, Culture, and Technology project, which was conceived to connect teenagers with adult artists, musicians, filmmakers, computer specialists, and radio technicians in a center equipped with music, painting, and sculpture studios, high-tech recording equipment, computer labs, and a community FM radio station. Some artists will live in the facility, a historic structure on Westcott Street scheduled to undergo large-scale renovation in 2001. A third promising project remained on the drawing board at the end of 2000. It would employ neighborhood teenagers as workers to help rehabilitate houses that the neighborhood association would purchase and sell to live-in owners. The youth would earn money and learn new skills. Thirty residents pledged a thousand dollars or more to buy the first house, but the project has been delayed because of legal issues involved with incorporation and liability.

Policy

Strengthening the core of family responsibility and generating new social capital through the kinds of enterprises described here are vital. But they are not enough. There are few examples of urban neighborhood rebirth in the United States. Westcott efforts may falter and give way to the spread of decay and the relentless pressures of drug-induced crime. The middle class in the Westcott neighborhood continues to shrink, as it has in the city as a whole, where a third of the children under eighteen are in poverty and 40 percent live in female-headed households. Vast areas of Syracuse are desolate, and the overall housing vacancy rate is near 10 percent. Although significant housing improvements have been made in the past decade, more blocks within the Westcott neighborhood are in decline than show signs of renewal.

This did not happen by accident. Some of it is the result of racism. Some of it comes of a natural desire by many Americans to enjoy life in a new home in the suburbs and to avoid neighborhood conflict of the sort described in this essay. And much of it is the result of public policy. This brief history of the Westcott neighborhood serves as a case study of misbegotten public policy. It began with urban renewal that was comparable to doing brain surgery with a meat axe. No consideration was given of how to preserve the social capital of the old Fifteenth Ward through historic preservation and more precise surgical relocation. The contours of the present Westcott neighborhood were decisively cast by the creation of a "black township" that isolated the poorest African-American families and concentrated them in ways that bred dependency and distrust. Federal housing policies encouraged white flight with low mortgages and tax breaks in the suburbs while redlining many neighborhoods in the city. There were subsidies for exit but a pittance for genuine renewal of the infrastructure of cities like Syracuse. In Syracuse, as in most of the northeastern United

States, suburbs used their jurisdictional powers to virtually zone out the poor and the black. By 1990 only 1.4 percent of the 305,113 persons living in the Syracuse suburbs were black and 4 percent were in families below the poverty line. One-fifth of those in the city were black and 23 percent in poverty including 39 percent of children younger than six.

The burden of school desegregation was borne almost entirely by the city. Policies designed to accomplish desegregation in Syracuse may have been more effective than in many cities in the Northeast (with a higher than average number of schools in racial balance in the nineties), but they were still crude. It was policy designed by social engineers and lawyers concerned with bus schedules and quotas. Teachers were poorly prepared to deal with the realities and traumas of desegregation. Too little thought was given to ways of reconstructing the social capital that was depleted by massive changes in relations between families and schools. While recognizing that no amount of planning could have avoided the inevitable pain and sense of loss that accompanies any social revolution, the outcomes would have been better if school desegregation had been a metropolitan rather than a city-only burden. I suspect that studies would show that black children fared better in places like Nashville and Raleigh than in Syracuse.

Although we cannot undo the policy errors of the past, we can learn from them. Major reinvestment in urban housing is needed to bring about new mixes of public and private investment in ways that avoid concentrating and isolating the poor.[17] Charter schools and other approaches should be pursued to foster integration of social classes as well as races across city-suburban jurisdictions.[18] Policing policies must continue to shift away from overreliance on 911 control centers to more emphasis on community policing. Creative ways should be encouraged to continue state support for experiments in faith-based social reforms in the inner city.

The most promising avenue for increasing the supply of social capital lies in the provision of universal preschool and after-school programs. For most of human history, education was a function of the home and the church. Massive public schooling was not invented until men left the home in the nineteenth century for work in factories and other places distant from home. Large numbers of children were no longer taught on farms or in household settings. At the beginning of the twenty-first century, more than three-fourths of all women have now also left the home for work, including a majority of women with children under six. It is just as necessary to establish quality child-care programs for all children now as it was to create public schooling for all a century ago. All-day child care should be provided for all children from birth to school age. After-school programs should be available for all children, every day, until parents come home from work, and through the summer as well. These should not be for poor children only; the charity schools for the poor did not work in the nineteenth century, and such a pattern of child care will not work now either. These day-care and after-school institutions should be more family-like than school-like, however. They need to develop more holistic and nurturing relationships with the child. They should be places where children can experiment with expressing different aspects of the self and achieve more intensity of involvement, whether in basketball or in ceramics. Most important, these must be places where children can experience some intimacy and develop mentoring relationships with adults who appreciate them as individuals with special gifts. In their study of effective youth organizations, Shirley Brice Heath and Milbrey McLaughlin argued that these programs make their most essential contributions through caring mentors who serve as coaches, advocates, and gentle but firm critics. They change attitudes and shape children's identities. They help the discouraged see alternative futures.[19] But like good parents, they don't give grades.

The story told here presents in microcosm the history of urban America. Nathan Glazer pointed out that the "urban crisis" ranked high on the national agenda in the 1960s and 1970s and then faded from view. He argued that the principal reason for the decline in attention to the problems of the inner cities was that many concluded that nothing much could be done about them.[20] If there is any value in this analysis, it lies in the utility of a good theory. By looking at these events through the lens of Coleman's theory of social capital, we see more clearly some things that can be done and why they are worth doing.

NOTES

I am grateful to the Spencer Foundation for support of research on the educational life of the community that informs this essay. I also wish to thank two research assistants who made contributions to this chapter, Jennifer Esposito and Donald Gates.

1. Gerald Grant, *The World We Created at Hamilton High* (Cambridge: Harvard University Press, 1988). The name of the school is fictional. Although its actual name has been revealed by some reviewers of the book, I will continue to describe it as Hamilton High.
2. James S. Coleman, *Foundations of Social Theory* (Cambridge: Harvard University Press, 1990), p. 300. Coleman acknowledges here his debt to Glenn C. Loury's formulation of a theory of social capital in "A Dynamic Theory of Racial Income Differences," chapter 8 of P. A. Wallace and A. Le Mund, eds., *Women, Minorities and Employment Discrimination* (Lexington, Mass.: Lexington, 1977).

3. Joyce Carol Oates, *What I Lived For* (New York: Plume-Penguin, 1995).
4. Kenneth T. Jackson, *The Crabgrass Frontier: The Suburbanization of the United States* (New York: Oxford University Press, 1985), p. 294.
5. Grant, *Hamilton High*, p. 35. The discussion here, for the purposes of illustrating the analysis of changes in social capital, necessarily collapses a complex account to be found in the first four chapters of *Hamilton High*.
6. Vanessa Siddle Walker, *Their Highest Potential: An African American School Community in the Segregated South* (Chapel Hill: University of North Carolina Press, 1996). Although she does not wish for a return to a segregated past, Walker's history of the Caswell County High School shows that it was a place of caring and high expectations, highly valued by its graduates. In *Getting Around Brown: Desegregation, Development, and the Columbus Public Schools* (Columbus: Ohio State University Press, 1998), Gregory S. Jacobs also discusses the loss of sympathetic and caring teaching suffered by many black students transferred to desegregated schools.
7. Coleman, *Foundations of Social Theory*, pp. 318–19.
8. James S. Coleman and Thomas J. Hoffer, *Public and Private High Schools: The Impact of Communities* (New York: Basic, 1987). In public schools, 14.3 percent of the sophomores left before graduating from high school; in the non-Catholic private sector, 11.9 percent left, but only 3.4 percent in the Catholic schools did so.
9. Donald Gates, "Potential Places of Informal Education Within a Neighborhood Community," unpublished paper, Syracuse University, 1997. Ray Oldenburg referred to places of informal interaction as "third places," with the home being the "first place" and work sites being "second places." See Oldenburg, *The Great Good Place* (New York: Norton, 1995). Gates, using city directories for relevant years, counted both work sites and informal gathering places.
10. This research was done by Jennifer Esposito, a doctoral student at Syracuse University. Names have been changed to ensure confidentiality.
11. Elijah Anderson, *Code of the Street: Decency, Violence, and the Moral Life of the Inner City* (New York: Norton, 1999).
12. Daniel Gonzalez, "Accusations Fly as Subsidy Cut: Syracuse Housing Authority Cites List of Neighborhood Complaints," *Post Standard* (Syracuse), June 10, 1999.
13. Christopher Jencks and Meredith Phillips, eds., *The Black-White Test Score Gap* (Washington, D. C.: Brookings Institute, 1998); Susan E. Mayer *What Money Can't Buy: Family Income and Children's Life Chances* (Cambridge: Harvard University Press, 1997); William Julius Wilson, *When Work Disappears: The World of the New Urban Poor* (New York; Knopf, 1997); Loury, "Theory of Racial Income Differences."
14. Fred Siegel, *The Future Once Happened Here: New York, D.C., L.A., and the Fate of America's Big Cities* (New York: Free Press, 1997), p. 169.
15. Peter C. Baldwin, *Domesticating the Street: The Reform of Public Space in Hartford, 1850–1930* (Columbus: Ohio State University Press, 1999).
16. The WENA News, a publication of the Westcott East Neighborhood Association, "Small Miracles on Harvard Place," winter 1999–2000, p. 2.
17. Some federal reinvestment with this aim has begun in Syracuse, although it will affect only a small portion of vacant and blighted housing in the city. Andrew Cuomo, secre-

tary of the U.S. Department of Housing and Urban Development, recently visited Syracuse to review initiatives under a $5 million HUD grant intended to leverage city and private development in four neighborhoods. Maureen Sieh, "Cuomo: City Strengthens Region; HUD Secretary Touts Private Money for Housing Stock," *Post Standard* (Syracuse), January 25, 2000.

18. I have opposed most voucher programs because they have been so minimally funded that they amount to tax breaks for the middle class and do not go far enough in the direction of increasing social class or racial integration. Nor do I believe it would be wise to institute any national voucher programs analogous to the GI Bill. We do not know enough to predict the long-term effects on public schooling. But experiments in several states along the lines of the Coons-Sugarman initiative in California are justified. That initiative stipulated that vouchers should be equivalent to 90 percent of the public school per-pupil expenditure and that any school that accepted a voucher must reserve at least 25 percent of its places for children in families below the poverty line.

19. Shirley Brice Heath and Milbrey W. McLaughlin, eds., *Identity and Inner City Youth: Beyond Ethnicity and Gender* (New York: Teachers College Press, 1993). This paragraph also draws on James S. Coleman, "Families and Schools," *Educational Researcher,* August–September 1987.

20. Nathan Glazer, "How Social Problems Are Born," *The Public Interest,* spring 1994.

Chapter 5 To Not Fade Away: Restoring Civil Identity Among the Young

William Damon

The death of democracy is not likely to be an assassination from ambush. It will be a slow extinction from apathy, indifference and undernourishment.
Robert Maynard Hutchins

Success often breeds the seeds of its own demise—just as, in coastal areas, hot weather eventually consumes itself by raising a cooling fog from the sea. Complacency is a common mechanism for success-born self-destruction in human affairs. It has the curious effect of creating conditions for eventual collapse at the same time as fostering the delusion that it could never happen. The more secure the sense of complacency, the more dense the reverie and the greater the peril. Among the most hazardous and oblivious senses of complacency are those that pile up across generations. Family histories come replete with stories of younger generations who have squandered wealth out of the naively entitled belief that their good fortune could never end.

The late twentieth century proved a triumphant time for democracy. Before World War II, only 28 percent of the world's nations claimed to be democratic. By century's end, after tyranny upon tyranny has fallen, this figure had risen to 62 percent. Perhaps this will prove to be the most important societal change of our time: although contemporary social theorists tend to portray the late twentieth century as an era of rapid technological innovation and economic globalization, future historians may characterize it as the watershed period when democracy became recognized as the world's governance model of choice.

But whether history will in fact be written this way will depend on a matter that may seem insignificant in relation to the grand scale of international politics. It is on the inauspicious front of young people's minds and morals that the battle for democracy will be won or lost in the coming years.

On this front, in contrast to the geopolitical one, the tide has not been turning the right way. Young people across the world have been disengaging from civic and political activities to a degree unimaginable a mere generation ago. The lack of interest is greatest in mature democracies, but it is evident even in many emerging or troubled ones. Today there are no leaders, no causes, no legacy of past trials or accomplishments that inspire much more than apathy or cynicism from the young.

In the United States, eighteen-year-olds were given voting privileges before the 1972 presidential election, and 47 percent of young people in the eighteen- to twenty-four-year age range voted that year. With the exception of an insignificant blip in 1992, voting rates in this age group declined consistently until the 1996 presidential election, when only 27 percent voted—barely one in four. Early analyses from the national election of 2000 suggest a further decline from even this insubstantial rate—and this was a hotly contested race.

Nor is the disaffection confined to a national level—as if it were in reaction, say, to past presidential crimes and peccadilloes. There has never been a time in American history when so small a proportion of young people aged twenty to thirty have sought or accepted leadership roles in local civic organizations. On opinion surveys it is hard to find a public figure on any level whom the young admire, let along wish to emulate. In fact, many of today's young show little interest in civil life beyond the tight circles of their family and immediate friends. Their lack of interest is reflected in the sorry state of their knowledge. In recent Department of Education assessments, only 9 percent of U.S. high school students were able to cite two reasons why it is important for citizens to participate in a democracy, and only 6 percent could identify two reasons why having a constitution benefits a country.[1]

It would be misleading to paint too bleak a picture of today's young. Many are thriving, most are staying out of trouble, and some are positively engaged in the broader civil society. Even the vast majority who have little interest in civic affairs often discover pockets of civil concern. One shining light of youth civil engagement these days is community service. Young people are out helping those in need to an extent that is impressive by any standard: almost half of American high school students devote time to charitable works at least once a month; about half of those do so weekly.[2] Other embers of youthful social affiliation still glow: family ties, peer friendships, sports teams, after-school clubs, communities of aesthetic, spiritual, and religious activity, study groups and other school-based organizations.

The problem is that a great many of today's young do not avail themselves of such opportunities. Far too many young people are drifting into *anti*social engagements, as I (among many others) have documented in recent writings.[3] But there is another problem, just as serious for the futures of the young and the society that they will inherit. Even for those youngsters who are staying on a positive track, there is something gone awry, something missing or fading away, from the seemingly propitious track that they are on. With astonishingly few exceptions, even the most positive of today's youth affiliations are unaligned, for the present and likely for later, with the public domain, where our democratic society is composed and sustained.

THE DEDICATION GAP

Periodically, my Center on Adolescence at Stanford conducts interviews with adolescents and young adults in order to explore their views about themselves and society. In spring 1999 we collected a few in-depth interviews with youngsters aged fourteen to eighteen living in some heartland American communities.[4] We also examined essays that these and hundreds of other students had written about the laws and purpose of life in today's world.

What struck us was not only what these young people said but also what they did not say. They showed little interest in people outside their immediate circles of friends and relatives (other than fictional media characters and entertainment or sports figures); little awareness of current events; and virtually no expressions of social concern, political opinion, civic duty, patriotic emotion, or sense of citizenship in any form.

For example, when asked what American citizenship meant to him, one student replied, "We just had that the other day in history. I forget what it was." Another said, "I mean being American is not really special. . . . I don't find being an American citizen very important," and yet another said, "I don't know, I figure everybody is a citizen so it really shouldn't mean nothing." One student said directly: "I don't want to belong to any country. It just feels like you are obligated to this country. I don't like the whole thing of citizen. . . . I don't like that whole thing. It's like, citizen, no citizen, it doesn't make sense to me. It's like to be a good citizen, I don't know. I don't want to be a citizen. . . . It's stupid to me." Although such statements are by no means universal, neither are they atypical. In fact, they are strikingly similar to sentiments that I hear from students in every formal or informal setting that I visit.

To the extent that political life showed up on these students' radar screens at all, it was viewed with suspicion and distaste. "Most [politicians] . . . are kind of crooked," one student declared. Another student, discussing national politics, said, "I feel like one person can't do that much, and I get the impression that [most people] don't think a group of people can do that much." The cynicism carried over to political action at all levels, even school. When talking about how school government works, one girl said, "The principal and vice principals probably make the decisions and say what is going on and don't worry about it." A palpable feeling of futility—a "what's the use?" sensibility—ran through all the students' attitudes about political participation. The following excerpt from one student's interview is illustrative. Before the statements below, the girl had been complaining that her school's dress code was arbitrary and unfair.

Q. Why do you think there's no action on it?
A. I guess because [the students] think that even if they do try to do it, they will not change it. It's a rule and it's going to be there forever. It's not going to change. We've always had that rule. You come here you have to abide by our rules. We're not going to change it just because you want to change it.
Q. Do you feel like there is any democracy at all at your school?
A. I don't know.
Q. Do you vote on anything other than electing representatives?
A. Nope.
Q. Do they vote on anything?
A. I have three representatives in my class, but I don't really ask them about this stuff and they don't really tell us about that. I mean, they might vote on stuff. I don't know that they do though.

When asked what they would like to change in the world, the students mentioned only such personal concerns as slowing down the pace of life, gaining good friends, either becoming more materially successful or less materially oriented (depending on the student's values), and being more respectful of the earth, animals, and other people. None of the students expressed concerns about the civic and political worlds, domestic or foreign. If they had expressed such interest, they would have few tools to pursue them: they lacked even minimal knowledge of topics in national and world affairs.

Although some of the students considered themselves to be leaders among their circles of close friends, almost none desired to be a civic leader. (There was a lone exception in our sample.) One boy, for example, dismissed the idea by saying, "It just doesn't seem like a very good job to me. I'd rather be concentrating on more artistic efforts rather than civic efforts or saving the world or something."

Is this unusual, or remarkable in any way? Hasn't youth always been a time for the pursuit of personal pleasures and intimate relationships rather than participation in the broader civil society? Have the young ever been driven by a sense of civic duty or dedicated to social and political purposes beyond their own everyday lives? Indeed, is there not plenty of time in later life to get interested in such things?

The uncomfortable answers to these rhetorical questions are: (1) yes, young people's current lack of dedication to broader civil purposes is unusual by any historical standards that we have; (2) no, youth traditionally has not been a time of exclusively personal and interpersonal goals to the exclusion of civic ones; and (3) yes, young people normally have been drawn to civic and political affairs by the time of late adolescence. In fact, there is reason to believe that a person's crucial orientations to life incubate during adolescence. If civic concern is not among them, it may never arise.

We all have memories, of course, about times in our own recent history when young people in numbers threw themselves into the political fray. They joined the civil rights movement, campaigned for political candidates, lobbied for environmental protection, and protested government actions that they did not like, such as the Vietnam war and the Watergate abuses. One sociological study has shown that young people who marched for civil rights in the 1960s were far more likely than their peers to later join civil associations, assume positions for civic leadership, and vote.[5] We also are aware (at least from old Hollywood films, if not from family lore) that in our country's more distant past young people have signed up with ardor for military and public service when wars and other threats to their society have emerged.

But there is far more evidence for a tradition of youthful civil engagement than these few scattered data points. Virtually all the classic theories of human development—of Jean Piaget, Erik Erikson, Jane Loevinger, and Harry Stack Sullivan, among many others—portray adolescence as a period when young people formulate their personal, social, and civil identities. A civil identity is an allegiance to a systematic set of moral and political beliefs, a personal ideology of sorts, to which a young person forges a commitment. The emotional and moral concomitants to the beliefs are a devotion to one's community and a sense of responsibility to the society at large. The specific beliefs and commitments, of course, may change over the subsequent years, but the initial formulation of them during adolescence always has ranked as a key landmark of human development. Piaget found evidence for this in the young people's diaries, Erikson and Sullivan in clinical encounters, Loevinger in psychometric measures and surveys. This is a part of a large data base spanning many countries and several generations of youngsters.

A civil identity is by no means the province of the privileged in society. Nor is it totally extinct in our own society. I quote here from an interview conducted a few years ago by my former student and frequent collaborator Daniel Hart. The interview was conducted with a seventeen-year-old African-American boy living in an extremely disadvantaged section of Camden, New Jersey. David, the subject, expresses an affiliation with his community and a sense of responsibility for it that still exists, though it has become increasingly rare among advantaged and disadvantaged youngsters alike.

Q. How would you describe yourself?
A. I am the kind of person who wants to get involved, who believes in getting involved. I just had this complex, I call it, where people think of Camden as being a bad place, which bothered me. Every city has its own bad places, you know. I just want to work with people, work to change that image that people have of Camden. You can't start with adults because they don't change. But if you can get into the minds of young children, show them what's wrong and let them know that you don't want them to be this way, then it could work because they're more persuadable.

A number of young people from all backgrounds still acquire a solid civil identity, and the possibility is still very much alive for the many who are not doing so. It is still the case that neurological and cognitive growth around the time of puberty, combined with the expansion of social roles and educational experience that the secondary school years brings, sets the stage for the adolescent's formulation of civil identity.

But what happens when young people choose not to walk upon the stage that has been set for them? To put it frankly, we do not know. We do not know how the abnegation of civic concern on the part of a young person will affect his or her later development; nor do we how it will shape the society that a cohort of similar young people will inhabit. It is as if we had launched two daring experiments, one psychological and one sociological, asking the twin questions: how will it turn out for the individual, and how will it turn out for the society, if we skip over (or perhaps try to postpone) the traditional developmental process of forming civil identity during the adolescent years?

As a social scientist, I generally welcome experiments, especially ones that explore the vagaries of human development and social change. But this is not an experiment that I can support. For the continued health of a democracy that counts on the dedication of a prepared citizenry, the stakes are simply too high. If the results are not to our liking, it might not be so easy to reverse the experimental conditions.

IMPOLITE WORDS AND YOUTH CHARACTER FORMATION

In earlier writings, I have made the case that an unfortunate combination of cultural forces in contemporary society has obstructed the formation of moral commitments among many young people.[6] I identified two conditions in particular: a failure to communicate high moral standards to the young at a time in their lives when their character development requires unambiguous guidance; and the isolation (or worse, division) among people and institutions who are responsible for providing coherent guidance to the next generation.

Civil identity is a part of youth character formation. It develops—or does not develop—through many of the same processes that shape moral character. If we are to foster civil identity among today's young, we must start by understanding what has gone wrong in our efforts to guide young people's character formation. I will start with a story. It was told to me by a Washington, D.C., mother who called in to a National Public Radio program on which I recently spoke.

The week before, the mother received a note from her son's school. In her son's class, someone had been taking lunch money out of students' backpacks, and the authorities had just caught the culprit—her son. Distressed, the woman called the boy's teacher to see what she could do to make sure that the boy did not continue to steal. According to this parent, the teacher said something to this effect:

Mrs. Jones, we sent you a note because we must keep you informed, but now we must ask you to stay out of this. We held a teacher's conference to decide what to do, and we are handling the situation in a professional manner. We are not calling your son's behavior "stealing." That would only embarrass him. It would make him think of himself as a thief. We have told your son that this is "uncooperative behavior." We have explained to your son that he will not be popular with the other students if he continues to act this way.

Mrs. Jones reported that the boy now dismisses her efforts to communicate with him about the matter. In fact, she suspected that he had "blown the whole thing off" without learning anything from it at all.

Now, *stealing* is an impolite word, carrying with it a moral accusation that indeed should embarrass anyone with a sense of right and wrong. But that, of course, is the point—it *is* a matter of right and wrong. If we remove the moral meaning behind it, its potential to evoke shame or guilt, the concept carries nothing more than an instrumental meaning. If you get caught stealing, you may get punished or become unpopular. If you don't get caught . . . well, so what? This is the opposite of moral education—in fact, it qualifies as moral *mis*education.

An essential part of moral education is reaffirming the emotional sense of moral regret that young people naturally feel when they harm another person or violate a fundamental societal standard. Every child is born with a capacity to feel upset when another person is harmed (empathy), with a capacity to feel outrage when a social standard is violated, and with a capacity to feel shame or guilt when he or she has done something wrong.[7] This is the emotional basis for the child's moral character; but it will quickly atrophy without the right kinds of feedback—in particular, guidance that supports the moral sense and shows how it can be applied to the range of social concerns that one encounters in human affairs.

Yet there is hesitancy today to assert the moral sense, or to use a moral language at all, in many homes and schools. There are several reasons for this: some adults worry that shaming children wounds their self-esteem; some believe that moral teaching does not belong in schools; some believe that there are no moral truths anyway, or that it is hypocritical to preach them to the young when so many adults ignore them, or that in a diverse society one person's moral truth is another's moral falsehood.

The result of this hesitancy is a prevailing, and debilitating, climate of moral uncertainty in many of the places where young people look to adults for guidance. In recent visits to schools I have been increasingly struck by how readily a school can be paralyzed by a common breach of standards such as cheating. Over the past few years, I have been called into several secondary schools—

many of them elite—to help resolve cheating scandals. In every case, the ambivalence of the teaching staff about the moral meaning of the incident was palpable at the time of my arrival. Many, if not most, of the teachers publicly expressed the opinion that it was hard for them to hold students to a no-cheating standard in a society in which people cheat on taxes, the president cheats on his spouse, and so on. Many sympathized with the cheaters because the tests were somehow flawed, or because the cheaters had been acting out of loyalty to their friends by secretly sharing the information. It can take days of intense discussion, and some arm-twisting, to get the teaching community solidly behind the moral bases for a no-cheating standard—namely, that cheating is wrong because (1) it violates trust between teacher and student, (2) it gives students who cheat an unfair advantage over those who do not, (3) it encourages dishonest behavior, and (4) it undermines the academic integrity, codes of conduct, and social order of the school.

Adult solidarity on the side of clear moral standards is precisely what guides character formation in the young. I am not referring to an arbitrary, imposed set of commands regarding debatable issues but rather a sense of shared values concerning fundamental norms of human behavior: honesty, fairness, common decency, respect for legitimate authority, compassion, and the like. I have worked with parents from just about every ethnic group and socioeconomic background, and I have yet to encounter groups that do not want to see their children behave according to such standards. Nor, in my reading of the anthropological literature, have I found significant variation from these shared standards across cultures.[8]

After all, what society could long exist if it explicitly promoted, say, dishonesty rather than honesty in human communications, cruelty instead of compassion, or disrespect rather than respect for legitimate authority? One reason that moral standards are not arbitrary is that they are deeply functional, at least in the long term. Another reason that they are not arbitrary is that they reflect a consensus, a living tradition of past and present judgments, about what people in society consider to represent the good in human affairs.

The belief that moral standards are not arbitrary, that they reflect basic human truths *and therefore merit a sense of certainty,* is the essential message that must be passed down across the generations if the ethical center of society is to be preserved. This is, in large part, an emotional message: it engages the heart as well as the mind and fosters the sustained devotion to society that, as Durkheim originally noted, is the necessary prerequisite of all moral education.[9]

Yet this is precisely what has been missing from a culture that has come to favor moral relativism over moral certainty. And this culture is very much present in the classroom: although it may seem that the average schoolteacher is a long way from the literary and academic circles where postmodern thinking holds sway, today's intellectual trends have reached every corner. Our teachers have eyes and ears, they are bright and curious, and most are right in tune with the prevailing cultural notes. Moreover, many of the teachers, and especially the younger ones, have studied education in current programs that promote what I have described as an "anything-goes constructivism."[10] This approach (a bastardized version of Piaget's theory) stresses the importance of the child's autonomous discovery and discourages discipline, external feedback, and objective standards: in short, it is ideologically in sync with postmodernist views on cultural transmission in general and moral learning in particular. Not surprisingly, the great majority of the teachers I meet believe that young people must work out their own values, and they question whether there are any solid moral truths that they ought to impart to students.

In this climate of moral relativism, expressions of moral sentiments become not only impolite but dangerous—they may in fact become fighting words. A teacher's reprimand to a student, when phrased in a moral language of right and wrong, can and does lead straight to litigation in today's school world. A growing number of public schools in the United States are being sued by parents who believe that their children have been unfairly accused of a moral infraction.[11] I have seen this happen in a number of cases—often in matters related to honesty (cheating, lying to a teacher, forging excuses from a parent), but also in matters related to seriously harmful behavior (racial or ethnic slurs, harassment, violent assault).

It is hard to imagine a young person learning a firm moral code in a society that embraces no common values; and yet this is precisely the condition that we offer young people when moral instruction in the school is hesitant, haphazard, and wholly uncoordinated with the core values of the home and the community. The development of moral commitment among young people thrives on coherence in the social environment. Studies of adolescents from a variety of American cities and towns have found high degrees of prosocial behavior and low degrees of antisocial behavior among youngsters from communities that are characterized by widespread consensus in moral standards for young people.[12] The opposite is true of communities characterized by conflict, divisiveness, and lack of shared standards for the young. For a young person's moral character, a coherent set of social influences that reflect a set of core common values is a far more telling condition than affluent material conditions.

Young people need to hear clear and consistent messages from all the respected people in their lives if they are to take the messages to heart. Enduring moral commitments—ones with an emotional as well as a cognitive foundation—are acquired through repeated exposures to core standards in multiple settings. Even though children are born with emotional predispositions toward empathy and other moral orientations, social guidance is needed for further growth. To have a lasting impact, the guidance must come from many sources and take many forms. A student best learns honesty when a teacher explains why cheating undermines the academic mission, a parent demonstrates the importance of telling the truth for family solidarity, a sports coach discourages deceit because it defeats the purpose of fair competition, and a friend shows why a lie undermines the trust necessary for a close relationship. The student then acquires a living, felt sense of why honesty is important to all the human relationships that the student cares about.

Because of increased public awareness that many young people's moral and behavioral standards are not what they should be, character education programs have proliferated in schools across the United States. There are more than 150 independent organizations producing materials, and the market for the materials is growing yearly. I am generally in favor of this effort. At the very least, it makes a public statement to young people that morality once again is an educational priority for our society. (Moral education "came with the territory" for the first century of American schooling.)

Still, in reviewing these programs, I have had to conclude that their effectiveness is undermined by mixed moral messages that students receive in other parts of the school day.[13] It does little good for students to discuss the virtues of honesty in a class on character development when one period later an English teacher looks the other way while students copy material for their papers from an encyclopedia. The moral atmosphere that students actually experience in their schools—the manner of their teachers, the integrity of the school codes, the quality of the peer relationships that they form—has more influence on character growth than do academic programs.[14] This is especially the case when these programs are at odds with the culture of the school. In the end, the school culture will overwhelm any isolated effort, because it is the culture that shapes the social relationships that students participate in. It is through these relationships that students acquire the norms and values that they eventually make part of themselves. A student's moral identity is forged from the felt reality of many such relationships, and the moral identity will be strongest when the relationships tend to support the same high standards of behavior.

The same can be said for the student's positive affiliation with civil society: to be learned, it must be felt as well as imagined, and it must be fostered through multiple relationships that all show the student why such an affiliation should play an important part in the student's life goals. Civil identity is a part of moral identity, acquired through similar developmental processes.

In my previous writings, I have discussed the problem of nurturing moral identity in young people growing up in a culture infused with moral relativism.[15] Here I turn to the equally urgent problem of fostering civil identity among young people growing up in a time of skepticism about public life and public service. The civil disaffection felt by many of our young resembles their moral confusion in many ways: it has led to a similar sense of indirection—indeed, paralysis—and it feeds on the same general sense of skepticism and uncertainty. But there are additional cultural currents that must be directly addressed if our civic engagement problem is to be solved. In order to do so, I will need to invoke another impolite word, *patriotism,* or the love of one's own society.

PATRIOTISM, THE EMOTIONAL ANCHOR OF
CIVIL IDENTITY

Intellectual trends, as I have noted, do not confine themselves to circles of intellectuals, at least not these days. In this era of universal education and mass communication, the most cutting-edge trends reach into every corner of our culture. This includes, of course, the public schoolroom, where teachers impart, for better or for worse, the particular ways that they interpret the ideas of the day.

In many intellectual circles, including much of education, the notion of patriotism has been out of fashion since at least the days of the Vietnam war. This may be understandable, at least when patriotism is confused (as it has been) with the kinds of chauvinistic and supermilitaristic passions that have spawned such evil nationalisms as National Socialism. It is not that patriotism itself has been abandoned: most educators no doubt feel a sense of it in their own lives. But it is rarely advocated as a legitimate goal of education or promoted as an essential virtue to pass on to the younger generation. Much like the notion of moral truth, it is honored in personal practice but held on tenterhooks when talked about in professional circles. Most often, it is not talked about, at least not without doubt and skepticism.

When patriotism does come up in education, the goal is usually to find ways to guard against its dangers. Many educators see patriotism as antithetical to a more global perspective on humanity and thus as the enemy of such humane conditions as peace and justice. Influential educators have urged schools to teach children to become "cosmopolitan" or "citizens of the world" rather than to identify themselves with any particular nation-state. One prominent advocate of cosmopolitan education is the University of Chicago professor Martha Nussbaum, whose work has been celebrated in academic reviews and the popular press alike. Nussbaum has written that we must avoid instilling in students an "irrational" patriotism "full of color and intensity and passion." She writes that "through cosmopolitan education, we learn more about ourselves." Nussbaum goes on to explain: "One of the greatest barriers to rational deliberation in politics is the unexamined feeling that our own preferences and ways are neutral and natural. An education that takes national boundaries as morally salient too often reinforces this kind of irrationality, by lending to what is an accident of history a false air of moral weight and glory. By looking at ourselves through the lens of the other, we come to see what in our practices is local and nonessential, what is more broadly or deeply shared. Our nation is appallingly ignorant of the rest of the world. I think that this means that it is also, in many crucial ways, ignorant of itself."[16] For such reasons, Nussbaum wonders why we would ever teach American students to see themselves first and foremost as U.S. citizens, with all the rights and responsibilities that would then accrue: "Most important, should they [our students] be taught that they are, above all, citizens of the United States, or should they instead be taught that they are, above all, citizens of a world of human beings, and that, while they happen to be situated in the United States, they have to share this world with citizens of other countries?"[17]

The posture that one simply "happens to be situated in the United States" seems about as far away from a sense of national affiliation as one can get. But Nussbaum is no more extreme in her distaste for U.S. (or any other) citizenship than are many other prominent educators today. In a well-received book called *Banal Nationalism,* the social scientist Michael Billig warns against all messages, explicit or symbolic, that communicate a sense of national identity across generations: "Banal," Billig writes, "does not imply benign. . . . In the case of the Western nation-states, banal nationalism can hardly be innocent: it is reproducing institutions which possess vast armaments."[18] Such sentiments have drawn criticism from some, yet they are by no means anomalous.[19] More to the present point, they are widely shared by teachers in the ranks of our public and private schools. In fact, in my own informal observations, they set the tone for much of what is taught in social studies curricula across the United States.[20]

Why should this be troublesome? After all, the notion of global citizenship is a benign one, especially in a world that is growing closer together every day. Moreover, spirited criticism of our own country is healthy, absolutely in line with the best parts of our democratic tradition. My concerns are not with the ideology or criticism per se but rather with their uses in educating the young. Here I will make two assertions, based upon my own understanding of the developmental needs of young people during their primary and secondary school years:

1. A positive emotional attachment to a particular community is a necessary condition for sustained civic engagement in that community. For full participatory citizenship in a democratic society, a student needs to develop a love for the particular society, including its historical legacy and cultural traditions.

2. The capacity for constructive criticism is an essential requirement for civic engagement in a democratic society; but in the course of intellectual development, this capacity must build upon a prior sympathetic understanding of that which is being criticized.

My first assertion stems from the same developmental perspective that I have used to discuss moral commitment and character formation in general.[21] My argument is that consistent moral action requires commitment; commitment is a function of identity; and identity is the way that a person organizes all the personal identifications, ideas, and feelings that have continuing importance in the person's life. Hence the importance of fostering a positive emotional attachment to a community, a sense that "I care about the community in the way that I care about myself," if we are to expect sustained moral action on its behalf.

In order to understand a person's behavior, we must know not only what he or she believes but also how important that belief is to the person's sense of self—that is, why (or even whether) it is important for the person to act according to the belief. All our studies of moral behavior have shown that a person's answers to the second set of questions, pertaining to self-identity, prove to be the best predictor of the person's actual conduct.[22] And a person's emotional experience is a central part of the person's self-identity, implicated in every decision about "who I am" and "who I want to be."

On the matter of civic engagement and civil identity, psychological research has been thin to date, but recent writings in the philosophical literature support the argument that I am making here. Reacting to the idea of educating students according to the "cosmopolitan ideal of world citizenship," my colleague Eamonn Callan writes:

> The patriotic sentiment runs deep in many contemporary societies, and in its liberal form it can mitigate against the civic alienation and ethnic chauvinism that are among the most serious threats to the viability of mass democracy. If the sentiment is somewhat weakened or, worse still, remains strong but comes to be regarded as a civic bond divorced from the principles of universal justice, our loss may be great. The USA is a revealing case because even though patriotism has commonly been implicated in the worst of American history, it has also had no small role in the best. The struggle against slavery, the Civil Rights movement, and even oppositions to the Vietnam war were animated by a commitment to a universal justice. But the commitment was commonly mediated by a love of American democracy and its founding principles. To give up on the task of perpetuating that love from one generation to the next in the name of world citizenship is to forego the moral power of a live tradition for the charms of an imaginative construction.[23]

The "task of perpetuating that love from one generation to the next" is the responsibility of adults who raise and educate the young. It is the central mission of civic education, or at least it should be. Regrettably, present-day civics instruction in our schools is not taking up this task; and, in any case, schools alone could never succeed in "perpetuating that love" in the face of a hostile or indifferent culture. Just as a child's moral identity is forged through direct experiences in multiple social settings that together reflect a coherent set of standards, a child's civil identity can be acquired only in the course of many actual encounters, and reasonably congruent reflections on those encounters, that touch the child deeply.

My second assertion also indicates a developmental reality not widely recognized in today's educational practice: teachers can be as egocentric as their students.[24] Often in their instruction, teachers will emphasize the issues that they themselves find problematic and have worked through in their own thinking as adults. A prototypical case of this is the beginning professor who dwells on a specialized dissertation topic while lecturing undergraduates. I have complained about the way that this egocentric error has distorted much teaching today. As one example, teachers often try to spur children's creativity by urging them to ignore structure, forgetting that the most wildly creative geniuses in all fields begin by mastering their disciplines. (Picasso drew horses that looked just like horses when he was a child.) As another example, so much effort in the humanities is directed toward deconstructing texts for purposes of social criticism that students are never taught the truth and beauty of the text itself—that is, the reasons why readers have loved the text and why educators have believed it worth teaching to the next generation. In all teaching, the first effort must be to give students reasons to cherish the material enough to invest their attention in it and, eventually, to pursue it on their own. Without this prior positive investment of attention, any critical exercise will be pointless.

Students need a positive exposure to the history, cultural heritage, core values, and operating principles of their society if they are to become motivated to participate as citizens in that society. They need to acquire a love of their society, a sense of pride in its best traditions, an emotional affiliation with the broader community of state, a sense of patriotism in the benevolent and inclusive senses of that word, if they are to develop a civil identity. What is more, students need to be given a sympathetic introduction to the workings of a democracy if they are to become good critics of the democracy. All this must be done through action as well as words, in multiple contexts, and in ways that inspire students on the emotional as well as the intellectual plane.

WHAT OUR SCHOOLS CAN DO

The problems that I have been describing are ideational in origin and emotional in effect. In a sentence, we have been failing to impart to children the kinds of inspiring messages that they need to hear in order to develop strong civic commitments and an enduring civil identity. By "inspiring messages" I mean knowledge about their society set in a context of appreciation for the best contributions of their society over time. In the United States, some obvious themes would be our traditions of democracy, liberty, opportunity, justice for all, pluralism, optimism, and generosity. Although such themes show up in our popular culture and mass communications, they are rarely emphasized in the systematic school instruction that many children receive every day. In my observations of present school practices, these positive themes most often are buried beneath critical perspectives on the damage that our society has done, or is doing, to sectors of humanity or the planet as a whole.

If children are to take such messages seriously, in ways that move them emotionally, they need to encounter the messages in multiple settings, coming away with a sense that the messages are authentic and fundamentally true. It is not that children cannot handle critical perspectives. In fact, it is essential for their intellectual development that they learn to handle complexity, and it is essential for their moral development for them to learn that there are shades of gray. But there is a time and a place for everything. When students are introduced to an idea, they can make sense of it only if it is presented in a coherent way. If it is a powerful idea that we hope that they will live by—an idea that reflects our deepest beliefs about goodness, truth, and beauty—it is all the more important to convey a sense that the idea is in fact a part of what it means to acquire the culture, to become a full participant in the society.

Do we, in our pluralistic society, have ideas that we can impart to the young in such a wholehearted way? The answer is yes, we do, although we do not always realize it. As I have written on many occasions, our moral universe is full of shared values: parents everywhere want their children to be honest, respectful, kind, responsible, law-abiding, fair-minded, and so on.[25] There are differences in emphasis and interpretation, but these differences pale in comparison to the commonalities. A 1999 Public Agenda survey of eight hundred parents living in the United States, for example, reveals high levels of agreement about what the parents want children to learn about America. One-quarter of the parents were foreign-born, but this made little or no difference in their perspectives on what messages to give children about U.S. citizenship. Among the findings of the Public Agenda survey are:

- Foreign-born and native-born parents, including whites, African Americans, and Hispanics, share a belief that the United States is a special country and, in a number of findings, express thankfulness for being here. They voice a new patriotism that is calm and inclusive.
- The chief components of the American ideal—identified by all groups with very strong majorities—are individual freedom and opportunity, combined with a commitment to tolerance and respect for others.
- Parents also express somewhat submerged fears that others—and sometimes they themselves—take the country for granted and that there is too much emphasis on "the things that divide us."
- Large numbers of both U.S.- and foreign-born parents expect the schools to teach all children about the ideals and history of the country.[26]

If the Public Agenda survey is accurate, parental values concerning U.S. citizenship may be poorly aligned with what our schools are teaching on the subject. This is by no means the only place that such a gap exists. I have written about similar misalignments in the areas of language learning, academic achievement, and behavioral standards. Bellah and his colleagues have attributed such gaps to the increasing tendency of modern schools to position themselves as enclaves of expertise, separate from their communities.[27] In my view, this kind of separation does children no favor in any area of their development: in intellectual areas, for example, students will become most motivated to learn when their family and friends support their academic achievement. In the areas of moral and civil identity, where the student's relationship to the community is itself the subject matter to be mastered, separation can be especially detrimental to growth. Even more costly is the discord that often accompanies separation.

In order to foster civil identity in our young, schools must join with their communities in the effort to impart to young people a sympathetic understanding of our democracy and a deeply felt love of their country. Now I am aware that when I write this, I risk being accused of trying to indoctrinate children by brainwashing them with a whitewashed picture of America. But whitewashing is not at all what I have in mind. For one thing, it is a necessary part of character education to teach about the mistakes that have been made and the problems that persist. It is never helpful to pretend that any person or society is perfect: a far more useful message for a child's character formation is that none of us is perfect but we can always do better if we try. For another thing, dissent is one of democracy's proudest traditions—and it can be taught that way, enhancing rather than decreasing respect for the nation's heritage.

The point is not to paint for children a falsely glowing picture of their country but rather to present the country's shortcomings within a positive framework—that is, in perspective of its noblest aspirations (whether or not fulfilled), traditions, attainments, and ideals. For fostering true understanding, context is all. Students rely on guidance from their teachers to provide a context of meaning for all the otherwise disconnected bits of information that the world throws at them. A landmark civil rights demonstration can be presented either as an indicator of our society's racism or as a sign that there have been people in our society who have been determined—and permitted by our democratic system of governance—to correct that racism. Which orientation is more likely to encourage students themselves to get involved in constructive civil action? Which is more likely to instill civic affiliation rather than cynicism and apathy?

Educational guidance that helps students find enduring reasons to devote themselves to their vital communities—national as well as local—will promote affiliation, civic engagement, and participatory citizenship. A truthful rendering of a society's successes and failures can always be presented in a context of appreciation for the society's highest ideals. This is especially true for one of the world's great democracies.

What forms can this kind of guidance take? The most effective character education programs blend opportunities for constructive action with guided reflection. Civics education should follow the same principle. Schools and communities must work together to create opportunities for young people to participate in civic and political events at every level, from the school to the broader society. In the classroom, coursework should make connections between these lived experiences and the challenges faced by historical or present-day civic leaders. Within and beyond the classroom, young people should be given a sense of their own potential roles in the continuing drama of their society's search for a more exemplary democracy. This will require conveying to the young a firm faith in the fundamental mission of democratic governance as well as high expectations for young people's capacities to improve it once they have gained their own understanding and commitment.

NOTES

1. "35% of High School Seniors Fail National Civics Test," *New York Times,* November 21, 1999.
2. James Youniss and Miranda Yates, *Community Service and Social Responsibility in Youth* (Chicago: University of Chicago Press, 1997).
3. See William Damon, *Greater Expectations* (New York: Free Press, 1995). In the aggregate, young people's behavior has grown increasingly uncivil year by year according to practically every indicator that we can muster: physical assault, verbal aggression, cheating, lying, stealing, sexual harassment, vandalism, drunkenness, discourtesy, and so on, down a panoply of major and minor assaults on the social fabric. Of course, these are normative trends and do not apply to every young person, many of whom continue to be exemplary citizens in every sense. Our sensationalistic media focus on the most horrific (and, fortunately, still rare) examples of this trend, such as the Columbine school shootings, but the problem goes far beyond such atypical incidents.
4. Susan Verducci and William Damon, "The Outlooks of Today's Teens," in Richard Lerner and Jacqueline Lerner, eds., *Adolescents A to Z* (New York: Oxford University Press, forthcoming).
5. Doug McAdam, *Freedom Summer* (Oxford: Oxford University Press, 1990).
6. Damon, *Greater Expectations.*
7. William Damon, *The Moral Child* (New York: Free Press, 1990).
8. Richard Shweder et al., "The Cultural Psychology of Development: One Mind, Many Mentalities," in William Damon, ed., *Handbook of Child Psychology,* vol. 1 (New York: Wiley, 1998); Richard Shweder, Milpitra Mahapatra, and Joan Miller, "Culture and Moral Development," in Jerome Kagan and Sharon Lamb, eds., *The Emergence of Morality in Young Children* (Chicago: University of Chicago Press, 1987).
9. Emile Durkheim, *Moral Education: A Study in the Theory and Application of the Sociology of Education* (New York: Free Press, 1961).
10. Damon, *Greater Expectations.*

11. I have heard varied estimates of this, as high as one-third in the past decade, but I have not been able to come up with a reliable figure.

12. Francis Ianni, *The Search for Structure: A Report on American Youth Today* (New York: Free Press, 1989).

13. William Damon and Anne Gregory, "The Youth Charter: Towards the Formation of Adolescent Moral Identity," *Journal of Moral Education* 26 (1997).

14. As for moral education programs, by far the most effective are those that engage students directly in action, with subsequent opportunities for reflection: community service, for example, has proven to be one of the most reliable means of triggering positive change in students' values and commitments; see Youniss and Yates, *Community Service and Social Responsibility in Youth.* The reason, again, is that students respond to experiences that touch their emotions and senses of self in a firsthand way.

15. William Damon, *The Youth Charter: How Communities Can Work Together to Raise Standards for All Our Children* (New York: Free Press, 1997).

16. Martha Nussbaum, with respondents, *For Love of Country: Debating the Limits of Patriotism* (Boston: Beacon, 1996), p. 11.

17. Ibid., p. 6.

18. Michael Billig, *Banal Nationalism* (Thousand Oaks, Calif.: Sage, 1995), p. 7.

19. In the book of essays responding to Nussbaum's notion of a cosmopolitan education (Nussbaum, *For Love of Country*), several scholars ended up defending the benefits of loving one's country, though the defense was ambivalent in most cases. The most unambivalent defense came not from a scholar but from the poet Robert Pinsky, who found Nussbaum's cosmopolitan position "arid" and "sterile." Pinsky wrote that the cosmopolitan formulation "fails to respect the nature of patriotism and similar forms of love" (p. 88).

20. I know of no data on teachers' views on this matter, but I have discussed it with many whom I have met in my visits to schools in many parts of the United States. Also, I have had my own unintended litmus test: every now and then in a lecture or conversation, I introduce the idea of patriotism. It is, invariably, the least popular thing I say—and I tend to make controversial statements. In professional circles, I cannot count the number of times that friends and colleagues have counseled me to rethink the idea or, at the very least, to "find a different word."

21. Damon and Gregory, "Youth Charter."

22. Anne Colby and William Damon, *Some Do Care: Contemporary Lives of Moral Commitment* (New York: Free Press, 1992).

23. Eamonn Callan, "Reply," *Studies in Philosophy and Education* 18 (1999).

24. Jean Piaget, (1928) *The Child's Conception of the World* (London: Kegan Paul, 1928).

25. Damon, *Youth Charter.*

26. "A Lot to Be Thankful For," a report from Public Agenda, 1999.

27. Robert N. Bellah, Richard Madsen, William M. Sullivan, Ann Swidler, and Steven M. Tipton, *The Good Society* (New York: Vintage, 1992).

Chapter 6 Moral Disagreement, Moral Education, Common Ground

Warren A. Nord

Discussions of moral education almost inevitably hit the rocks over the problem of moral disagreement: whose morality, whose values do we teach? After all, we disagree, often deeply, about morality; common ground is elusive. In private schools, of course, common ground can be found by limiting the constituency to those who accept the mission and values of those schools. This option isn't open to public schools, however; their constituency, after all, is everyone—and even the smallest, traditionally homogeneous school districts are becoming culturally and morally pluralistic. I want to suggest a simple solution to this problem—simple, at least, in broad outline. (Inevitably, the devil will be in the details.)

First, we should remember that for all our pluralism and disagreement, we still agree about a good deal: about the importance of honesty, the need for integrity, and the value of democracy, for example. No doubt we disagree about issues around the edges of these virtues and values—hard cases, as it were. But *of course* people should be honest and have integrity; *of course* we should nurture democratic virtues and institutions. There is common ground here that provides a foundation on which public schools can and should construct programs of character education.

But (of course) we also disagree about a great deal: about politics and economics, abortion and homosexuality, for example. Even more important, perhaps, we disagree about the nature of morality itself. When we disagree, I suggest, the only way to find common ground is to draw the circle wide enough to include everyone in the conversation. (Well, nearly everyone; there are limits.) This, then, is the second prong of my proposal: that we find common ground when we disagree by teaching about the alternatives, taking everyone seriously, and remaining neutral. How we might actually do this is a bit of a challenge, as we shall see. A part of my task is to say something about what it means to take different moral points of view seriously.

Folks on the Right are often wary of the second prong of my proposal, fearing cultural fragmentation and moral relativism; folks on the Left are often wary of the first prong, fearing traditionalism and the oppression of minority subcultures. I will argue that there are principled civic and educational reasons for my two-pronged approach, but there is also a powerful consequentialist reason: it is the approach most likely to secure deep support for public education, for it is the approach that takes everyone (on the Right and the Left and everywhere else) seriously.[1]

CHARACTER EDUCATION

After several frustrating decades of values clarification, many educators have, over the past decade, embraced the character education movement, which has reasserted the importance of nurturing the development of basic, putatively universal moral virtues and values. As a practical matter, character education programs often proceed by way of local efforts to identify those widely shared virtues and values on which people can agree.

According to the Character Education Manifesto, "schools have the obligation to foster in their students personal and civic virtues such as integrity, courage, responsibility, diligence, service, and respect for the dignity of all persons." The goal is the development of character or virtue, not correct views on "ideologically charged issues." Schools must become "communities of virtue" in which "responsibility, hard work, honesty, and kindness are modeled, taught, expected, celebrated, and continually practiced." An important resource is the "reservoir of moral wisdom" that can be found in "great stories, works of art, literature, history, and biography." Education is, fundamentally, a moral enterprise in which "we need to reengage the hearts, minds, and hands of our children in forming their own characters, helping them 'to know the good, love the good, and do the good.'"[2]

Character education nurtures those common virtues and values that are essential if our society and our schools are to survive and thrive. Surely we are on common ground here?

Not so, its critics charge, for the advocates of character education have an ideologically conservative (and, therefore, deeply controversial) agenda. So, for example, Henry Giroux charges that "there is no talk of conflict within this discourse, no mention of the 'messy' social relations of sexism, racism, and class discrimination. . . . It is the discourse of uneasy harmony, one that smoothes over the conflicts and contradictions of everyday life." Thus while "individual virtues are praised as the basis for moral behavior . . . these virtues at best simply become a convenient and almost totally transparent apology for the status quo."[3] The character education literature draws heavily on Plato and Aristotle but ignores Marx and Foucault; it emphasizes honesty and integrity but says little about social and economic injustices that are central to leftist critiques of mainstream American and Western culture. It nurtures, in effect, a "morality of compliance." Indeed, so this critique goes, claims made by character educators for universality ignore minority subcultures and mask the cultural particularity of the chosen virtues.

It might be said in response that whatever the ideological commitments of the leaders of the movement, character education programs are typically grounded in practice in local agreement about virtues and values. This is, in part, a tactical matter: if character education programs are to be successful, they can't be controversial. Consequently, communities are encouraged to choose those virtues and values they wish to nurture in their schools. But, critics respond, this approach emphasizes commonality (the *unum*) and deemphasizes the differences (the *pluribus*) of American life, and in our current cultural politics, this too looks conservative.

Granted: character education *is* a conservative approach to moral education. Still, however conservative (and, consequently, controversial) some advocates of character education might be, it remains true that there *are* common, perhaps even universally shared, virtues and values, and it *is* tremendously important that students acquire them. No doubt they will be understood and justified somewhat differently from different moral perspectives; no doubt they will have somewhat different implications, at least along the margins, depending on our ideological commitments. Still, some sense of honesty and integrity, kindness and responsibility, are essential to the survival and well-being of society and to being a good person. Surely we agree that the democratic virtues of our constitutional tradition are worth nurturing. *This* shouldn't be controversial.

In any case, as we shall see, an adequate theory of moral education must maintain a balance between tradition and community on the one hand and criticism and pluralism on the other. Character education provides cultural ballast that balances the more liberal and liberationist goals of a liberal education, as we shall see.

There is a second kind of criticism we need to consider. A distinction is often drawn between education on the one hand and socialization, training, and indoctrination on the other. Soldiers are trained to march and are socialized to follow the orders of their officers. Children are toilet-trained (rather than educated in toiletry), and, with some luck, they are socialized to obey their parents. In each of these cases, learning is more a matter of drill, discipline, and habit than of critical thinking. In matters of morality, politics, and religion we often use the word *indoctrination* rather than *training* or *socialization*. We indoctrinate children (or adults) when we teach (or socialize) them to accept doctrines, or a point of view, uncritically. We educate them, by contrast, when we provide them with a measure of critical distance on their subjects, enabling them to think in informed and reflective ways about alternatives. Public schools inevitably and properly train and socialize children: learning the basic skills of reading, writing, and arithmetic, for example, is largely a matter of training and drill; learning to be tidy and on time is largely a matter of socialization.

Much character education might better be called character training or socialization, for the point is less to teach virtue and values by way of critical reflection on contending points of view than to structure the moral ethos of schooling to nurture the development of those moral habits and virtues that we agree to be good and important, that are part of our moral consensus. Character education does appeal, as the Character Education Manifesto makes clear, to a heritage of stories, literature, art, and biography to inform and deepen students' understanding of, and appreciation for, moral virtue. Often such literature will reveal the moral ambiguities of life, and discussion of it will encourage critical reflection on what is right and wrong. But if the literature is chosen to nurture the development of the "right" virtues and values, it may not encourage informed and critical thinking about contending values and ways of thinking and living. (I should say that training can require a great deal of intellectual sophistication: much of what we do in professional schools is train doctors and lawyers and accountants to think and act within a particular tradition or set of practices, without educating them about alternative traditions or practices.)

But even if character education proceeds largely by way of socialization and training, this need not be a criticism. Children must be morally trained before they reach the elusive age of reason (an age some people, alas, never reach).

A third criticism: no matter how philosophically sophisticated its advocates might be, in practice character education tends to be intellectually superficial, in part, at least, because it emphasizes consensus and training. It doesn't deal well with questions of deep justification—those existential, philosophical, and religious questions about the human condition, the nature of morality, and the worldviews that make sense of, and ground, consensus moral virtues and values—because they are, after all, controversial. Moreover, character education programs tend to emphasize personal morality and deemphasize those social, ideological, and institutional dimensions of our moral life that complicate moral decision making and are controversial.

This criticism can be overstated. No doubt some "virtue of the week" programs manage to avoid both substance and subtlety, though much literature used in character education programs is historically and culturally rich—and reveals something of the motivations and traditions that do provide deep justifications of our moral virtues and values. Of course, it is this literature that critics charge is conservatively biased. Still, the history and literature that is used in character education programs might be (and sometimes is) chosen to point to the diverse ways in which people and cultures make sense of moral virtues and values—not for the purpose of raising critical questions about them but simply to make students aware of the differing moral and cultural grounds people have for acting morally.

No doubt character education programs can be superficial and ideologically biased. Good character education programs are tremendously important, however, for nurturing those virtues and values that we agree are important and, in so doing, sustaining a sense of moral community in an increasingly pluralistic culture. This said, I want to argue that students—of a suitable age and maturity—must also be initiated into the rough and tumble of moral controversy.

THE EDUCATIONAL ARGUMENT

If we agree that it is important for schools to nurture the democratic virtues that sustain democracy, we don't agree that schools should nurture the "Democratic virtues" that sustain the Democratic Party. We are, after all, deeply divided about politics. If we taught students in schools only the views and values of Democrats (and ignored or constantly criticized Republicans) it would be fair to say that we were indoctrinating (or socializing or training) them rather than educating them. If students are to be educated about politics, if they are to think critically about politics, they must learn, fairly, about both parties.

In most domains of life we believe that the truth is most likely to be found when we hear both (or all) sides of the story. If students are taught only one way of thinking about something controversial they will not be given the critical distance they need to make educated judgments about it—even if they are given the true view. It is, after all, one thing to believe (what one takes to be) the truth; it is another thing to be educated to be able to make critical judgments about it—to believe it for good reasons. So, I suggest, to be able to think critically about the moral domain of life, students must know something about the alternatives when we disagree.

One of the much-touted virtues of the old values clarification approach was that it freed students from official orthodoxies to think critically about values. But of course that approach was hopelessly superficial because it left students essentially on their own in doing so. We are not, after all, social atoms, free or even able to create a moral universe out of our own resources; we are born into communities and traditions, into a world rich with theories and practices on which we can and must draw in order to think in an informed and truly critical way. Morality is not intellectually free-floating, a matter of arbitrary choices or merely personal values. Moral judgments and conceptions of morality are rooted in historical, cultural, and intellectual contexts that make sense of them. They are entangled with our convictions about human nature, the law, our feelings of guilt and love, our religious experiences, our assumptions about what the mind can know, and our convictions about the meanings of life.

So, for example, our deep disagreements over homosexuality are rooted in different conceptions of human nature (Is there a homosexual orientation? Is normative moral law built into human nature?); in the authority we grant (or do not grant) to religious Scripture and in different ways of interpreting Scripture; in differing commitments to traditional institutions (like the family) and degrees of openness to change; in different conceptions of what is appropriate for courts to rule; in the different values of the subcultures in which we were raised. Moral judgments are inevitably entangled in a complex web of conceptual relations.

A good liberal education will make students aware of a variety of moral and social practices and institutions; it will give them imaginative insights into the hearts and minds, the joys and suffering, of people in different times and places; it will provide them with contending ways of interpreting their experiences.[4] It will provide a richly textured background understanding of the different moral judgments people make. In doing this, students will inevitably learn that the disagreements among us run deep: we often disagree about the meaning and lessons of history. We disagree about how to make sense of the world. Indeed, we often disagree about what the relevant facts are—or, even more basically, what counts as a fact, as evidence, as a good argument precisely because we identify with different subcultures, we are part of different traditions, we are committed to quite different worldviews.

I have suggested that character education is often little more than training or socialization (which, again, is not to belittle its importance). A good liberal education, by contrast, initiates students into a conversation in which they hear a variety of contending voices, acquiring, in the process, the perspective that allows them to think critically about the moral domain of life in all of its complexity and controversy. As students mature and proceed through the grades, the extent to which they are trained or socialized should diminish, while their education, properly conceived, should take root and grow. A liberal education initiates students into a conversation in which they are taught to understand, to take seriously and think critically about, the major ways people have devised for talking about morality and the human condition.

THE CIVIC ARGUMENTS

There are also civic reasons of justice and community for teaching students about different views when we disagree. It would be profoundly *unjust* if public schools disenfranchised either Democrats or Republicans by privileging or ignoring one or the other party. Because we disagree deeply over politics, schools shouldn't take sides; there shouldn't be Democratic or Republican schools, or texts, or teachers. The solution, happily, is simple: students should be taught *about* the policies and values of each of the major political parties. This is a matter of justice: when the public is deeply divided, public schools should ensure that all of the major voices in our cultural conversation about politics are included in our curricular conversation, and that none be privileged. Public schools must remain neutral; they must be built on common ground.

Similarly, the traditional exclusion of women's and African-American history and literature from the curriculum was unjust; it relegated many children to second-class status, and massive efforts have been made over the past several decades to integrate public schools culturally, rebuilding them on common (rather than segregated) ground. If the voices of people of a particular gender or culture or class are excluded from the curricular conversation, those people are disenfranchised—much as if they couldn't vote. This is not a matter of nurturing self-esteem but of requiring justice: when we disagree, when we interpret the world differently, then in a democracy people have a right to participate in the discussion—both politically, by means of voting, and educationally, by means of having their voices heard in the curriculum.

Indeed, if we are to live together in spite of our deep differences, if the cultural politics of schooling is not to become dangerously polarized, if students are to take seriously different points of view (as a good liberal education requires) then schools must nurture the virtue of civility. According to the Williamsburg Charter, how we debate our differences is almost as important as what we debate. This requires, in turn, that "those who claim the right to criticize should assume the responsibility to comprehend" those whom they would criticize.[5] Of course, comprehending others doesn't mean agreeing with them; it does mean understanding their ideas, values, concerns, and needs—as they understand them. (Don't we want others to understand us in this way?) Mutual understanding is a civic obligation—one that might well be nurtured in character education programs.

It is often argued that rights-based ideologies, multiculturalism, and an emphasis on differences can (and often do) lead to cultural fragmentation and warfare, but the civic virtues of civility and mutual understanding can bind us together.[6] If there is to be social peace, if the landscape of American education is not to be a battleground of warring ideologies and subcultures, we must build schools on common ground, and the only way to do this is to agree to take each other seriously (even as we disagree about matters of great importance), debate civilly with each other, learn about each other, and in so doing establish that trust that is necessary to live together with our deepest differences.[7] Again, the only way to find common ground when we disagree is to draw the circle widely enough so that we include everyone in the conversation.

DIVERSITY

Do I really mean that we must include everyone in the conversation? Well, no. Although the ideals of liberal education and civic justice both require the greatest possible inclusiveness, there are at least three criteria that can limit the number of voices in the conversation. (As I said above, the devil is in the details.) At best, I can only sketch in crude strokes what I take to be at issue here.

First, it simply isn't possible to include all voices in the curriculum; the numbers of available textbook pages and classroom hours impose limits. Indeed, there will always be trade-offs: the more voices considered, the more superficial the discussion. Consequently, it is inevitable (and proper) that the major—that is, the most influential—voices be heard, though decisions about inclusion must be made with sensitivity to local minorities. A local minority that is small on the world stage may still be relatively influential, and warrant inclusion, on the local stage.

I should also say that I am not arguing for equal-time or balanced treatment for all (major) views; to some considerable extent the degree of influence of different views rightly determines how many pages they get in the text.

Second, it is justifiable, educationally, to discriminate on the grounds of what I will call "intellectual seriousness." When voices speak out of the context of a rich and reflective intellectual background, there is more reason to take them seriously than if they express (relatively) superficial ideas or ideals—no matter how common, relevant, or influential. So, for example, even though polls show that perhaps a quarter of Americans believe in astrology, there is now (as opposed to several centuries ago) only the most superficial intellectual tradition connected with it. (Of course, one could also argue that astrology doesn't actually make much difference in how people live their lives, so it isn't really influential.)

There is a danger, of course, of defining intellectual seriousness tendentiously. I reject, for example, the conviction among educators that only their views should be taken seriously, that the conventional wisdom of the various disciplines should limit the alternatives presented to students. There are serious moral and intellectual traditions in our culture that are not taken seriously among educators. (I will say a good deal about religious traditions, as an example of this, shortly.) It is not the task of public schools to initiate students uncritically into the conventional wisdom of any (or all) academic disciplines but to provide a liberal education—one that initiates them into our ongoing cultural conversation about matters of importance. The point is not to enable students to navigate the waters of academe but to enable them to think their way though the complexities of life. The point is not to train historians or literary scholars or scientists but to educate students about various ways of making sense of the world when we disagree.

We must also be wary of using intellectual seriousness to define out-of-bounds the views of oppressed people who have not had the opportunity to create or sustain a rich intellectual tradition (or make known the tradition they do have). The criterion of intellectual seriousness is meant to allow the exclusion of morally and intellectually superficial ideas and ideals.

Finally, a great deal depends on context: are we talking about a course in British literature or American history or economics—or the curriculum as a whole? Some voices (some traditions, some subcultures, some worldviews) are more or less relevant depending on the course, and no individual course could or should take seriously all the (major) contending voices in our current cultural conversation. It is important, however, that the curriculum as a whole be defined broadly enough to take account of the major ways humanity has devised for thinking about the world and living their lives.

NEUTRALITY

I have argued that teachers, texts, and schools must not be neutral about those moral and civic virtues and values about which there is broad consensus. Students must be taught the importance of honesty and integrity; schools must nurture the democratic virtues of good citizenship.

Similarly, students must learn that some actions are morally wrong, and that some views are beyond the pale. Lying and stealing are wrong; the views of Nazis and the Klan are beyond the pale. (Happily, such values and views are almost never sufficiently influential or intellectually serious to be taken seriously as candidates for the truth.) It is true, of course, that students should learn something about criminals, Nazis, and the Klan, not because their values and views might be the right ones but to better understand the causes and dangers of evil. When there is deep moral disagreement, however, teachers and schools should take the alternatives seriously as contenders for the truth. Must they also remain neutral?

I have argued that a good liberal education will take seriously alternative ways of thinking about the world when we are deeply divided; it requires fairness. But it doesn't require neutrality of teachers. Just as a judge might be fair to (that is, take seriously) the opposing parties in a trial before passing judgment, so teachers or texts might be fair to the contending points of view and then pass a reasoned judgment. Indeed, it is one important task of education to guide students through the maze of contending claims and theories they encounter by way of informed and judicious appeals to evidence and argument.

I have argued, however, that justice, and the nature of schools as public institutions, require neutrality when we are deeply divided—as we are about politics, abortion, social justice, and homosexuality. In such cases, teachers must include all of the major voices in the conversation, and withhold judgment. If we are to take each other seriously, sustain community and maintain peace among ourselves, then it is imperative that we agree to disagree and not align the classroom or schools with any one of the contending views. Schoolrooms cannot become captive to any particular (controversial) view if schools are to retain their civic legitimacy and maintain broad public support.

This doesn't mean that teachers may never express their personal views, at least when asked to do so, so long as they are carefully characterized as such, and so long as the students are sufficiently mature. Pedagogically it is sometimes helpful for teachers to speak personally or autobiographically; indeed, it may be good for students to see that teachers can believe something, perhaps strongly, yet be fair to opposing points of view. It is essential, however, that students be mature enough to distinguish such personal opinions from the "official" conclusions they are expected to accept and repeat on tests.

Happily, matters of considerable controversy sometimes become matters of consensus. Not so long ago, racial integration was a matter of deep controversy; now it is a matter of consensus (even while we continue to disagree about busing and affirmative action). At one time it would have been right to teach about the conflicting positions; now it is important to teach students that the civil rights movement and racial integration were morally necessary. (Indeed, had robust discussion of the alternatives been allowed during the era of segregation, integration might well have taken place more quickly and with less pain.)

On some matters, however—abortion is an example—there has been little movement toward consensus over the recent decades. And on even more fundamental questions relating to the ground and nature of morality itself there continues to be and will probably always be deep disagreement, for our differences are rooted in different worldviews, and worldviews are notoriously difficult to falsify or verify. In fact, there is nothing close to agreement about how to think about morality even among scholars and educators; the differences between and among evolutionary biologists, developmental psychologists, sociologists, anthropologists, and philosophers (for example) are huge, and when we add to the mix theologians (who are not allowed onto school grounds or the campuses of public universities), the disagreements become even more profound. I think it fair to say that it is not at all obvious where the truth about morality lies, particularly when contending worldviews are at issue; consequently, a measure of humility—and rough neutrality—also seems to be required on philosophical grounds.

Does this mean that we should simply line up the alternative values and views, give each equal time, and let students pick and choose as they will? Of course not. What I have elsewhere called the Principle of Cultural Location and Weight requires that teachers and texts locate moral arguments and positions culturally, indicating what weight they carry and for whom. Which views and values are dominant or orthodox in a discipline or subculture, and which are the minority views? How much influence do different moral positions or traditions have within our culture generally? If students are to learn how to assess disagreements, they must have some understanding of the "location" and "weight" of the cultural and intellectual traditions that make sense of the alternatives. Of course, this is a purpose of a liberal education: to provide a richly textured understanding of our moral situation against the background of which students can make informed, reasoned moral judgments.[8]

It is also important that students encounter the alternatives not simply as static entities but as engaged contenders in cultural disputes, responding to each other as well as to various cultural and intellectual developments. Moral education properly takes the form of a conversation, in which advocates of different views respond to each other. Students should encounter arguments, not abstract positions.

Of course, school boards and the state have to take official positions on a host of controversial public policy issues—on affirmative action or on busing to achieve racial balance, for example—and students must learn what the courts and the law require. (They should also learn that obeying the law is morally obligatory—we all agree about that general principle, though we disagree about when civil disobedience may be justifiable.) But schools shouldn't teach students that any particular position on affirmative action or busing is morally correct; they should teach the alternatives, provide as much historical, cultural, and moral context as possible to make sense of them, encourage discussion, and then leave it at that.

Finally, a reminder. One of the most difficult tasks teachers have is to convey to students the difference between pluralism (and respecting people who hold different views) on the one hand and relativism (the idea that no moralities or moral principles are more true, or objectively justifiable, than others) on the other. It is important to remember—and to remind students—that moral disagreements are almost always disagreements about what the truth is, what justice actually requires. True, many philosophical naturalists and postmodernists hold that the idea of moral truth makes no sense, and older students should be introduced to such views too in the proper time and place (though even here there is often a pragmatic moral consensus about basic virtues and values). If students come to believe that choosing a moral (or religious or political or scientific position) is like choosing what to eat from a buffet line, they will have misunderstood the nature of morality badly. From within each tradition, some foods are poisonous; others are healthful, and they are certainly not to be chosen on the basis of appearances or taste. Schools should take seriously all the major voices in our cultural conversation and should not take positions on controversial issues, but this doesn't mean that all moral positions are equally true or equally false. That is another thing entirely—and students must understand the difference.

THE CONVERSATION

Moral education—in contrast to character education—is the initiation of students into our cultural conversation about goodness, justice, public policy, and, ultimately, the meanings of life. It is essential that the conversation be an informed one: for both civic and educational reasons students must learn to understand the different voices in the conversation, appreciating them in context. Only in this way do they acquire a truly critical perspective on our differences; only in this way do they take others seriously. That is why we must understand the conversation in terms of a truly liberal education—one that is sufficiently rich and textured to make this task possible.

Unfortunately, what often passes for a liberal education falls well short of the mark, for three reasons: first, it divides the curriculum into disciplines rather than subjects; second, there is little that is conversational about it; and third, many of the most important voices in our cultural conversation aren't included in the curricular conversation.

First, it is often thought that a liberal education is one that requires students to study a variety of subjects. But students don't typically learn about subjects (which are open to different interpretations) in their schooling so much as they are taught disciplines, particular ways of thinking about their various "subjects." So, for example, they don't learn about the subject of economics, which is open to various interpretations (conservative and liberal, secular and religious); they learn instead to think about the economic domain of life as it is interpreted by mainstream economists, typically employing neoclassical economic theory. And this is almost always done uncritically. Economics textbooks devote few pages, if any, to justifying their methodological assumptions and their interpretive framework for making sense of the subject at hand, or to discussing, much less taking seriously, alternatives. That is, students are given little critical perspective on the philosophical assumptions that shape economics as a discipline. And so it is with every discipline. We don't liberally educate students so much as we train them in a succession of disciplines.

Second, although it is true that students encounter somewhat different ways of making sense of the world in studying the different disciplines, they are unlikely to encounter any serious interdisciplinary conversation in the course of their studies. Are there tensions or conflicts between what they learn about human nature and the moral dimension of our lives in studying biology, economics, Shakespeare, and sex education? The literary critic Gerald Graff has argued that curricula are typically separatist, "with each subject and course being an island with little regular connection to other subjects and courses."[9] We do not initiate students into a curricular conversation about how to make sense of the world (or the "subjects" they study) so much as we provide them with a sequence of monologues, each conducted in isolation from the others. Graff's solution, one I endorse, is to "teach the conflicts"—indeed, to use this as an organizing principle for a liberal education.[10]

Third, not all of the (major, intellectually serious) voices in our cultural conversation make it into our curricular conversation (such as it is). For most of our history, women and African Americans were essentially voiceless, though the multicultural movement has done a great deal to remedy this situation. The largely conservative thrust of public education long kept leftist political voices out of the conversation. Nowadays religious voices are particularly conspicuous by their absence.

In fact, moral education is a profound problem for the educational establishment because to some considerable extent it has allowed the academic disciplines to define the content of the curriculum in ways that rule moral and religious ways of thinking out-of-bounds and make truly interdisciplinary conversations all but impossible. Perhaps I can best make my point by way of two brief case studies: the first deals with the exclusion of religious voices from the curriculum, the second with the notably illiberal way in which economics is taught.

RELIGION

I have suggested that religious voices are conspicuous by their absence from the curricular conversation of public education. Much of the concern over moral education in public schools is expressed by religious conservatives who believe that their beliefs and values are not taken seriously—and they are right. Of course the beliefs and values of religious liberals aren't taken seriously either—though most religious liberals seem oblivious to this fact.[11]

To get some sense of how seriously religion is taken in public schools, I have reviewed, over the past few years, eighty-two high school textbooks in history, literature, economics, home economics, health, and the sciences. I've also reviewed the national content standards for eleven core areas of the curriculum. With a single exception (the civics standards), the texts and standards essentially ignore religion except in the context of fairly distant history.[12]

The idea that we need to consider religion only in historical contexts implies, of course, that religion is a thing of the past. No academic discipline uses, or even mentions as possibilities, religious interpretations of its subject matter. The unquestioned assumption is that religion is irrelevant to interpreting every subject of the curriculum—a deeply controversial claim in our culture. Students are systematically and uncritically taught to think about physical nature, human nature, society, economics, sexuality, morality, and history in exclusively secular ways. As a result, public education nurtures a secular mentality and marginalizes religion both intellectually and culturally.

I am not claiming that educators intend any hostility to religion—but, of course, discrimination need not be intended to be real. The problem lies in the naturalistic philosophical assumptions, the secular worldview, that shapes the academic disciplines and the curriculum.

No doubt it can be controversial to include religious voices in the curriculum, though it need not be nearly so controversial as is often feared.[13] It is also true that most teachers aren't prepared to teach about religion; this is a more serious problem, given the indifference of most schools of education. Be that as it may, there are powerful (secular) reasons for including religious voices in the conversation—the first two of which we have already encountered.

First, it is profoundly illiberal to ignore religious ways of thinking about the world. As I have argued, a good liberal education should introduce students—at least older students—to the major ways humankind has developed for making sense of the world and their lives, and some of those ways of thinking and living are religious. Indeed, if students are to be able to think critically about the secular ways of understanding the world that pervade the curriculum, they must understand something about the religious alternatives.

Second, it is unjust to ignore religion. Religious parents are now, in effect, educationally disenfranchised; their ways of thinking and living aren't taken seriously. Just as we have learned that texts and curricula that said virtually nothing about women and African Americans were discriminatory, so we need to recognize that it is discriminatory to exclude voices of religious subcultures from the curricular conversation. (Ironically, the multicultural movement has been almost entirely silent about religion.[14])

Third, it is unconstitutional to ignore religion. (This may come as a bit of a surprise to some.) It is, of course, uncontroversial that it is constitutionally permissible to teach about religion in public schools—when done properly. No Supreme Court justice has ever held otherwise. But I want to make a stronger argument.

The Court has been clear that public schools must be neutral in matters of religion—in two senses. They must be neutral among religions (they can't favor Protestants over Catholics, or Christians over Jews), and they must be neutral between religion and nonreligion. Schools can't promote religion; they can't proselytize; they can't conduct religious exercises. But neutrality is a two-edged sword. Just as schools can't favor religion over nonreligion, neither can they favor nonreligion over religion. As Justice Black put it in the seminal 1947 *Everson* ruling, "State power is no more to be used so as to handicap religions than it is to favor them."[15] Similarly, in his majority opinion in *Abington Township v. Schempp* (1963), Justice Tom Clark wrote that schools can't favor "those who believe in no religion over those who do believe."[16] And in a concurring opinion, Justice Goldberg warned that an "untutored devotion to the concept of neutrality" can lead to a "pervasive devotion to the secular."[17] Of course, this is just what has happened. An "untutored" and naive conception of neutrality has led educators to prohibit smoking guns, explicit hostility to religion, when the actual hostility has been philosophically rather more subtle—though no less substantial for that.

As we have seen, the only way to be neutral when all ground is contested ground, is to be fair to the alternatives. That is, given the Court's long-standing interpretation of the Establishment Clause, it is mandatory for public schools to require the study of religion if they require the study of disciplines that cumulatively lead to a "pervasive devotion to the secular"—as they do.

If schools are to be built on common ground, if religious subcultures are to be treated with respect, if schools are to be neutral in matters of religion, and if students are to be liberally educated, then religious voices must be included in the discussion.

Advocates of character education sometimes claim (rightly) that such virtues as honesty and integrity are universal and are found in all the world's religions. Nonetheless, because religion can't be practiced in public schools and because it is often controversial, the character education movement avoids it.[18]

Clearly the moral ethos of public schools must be secular rather than religious. Character education cannot use religious exercises to nurture the development of character, nor may teachers invoke religious authority to teach good behavior. At the same time, however, character education cannot implicitly convey the idea that religion is irrelevant to morality. As is the case elsewhere in the curriculum, ignoring religion marginalizes it; students learn that religious tradition and authority are morally unimportant and are unnecessary for moral guidance. This is, of course, an extremely controversial claim. At least some of the literature and history used in character education programs should make clear that as a matter of fact many people's and cultures' moral convictions are grounded in religious traditions.

When students study controversial moral issues, a good liberal education will expose them to religious as well as secular interpretations. Consider abortion, for example. For many religious people, abortion is the most important moral issue of our time, the most important consequence of many unwanted pregnancies and much sexual promiscuity. Yet most sex education ignores abortion, in large part, no doubt, because it is controversial, though this has the effect of conveying a biased conception of what is important in sex education. Of four health texts I reviewed recently, only one mentioned abortion—devoting a single paragraph to explaining that it provides a medically safe alternative to adoption. That paragraph concludes: "This procedure has sparked a great deal of controversy."[19] Well, yes. But I suggest that to be an educated human being in America at the beginning of the twenty-first century one must understand the abortion controversy; indeed, its relevance to sex education is immediate and important.

So what would it mean to be educated about abortion? Certainly students should understand the point of view of the Roman Catholic Church and those religious conservatives who believe that abortion is murder. They should also understand the point of view of those religious liberals (from various traditions) who are pro-choice. They should understand feminist positions on abortion. They should learn about the key Supreme Court rulings and different ways of interpreting the implications of political liberty for the abortion debate. Students should read primary source documents written from within each of these traditions. And, of course, teachers and texts should not take positions on where truth lies when we are so deeply divided.

But as I have argued, our disagreements aren't just about moral issues; they cut much deeper. They are about human nature, the nature of moral authority, and our understanding of ultimate reality. From within almost any religious worldview, conservative or liberal, people must set themselves right with God, reconciling themselves to the basic structure of a reality. Scripture is taken to be a source of moral insight and knowledge. We are required to act in love and justice and community, being mindful of those less fortunate than us. All of this is likely to stand in some tension with what is typically taught in history and psychology and health and economics and literature courses.

Of course, if students are to understand religious positions on moral issues, they must see them within the contexts of the traditions and worldviews that make sense of them. This isn't going to happen as a result of the two or three pages on the "basic teachings" of a religious tradition in the context of studying ancient history. All textbooks that deal with religiously controversial material should at least acknowledge that fact in an opening chapter that maps the relation of the discipline at hand to other disciplines and domains of culture—religion included. They must nurture a conversation.

But although textbooks could be more sensitive to religion, the "natural inclusion" of religion in the existing curriculum isn't likely to solve the problem. If religion is to be taken seriously, there must be courses in religious studies that expose students to a variety of religious traditions, not just as cultural artifacts of the distant past but as living traditions that offer alternative ways of making sense of nature, history, psychology, sexuality, economics, and morality. Indeed, I would require of all high school students one year of religious studies. Because religious voices continue to shape our cultural conversation, they must also be heard—and studied in some depth—as part of the curricular conversation.

ECONOMICS

It is a little surprising that there has been no controversy over economics education, because economics is, in our culture, deeply controversial, often on moral and religious grounds. Although economics courses may deal with relatively uncontroversial matters like balancing a checkbook and taking out a home mortgage, most texts and courses deal with controversial questions of human nature, values, decision making, and the structure of economic institutions.

A part of the problem is what the texts and the new national standards leave out. They say little about poverty, especially as a moral or spiritual problem. They are usually silent about the moral relation of the First and Third Worlds. They typically ignore the effect of economics and technology on the environment. They are oblivious to the moral and spiritual problems of consumer culture. They ask no questions about dehumanizing work. They emphasize the importance of the profit motive and competition but say nothing about the possibility of excess profits or the possible costs of competition. They never appeal to the dignity of people, the sacredness of nature, or obligations to any larger community (or God). That is, they demoralize and secularize the economic realm.

The problem isn't just what's left out, however; it's also what's included. The texts and the standards teach neoclassical economic theory: economics is a "value-free" science, and the economic world can be defined in terms of the competition of self-interested individuals with unlimited wants for scarce resources; values are subjective, personal preferences; decisions should be made according to cost-benefit analyses that maximize whatever it is that we value and that leave no room in the equation for duties, the sacred, or those dimensions of life that aren't quantifiable. Economics is one thing, morality is, quite clearly, another. (It is not irrelevant that a number of studies by economists have shown that students who study neoclassical economic theory end up more self-interested than when they began.[20])

The texts often include some discussion of Marxism and socialism in historical context—though it is clear that the texts don't take them seriously as live options for their readers. The national standards, however, are silent on all alternatives to neoclassical theory, even in historical context. Of course, even with the collapse of the Soviet Union and the virtual end of world communism, there continues to be a leftist, Social Democratic critique of capitalism in the industrial democracies, though students would never know it. Nor do the standards or texts make students aware of communitarian or traditional conservative critiques of the radical individualism of capitalism and neoclassical theory.

Of course, the Scriptures of all religious traditions address justice and the moral dimensions of our social and economic life. What may be less appreciated is the vast religious literature on justice and economics of the past hundred years.[21] What is central to this literature is the claim that to understand the world of economics we must use moral and religious categories. Economic decisions must take into consideration the dignity of people and respect for what is sacred. People are by nature social beings, born into webs of obligation to other people and to God. If we are by nature sinful, it is also incumbent on us to rise above self-interest. Religious traditions have emphasized cooperation over competition and are deeply wary of the corrupting influence of wealth, materialism, and our consumer culture. All religious traditions pay special attention to the needs of the poor—the widow, the orphan, the alien. Needless to say, economics textbooks say nothing about religious ways of understanding economics.

Should students be exposed to alternatives? According to the national standards, students should be taught only the "majority paradigm" or "neoclassical model" of economic behavior, for to include "strongly held minority views of economic processes [only] risks confusing and frustrating teachers and students who are then left with the responsibility of sorting the qualifications and alternatives without a sufficient foundation to do so."[22] (So much for liberal education!) Robert Duvall, president of the National Council on Economic Education (which issued the national standards), has fretted that many parents and educators fear that the study of economics must be politicized and will prove controversial; hence he has reassured us that the study of economics need have no ideological content.[23] But of course neoclassical economic theory is hardly nonideological or uncontroversial.

The texts and the standards approach economics not as a subject, open to various moral, political, and religious interpretations, but as a discipline, as a "hard" social science. In the process, they convey uncritically to students a particular way of thinking about values, human nature, and social institutions that is deeply controversial.[24] I am not so quixotic as to recommend that economics courses balance neoclassical theory and social science with moral philosophy or theology at every turn; but I do think that economics texts should be at least minimally fair by acknowledging, and outlining, alternatives to neoclassical economic theory. If there is to be a true curricular conversation about economics, morality, and religion, I suspect it will have to take place in a course devoted to morality or religion.

Finally, I need to note the moral significance of the larger ways in which economics shapes public education. For more than a century, but particularly after the reform reports of the 1980s, public schooling has been oriented more and more to economic purposes and has been governed more and more by economic conceptions of organizational structure. We don't have to go so far as Henry Giroux, who has argued that "educational reform has become synonymous with turning schools into 'company stores,'" to appreciate the fact that the ethos and context of schooling have changed in ways that have implications for the moral and spiritual dimensions of schooling.[25] Certainly the moral education of students requires that they understand something of the public debate over the economic purposes and structure of their own educations.

MORALITY IN COURSES,
COURSES IN MORALITY

It is no mean feat to make our ongoing cultural conversation about the moral domain of life intelligible to students. There are many moral theories and traditions, and the evidence and arguments are complicated, grounded as they are often are in contending worldviews. This complexity dictates yet another two-pronged approach.

First, textbooks and teachers must acknowledge contending voices when they deal with morally contested issues and themes. All texts should have an opening chapter (at least!) that provides some sense of the larger cultural conversation within which the disciplinary approach of the course is embedded. When particularly controversial issues are discussed, texts and teachers should give students some sense of the controversy (in accordance with the Principle of Cultural Location and Weight).

Given the authority of professional and academic organizations, however, there can be little hope they will open the pages of their textbooks to a conversation in which (from their point of view) intellectually irrelevant—and perhaps disreputable—voices would be taken seriously. Nor are most teachers likely to be prepared to deal with the conceptual, philosophical, and religious issues that they would need to address. At best this approach will yield a minimal rather than a robust fairness. And so—this is my second prong—there must be at least one course required of high school students, taught by a teacher competent to teach it, that takes the moral domain of life seriously in all its complexity and controversy.

As important as we all agree morality to be, it is striking that courses on morality or ethics are not an option thought worth offering in public schools. Indeed, what could be more helpful to students than to bring together the disparate strands of their education in a capstone course they would take as seniors, focusing their attention on the implications of our cultural conversation for the kind of person they should be, and how, in their life's work, they might make the world a better place.

Such a capstone course should not be taught as just another course in a specialized discipline—ethics—though it should certainly expose students to major moral theories. It is astonishing, after all, that we require students to understand a welter of highly complicated scientific theories but allow them to remain totally ignorant of even the most basic ethical theories: how many high school graduates could give any account whatsoever, for example, of utilitarianism, Kantian ethics (Immanuel Kant being widely considered the greatest moral philosopher of modernity), feminist ethics, or liberation theology (the moral theology that is dominant in most mainline seminaries)? How many have even heard of John Rawls, perhaps the most influential moral and political philosopher of the twentieth century?

I would have such a course be broadly interdisciplinary, drawing on texts from across the curriculum—from literature and the arts, history and religion, the social sciences, and, of course, ethics. Its purpose should be, in part, to make explicit the moral claims, connections, and tensions to be found in the curriculum. It should deal with some mix of practical moral problems (race, poverty, abortion, or sexuality, for example), existential concerns (love, loneliness, suffering, death) and those traditions and theories that enable students to think critically and systematically about their experience. Ideally, such a course should also have a service component, not because students should be required to help others but because of the educational value of such experiences. Of course students should read a good deal of primary source material, including imaginative literature, written from different points of view.[26]

Such a course would logically follow the course in religious studies I have proposed. No doubt many educators will point out that there is no time for such courses. I would point out, in response, that it is astonishing that we find time for twelve years of mathematics but no time for any kind of serious study of morality or religion.

CONCLUSIONS

Whose morality? This is, of course, the inevitable question: if we are going to teach moral virtues and values, whose morality are we going to teach? The answer is simple, at least in principle: we teach everyone's morality. Where we agree, we teach the importance and rightness of our consensus values and nurture the development of the relevant moral virtues (as good character education programs do). Where we disagree, we teach about the alternatives, fairly, taking everyone seriously (as a good liberal education does)—withholding official judgment.

A fundamental problem with most theories of moral education is that they privilege particular, highly controversial, theories of morality—as have advocates of values clarification, Kohlberg's theory of moral development, and the "critical pedagogy" of the Cultural Left, for example—employing them uncritically. (Similarly, schools often adopt controversial multicultural curricula and teach them uncritically.) But because we disagree about morality and moral education (and multiculturalism), it is necessary for educational and civic reasons to teach students—at a suitable level of maturity—about our ongoing cultural conversation about morality and moral education. Programs of moral education cannot uncritically assume and convey a particular, highly controversial conception of morality to students. Justice and liberal education require that contending accounts of morality be taken seriously and that we teach the conflicts—even if they be conflicts about the nature of moral education.

Perhaps the greatest merit of my account of moral education is the degree of overlap between the requirements of a liberal education (and critical reasoning), of justice, of the Establishment Clause, and of practical politics. A liberal education requires that students come to understand, in some depth, the major contending ways in which humankind has made sense of reality and the moral dimension of life. In our democracy, justice requires that public education take the public seriously by including all the major voices in its curricular conversation. In requiring neutrality between religion and nonreligion, the Establishment Clause requires fairness to contending secular and religious alternatives. And, it seems to me, this is the proposal most likely to secure the broad level of support that public education requires if it is to survive, because it takes everyone seriously.

Much of the opposition to public education comes from people who believe that their voices and values aren't taken seriously by educators. And, of course, public education *doesn't* take everyone's beliefs and values seriously. Not surprisingly, people are resentful when they don't have a place at the table, when their deepest beliefs and values aren't acknowledged. Happily, including everyone in the conversation is not only the politically expedient thing to do; it is what justice and a good liberal education require.

Moral education must, then, maintain a delicate balance. Character education properly nurtures those often conservative virtues and values that we share. Liberal education requires that we understand and think critically about those moral values, theories, and traditions that are controversial and divide us. Schooling must nurture and sustain both tradition and community on the one hand and give students the resources to think critically about those traditions and communities on the other. And of course a good liberal education allows us to maintain a balance between the sacred and the secular (just as justice and constitutional neutrality require).

If schools are to be built on common ground, there need be no requirement that we agree with each other about all those moral, political, and religious ideas and values that divide us. It is essential, however, that we agree about how to disagree—with civility and fairness, taking each other seriously. Happily, there is also a good deal, morally, about which we still do agree—including, I would like to think, the fundamental moral and civic value of fairness. If this is the case, then common ground may just be a possibility.

NOTES

1. My proposal—and this essay—draw on and develop earlier attempts to work out a theory of moral education in the context of dealing with the role of religion in public education. See Warren A. Nord, *Religion and American Education: Rethinking a National Dilemma* (Chapel Hill: University of North Carolina Press, 1995), especially chapter 11, and Warren A. Nord and Charles C. Haynes, *Taking Religion Seriously Across the Curriculum* (Alexandria, Va.: ASCD Press, 1998), especially chapter 9.

2. The Character Education Manifesto is printed in *Character* 4 (1996), a publication of the Center for the Advancement of Ethics and Character at Boston University, and is available from the center.

3. Henry Giroux, *Schooling and the Struggle for Public Life: Critical Pedagogy in the Modern Age* (Minneapolis: University of Minnesota Press, 1988), pp. 19, 50. Similarly, Robert Nash has noted that each of the ten virtues that William Bennett has highlighted in his *Book of Virtues* and "the vast majority of the readings he has chosen to illustrate these virtues, are irrefragably conservative, calculated to reinforce a sociopolitical (and moral) status quo." Indeed, "if the truth be told . . . most writing in the character-education genre smacks of ultra-conservative special pleading." *Answering the Virtuecrats: A Moral Conversation on Character Education* (New York: Teachers College Press, 1997), p. 48.

4. No doubt much of what we call a liberal education serves a "conservative" role, for in teaching students history and civics and literature we provide them with a past, with roles in developing stories, with civic and cultural identities, with inherited rights and obligations that are constitutive of traditional institutions and practices. Such education gives depth to character education. Bruce Kimball has helpfully shown that historically there are two quite different conceptions of liberal education. The first, which Kimball calls the "liberal arts" model, is akin to what we might call a classical education; it initiates students into a cultural tradition and is more or less conservative. The second, which Kimball calls the "liberal-free" model, emphasizes questioning, experimentation, and critical thinking, and is, by contrast, liberal or liberating. Each can be traced back to the Greeks—the first to Isocrates, the second to Socrates—and each has played a powerful role in Western history. See his *Orators and Philosophers* (New York: Teachers College Press, 1986). I am closer to his second model here.

5. The Williamsburg Charter, reprinted in Charles C. Haynes and Oliver Thomas, eds., *Finding Common Ground: A First Amendment Guide to Religion and Public Education*, rev. ed. (Nashville: Freedom Forum First Amendment Center, 1994), appendix A, pp. 6, 12. The charter was signed by American religious, educational, civic, and political leaders (including two presidents and two chief justices of the Supreme Court) in 1986, on

the two hundredth anniversary of Virginia's call for a bill of rights, to reaffirm the importance of freedom in matters of conscience and religion.

6. Jean Bethke Elshtain has expressed a common concern in claiming that "over time the stripping down of the individual to a hard core of an isolated or a suspended self, the acceleration of a version of radical autonomy, casts suspicion on any and all ties of reciprocal obligation and mutual interdependence." *Democracy on Trial* (New York: Basic, 1995), p. 12.

7. K. Anthony Appiah has argued that multiculturalism is necessary to "reduce the misunderstandings across subcultures." It is "a way of making sure we care enough about people across ethnic divides to keep those ethnic divides from destroying us." Consequently, it must be "a central part of the function of our educational system to equip all of us to share the public space with people of multiple identities and distinct subcultures." "Culture, Subculture, Multiculturalism: Education Options," in Robert Fullinwider, ed., *Public Education in a Multicultural Society: Policy, Theory, Critique* (New York: Cambridge University Press), p. 84.

8. The Principle of Cultural Location and Weight is also important for assessing the differences between academic and nonacademic approaches to morality in two ways. First, it is important that students understand what it is academically respectable to say about morality (of course this will vary from discipline to discipline). It is also important for students to know that there are culturally important alternatives that, from within different traditions, can throw critical light on the academic positions.

9. Gerald Graff, *Beyond the Culture Wars* (New York: Norton, 1992), p. 13. Graff is discussing undergraduate education, but his arguments apply with even more force to high school education.

10. Ibid., p. 12.

11. There are a number of reasons for this. See my (regrettably mistitled) essay "Religion-Free Texts: Getting an Illiberal Education," *Christian Century*, July 14–21, 1999.

12. See Nord, *Religion and American Education,* chapter 4, and Nord and Haynes, *Taking Religion Seriously,* passim.

13. Over the past decade more than a half-dozen "common ground" statements concerning various aspects of religion and public education have been endorsed by a wide range of religious, educational, and civil liberties groups. At least at the national level, there is considerable consensus about the role of religion in public schools. A number of these documents are collected, with accompanying essays, in Haynes and Thomas, *Finding Common Ground.* Also see Nord and Haynes, *Taking Religion Seriously,* pp. 9–10, 36–37.

14. See Warren A. Nord, "Religion and Multiculturalism," in Carlos J. Ovando and Peter McLaren, eds., *The Politics of Multiculturalism and Bilingual Education* (New York: McGraw-Hill, 1999).

15. *Everson v. Board of Education,* 330 U.S. 1, 16.

16. *Abington Township v. Schempp,* 374 U.S. 203, 225.

17. Ibid., at 306.

18. Thomas Lickona has recently provided a helpful exception to this rule. See his essay "Religion and Character Education," *Phi Delta Kappan* 81 (1999). Also see Nord and Haynes, *Taking Religion Seriously,* chapter 9.

19. Leroy H. Getchell et al., *Perspectives on Health* (Lexington, Mass.: D. C. Heath, 1994), p. 163.

20. See Robert H. Frank, Thomas Gilovich, and Denis Regan, "Does Studying Economics Inhibit Cooperation?" *Journal of Economic Perspectives* 7 (1993).

21. In Christianity, for example, economic issues have continuously been at the heart of moral theology—from Pope Leo XIII's great 1891 encyclical, *Rerum Novarum,* through the Social Gospel movement, Reinhold Niebuhr's Christian Realism, Michael Novak's work on democratic capitalism, and liberation theology, to Pope John Paul's encyclical *Centismus Annus.* Indeed, most mainline denominations and many ecumenical agencies have official statements on economics and justice.

22. National Council on Economic Education, *National Content Standards in Economics* (New York, 1997), p. viii.

23. In a *Parade* magazine story Duvall is quoted as saying that "teachers, parents and others are often afraid that economics can't be separated from ideology and politics." The author then writes: "That's not true, Duvall adds. Indeed, the National Council's standards for an economics curriculum are basic principles with no ideological content. . . . These principles are just common sense." Lynn Brenner, "What We Need to Know About Economics," *Parade,* April 16, 1999.

24. Compare, for example, the Catholic bishops, who, in their powerful 1986 statement on the economy, warned against a "tragic separation" between faith and our economic life. People cannot "'immerse [them]selves in earthly activities as if [they] were utterly foreign to religion, and religion were nothing more than the fulfillment of acts of worship and the observance of a few moral obligations.'" Economists, like all of us, must realize that "economic life raises important social and moral questions. . . . [It] is one of the chief areas where we live out our faith, love our neighbor, confront temptation, fulfill God's creative design, and achieve our holiness." National Conference of Catholic Bishops, *Economic Justice for All: Pastoral Letter on Catholic Social Teaching and the U.S. Economy* (Washington, D.C.: United States Catholic Conference, 1986), pp. vi–vii.

25. Giroux, *Schooling and the Struggle for Public Life,* p. 18.

26. It is tremendously important to remember that the world—and any particular moral tradition—will look one way when viewed from the "outside," using the categories and conceptual nets of an outsider—a social scientist, perhaps, or the adherent of a rival tradition—but will look quite different when viewed from the "inside," using the moral, cultural, and philosophical categories of that particular tradition. Indeed, if we are to be fair, we must let people speak for themselves, using the conceptual resources of their own traditions. This is best done through the use of primary sources. And because moral virtues and values are grounded in traditions and worldviews that may be foreign to students, teachers and textbooks must provide sufficient context (enough time and pages) to make sense of them. Needless to say, this also requires some sophistication on the part of teachers.

Chapter 7 Some Problems in Acknowledging Diversity

Nathan Glazer

The central issue that is brought to mind when we consider the relation of civil society to education is whether civil society today, fragmented as it is by different dominant assumptions, can properly support the enterprise of education. How effective can this support be when civil society is fractured and divided over such central issues as the significance of authority in the education of children, the place of the family in the moral shaping of children, whether a role of strict neutrality in the realm of values is the proper stance of state and school, the role of religion in education, the degree to which traditional sexual morality should be supported by society and its institutions, and indeed the very central issues of what education should be, what makes it effective, and who should be responsible for answering these questions?

Civil society is a somewhat diffuse and murky term, and even in eschewing as I will any extensive effort to define how it is used here, some preliminary remarks are necessary, particularly because I make the claim that civil society is divided over key issues affecting education. Civil society in its largest sense consists of all those social institutions outside of and independent of government, and outside of and independent of the economy.

There are many useful definitions, but as William A. Galston elegantly and succinctly puts it, civil society is the "realm of nonprivatized collective action that is voluntary rather than compulsory and persuasive rather than coercive," and it "provides a basis for criticizing the excesses of both the state and the market."[1] Government is characterized by the ability to use power and compulsion directly; the economy is characterized by its emphasis on efficiency, which can be measured by the common coin of the economy, money. Civil society is characterized neither by the ability to resort to direct compulsion nor by the requirement to measure its effectiveness in terms only of efficiency. Admittedly, some use of power and compulsion is to be found in civil society (social ostracism is one example), and the institutions of civil society must take into account economic considerations in their processes and enterprises.

Nevertheless, we can roughly define a realm in which neither direct state power and compulsion nor considerations of efficiency are dominant. Nonstate civil associations are the most unarguable and generally accepted components of civil society. Religious institutions are also included among civil institutions, particularly where church is divided from state. Education, though everywhere to some degree a state function, is itself part of civil society. In some societies (such as the United States), much of it is nonstate, but even where it is a state function, persuasion rather than compulsion, we generally believe, should be its chief mode of operation, with some peripheral exceptions, such as truancy laws. As Galston's reference to a realm of "nonprivatized collective action" alerts us, there is some uncertainty over whether the family is one of the institutions of civil society. It is generally so considered because of its independence of government and of purely economic considerations in its internal operations and in the relations between parents and children, though there is some debate as to whether it is properly so included. Increasingly, it is, and in this discussion I do include it as an institution of civil society.[2]

A LOST CONSENSUS

The question of the relation between civil society and education becomes urgent because of the widespread conviction that the civil society of the past was more integrated, more unified, more coherent than the various forms in which civil society appears today. The degree to which civil society has changed, and how it has changed, is itself a disputed question, and I will not take the change for granted in this discussion. I shall briefly discuss various positions on this matter, but my conclusion is that the change has been substantial. The culture of families, neighborhoods, ethnic groups, churches—civil associations of all types—has indeed undergone significant change. These changes affect the culture of the school, its ability to be effective in achieving the task of educating the young, and how it must go about this task.

Many argue that the coherence and integration of civil institutions that we believe we see in the past is illusory, a product of nostalgia, and in part it is. Yet I think the common perception that there has been such a change is not illusion. Consider one kind of evidence, current as I write, of what I consider a divided civil society: the issues that become litmus tests in presidential contests. In what presidential primary campaign previous to that of 2000 has the issue of belief in Jesus Christ and a salvationary experience become a talisman for some candidates, while others resolutely refuse to join in this self-exposure and direct reaching out to one element of our society? For some time now, the issue of one's stand on abortion has been a key test for Republican candidates, and one's stand on gay and lesbian rights has been a key test for Democratic candidates.

One might argue that the emergence of such divisive issues in the past two decades need not affect the tasks of the common school, despite the role they play in presidential primaries, for how can they impinge on the key functions of teaching skills? Yet as we know, it is because the public schools take or rather do not take positions on such issues and on the broad ground of moral considerations of which these issues are particularly salient and abrasive expressions that fundamentalist Christian schools have thrived, home education has become more common, and support has grown for charter schools and vouchers. Division on the values taught or not taught in the public schools is only one reason for the growth of such alternatives to the public school, but it is an important one. One chancellor of the New York City schools was brought down because of his willingness to include in his multicultural curriculum the teaching of tolerance for and acceptance of gay and lesbian relationships and families.

Of course, divisions over key issues affecting the public schools have existed in the past too. Indeed, the most substantial split in the history of American public education arose 150 years ago from the unwillingness of dominantly Protestant public schools to respect the faith of their Catholic students and the unwillingness of Catholics to commit the teaching of their children to the public schools. And there have been other severe conflicts in the public schools over a range of issues.[3] But for some decades—let us say from the 1920s to the 1960s—a common understanding on key moral issues was so prevalent that it was unnecessary to raise these issues in public discussion. The Catholic schools, the great example of a split over religious issues, which of course must also impinge on moral issues, became just another version of the public school of the time, indeed an almost exemplary version.[4]

In these decades, a remarkably uniform culture was expressed in public schools of remarkable uniformity. One may note that during those years the superintendents of U.S. public school systems generally stayed in office for a long time—in the case of New York City, until death or retirement on grounds of age. No public issue seemed significant enough to lead to any challenge to their authority. This was one expression of the uniformity or harmonization of values affecting school administrators, parents, and political leaders. The schools were, from a modern point of view, divorced from contentious political issues. Note that even so energetic a mayor as Fiorello La Guardia did not discuss education or the public schools or take stands on any issues that might arise in connection with them: there is simply no reference to public education in the various biographies of Fiorello La Guardia. The contrast with his equally energetic successor, Rudolph Giuliani, is striking.

Schools could be then removed from politics because school authorities, parents, and politicians for the most part agreed on what schools should do. Looking back from the point of view prevalent today, the fact that this consensus ignored issues of race and culture in the schools would be considered scandalous. The straightforward pursuit of assimilation—"Americanization," as it was then called—evoked almost no resistance from immigrant parents.

In contrast with that period, for some years now, views on abortion, on gay and lesbian rights, on assimilation, integration, pluralism, and multiculturalism and other public issues have become litmus tests for different segments of our society for judging school leaders and schools. The conflicting points of view, centrally shaped either by traditional religion or by modern sensibility, have played a surprisingly large role in politics and public discussion. The social soil out of which such differences arise is marked by different views of society and of how children are to be shaped. It is inevitable that such divisions in society affect public education, and they affect it even when public education, as is commonly the case, is designed to be neutral on traditional morality. Neutrality on such issues will not satisfy large parts of our society.

Was there truly more unity and coherence in the values of the past? The issues of class division and class conflict that were more prominent in the middle decades of this century divided society as sharply as the moral issues that today appear more prominent. Class divisions—consider the hatred of Roosevelt among the upper or upper-middle classes, the intensity of the attack on big business and inequality during the same years and the early postwar years by Roosevelt and Truman—were as fierce as or fiercer than moral divisions today. Labor strikes could become as violent and raise as strong and murderous passions as the picketing of abortion clinics today. These class and ideological divisions were as substantial a rupture in the order of civil society as those we find today between the religious and the nonreligious, the traditional and the modern, or the modern and the postmodern.

But the issues of the past, however deeply felt, however divisive, were issues that were resolvable in ways that the issues of today seem to resist. One could, when it came to economic issues, "split the difference," unless the very principles of a free-market capitalist society were challenged, and in American history such challenges have come from small and insignificant groups. The culture of the challengers of the status quo was in any case generally more coherent with the larger culture of mainline civil society than we see today. The challengers of free-market economics and capitalism in the past were generally culturally conservative, as all who were involved in such groups can testify.

Rosemary Salomone stretches the period of value consensus over the schools farther into the past and argues that despite the conflicts over public schools in the past century, commonly accepted values were dominant until the past few decades. She notes the "narrow range of socially acceptable values and lifestyles" that prevailed "throughout the 100-year span [during which] Horace Mann and John Dewey . . . sequentially influenced educational thought and practice (Dewey was born the year Mann died). . . . Government and other welfare institutions reflected the values of the social and intellectual elites, who used these institutions to impose traditional standards on the uneducated and the less powerful. The underclass, in turn, silently resisted educational efforts on their behalf or quietly acquiesced in their eagerness for assimilation and social acceptance."[5] I believe that Salomone is right: that is the picture that emerges from the important social research on schools in the 1940s and 1950s, and that is the experience that some of us who underwent education in big-city schools during that period can recall.

A recent account of a current immigrant neighborhood in New York focuses on some key aspects of difference from the immigrant neighborhoods of the past, and one relevant to our consideration of the relation between civil society and education:

Those [older] New York ethnic neighborhoods, the stuff of the city's literature, its memoirs and founding myths, were once urban villages of a few square blocks where immigrants lost their accents and joined the American mainstream, where everyone worshipped in the same few churches or synagogues, learned the same lessons in school and exchanged gossip at the same corner drug store.

If they were never quite as homogeneous as the old-timers remember, these neighborhoods did bespeak the influence of one dominant group. For much of this century, if you were Irish-American in Woodside, Italian-American in Bensonhurst or a Jew of Russian heritage in Brighton Beach, the neighborhood felt like your turf.[6]

Such accounts of the past, as well as those of our current situation that emphasize the degree of division that we find today in our society, are matters of dispute. Thus the educational historian David Tyack assures us that the change is not as great as much public discussion assumes, and that there is a large area of common ground in American education today: "Historian Michael Frisch of the [State] University of New York at Buffalo has found that the traditional American heroes are alive and well in the memories of his students." A survey by Public Agenda reported that

a majority of both teachers and the general public believed that teaching common-core moral values was more important than teaching academics. . . . 95% of teachers thought honesty an essential value to teach; 90%, punctuality and responsibility. About three-quarters . . . thought that studying American history and learning "habits of good citizenship such as voting and caring about the nation" were "absolutely essential." . . .

Teachers strongly supported toleration of social differences but thought at the same time that the duty of the school was to acculturate students to a common pattern. Ninety-six percent said they believed in "Teaching respect for others regardless of their racial and ethnic background." . . . Relatively few teachers (6 to 13 percent) wanted to introduce divisive issues into their classrooms, such as "arguing that racism is the main cause of the economic and social problems blacks face today," "bringing in a speaker who advocates black separatism," or "a speaker who argues that the Holocaust never happened."[7]

In his important survey of middle-class opinion, both upper-middle and lower-middle, in eight suburbs scattered through the United States, Alan Wolfe also concludes that we are "One nation, after all." Tolerance or nonjudgmentalism is the key value he finds throughout the United States, even among those with strong religious commitments. Even he, however, finds some areas in which the prevailing nonjudgmentalism wears thin, and there is some substantial division.

The issue on which he finds the most extensive divide is the degree of tolerance or acceptance of the legitimacy of homosexuality. "There is no doubting
the matter; the question of homosexuality reveals two genuinely different
moral camps in America, which disagree profoundly about the fundamental
nature of what they are contesting."[8]

Against Alan Wolfe, Gertrude Himmelfarb has recently compiled in impressive fashion the evidence that demonstrates that though we may be one nation,
we are certainly two cultures, and these two cultures inescapably must affect the
schools. She agrees with Wolfe that "The reluctance to be judgmental pervades
all aspects of life." But she turns it into key evidence for the split between the
two cultures: "In the university, [this nonjudgmentalism] takes the form of
postmodernism. In scholarly books and journals, 'truth,' 'objectivity,' 'knowledge,' even 'reality,' commonly appear ensconced within quotation marks, tes-
tifying to the ironic connotation of such quaint words. . . . The language of
'right' and 'wrong,' 'virtue' and 'vice,' are made to seem as archaic as the language of 'truth' and 'objectivity,' 'knowledge' and 'reality.'" As the absolute
ground of truth and morality weakens, one will find students (and teachers)
who will question the automatic disapproval of practices once considered abhorrent (human sacrifice among the Aztecs?) because they have been taught
that every culture has its own standard, and that there are no absolute grounds
for judgment.

As against the nonjudgmental culture that she sees as the heir of the cultural
revolution of the 1960s, Himmelfarb argues, "There is . . . another culture (or
loosely allied sub-cultures) that coexists somewhat uneasily with the dominant
culture. This might be called the 'dissident culture'—the culture not of the
three-quarters of the public who redefine family to consist of 'significant others,' but of the one-quarter who abide by the traditional definition; not of the
55–60 percent who think that premarital sex is acceptable, but of the 40–45
percent who think it is not." Her numbers refer to percentages cited in public
opinion polls.[9]

But why should all this affect the public schools, one may counter? Could
educators not agree to ignore these controversial matters, in a kind of educational version of "don't ask, don't tell"? That was their posture in the past, and
it is probably the dominant posture today. But there is no escaping such issues,
even those once considered as marginal as the rights of homosexuals or the nor-
mality of homosexual couples raising children. Recall the fate of Chancellor
Joseph Fernandez in New York City: what brought him down was a curriculum

preaching multicultural tolerance. There was little disagreement that tolerance was a positive goal in principle, but then what was one to do about gays and lesbians, about gay and lesbian parents, and in what grade should one do it? If there is a mandate to teach about AIDS, as there often is, it may be a requirement to teach about AIDS to young schoolchildren, and then what is one to do about the inescapable connection between AIDS and homosexuality? An issue that was once confined to a corner of our lives and that could be shoved under the carpet thus begins to spread, and becomes unconfinable.

The issue of abortion raises similar questions. Why is it so important that every presidential candidate must define his or her position in the most excruciating detail, that almost every state legislature must deal with the when and why and kind of abortion that is acceptable, and that every such decision is in principle submitted to the decisions of our substitute for an established church and an unquestioned authority, the Supreme Court? This once-marginal issue becomes significant for a number of reasons. It points to other and larger issues: the role of women in society, the rights of women, the place of personal fulfillment and personal expression as against religious prohibitions. Of course, the best approach in a divided and litigious society is to evade these issues, and that is what educators in the public schools try to do. But that evasion does not satisfy a large part of the American people.

There is indeed a good deal of common agreement on what public schools should do. After all, nearly 90 percent of children in the United States attend them, and their parents indicate for the most part satisfaction with the schools their children attend. If education has become an issue in political campaigns, the apparent and direct cause of that politicization, it can be argued, is strictly the issue of academic standards, academic curriculum, and academic effectiveness. But such disagreement itself is based on a significant split in how people see the world. One may begin narrowly with phonics against whole language, or new mathematics and calculators versus old mathematics and manual long division, or bilingual education versus rapid induction into English, but these divisions are not purely technical, even if technical considerations are part of what makes the division. They reflect a deeper split dividing the traditional from the contemporary, between what Himmelfarb calls the culture that emerged from the 1960s, now dominant among the educated and the elite, and the "dissident" culture that still preserves substantial strength among a large part of the population.[10]

The one issue that tends revealingly in surveys to show the greatest discontent with public schools is discipline: and disagreement over discipline, its necessity, its forms, its relation to education, is one of the key markers of the difference between the two cultures, the culture of the nonresisting acceptance of assimilation into a world of common and traditional American values, and the culture of individual expression and realization and of challenge to the certainties and acceptances of the past. The elites in education clearly stand with the latter culture. Himmelfarb notes strikingly from a survey: "Professors of education are . . . more permissive than either parents or teachers. Only 37 percent think it important to maintain discipline in the classroom; 19 percent to stress spelling, grammar, and punctuation; 12 percent to expect students to be on time and polite."[11] We do find a large measure of common agreement on the adequacy of the public schools as indicated by the great majority's general approval of them, despite the various dissident movements that support home schooling, charters, vouchers, and the like. But that is owing to the fact that the American people for the most part live in areas of homogeneous values in which the public schools can without great conflict express those common values, even those whose public expression has been outlawed by the Supreme Court (such as prayer). Suburbs and small towns and rural areas are more likely to be areas where common values prevail, though even in what might appear to be the most homogeneous areas severe conflicts over the schools do break out.[12] But the discontent is greatest in the big cities, with their large and diverse populations, and is particularly strong among the African-American population.

That discontent has heartened those who criticize, on a variety of grounds, from religion to efficiency, the public school monopoly or dominance, and who call for charter schools and vouchers. It constitutes evidence that this dissident movement is not a cover for a new resegregation, is not a grab for public funds by those who already do better in school and come from higher socioeconomic backgrounds. But it also raises some questions that have not as yet been given great attention. What happens when civil society splits and divides, and when some of its elements want to maintain schools for their children in which their values, dissident or dominant, are more directly expressed or realized?

THE CONSEQUENCES OF A DIVIDED CULTURE

One central question has taken the largest role as we debate the prospect of a society in which the once-common school of a common civil society is no longer so common, and is in measure being replaced by different schools selected by parents who hold different values and different orientations on schooling and society. That question is: What then happens to the national culture, the national unity for which the common school was designed and which in large measure it created? What will be the effect of such schools as they reflect directly the facts of a divided civil society? Those who favor the largest degree of parent choice could answer the question effectively by bringing up the example of the parochial schools, which produced Americans as loyal as those from the public schools, or the example of other democracies, such as the Netherlands or Israel, which have always had divided school systems expressing the distinctive religion or values of a part of their population, seemingly without fatally undermining a necessary national unity.

Historical experience shows that such school systems are not inconsistent with patriotism and unity in significant national causes. One can argue that a more divided school system would not have more serious effects in the United States, where we also have, as a partial substitute for the common culture created by a common school, a powerful mass culture that affects all groups. We have, furthermore, a strong commitment to the rules of a common democratic polity, with unchallenged constitutional arrangements for bringing closure to, or at least temporary settlement of, major issues in dispute. The recognition of conflicting cultures and values in the United States today does not mean religious war, in the style of the sixteenth and seventeenth centuries, in which neither side was willing to grant tolerance to the other. Except for tiny sects, that is not the situation today.[13]

Still, the matter cannot be put aside so easily. In Great Britain, which has for a long time supported with state funds Catholic and Jewish schools, the question of whether Muslim schools should also get support has raised considerable uneasiness. Some have suggested that such schools break the outer limit of a necessary minimal degree of unity. In the United States, the issue of charter schools and vouchers will have to confront the question of what kinds of schools get support, and whether schools which in their orientation transgress what seems to be a necessary minimal agreement on common norms will be allowed to get charters or enroll children with vouchers from public funds. The matter cannot be settled by resort to the presumed constitutional prohibition of state support for religion, for there are other than religious bases for division, and even religious bases of division can be concealed to appear publicly as something else. Thus a charter school that is to open in New York State plans, according to a news item, to "teach students about creationism as a scientifically based theory competing with the theory of evolution."[14]

The issue is not only the reinforcement of the divisiveness of a divided society. One must also consider what kind of education children will receive in the great range of schools that choice makes possible. Will it be one in which children not only have very different views of their society but believe very different things about nature and the world, with some of those beliefs affecting the essentials of what we consider an educated person?

As we think of the educational effects of schools that reflect the fragments of a fragmented civil society, educational issues will arise that must give us some pause. I take it as given that a major cause of the discontent with public schools among the minority population of the large cities is their ineffectiveness in bringing the children of these populations to a suitable level of academic competence, universally accepted as the necessary platform for economic and social mobility. The schools that are chosen by minority inner-city parents range from Catholic schools, where permitted by vouchers, to Afrocentric schools, which have been created under charter in Washington, D.C., and have been chosen by children receiving vouchers in Cleveland. We may be willing to accept the teaching of doubtful views of the history of the United States and the world if they are accompanied by a passion for reading and learning that improves basic skills. We are less likely to accept as a trade-off for the uncertain improvement of basic skills the teaching of views that challenge received biological and physical science.

But the educational effects are likely to go beyond that. As children are concentrated in schools that reflect a distinctive culture and distinctive values, must we not expect that this will have an effect not only on the content of what is taught but also on the effectiveness in transmitting the basic skills? This is a key problem that the schools that reflect a divided civil society will raise.

In addition to concerns about basic skills, the values taught or not taught in the public schools constitute a major reason for discontent and affect those with strong commitment to the traditional culture. There is a substantial overlap between the populations that are affected by these two failures of the big-city public school: a large part of the African-American population, discontented with the level of academic achievement, also holds traditional values. Many of those who hold traditional values—populations as various as fundamentalist Christians and Orthodox Jews—create their own schools.[15] With the opportunity offered by charters and vouchers, we may expect more schools to be created that reflect minority orientations. The two discontents work together. If one is unsatisfied with the level of academic achievement of one's children, one may ascribe the failure to many causes, but among those causes are some that directly reflect the great cultural change that has transformed the

United States: inadequate discipline; the abandonment of traditional and tried methods for new ones that assume a greater level of autonomy, creativity, and independence in the child; teachers who do not assert or illustrate authority.

Adherents to the movement that is trying to facilitate the creation of more diverse schools expect that these schools will be chosen both to enhance educational achievement and to provide an environment more coherent with the values of parents and the values they see as important for education. The new public policies or philanthropic enterprises that are beginning to make such parent choices possible are limited for political and practical economic reasons to the low-income population, which in the big cities means primarily the minority population. This has been the group targeted by voucher experiments in Milwaukee and Cleveland, and by the programs that have been launched by individual philanthropists in other cities. The effect of such programs is that we will have more schools that are coherent with the culture and values of the parents that choose them. This does not necessarily mean a direct reflection of this culture and these values: many black parents prefer Catholic schools because of their more effective discipline, not because they are Catholics themselves. But one will find the fitting together of the values of school administrators and teachers, parents and children that generally marks a more effective school.

Whether these schools will show a marked improvement in the academic achievement of those groups whose low level of achievement is now such a major and pervasive public concern is still uncertain. We will find two effects in such schools, working in possible contradiction. One effect will be the improvement characteristic of schools with greater social capital, as has been demonstrated by the research of James Coleman and his colleagues and others on Catholic schools: the social capital in question is the involvement of parents and the community they reflect or create in the work of the school. Their involvement may be as minimal as choosing it, but even that brings as a consequence—and indeed this may be required by the school—visiting it, participating in parent meetings, helping to raise money for it, politically supporting it, and the like. All this provides the "social capital" that is a factor in improving the effectiveness of the school. Commitment becomes a requirement. This is true of all private schools, whether they are for the elite or for poor children. Both kinds call on parents and the community of parents that the school reflects or creates for support of the educational enterprise.

But a second effect that may work together with the first one or in contradiction to it is the culture that the concentration of parents choosing a distinctive school bring to it. The word *culture* is as disputed as *social capital* or *civil society*, but it is the best one can do in trying to understand why children of different social classes and ethnic groups perform differently academically. We have tried for a long time to evade the effects of culture by burying it under effects that are easier to understand, and more acceptable to our prevailing liberal orientations, such as socioeconomic differences: differences in income, occupation, education. That these should have consequences for the educational achievement of children is easily understandable. What is less understandable is why children of similar socioeconomic background within different ethnic or racial groups achieve so differently in school. Even more difficult to understand are the cases in which children of a group of low socioeconomic standing do well even as children of a group of higher socioeconomic standing do poorly, and yet such results are increasingly evident in research. And so the children of Vietnamese immigrants surprise us by doing well, even when they do not come from middle-class backgrounds.[16] As a society, we are more concerned with why African-American children do worse than can be explained simply by socioeconomic background. They are the group principally targeted by voucher experiments in Milwaukee and Cleveland. We expect that these experiments will permit their parents to choose schools more coherent with their values and their culture. With what effect?

The most elaborate effort to deal with the black-white test-score gap is cautious in invoking culture, but this is more or less what emerges as significant in trying to understand this gap. As Jencks and Phillips have written in their summary of the research collected in their edited volume, *The Black-White Test-Score Gap:* "The number of affluent black parents has grown substantially since the 1960's, but their children's test scores still lag far behind those of white children from equally affluent families. Income inequality between blacks and whites appears to play some role in the test score gap, but it is quite small."[17]

There seem to be significant differences in parenting practices that affect educational performance. The large data set used in the Jencks and Phillips effort to trace the reasons for the differences in black and white test scores asked "parents what they did and . . . [asked] interviewers how mothers treated their children during the interview. . . . Even with parental education, family income, and mother's AFQT [an intelligence test] controlled, racial differences in parenting practices account for between a fifth and a quarter of the racial gap on the PPVT [a vocabulary test used to score children's achievement]. This suggests that changes in parenting practices might do more to reduce the black-white test-score gap than changes in parents' educational achievement or income."

But what in parenting practices? Not many details emerge from the research Jencks and Phillips are summarizing and reporting, but they write:

> Upwardly mobile parents often raise their children the way they themselves were raised. Phillips and her colleagues find that racial differences in parenting practices are partly traceable to the fact that even when black and white parents have the same test scores, educational attainment, income, wealth, and number of children, black parents are likely to have grown up in less advantaged households. [They] also find that this can lower black children's test scores. In other words, it can take more than one generation for successful families to adopt the "middle-class" parenting practices that seem most likely to increase children's cognitive skills.[18]

A "grandparents" effect is emerging in the explanation of the black-white test score gap, but the grandparents effect that Jencks and Phillips have pointed to does not specify just what in the details of parenting practice might lead to the differences that emerge in lower than expected test scores. It tells us only where statistical analysis leads us in trying to determine what contributes to those differences in parental practices. Other research suggests to us in greater detail what those differences might be. The research of Elsie G. J. Moore, for example, explores the differences in the rearing of black and white children in similar socioeconomic positions, specifically black adoptees in black and white homes. L. Scott Miller summarizes these findings:

> Moore found that the adopted children in the white and black homes had very different response styles and that the ways in which the mothers assisted their children with the cognitive tasks were very different. The children in the white homes were much more apt to demonstrate an assertive approach to the test questions, to offer voluntary elaborations of their answers, and to attempt to solve a difficult problem, even when they were likely to be wrong. And they seemed to enjoy the test process more than their adoptive peers in the African American homes. . . . The white mothers typically adopted very encouraging and supportive demeanors in their interaction with their children. They smiled, joked, offered suggestions (usually in the form of hints), and they indicated that it was all right for their children to be wrong. In contrast, the black mothers were more likely to scowl, to offer negative evaluations of how the children were doing, and to offer very specific instructions as to what to do.[19]

These findings are similar—not, to be sure, in every detail—to the kinds of differences that emerged in research of the 1950s and 1960s on differences in the rearing of working-class and middle-class children. Our research focus then was on class differences in school performance, and research pointed to differences in parent-child relations that seemed important. Here we find somewhat similar and important differences in how parents relate to children. Tracing back these differences statistically, we find that parents of the same general socioeconomic status today will not have parents of the same socioeconomic status. Miller notes the same grandparents effect in other research.[20] We could also call it a difference in culture, for what is culture but the effects of a differential history? We are only at the beginning of trying to understand these differences and their pervasive effects on educational achievement.

Such findings must raise questions as to the effects of schools that reflect and make use of the distinctive social capital of different communities. This, after all, is what the emphasis on freedom to choose, by means of charter schools or vouchers or school choice within the public school system, means. It means the recognition of communities that want something distinctive and more effective in the schooling of their children. It encourages the creation of communities that gather around a school on some basis of connection—cultural, religious, interest, or the like. But in reflecting different communities, in giving them voice, the new freedom to choose also means that the values and practices of distinctive communities will have a more direct reflection in school practices, in curriculum, in teacher-student relations. We have focused quite properly on the upside of such opportunities. But depending on what community is reflected or strengthened by the school, we must realize that we also open the gate not only to higher levels of achievement—I have no doubt that that will be the effect in many schools—but to less positive educational results. Freedom and equality are always in some degree of tension. Freedom to choose means the freedom to be different. There is no guarantee that all the differences will improve upon the present abysmal level of most current public schooling of poor children.

Social capital, that desirable product of a strong civil society, will be generated to some extent by the mere process of creating a school, recruiting a student body, involving parents. But social capital also exists outside the school environment, in church and civil associations and neighborhood and family, and it serves to contribute to the success—or failure—of the school project. The social capital that Coleman cites to explain the relative success of the parochial school exists in the Catholic neighborhood, with its church-parishioner relationship, its acceptance of church authority and traditional values. But that is only one version of social capital, and not all versions will be as benign.

The preexisting social capital of a distinctive ethnic or religious group that may be drawn upon by the schools may be called "ethnic capital." It is so named by George J. Borjas in his study of immigrant adaptation, *Heaven's Door*. He finds differences in school achievement that can be explained only by ethnic background. Econometric analysis shows ethnic capital to be effective in explaining group differences in school achievement. The effect will remind us of the grandparents effect in the Jencks-Phillips research, but it is not the same thing.

Borjas writes, on the basis of his research, that "ethnic differences dissolve slowly over time. The historical record of earlier immigrant waves shows that over half the skill differences between any two ethnic groups in the first generation persists into the second, and over half of what remains persists into the third." He points out that "the connection found in research between various measures of parental socioeconomic achievement—such as education and earnings—and the children's achievement may not be very strong." This parallels the Jencks-Phillips conclusion.

> The evidence presents a puzzle. How can one reconcile the relatively weak transmission that takes place between parents and children with the relatively strong transmission in ethnic socioeconomic characteristics [that my research shows]? In other words, how can it be that only 20 to 40 percent of parental differences in skills are transmitted to the children, but at least half of the ethnic differences in the immigrant generation survive into the second generation?
>
> To solve this puzzle, I will argue that a person's ethnic background—*in and of itself*—influences the process of social mobility. In particular, the skills of the next generation depend not only on what the parents do, but also on the characteristics of the ethnic environment in where the children are raised. A highly advantaged ethnic environment—where most parents are college graduates, for example—imbues the children who grow up in that environment with valuable characteristics that enhance the children's socioeconomic achievement later in life. In contrast, disadvantaged ethnic environments—where most parents may be high school dropouts or welfare recipients—imbue the children raised in those environments with characteristics that impede future socio-economic achievement. In effect, the ethnic environment is like glue in the process of social mobility.[21]

Borjas then proceeds to demonstrate this effect statistically, but just what it is in the "ethnic environment" that produces these effects will require more than econometric research.

Whether we deal with a grandparents effect or an ethnic-capital effect, we will have to recognize that grandparental generations and ethnic groups can be quite various. And the effects of these differences can be sustained over a number of generations. When we offer the opportunity for communities and groups of all types, constituted on a variety of bases, from interest to heritage to common values to whatever, to cohere and influence schools, we will have to recognize that these influences are various. We will want to hold each to account in terms of some common level of achievement that all agree is socially desirable. But many schools will fall below that level. Every school that escapes the restraints of the typical big-city school bureaucracy, and that calls on teacher and parental energy to create a school that engages student interest more effectively, will offer educational advantages. I am not so sure that all will show improved basic skills, which among some groups have been resistant to the reforms of various types we have tried in different degree over the past twenty years.

Accommodating the divisions that have broken the more uniform civil society of the period before the 1960s seems to me to be not only a matter of equity and justice.[22] It also promises to deliver a more effective education. At the same time, however, the school that takes account of a distinctive cultural or religious environment must deal with the consequences of that culture or religion and how they affect educational achievement. The culture and religion and ethnic background recognized or acknowledged or fostered in the school may enhance educational achievement; the effects may also run the other way.

From the point of view of educational achievement, we cannot predict what the effects of the accommodation of and response to a fractured civil society will be. To make this accommodation is certainly to "choose equality" in one sense: the equal treatment of those with diverse religious, cultural, and group orientations. To what extent it will mean more equality in educational achievement among groups is, in the present state of our knowledge and experience, less certain.

NOTES

1. William A. Galston, "Civil Society and the 'Art of Association,'" *Journal of Democracy* 11 (2000).
2. Note the extended discussion of the place of the family in civil society by Jean L. Cohen, "Does Voluntary Association Make Democracy Work?" in Neil Smelser and Jeffrey C. Alexander, eds., *Diversity and Its Discontents* (Princeton: Princeton University Press, 1999), pp. 277–83. Cohen asserts that Robert Putnam, a central figure in the current discussion of civil society, initially in his important book *Making Democracy Work: Civic Traditions in Modern Italy* dismissed the family "as a primitive substitute for social capital, not a source of it," while in his later influential article "Bowling Alone," "we are suddenly told that 'the most fundamental form of social capital is the family'" (Cohen, pp.

282–83). "Social capital" is closely linked to, and seen as the product of a healthy, civil society.

3. For a key discussion of these conflicts see Diane Ravitch, *The Great School Wars* (New York: Basic, 1974).

4. See, for example, in Alan Ehrenhalt, *The Lost City* (New York: Basic, 1995), his account of a Catholic parochial school in Chicago, in the 1950s.

5. Rosemary Salomone, *Visions of Schooling: Conscience, Community and Common Education* (New Haven: Yale University Press, 2000), p. 34. I assume that by "underclass" Salomone means the entire lower and working class, not only the group particularly subject to serious social problems that bears that label today.

6. Susan Sachs, "From a Babel of Tongues, A Neighborhood," *New York Times,* December 26, 1999.

7. David Tyack, "Preserving the Republic by Education 'Republicans,'" in Smelser and Alexander, *Diversity and Its Discontents,* pp. 78–79.

8. Alan Wolfe, *One Nation After All* (New York: Viking, 1998), p. 79.

9. Gertrude Himmelfarb, *One Nation, Two Cultures* (New York: Knopf, 1999), pp. 122, 124.

10. For a lively and persuasive description of the cultural change, see David Frum, *How We Got Here: The 70's* (New York: Basic, 2000).

11. Himmelfarb, *One Nation, Two Cultures,* p. 119, citing the *Chronicle of Higher Education,* November 7, 1997.

12. See, for example, Salomone, *Visions of Schooling,* chapters 5 and 6.

13. For a strong argument defending the position that a basic unity still binds the United States, see John A. Hall and Charles Lindholm, *Is America Breaking Apart?* (Princeton: Princeton University Press, 1999).

14. Edward Wyatt, "Charter School to Present Creationism as an Alternative to Evolution," *New York Times,* February 18, 2000.

15. It is of interest that American Jews, the strongest supporters of the public school in the past (and perhaps today, too), are increasingly drawn to private Jewish day schools. The Orthodox were once the almost exclusive patrons of such schools, but increasing numbers of Conservative and even Reform Jews now patronize them. Perhaps as many as one-third of Jewish children now attend such schools. The reasons are those that commonly account for discontent with public schools: concern over academic standards and over discipline and safety. But there is also the desire to transmit the distinctive culture.

16. See Min Zhou and Carl L. Blackstone, *Growing Up American: How Vietnamese Children Adapt to Life in the United States* (New York: Russell Sage Foundation, 1998).

17. Christopher Jencks and Meredith Phillips, "The Black-White Test Score Gap: An Introduction," in Jencks and Phillips, *The Black-White Test Score Gap* (Washington: Brookings Institute, 1998), p. 9.

18. Ibid., pp. 24–25.

19. L. Scott Miller, *An American Imperative: Accelerating Minority Group Educational Advancement* (New Haven: Yale University Press, 1995), pp. 196–97, summarizing research by Elsie G. J. Moore, "Family Socialization and the IQ Test Performance of Traditionally and Transracially Adopted Black Children," *Developmental Psychology* 22 (1988), and

"Ethnic Social Milieu and Black Children's Intelligence," *Journal of Negro Education* 56 (1987).

20. Miller, *An American Imperative,* pp. 166–69.

21. George J. Borjas, *Heaven's Door: Immigration Policy and the American Economy* (Princeton: Princeton University Press, 1999), pp. 146–47.

22. On this aspect of the issue, see Joseph P. Viteritti, *Choosing Equality: School Choice, the Constitution, and Civil Society* (Washington, D.C.: Brookings Institution Press, 1999).

Chapter 8 Education and Citizenship in an Age of Pluralism

Mark Holmes

Although the idea of the common school for all was first realized in Scandinavia, the earliest strong prototype among the English-speaking democracies was developed in the United States, both in fact—in the towns and rural areas of the Northeast and Midwest—and in the minds of its people.[1] In the first half of the twentieth century, while the secondary school in the Scandinavian countries developed along generic northern European lines (with separate provision for the academically talented), the myth, if not the reality, of a "democratic" school representing a national sense of citizenship took hold in the United States. Writing in the early 1980s, David Tyack and Elisabeth Hansot quote from the AASA Yearbook of 1933 that public school leaders have the responsibility "to mold character and to ameliorate the whole intellectual, moral, civic, and economic status of their fellows." Tyack and Hansot see 1960 as a turning point when that all-embracing vision ceased to be consensual in the United States. In the years following World War II, the American vision, exemplified by the comprehensive high school, had widespread influence—in Canada, in American-occupied Japan, in social democratic Sweden, and in Labour-governed Britain.

Emile Durkheim, the French educator and sociologist, had provided, in the early twentieth century, a coherent statement of the context and implications of the common school and its social setting. He interpreted the changing norms of social solidarity, from organic to mechanical, within the school. While solidarity had earlier been founded on kinship and local geographical community, it was by the twentieth century coming to depend on external contractual obligation. The modern school would treat all children the same, irrespective of their family and social background. Durkheim fully understood that the mechanical solidarity of the school would require moral or ideological meaning beyond the processes designed to provide required workplace and social skills. He accepted the replacement of religious tradition, which had been embedded, explicitly or implicitly, within the school's ethos, by a secular morality. Education should be based on society's ideal sense of itself, an approved notion of citizenship. He recognized that removal of the religious nature of the sacred demanded some substitute. Without the sacred, "One is . . . inclined to deny morality." In order to develop a form of secular morality, "We must discover those moral forces that men, down to the present time, have conceived of only under the form of religious allegories. We must disengage them from their symbols, present them in their rational nakedness. . . . We want moral education to become rational and at the same time to produce all the results that should be expected from it."[2] The term *citizenship* is used here to refer to the anticipated moral and attitudinal outcomes rather than to the more objective knowledge and understanding of the democratic process.

It is possible to appreciate Durkheim's ideal and the American myth and at the same time recognize that they are obsolete and counterproductive in the contemporary pluralist society. It is also important to bear in mind that the myth has never approached universal application and approval, even in the United States. Formal racial segregation was succeeded (or accompanied) by informal separation, on the basis of income, ethnicity, and language as well as race. Even Sweden, homogeneous both in ethnicity (despite its established Finnish minority and more recent immigrants) and in political values compared with the Western English-speaking democracies, now funds a wide choice of schools. Clearly, there are problems for the transmission of citizenship, for the attempt to convey an ideal sense of society, when disparate schools disseminate inconsistent worldviews.

Two central issues emerge in the context of this essay. What are the consequences of an attempt to cling to a common school ideal based on an assumption of social and moral homogeneity when society has become pluralist? Does the abandonment of the common school imply the end of citizenship as a goal of formal education?

THE COMMON SCHOOL AND
THE PLURALIST SOCIETY

In the United States, Canada, and England the problem of the common school has emerged in three distinct ways. First, there is the inevitable problem of choosing the values (and their relative priority) to be represented in the school; it is one thing to select values centrally based on research and surveys, another to deliver them equally to Hispanic, African-American, Mennonite, and affluent white communities. Second, there is the superficially manageable problem of a conflict between the selected values of the school's public and the values held by its teachers. Third, public schools are evidently not "common" irrespective of official claims and academic argument.

In the United States, differences in values have been most publicized in the case of fundamentalist Christian communities, whose beliefs are inconsistent with the secularism of the public school. That conflict is familiar because it has resulted in numerous disputes, with parents pitted against educators. The school wars have been well documented by Barbara Gaddy, William Hall, and Robert Marzano. In spite of the fierce mutually exclusive beliefs of each side, the authors argue that compromise is still possible, but their example is unconvincing. The cited set of conclusions from a case study include that science teachers will present evolution as theory; creationism will be discussed in religious studies; phonics will be available for children who need it; abstinence will be encouraged as a preferred mode of sexual behavior; and information about contraception will also be taught with the consent of parents.[3]

That agreement, as well as being intellectually confusing, is likely to lead to dissatisfaction when translated into action. Consider two examples. First, advocates of phonics believe that it is a necessary introduction to reading for nearly all children. Educators claim that schools provide phonics when needed; the problem is that the need is often not recognized until three or four years of failure. Second, there is an ethical problem in requiring teachers who enjoyed sexual activity in adolescence and continue to change partners frequently to teach abstinence. It may simply not be possible to find enough teachers in some schools to teach sincerely the importance of sexual abstinence outside marriage.

My study of the educational worldviews of groups of educators and similarly educated members of the public in Ontario showed important differences among and between educators and educated laypersons with respect to educational priorities.[4] Overall, asked to rank six educational worldviews, the highest proportions give priority to the technocratic and cultural, measured by first or first and second choices. If a similar finding were found overall within a society developing a common program, its core would emphasize academics required for postsecondary education together with preparation for employment. Substantial minorities, however, reflecting the school wars, give first or second priority to the traditional worldview, defined as emphasis on the development of good character and personal responsibility.[5] It is intellectually possible (and practically feasible in some circumstances) to combine the traditional perspective with the technocratic and cultural, but many of those favoring the two also rank the traditional low or reject it altogether.

If one accepts that the public school reflects educators more than it does parents or the public, then the gap between the worldviews of educators and laypeople assumes considerable significance. According to my surveys, 38 percent of superintendents of schools ranked the progressive (Deweyan child-centered) worldview first, more than twice the proportion choosing any other; 57 percent ranked it either first or second. They ranked the traditional fifth. The three lay samples (a comparison group matched by age and education, nurses, and engineers), though differing among themselves, ranked progressivism behind not only the technocratic and cultural but the traditional worldview. The differences between teachers and the public were less striking. However, educators (that is, teachers and administrators combined) expressed a first or second preference for the progressive worldview greater by 15 percentage points than that of the combined lay groups. (Secondary teachers were much less supportive of progressivism than superintendents, principals, and elementary teachers.)[6]

School wars between progressivism and a more academic, disciplined, and traditionally moral point of view have been seen in England, where the Thatcher government had great difficulty in finding educators to develop and implement its new common curriculum in the late 1980s; in California, where there continue to be skirmishes between educators and the state (centered on whole language); and in parts of Canada. Overall, the divide between progressive teachers and instrumentalist parents is less publicly obvious than the chasm between secularism and fundamentalist Christianity, though the two issues sometimes coalesce. The attitudes of teachers may change over time, but there are obstacles. Teachers' worldview is an integral part of their sense of professionalism, reinforced by faculties of education. Central attempts to convert them, however justified in terms of public will, are seen as "political" interference.

Parents are likely to react to situations that directly affect their children, rather than fight for more general educational causes. Evidence of that is the increasing enrollment of independent schools in England and Canada, as well as in the United States. Independent schools are generally more characterized by academics, strong discipline, and a code of traditional morality than are state schools; in North America, most are officially religious. Perhaps more important than the war within schools is the flight to the independent school; the former implies an implicit if reluctant acceptance of the public school, the latter its explicit rejection.

It is probably the case, however, that the common school ideal has died less as a result of the manifestation of educational choices by parents and teachers than from the inexorable march of pluralism and modernism in all areas of social activity. The foundation of the American common school lies in the small town, or a smaller center serving a surrounding rural community. Those schools are (or were) relatively small, with members, staff and students, recognizing every other member. They enroll everyone, from all social backgrounds, and form a focal point for the neighborhood served by the school, which usually accords with traditional boundaries.

Over the second half of the twentieth century, that mythical community school, never universal, became unusual. The growth of cities and suburbs and the increasing colonization of the countryside by city folk, have had two influences, with the same outcome.

First, dense populations have concretized the differentiation by family income in choice of residence. August Hollingshead showed, more than fifty years ago, that even small-town students came from different sides of the track, and that the social hierarchy was replicated in high school programs.[7] Today, residential developments and entire municipalities are layered according to the social categorization of their inhabitants.

Second, the growth of automobile ownership in suburbs and wealthy rural areas increasingly makes school choice viable, independent of public provision of transport. So those with the means to choose where to reside increasingly live with people like themselves. Those who do not are able to select a school, public or independent, that approximates their own values, outside their immediate school zone. The effect of increasing residential separation (I distinguish between voluntary choice and regulated segregation) and of increased mobility is to make the common school, as a microcosm of the larger society, obsolete. Whether or not the new pattern is democratic depends on one's definition, but it is hard to see it as reflecting the ideals of John Dewey, his contemporary supporters, or Durkheim's interpretation of moral education.

The implications for the school board are important. Developed in America and Canada as a buffer between the state or province and the local community, it has frequently become a travesty of its former self. If individual schools often no longer serve communities (in the traditional sense), how much less do large urban and suburban school districts? The social differentiation within a single school district frequently exceeds that between school districts. The Canadian province of New Brunswick has abolished locally elected boards altogether, replacing them with regional offices. Ontario has increased the size of boards (and decreased their number and powers) to the extent that they have become irrelevant bureaucracies with little purpose. England's Labour government, following New Zealand's example, announced in June 2000 that school boards, never as powerful as their U.S. counterparts, would be abolished entirely.

Increasingly, neither the school board nor the local school represents a distinctive community. That statement appears to contradict the claim that parents typically choose to live in homogeneous residential developments with their local school, reflecting their social status. Indeed, there are examples of schools serving homogeneous populations that can possibly be described as communities. Most often, however, the homogeneity is limited and superficial; it is also relative to a more heterogeneous society as a whole, not to times past. In Durkheim's terms, mechanical solidarity has almost erased organic solidarity—even within the strongly separate, gated, residential "community." The new homogeneity essentially rests on material parity; values, faiths, and a sense of moral citizenship commingle uneasily. Urie Bronfenbrenner, comparing the United States and Russia thirty years ago, observed the acid test of community; will adults reprimand (as distinct from notifying the police or looking the other way) youths who are misbehaving in the neighborhood?[8] A major theme of his book is that American children were then becoming subjected more to the influence of peers than to that of adults, with an accompanying decline in standards of citizenship.[9] The decline of traditional community is closely linked to the disappearance of the common school, the changing patterns of modern social life, and the growth of individualism.

COMMUNITY AND INDIVIDUALISM

The two concepts are not necessarily mutually exclusive in the larger social environment. Durkheim's *anomie,* which so aptly captures the pathology of the disenchanted adolescent, is related not only to being disconnected from community but also to a lack of a strong sense of personal identity. Nevertheless, there is inevitable tension between the two ideas within any organization.

It would be difficult to develop a densely populated, significantly closed organization avoiding all sense of community. The vacuum left by the erosion of traditional, school-level community is quickly filled by ad hoc subcommunities. In the same way, the modern residential development has few of the characteristics of traditional community, but subcommunities develop within it to reflect shared values and interests. Adults' activity in sports (directly with other adults or vicariously through their children) or in work for a religious faith are important examples.

The growth of subcommunities among young people is most evident in the large comprehensive high school, where the anonymity of size and individualized schedule coincide with developing adolescent independence of family. Undoubtedly, many students in the contemporary atomized society actively prefer the autonomy permitted by their high school. At the same time, other students, lacking a sense of belonging, seek any clique that will accept them as members. The activity of cliques has been portrayed in popular film and media publicity in the aftermath of sporadic acts of violence. The most popular subcommunities are related to immediate adolescent interests, which only occasionally mirror the activities most consonant with the educational goals related to citizenship. Sporting activities provide an interesting case. Advocates claim that sport provides a healthy outlet for adolescent energy, encourages team membership and cooperation, and develops loyalty to the larger school community. It can also be seen as promoting violence, distraction from the school's central purposes, and a division between the athletic cliques and the lower-status students lacking the requisite athletic strength, skills, and enthusiasm.

There are reasons for concern about the absence of community consistent with the school's overall goals—in the areas of both citizenship and academics. Outside sports, the subcommunities filling the central void are typically either peripheral or antagonistic to traditional educational values. Patterns of dress and decorum indicate a defiance of authority, a complicity with the peer group, occasionally with strains of violence and criminality; instead of reinforcing the school's community, they represent the statements of disparate, sometimes belligerent factions. Groups coalesce around the values of taste in popular music, partying, rebellion, dress and hair style, sexual achievement, social status within the school or neighborhood, and academic detachment (indifference to the school and its organized activity).

Internal relations within the high school are expressions of ongoing processes in society. Educational policy over the past forty years has eroded traditional expressions of community. Some evident factors are the increasing size of schools and their computerized schedules; the assault on the privileged place of heroic "dead, white, European males" previously dominant in history and literature; the dilution or disappearance of Judeo-Christian values (such as cleanliness, purity, and sobriety); and an increasing respect for students' individual rights, as against the interests of the student body as a whole. All of this takes place in a context where the student body does not belong to a coherent external community expressing shared values.

Most often, the weakening of community has been a by-product of policies chosen for entirely different reasons. The very fact that community has disappeared more from oversight than from cunning suggests that it has not been much missed, probably because it has also disappeared from most other areas of life. If parents themselves are significantly individualized, then they will hardly be upset, or notice, that their children lack community. If they recognize symptoms—their children lack genuine friends and have "nothing to do" when they face an unorganized moment—then the answer is a quick fix, membership in the gymnastics club or an invitation to instant "friends" from the neighborhood.

Individualism lies at the heart of contemporary society. It would be absurd to imagine that pluralism in the West simply means the replacement of an exclusive myth of patriotic and Christian community with choice from a closed set of coherent and discrete moral frameworks. To the question "Which of the following strong communities would you like to join?" the answer will often be, "None of the above." I am not alone among those who deplore the loss of community while being myself a fundamentally imperfect exemplar of community membership. The aroma of individualistic freedom cannot be captured and returned to the jar.

But what of citizenship and moral purpose? What about social capital?

Homes can supply much of that center of culture to their children, particularly if they are supported by relatives, friends, and neighbors. Francis Fukuyama argues that social conservatives who see social capital as being depleted during the twentieth century are simply wrong.[10] He claims that any lawful social exchange, however materialist, renews social capital. No clear distinction, he continues, can be made between doing the right thing for extrinsic and intrinsic reasons; practice of the former motive may lead to adoption of the latter. Even if he is correct on both counts, his conclusion that a new period of strong social order is assured because human beings naturally incline toward order does not necessarily follow. There are numerous historical records of extended social upheaval accompanied by the rejection of traditional norms. The freedom and affluence enjoyed by adolescents today (with the attendant mobility, consumption, and autonomy) are unprecedented.

If the school is to contribute to the reconstruction of social order, to a better and stronger sense of citizenship, then both the content of good citizenship and the mechanisms by which it can be promoted must be established, once intuition and osmosis are deemed insufficient. The public school attended by most young people is no longer, if it ever was, a common school. It is impractical to even consider the establishment of a strong, patriotic, and unified ethic, because that change would require the destruction of many of the schools most loved by parents, together with the compulsory mass transportation of young people to assure that every school is a reasonable social microcosm of the larger society.

The central characteristics of the current system are relics. The structure of zoned public schools, elected school boards, and a state bureaucracy reflects a time when there was, or was assumed to be, a central consensus on the values inherent in schooling. Those central values were to be moderated by the local school board to reflect the local community. There is now neither central consensus nor local community. Examples of areas of diverging belief include the role of government; the status and qualities of organized religions; the place of the classics in literature and the arts; sex education; environmentalism (including climate-change and energy conservation); and the traditional virtues. The values represented in the school depend on numerous factors, including state and local programs, the leadership provided by administrators and teachers, individually and collectively, and the interest and action of parents. The values transmitted to students are both muffled and strident, confused and conflicted, varying with the teacher and the school.

Underlying the disorder that schools represent, in purpose if not always in practice, are three related fundamental values. That low-level doctrine consists of nonviolence, consideration of the other person, and tolerance. A semblance of those values is required to get to the end of the day. Perhaps the most frequently mentioned value—by educators—beyond the basic triad is the enhancement of self-esteem. Although no parent is likely to object in principle to the triad, many (including nonsecularized adherents to established religion) do demur from the addition of self-esteem, the antithesis of the traditional virtue of humility. In practice, widely distributed additions to the triad are difficult to establish.

Florida is one state attempting to return citizenship to the curriculum. Broward County asked residents to rank twelve traits (from an original pool of eighty-nine), of which eight were to be selected for instruction over consecutive months.[11] The three most favored were respect, responsibility, and honesty. Respect is an aspect of consideration for others (the foundation of the triad). Responsibility runs counter to the litigious trend of U.S. society, whereby anyone accused is automatically expected to deny responsibility until an accusation is proven. It will not be easy to persuade teachers to inculcate a value that they do not hold; teachers' representatives routinely attribute any shortcoming in student achievement and behavior to the home background, with little responsibility to be borne by the student, and less by the teacher. As for honesty (a part of the greater virtue of truth), teachers have been widely encouraged not to cause confrontations over factual disagreement but to concentrate on the task at hand and the diminution of conflict. Courage, incidentally, on which truth depends for survival and which frequently implies conflict, was not ranked in Broward's eight values. Justice was not included in the longer initial list. Alasdair MacIntyre, the contemporary philosopher who has done most to reintroduce virtue to an increasingly hedonist and individualist society, uses truth, courage, and justice as his starting point, on which the remaining virtues significantly depend.[12]

Overall, one must question whether Florida's worthy intentions have practical value. Can a state monopoly of schooling successfully inculcate values that are foreign to the larger society? To what extent are the major authority figures in Florida (or any other state or province in North America) characterized by the values of, for example, responsibility, integrity, cooperation, self-discipline, and compassion (from the intermediate list of twelve), let alone the traditional core virtues of truth, courage, justice, humility, and diligence, without which, according to MacIntyre, chosen values of the day are nothing more than emotivism?[13]

If the common school is moribund beyond possible resuscitation, if the larger society is divided between those who hold to evanescent emotivist and secular values and others belonging to religious and ethnic minorities with distinctive, sometimes incompatible values; if individualism and the changes in social life have erased both the local community (defined in terms of shared values as distinct from levels of income) and its patriotic links to a national manifestation of society; and if the traditional Judeo-Christian tenets on which the public, common school was originally built no longer hold, even in diluted form, is it reasonable even to consider the implementation of an ambitious program of moral citizenship? In a pluralist society, connected more by shared consumption and entertainment than by a sense of the virtuous life, can there be agreement on the meaning of good citizenship?

SURVIVING THE WRECKAGE OF
THE COMMON SCHOOL

Outwardly, public schools are not much changed. The bureaucratic order is much the same, students are organized in large groups, and they are assessed on the basis of persistence over time and a variety of measures of achievement. Most children still attend their local school. The school is rather like a human body in a coma, hooked up to a machine—one that, in the school's case, supplies sustenance in the form of dollars per live body in nominal attendance. The body looks much the same, but the soul has long since departed.

Just as the human vegetable maintains some basic functions, so does the public school. The school, though increasingly lacking in agreed intellectual and moral substance, has served the same three essential functions for over a century, the ABCs. Schools serve to allocate students among an ever-increasing variety of futures; this function has become increasingly important. In England, for example, national examinations that were administered to just a quarter of the age cohort forty years ago have been expanded (in terms of levels of achievement and content) to serve three-quarters. The United States has an immense variety of postsecondary opportunities compared with seventy years ago. Although there have been critics of this function (without which the secondary school would not survive), alternative distributive mechanisms would be equally elaborate and possibly less equitable. While the erosion of nonscientific programs in the school (for example, history, literature, the arts, and citizenship) makes intelligent discrimination hazardous, allocation within the expanding technical and service fields becomes even more important.

Schools still teach the vast majority of children the basics. Although increasing numbers of parents teach their children entirely at home, supplement the school's work themselves, or pay for private after-schooling, the skills of reading, writing, and mathematics remain universal, despite the numerous attempts by progressive educators to trivialize them by defining them as patterns of natural growth rather than external qualities requiring focused instruction.

Most important of all, schools still provide generally benign custody, critically important in the case of adolescents. Of the three functions, the last is the closest to moral citizenship, and one impossible to avoid, even by default. Dysfunctional high schools may teach amoral citizenship; poor attendance, low levels of achievement, and parasitic work habits may be condoned or even rewarded. Few principals of large comprehensive high schools would claim that their high school graduates have demonstrated habitual reliability, punctuality, and honesty—qualities reasonably desired by employers. The negative case demonstrates the inevitable conjunction of custody and citizenship; the (custodial) home, too, provides either good or bad preparation for citizenship; there is no vacuum in attitude and behavior; even nihilism denotes both.

Underlying the three functions is the virtue of justice. Schools and postsecondary institutions have made great efforts to influence the allocation of high school graduates, by raising the aspirations of girls, particularly in math, science, and technology, as well as those of racial and ethnic minorities. In the name of equity, major efforts are made to improve preschool and elementary programs in a brave, if generally unsuccessful, attempt to provide the same level of basic skills to disadvantaged children as that reached by the advantaged. Legally enforced custody, in the form of compulsory attendance, testifies to the school's moral duty to provide young people below school-leaving age, irrespective of their background, with an education that will serve them and society well in the future. Without that concept, it would be impossible to justify enforced custody. I shall argue that the idea of equity has been transmuted into an unhealthy emotivist belief that perverts good citizenship; nevertheless, a sense of justice rightly lies at the heart of the publicly funded school, without which taxpayer support would be difficult to sustain.

Although the public school has deservedly lost much esteem in the eye of the public, and despite the demise of the common school, in whose image the public school was constructed, there remains some vestigial linkage between the school and the values of our democratic society, even in its pluralist form. Although justice (usually experienced in the language of equity), is the most generally evident, there are others. Consider two examples. Nonviolence is an important part of the low-doctrine school; that concept is easily transferred to the settlement of differences in the larger society, most importantly to the choice of government. The United States is an English-speaking country—its laws are written in English. California, faced with a growing Hispanic minority, has established English as the official language to be used in schools, thereby ensuring that the minority will be able to participate fully in state and national affairs. Canada, with its long-standing French-speaking minority, has established two official languages, ensuring that its many other minorities will be socially integrated, at least to the extent of making civic choices.

Although these vestiges do nothing to justify the retention of the myth of a common school, they do illustrate that citizenship is not entirely unrepresented, despite the low-level interpretation of the public school's sense of mission.

FILLING THE VACUUM

The Judeo-Christian tradition may have been first watered down and then erased, the vestigial values of the public school may be an insufficient low doctrine, but it does not follow that schools are necessarily lacking in values. The vacuum is often filled with passing enthusiasms—environmentalism, antiracism, and feminism are obvious examples. While I do not wish to disparage the principles and intentions behind those movements—I too oppose careless destruction of the environment, the differential assessment of people on the basis of race, and the subordination of women—I do not develop them as independent values outside a context of the fundamental values of good citizenship. Although they are important issues for today's schools, their expression outside a wider context of worldview may lead to injustice, unkindness, intolerance, and lack of consideration for others. An obvious educational example is the issue of quotas: why should a less qualified woman, Hispanic, or African American from a rich family be preferred on grounds of equity to a more qualified white male from a disadvantaged family? Groups as groups may merit special treatment (some organizations are given tax-free status, for example), but individual aspirants for a position should be treated on the basis of objective and relevant criteria; recent polls and electoral propositions suggest that this is a widely held principle among the people, if not the elites.

The most vigorous academic defense for the educational status quo stems from an interpretation of social equity. Its proponents often refer to their proposal as "democratic" education. Its best-known advocate is Amy Gutmann,

whose book *Democratic Education* is a standard reference.[14] More recent advocates have provided nuanced defenses of the educational monopoly. Eamonn
Callan allows that some exceptions (schools of choice) might be permitted, but
only if they meet his interpretation of a Rawlsian criterion of "reasonableness,"
the rejection of which, as a first principle, is the raison d'être of, for example,
fundamentalist schools.[15] Joseph Kahne provides a carefully developed defense
of the democratic school in the context of other possibilities, without denying
or ignoring its problems, but fails to come to terms with public will, the essence
of true democracy.[16]

Democratic education derives from Dewey; it emphasizes the importance of
building cooperation and sharing within the school. It envisages the development of schools as communities. There is little relation, however, between the
democratic community postulated for universal implementation and the traditional community referred to earlier. The imposed community requires the inculcation by the school of externally determined values, ones not necessarily
shared by the students' parents. The traditional community, in contrast, embodies the preexisting values of teachers and parents expressed in the bonds
limiting the behavior of all members of the community, as well as bounds sep-
arating the school community from those (geographically or ideologically) outside who do not share its norms and values. The two interpretations have little
in common. Advocates of the imposed community argue that it is precisely the
lack of community outside the school, the growing pluralism, that makes its
enforced presence inside necessary; children should be molded not according
to parents and their community but in the image of a manufactured ideal society.

James Coleman and Thomas Hoffer conclude from their research that traditional school communities are more effective, both in academic achievement
and in retention of students in school, than is the public school.[17] They distinguish between functional communities, the naturally occurring communities
exemplified by the turn-of-the-century small town (and in their study by Roman Catholic parochial schools), and value communities, schools selected by
like-minded parents. The two categories represent or attempt to recapture the
traditional archetype on the basis of parents' wishes. Despite the enormous
popularity of Deweyan, progressive, child-centered ideas among educators,
and their widespread implementation in England and Wales, Canada, and
parts of the United States in the latter part of the twentieth century, there is little or no evidence of the growth of community or citizenship; it is reasonable to
question whether community can be externally regulated without resort to to-

talitarianism, for the good reason that the very idea of the imposition of elitist prescriptions is authoritarian.

There is more, and less, to citizenship than the embrace of the democratic faith, but neither is it adequately represented by the low-doctrine triad. Although the imposition of progressive, democratic values in an individualistic, materialistic, and pluralist society is a formidable task, it would be equally challenging to deliver any other set of coherent values; certainly, any attempt to resurrect traditional values, with or without prayer in the classroom, with or without the intervention of the Supreme Court, is doomed to failure.

Although it is not feasible for a democracy to impose a minoritarian dogma, secular or religious, on an educational monopoly, the more important reasons for rejecting central direction of values are ones of principle. No democratic state prohibits private and home-schooling; none of the advocates of democratic education favors such proscription. They are left defending the dubious ethic of mandatory inculcation of democratic dogma in all children, except those fortunate enough to have affluent parents. Fifty years ago the principle was less problematic; the public school, frequently a common school, represented a perceived national consensus; independent schools either served tiny deviant minorities or provided the rich with a similar education in a different social setting. In the pluralist democracy, the interpretation of good citizenship is distinctive in the majority of independent schools, most having a religious connection.

A powerful argument for the common school was, and for the public school is, social equity. The definition of social equity has changed over time. From a vision of equal educational opportunity, with every child having the same right of access to the highest level of schooling, the purposes have moved in two ways. First, equal opportunity has been replaced by a belief in the virtue of equal outcomes among selected groups, usually defined by sex, race, ethnicity, or social class, but not by religion. Second, the specific goal of educational equity is subordinated to the larger purpose of achieving an egalitarian society. Although the original, and significantly achieved, ideal of equal access is rarely challenged, the goal of equal outcomes is politically divisive and practically futile. The achievement of equal outcomes from unequal groups requires, at the very least, massive state intervention, either in terms of differentiated treatment within a monopolistic system or through some form of quota.

Equal outcomes have been largely achieved between the sexes, but it is no coincidence that the idea of equal opportunity for boys and girls is generally held by parents. Most families encourage their boys and girls equally, and the sexes possess comparable if not identical intellectual qualities, both genetic and environmental. The same conditions do not hold among children from different social groups. Measured intelligence, egalitarian rhetoric notwithstanding, varies among groups and remains the most robust predictor of academic success.[18]

To the extent that intelligence is environmental in origin and that social factors other than intelligence influence success in school, the goal of equality of outcomes between groups differentiated by religion, ideology, race, or income remains absurd. It hangs on the assumption that it is both possible and ethical to prevent parents from helping their children. Once it is conceded that parents do and should promote their children's educational development, it follows that some parents are, and always will be, more effective than others, even if the differences between parents are reduced. At the same time as it has become obvious that state intervention has only a modest effect on relative group success, even within a state monopoly, it has become equally evident, unsurprisingly, that the educational system has little influence, in the context of democratic pluralist societies, on overall social equality.[19] As previously noted, choice of school is available in social democratic Sweden, as it has been (between various denominational and secular schools) in the Netherlands for seventy years. In the more capitalist Canada and the United States, where school choice, although growing rapidly, incongruously remains constrained by government regulation, the income gap between the first and last deciles has steadily increased over recent decades. The causes are to be found in the economic and political systems, not in the schools.

Attempts by the political Left and stakeholders in the educational monopoly to resuscitate the public school, usually in terms of an equitable, common, democratic school, have little substantive justification. Society has become increasingly pluralist over the past forty years, in terms of ideology, where polarization between free-market and governmental solutions has been accompanied by the growth of special interest groups interested in, as examples, environmentalism and a global economy; religion, where there are clear divides between mainline Christian denominations, fundamentalists and evangelicals, Islam, Judaism, and secularism; ethnicity, where immigration has changed the demography of California, Florida, and Texas; and race, where African Americans are less satisfied with integration and equal treatment as answers to their needs and are as or more likely to identify with their own communities. The implications for the teaching of citizenship in the school are immense.

Earlier, I used the conflict between strong religious belief and educational progressivism as the prime example of incompatible belief systems. It is unlikely that either would gain adherence from more than a quarter of the population, but each is deeply entrenched in its respective minority. There is no possible, principled consensus between those who believe in an absolute truth outside the human mind and those, following the pragmatic philosophy of William James and Dewey, who believe that truth, always tentative, lies in human behavior and experience. The strongest consensus that could be formed in the United States would be based on a combination of the great-books idea, a practical preparation for postsecondary education and work, and a much-diluted (Broward-style) version of selected Judeo-Christian virtues. Even if such a version could be developed and widely accepted by parents, implementation would be difficult because it would be opposed by large numbers of progressive teachers. The intended school would conflict directly with the interests and values of the progressive, democratic Left, as well as with those of the strongly religious, who are already excluded by the prevailing low-doctrine system.

It is not surprising in that context that an alternative solution is proposed for the public school in those societies where pluralism in lifestyle, worldview, and spirituality is accompanied by a strongly individualist free market. A logical alternative to the monopolistic imposition of a minoritarian expression of citizenship developed by an educated elite is the imposition of no citizenship at all. If there is no such thing as society, why not let individuals make their own way? The best government is no government; parents bear the responsibility for educating their children until they become autonomous adults.

The strongest and most persuasive advocate of a libertarian policy is James Tooley.[20] His argument is that not only should government get out of the content of education altogether, but it should not even provide funding. Vouchers contravene the free-market system (because individuals do not pay for them directly) and undermine the proper working of the capitalist system. He provides evidence that the private system was working quite well in the nineteenth century, in England and some American states, before the imposition of publicly funded systems for ideological reasons. He also demonstrates that private education is flourishing in competition with public schools in many developing countries, Brazil being his prime example.

The fundamental objection to a free-market system (whether the true market of Tooley or the watered-down version proposed by advocates of vouchers) is the same as the objection to the imposition of the dogma enjoyed by a privileged elite: there is no evidence that that is what the public wants; the two proposals are equally undemocratic. Confusingly, most parents, in the United

States and Canada, like the idea of the local public school. The inconsistency is that parents do not agree on what beliefs and practices the neighborhood school should represent.

There are strong objections of principle to a free market as a model for the provision of schooling. Crucially, the plan abandons citizenship as a central focus. It assumes that the interests of society (ignored or denied by libertarians) are trumped by those of the individual. But Durkheim was right when he argued that the school should represent an ideal version of the society we have; what he could not have known was that society a century later would not have a clear consensus based on secular values. Although the pendulum in education has swung toward the centralizing and self-serving influences of monopolistic bureaucracies and teachers' unions, there remains a generally recognized society with its essential values. Although parents should have a prior interest in the development of their children's values, society as a whole also has a legitimate interest.

MORAL CITIZENSHIP IN THE PUBLICLY SUPPORTED SCHOOL

Before attempting to map out the configuration of an educational system that reflects at the same time both the heterogeneity of an individualized society and the desire for community and sense of moral citizenship on the part of many of its members, I shall summarize the conclusions from which, I believe, future scenarios should flow.

The common, public school, if one accepts that it ever had genuine life, should be taken off its life-support system. It can survive only artificially, Soviet-style, by making those fundamentally opposed to its values (or lack of values) captive to the ideals of others. It is absurd to require that a single working mother of the Pentecostal faith, struggling to make ends meet, send her child to a secular school, while an affluent industrialist may send his to a school selected on the grounds that it will give her a head start in a material life by meeting more children like herself.

The neighborhood school remains popular partly because it does not teach an unwelcome central doctrine; to some extent, it accommodates, or claims to listen to, its clientele. But the crucial problem of principle remains the same. Dissident parents, unless they are wealthy or extremely self-sacrificing, are forced to accept an idea of citizenship to which they object. In some cases, the imposition may be even more objectionable than one emanating from the center; neighborhood schools in upscale suburbs may be overcome by the values of materialism—appearance, possessions, and immediate gratification.

A governmental decision either way, to select a one-size-fits-all model or to leave it to the market (with or without vouchers) to determine the nature of each child's formal education, equally undermines the naturally occurring communities that should be encouraged as potential contributors to citizenship.

Choice of school is a necessary corollary of, not just an alternative to, the neighborhood school. Communities, religious or secular, gated or organic, necessarily possess common bonds and bounds; they exclude as well as include even if their particularity is demarcated by culture rather than regulation. Even the most carefully balanced ideology in the neighborhood school will misrepresent the values of some. And such a genuinely representative school is hard to achieve because special-interest groups attempt to intervene.

The more deviant minorities the monopolistic school enrolls, the less citizenship it can represent, and the more it reverts to the low doctrine of nonviolence, consideration for others, and tolerance. As comprehensive schools increase in size and individualism, the more subcommunities develop and the more the larger entity loses any sense of purpose. A genuine citizenship is more likely to be found in a fundamentalist school, despite its intolerance, than in a comprehensive high school, with its tolerance of almost everything and parallel belief in almost nothing.

In short, the mandatory neighborhood school for all cannot inculcate a high level of moral citizenship—because it must be tolerant of minorities, however small. Even such a minor step toward shared citizenship as a school uniform is generally impossible, when objection is raised not only by libertarians but by Sikhs, Muslims, and Orthodox Jews.

There is a way out, and in differing ways, the pluralist democracies are already reaching for it. The starting point is to recognize in a formal way the need for moral citizenship. All but the most extreme libertarians recognize this—the problem arises when people attempt to install their own most fundamental articles of faith—whether it be love of God, of self, or of reason.

The way to begin is not to attempt to place everyone's most precious values in order of priority but to determine the essential, often subordinate, beliefs which all (or nearly all) share. The publicly funded school should accept the low-doctrine triad (nonviolence, consideration for others, and tolerance) not because it is sufficient but because it is necessary. Truth should be accepted as one essential ingredient in the school because no genuine education or worthwhile community can long survive a diet of dishonesty, hypocrisy, and public relations. To be sure, we shall never agree on a single interpretation of truth, but we should preclude the acceptability of lies by students to teachers or, even more important, by teachers to students. Democracy (that is, the principle of representative government on the basis of free elections and universal suffrage) should be taught as the best form of government for our society. As a corollary, the acceptability of the violent overthrow of a democratically elected government should not be countenanced. The schools should be prohibited from the teaching of hatred, of groups or individuals. They should not be allowed to teach the general superiority of any people on the basis of race, ethnicity, religion, sex, or ideology. That does not mean that all groups share the same characteristics (few do) but that none is intrinsically superior. The basic skills of mathematics and language, together with a general knowledge of the society, jurisdiction, and world within which young people live should remain a constant of every school—to provide a basic preparation for adult independence. English should be the foremost language of instruction in the United States (English and French in Canada). If all citizens are to be encouraged to participate fully in society (whether at the highest or lowest level of community), and if education is guided by truth, then it follows that students should have ready access to different versions of truth; in practice, that means a well-stocked library and resource center.

Those values, though not including the most important priorities of anyone's strong religion or ideology, are not trivial. They provide a preliminary picture of the minimal standards of an acceptable school. There are probably many schools that do not meet those standards (even the low-doctrine triad); they should be closed or radically reconstructed. I believe that MacIntyre's first virtues—truth, courage, and justice—are implicit in that prescription, but I would not make them explicit, because that would invite a Broward-style bidding contest. Doubtless, others would see their own most favored values as arising from the same list or a similar one.

In addition, two procedures are necessary if the state is to fund, partially or entirely, a broad range of schools. First, the state must be able to monitor compliance with the requirements of citizenship (for example, by inspection and forms of student assessment). Second, the state should require that any school receiving public funding extend admission to all bona fide students who (together with their parents) are willing to accept its culture and associated rules and norms. A Christian school would not be allowed to refuse applicants on the grounds that they lack appropriate baptismal certificates, but it would be able to expel students who refused to participate in activities related to the school's religious character.

Underlying those procedures is the ideal of equity. I earlier distinguished between the goal of social equality among groups and the goal of equal educational opportunity. It is reasonable for government to work toward the provision of universal access to a variety of available schools; it is unreasonable to assume that young people, irrespective of their parents and cultural environment, will take comparable advantage of those opportunities. Young people are inevitably influenced by their parents, not just at conception but continuously through childhood and adolescence.

If formal education is to balance the interests of parents and society, it is important that reasonable steps be taken to assure all children access to schools of all kinds. Moral citizenship is unlikely to result from state-run processes that systematically treat some children as being less worthy of opportunity than others. An example of a regulation that enhances the opportunities of the disadvantaged is the limitation of partial funding to those independent schools that spend no more per student than do equivalent fully funded public schools and that waive tuition for the indigent. Although the state should not hypocritically pretend to give unequal children an equal chance of admission to Harvard, it should take action to assure support to those who aspire to different conditions of life from those of their parents.

Readers with a strong belief in the mission of the school to deliver high standards of citizenship will see the foregoing as thin gruel. There is no mention of honor, integrity, perseverance, industriousness, humility, cooperation, sensitivity, purity, or temperance. It is important that the list is a minimum of common qualities, not a guarantor of a full and satisfying educational regime. If neighborhood schools survive the competition from schools with more explicit sets of values and missions, then they will probably do so precisely because they too represent something more than the minimum. I have suggested that the most likely consensual model for the neighborhood school is some combination of the traditional academic curriculum and a more utilitarian ethic of preparation for postsecondary or working life. Clearly, there are many virtues and values that can and should be incorporated in a renewed neighborhood school. There are parents who actively prefer a minimal set of values, arguing that it is their job, not the school's, to teach character; they may decide to choose an alternative school. Most parents, however, given the opportunity, will choose schools with a clear sense of mission, including citizenship.

Thus, although it is neither possible nor desirable for a pluralist society to legislate a tableau of right behavior, it can develop regulatory arrangements that make it easier for parents to realize their benign hopes for their children's formal education. Both society and parents have legitimate interests in the schooling of children. Society, with government as its agent, has a justifiable interest in assuring: the continuance of a democratic and civil larger community based on the rule of law; a high level of equality of educational opportunity, expressed as school and program accessibility; the encouragement and support of a high level of all aspects of educational achievement, including excellence at the postsecondary level; easy movement from school to work with an intent to minimize unemployment and unemployability among the young; a good level of basic skills; and an acceptable set of basic values, habits, and attitudes.

Parents, however, have a legitimate interest in choosing a distinctive interpretation of education, always within the limits of the fundamental premises of a pluralist democracy. There remains the important assumption that government has the will and foresight to overcome the self-interest and power of those who either benefit from the status quo or demand that all children be made captive to their own educational dogma. There is also an assumption that the problem of separation of church and state can be resolved in the interests of society as a whole. To a Canadian who assumes that separation of church and state requires the impartial treatment of all bona fide religious beliefs rather than their exclusion, it seems reasonable that a secular public system with parallel religious and secular choices for legitimate minorities does not offend that central principle.

There is no evidence to support the claim that the public school monopoly is a useful mechanism to prevent cultural differentiation, even if one were to accept that the culture and ideology enjoyed by elites should be the chosen one for all. In Canada, four provinces have had since their establishment parallel systems, one public (essentially Protestant until the 1970s) and one Roman Catholic, accompanied by lessening levels of religious friction. Over the past thirty years, various jurisdictions have provided partial funding to independent, mainly religious, schools; none among four Canadian provinces, all the Australian states, and England has experienced an upsurge of religious division. In contrast, the Soviet Union and Yugoslavia, two countries that attempted over decades of repression to erase religious and ethnic division and culture by means of common schools, failed spectacularly.

The most important assumption underlying this essay concerns the essential character of the pluralist society and its compatibility with some form of moral citizenship. Some readers may have mistakenly assumed that I am implicitly advocating the advancement and superiority of the pluralist, multicultural society. That misinterpretation would stem from a belief that one must be either for or against pluralism, for or against the metaphor of the melting pot.

I did begin with the premise that the United States, Canada, and England are pluralist as a matter of fact. All three countries have significant minorities that are distinct by some combination of culture, race, language, religion, and ethnicity. There are ongoing processes of assimilation (for example, in commerce and leisure) and others of continuing differentiation (for example, by formal and informal group identification and ethnic and religious activity). I assume further that no political action, least of all the totalitarian enforcement of common schools, will reverse the course of social development. My hope is the lesser one of keeping alive the flicker of virtue, at least within educational communities of choice, and enhancing standards of civility.

The dilemma facing society is not between embracing a nostalgic homogeneity and pumping up pride in multicultural difference. The polity can and should adopt an attitude of impartial acceptance. The presence of Hispanic culture and language in Florida and California, like the growth of black pride, is neither good nor bad, it simply is. It brings benefits to some and causes problems for others. The responsibility of central government should be neither to promote nor to deny cultural differentiation, but rather to assure that cultural minorities do not abuse their members or discriminate unfairly against nonmembers within the public domain.

The challenge of reconstructing a sense of moral citizenship is practical as well as ideological. Moral lines must be drawn. I have illustrated standards within all publicly funded schools. In addition, higher-level doctrines will be developed both for neighborhood schools freed from the impossible responsibility of representing every minority and, more readily, lacking the norms of recent experience, by schools of choice. Many in the modern Western world are covertly appalled at the thought of Muslim and Christian fundamentalist schools; they should bear in mind that the level of civility is not noticeably lower in the streets of Tehran and the Mennonite countryside of Pennsylvania than in New York or Toronto.[21] They are rightly fearful that the strict moral standards of religious minorities should be imposed upon others; as preachers of tolerance they should understand that religious minorities do not always welcome the imposition of the different moral standards of the public school. It is important to enshrine in our schools the core values necessary for citizenship in the contemporary democracy, and equally important to be tolerant of differing cultural traditions where they do not transgress those core values.

In this way, society develops by moderate accretion, building on its many conflicting traditions. The central qualities should be favored and harbored, but that does not preclude their being consensually enhanced or diminished at some time. However improbable it may seem at the moment, American society may, in the future, consensually determine that it wants to move toward a more homogeneous model. Such a decision would require the support of the most numerous minorities, by religion, race, ethnicity, and culture. The implication of the argument in this essay is that homogenization would be taking place long before it were formally embraced by authority. The problems in the realization of schools as agents of moral citizenship derive more from the inappropriate, inadequate, and outdated rules and regulations of governance than from the necessary and generally harmless incompatibility of different parents' wishes for their children.

The acceptance of pluralism should be accompanied by a concrete recognition in our schools of what it is that binds us together. The more strongly we can build community around the assumption of some common values and the pursuit of some common goals, the more likely is it that the attendant qualities will be represented in the larger external society.

It is often assumed that the progress of the modern democratic and individualistic state can be centrally determined by government, while children in school learn essential values by osmosis. The reality is the reverse; society changes incrementally, inattentive to the transient wishes of presidents and prime ministers, while children need direction if they are to grow into good citizens and moral adults.

How can good citizenship be assured in the Western world of the twenty-first century? One approach is to deny the problem and leave the domain of moral and ethical life to an individualized open market. Another is to attempt to impose an ideology favored by secular elites. Yet another is to assure the expression of the core values present throughout our pluralist, democratic society and accept, above and beyond them, the reasonable development of different images of our traditions.[22]

NOTES

1. The U.S. narrative is well told in David B. Tyack and Elisabeth Hansot, *Managers of Virtue: Public School Leadership, 1820–1980* (New York: Basic, 1982). The following quotation is from p. 7.
2. Emile Durkheim, *Moral Education* (New York: Free Press of Glencoe, 1961), pp. 10, 11.

3. Barbara B. Gaddy, T. William Hall, and Robert J. Marzano, *School Wars: Resolving Our Conflicts and Values* (San Francisco: Jossey-Bass, 1996), p. 225.

4. Mark Holmes, "Educated Dissent: Implications of Policy Disagreement for Educational Leadership," in K. Leithwood, ed., *Effective School District Leadership* (Albany: State University of New York Press, 1995).

5. The following summaries (of a fifty-word description) outline the other five worldviews provided respondents: cultural—cultivation of children's intellectual, esthetic, and social capacities; technocratic—preparation for future lives as citizens and workers; progressive—allowing children to grow healthily, to express themselves, to be tolerant, and to feel comfortable with themselves; individualist—challenging young people with the possibility of excellence to their limits; egalitarian—development of social equity by promoting harmonious and cooperative development of children irrespective of their social origins. The one-word labels were applied afterward. The original headings were The Child at the Center (progressive), Success in Future Life (technocratic), Intellectual and Cultural Development (cultural), Development of Good Character and Personal Responsibility (traditional); The Development of Individual Freedom (individualist); The Search for Social Equality (egalitarian). The last two were ranked lowest. I anticipate that if the ideas could be developed for the entire population, the popularity of the progressive and individualist would fall, that of the technocratic and traditional rise.

6. Holmes, "Educated Dissent," p. 265.

7. August deB. Hollingshead, *Elmtown's Youth* (New York: John Wiley, 1949).

8. Urie Bronfenbrenner, *Two Worlds of Childhood: U.S. and U.S.S.R.* (New York: Russell Sage, 1970).

9. James S. Coleman had illustrated this point in a famous study of ten high schools, *The Adolescent Society* (New York: Free Press, 1961).

10. Francis Fukuyama, *The Great Disruption: Human Nature and the Reconstitution of Social Order* (New York: Free Press, 1999), pp. 249–62.

11. "Broward Public: Respect Is Top Value to Teach," *Miami Herald,* Broward edition, February 9, 2000.

12. Alasdair MacIntyre, *After Virtue* (Notre Dame, Ind.: University of Notre Dame Press), 1981.

13. Ibid., pp. 22–33. Emotivism denotes feelings, beliefs, attitudes, and values that are developed ad hoc, lacking systematic roots in a philosophy or religion.

14. Amy Gutmann, *Democratic Education* (Princeton: Princeton University Press, 1987).

15. Eamonn Callan, "Common Schools for Common Education," *Canadian Journal of Education* 20 (1995).

16. Joseph Kahne, *Reframing Educational Policy: Democracy, Community, and the Individual* (New York: Teachers College Press, 1996).

17. James S. Coleman and Thomas R. Hoffer, *Public and Private High Schools: The Impact of Communities* (New York: Basic, 1987).

18. Richard. J. Herrnstein and Charles Murray refute the hypothesis of random distribution of measured intelligence in *The Bell Curve: Intelligence and Class Structure in American Life* (New York: Free Press, 1994), pp. 269–310.

19. Four consistent assertions of truth should be distinguished. First, increased equality of opportunity helped promote social mobility during the twentieth century, partly by encouraging more schooling for intelligent children in disadvantaged homes; that improvement has been accompanied by increasing proportions of the age cohort attending postsecondary institutions, giving an impression of even greater mobility. Second, level of schooling correlates well with future success and income. Third, parents (through their genes and home culture) significantly influence the character, level of schooling, and future success of their children. The effect of parents is mitigated by increased educational opportunity, but it would remain important even in the event of a hypothetical perfect equality of opportunity—that is, children of equal inherited qualities would have unequal outcomes related to differential parental influence. Fourth, intergroup differences in level of schooling are highly resistant to external manipulation (through formal intervention in preschool and school, for example) unless the parents' cultural patterns, values, abilities, and attitudes are consistent with the outcomes (for example, years of schooling and adult occupation) being used as the criteria of measurement.

20. James Tooley, *Reclaiming Education* (New York: Cassell, 2000).

21. It may be objected that Iran is not a fully fledged democracy, but elements of virtue and citizenship antedate modern democracy by more than two thousand years.

22. An underlying theme of this essay, that government should draw more from the common sense of the people and less from elitist programs, explicit in the final passages, is drawn from several sources. Adam Gopnik captures the spirit of Michael Oakeshott's union of strong principle and pragmatic policy making in "A Man Without a Plan," *New Yorker*, 21 October 1996. That combination was anticipated by Edmund Burke, interpreted by Conor Cruise O'Brien in *The Great Melody: A Thematic Biography of Edmund Burke* (Chicago: University of Chicago Press, 1992). Similarly, from a Christian perspective, the political scientist Glenn Tinder explains why, although planning is always presumptuous and inevitably unsuccessful, given the failings of all human actors, one still has the moral responsibility to choose wisely and incrementally, in *The Political Meaning of Christianity: The Prophetic Stance* (New York: HarperCollins, 1991), pp. 200–218. Christopher Lasch was a consistently powerful voice for the common sense of the people, most notably in *The True and Only Heaven: Progress and Its Critics* (New York: Norton, 1991).

Chapter 9 Common

Education and the

Democratic Ideal

Rosemary C. Salomone

A century and a half ago, education reformers conceived of the common school as the institution where our democratic and republican roots would come together. Designed to meet the needs of swelling European migration and rapid industrialization, mass compulsory schooling would develop in children the skills, understandings, and character traits necessary for them to participate as informed citizens sharing a public philosophy. Government-operated schools would develop civic virtue and national identity through a shared set of values reflected in the curriculum. This ambitious project assumed that Americans, old and new, could unite around a common set of public and private values and a vision of educational purpose and process. Both would serve as the groundwork for indoctrination and socialization.

Social and political events over the past century have put this grand scheme to the acid test. American society has transformed dramatically, and so has the knowledge base that informs educational policy and practice. Common school reformers could not foresee the rise of the administrative state emerging from the New Deal era, the concept of individual rights and liberties affirmed in the civil rights and women's rights movements, the cultural revolution of the 1960s, the political mobilization of religious conservatives, the widening gap between rich and poor, and the apparent failure of government intervention strategies to effectively address society's underclass. At the same time, sociological and psychological advancements in learning theory and child development have broadened the notion of schooling beyond anything imaginable in the mid-1800s. Progressive notions of educating the whole child, the increasing American emphasis on emotional well-being, the breakdown of the nuclear family, and the pressing needs of children in poverty have expanded the role of schools beyond education in basic skills and knowledge and into the social and even psychological realms. Sex, drug, and AIDS education; environmental and global education; visualization and relaxation techniques; and recognition of alternative lifestyles have gradually crept into the traditional curriculum over the past several decades.

Meanwhile, the rapid pace of technological development has led to the globalization of knowledge. Although we generally applaud the benefits of such progress, we are fast beginning to recognize its downside. The pervasive presence of the media and advanced telecommunications, particularly the Internet, has displaced the face-to-face talk that used to nourish community life. Young people now can pick and choose from among a broad menu of values, lifestyles, and influences that compete with those of their family and community. Adding to the diversity in values and worldviews, both secular and religious, is a mass immigration from Asia, Africa, Latin America, and eastern Europe, extending far beyond the mainstream Protestantism of the nineteenth century and even the Judeo-Christian framework of what we have come to regard as "civil religion." This changing pattern of migration has made it increasingly more difficult to draw on a common Western or European tradition as a source of collective identity. Following a typical pattern of "Americanization," immigrant groups initially confined to the cities are fanning out in the second generation into the suburbs. No longer can we assume that common residence brings with it a commonality of values and worldviews. As a result, the concept of the neighborhood school as an outgrowth of a functional community is slowly becoming a thing of the past.

This changing vision of educational purpose and substance, drawn on a changing American landscape, has become animated in the cries raised by religious dissenters, primarily but not solely Christian fundamentalists, who claim that the values taught in public schools are contrary to their religious beliefs. A growing number of these parents are educating their children in their own church-affiliated schools. In fact, Christian day schools have expanded at a faster pace than any other group within the private sector. Others, increasingly joined by liberals and by libertarians across the political spectrum, have abandoned institutional education and claimed the right to educate their children at home. Yet private and home schoolers constitute a relatively small group among the disaffected. The vast majority of religious conservative parents have doggedly remained within the public schools, struggling to navigate a system that they perceive as insensitive at best and hostile at worst to their fundamental worldviews. Many silently compromise their deeply held values and beliefs. With greater frequency, however, they challenge the system, often at considerable emotional and social cost to themselves and their children. Some have asserted what they consider a constitutional right to opt their children out of certain programs, materials, and textbooks, many of which are widely used throughout the country and some of which have won nationally recognized awards. Others have raised the specter of secular humanism and New Age philosophy to remove materials entirely from the school setting, evoking charges of censorship from the wider community.

Most Americans, including school administrators and board members, summarily dismiss these claims as baseless and troublesome, little more than religious extremism or even paranoia. Many communities, when confronted, circle their wagons against what they fear is the first step toward an organized takeover by the "religious Right." But regardless of whether we agree or disagree with the underlying concerns, it cannot be denied that these challenges lay bare the myth of the common school—that is, that the values we teach through the public school curriculum are indeed neutral and reasonable to all Americans.[1] The unswerving faith of these parents, their unwillingness to compromise their core values, and their politically visible attack on contemporary social norms promoted in the curriculum push to the extreme the ideal of education for democratic citizenship in a society that values pluralism and freedom of conscience along with civic understanding and commitment. The legal and policy claims they make and the remedies they seek provide a useful context for balancing these seemingly conflicting ends and examining the continued vitality of the common school concept juxtaposed against an alternative notion of common education.

LEGAL NARRATIVES

Over the past three decades, a startling number of school districts have been caught in gridlock over value conflicts and competing visions of the good life.

From condom distribution in the schools, to the debate over evolution versus creationism, to community service as a requirement for graduation, the media have brought into our homes the many dramas that have played out in communities and courtrooms across the country, all in the name of parental autonomy and most with a gloss of religious freedom. Both the stories and the legal issues they raise have captured the imagination and intellectual energies of political and legal scholars, generating rash of commentary on parental dissent and educational values. But of all the many cases that have reached the courts, two in particular have shaped the legal and political debate on religious accommodation in the public schools and the meaning of education in a liberal democracy.

The first, *Wisconsin v. Yoder*, recounts the efforts by Amish parents to gain complete release from state compulsory education laws beyond the eighth grade because the values taught in high school would undermine Amish values and their way of life. The second, *Mozert v. Hawkins County Board of Education*, tests the limits of *Yoder*. Here the conflict arose when fundamentalist parents requested school officials to exempt their children from a widely used reading program that offended their religious beliefs. Both groups based their legal claims in the free exercise clause of the First Amendment.[2] In *Yoder*, the parents found a sympathetic ear in the U.S. Supreme Court. In *Mozert*, the Court refused to hear the case, letting stand the decision of the appeals court denying parents their right to partially opt out of the curriculum. The conflicting and multitextured opinions generated in these cases shed equally distinct lights on the legal nuances, competing interests, and policy implications underlying religious accommodation in the context of the common school.

Yoder formed the basis for the legal claims in *Mozert*, as it has for numerous cases grounded in parental autonomy and religious accommodation. Here the Wisconsin law required six- to seventeen-year-olds to attend a public or private school. Jonas Yoder, Wallace Miller, and Adin Yutzy refused to enroll their three children between the ages of fourteen and fifteen in any school or equivalent instruction once they had completed the eighth grade in a local public school in Wisconsin. When the local district administrator learned that the Amish had opened their own elementary school, resulting in a loss of thirty-seven children and eighteen thousand dollars in state aid to the district, he signed a truancy complaint against them. Before trial, the attorney for the Amish offered state officials an alternative. They could permit the Amish to establish their own vocational training program similar to those initiated in Indiana, Iowa, Pennsylvania, and Kansas, but the superintendent of public instruction refused their proposal. This would have combined formal instruction in English, mathematics, health, and social studies in an Amish vocational school three hours a week with farm and household duties supervised by their parents. When the trial court fined the three fathers five dollars each, they appealed the criminal conviction through the state courts. The parents' key witness, Professor John Hostetler, a sociologist and anthropologist, captured the essence of the case in his trial testimony. Asked by the state's attorney whether the primary purpose of education is to prepare the child to "make his place in the world," Hostetler replied, "It depends which world."[3]

When the case reached the Supreme Court, at least eight of the Justices understood that nuanced response. Chief Justice Burger, speaking for the Court, relied heavily on the concept of the religious community, recognizing the serious issues that arise when democratic citizenship as the end and values inculcation as the means collide with distinct religious beliefs. The Amish parents feared that the values taught in the high school would lead to the disintegration of their insular community. In recognizing that fear, the decision is rich in the virtues of religious pluralism, parental rights, and group self-determinism. Nowhere before or since has the Court articulated such insight into the role that religious subgroups play as sources of values and control over their members and how that role stabilizes civil society.

In their arguments before the Court, the parents had relied on the following oft-cited quotation from *Brown v. Board of Education:* "[Education] is the principal instrument in awakening the child to cultural values, in preparing him for later professional training, and in helping him to adjust normally to his environment."[4] The state had also relied on *Brown,* arguing that, "the Amish child is being denied . . . [the] right [to equal protection] by the theocratic society into which he was born. Any desire for knowledge is stifled."[5] But whose cultural values, professional training, and environment—whose world—was each side talking about? Those of the religious community of Amish or those of the larger secular society? Here the Court turned the issue into one of parental preferences within a particular cultural context. The justices seemed to imply that education for citizenship in a democracy might mean different things to different communities depending on how actively the group participates in the larger democratic society. On closer examination, however, it appears that the Court was limiting parental autonomy and the respect afforded religious (and cultural) differences to those subgroups whose values are basically the same as those of the majority. The Court specifically commended the Amish for their long history as self-sufficient and law-abiding citizens and underscored the sincerity of their religious beliefs. The Amish would teach their children what the majority of Americans believe the public schools should teach: self-reliance, productivity, and respect for the law.[6]

The Court made clear that only religious and not secular philosophical or personal considerations (like those of a Thoreau) would satisfy the demands of the religion clauses. In fact, the Court so narrowed the decisive facts that it not only privileged organized theistic religious beliefs over more idiosyncratic ones of a nontheistic nature, but also privileged the Amish religion in particular over others. The Court expressly noted that "probably few other religious groups or sects" could make such a convincing argument supporting the adequacy of their alternative mode of vocational education.[7]

Justice Burger's opinion in *Yoder* continues to provoke heated debate among commentators. Some sharply criticize it for its lack of principled reasoning and for its failure to address the child's interests as compared to the parent's. Many express ambivalence toward it, agreeing with the ultimate decision but troubled by the narrow rationale supporting it. Nevertheless, two other opinions in the case, Justice Byron White's largely unnoticed concurrence and Justice William Douglas's highly controversial dissent, both raised equally important matters that prove helpful in thinking through parental dissent and educational purposes.

Justice White was less solicitous of the Amish than the Court majority, presenting a more balanced perspective on the group needs as compared with the individual needs of the Amish children. For him, the state had "a legitimate interest" in preparing children "for the lifestyle that they may later choose or at least to provide them with an option other than the life they have led in the past." Toward that end, he placed outer limits on parental discretion at the point where the education that parents choose for their children would leave them "intellectually stultified or unable to acquire new academic skills." Justice Douglas went much further. He warned that if Amish parents harness their children to their way of life and truncate their education, their entire life might be "stunted and deformed." In contrast, he urged that education expose children to "the new and amazing world of diversity that we have today."[8]

At first glance, *Yoder* appears to be an exemplar of religious tolerance and pluralism. Yet subsequent history has proven otherwise. In fact, the decision has been swallowed up by its exceptions, rendering its legal significance considerably more symbolic than real. Nevertheless, religious conservatives continue to rely on *Yoder* to support their right to educate their children, even though the decision loses its force when stripped of the unique circumstances surrounding Amish history and culture and the limited exemption they sought from the state. One such case occurred in the mid-1980s in Tennessee when Christian fundamentalist parents challenged the reading program used in the Hawkins County schools. *Mozert* presented a set of facts that have become increasingly familiar and burdensome to school officials faced with challenges spanning the curriculum. And while the case has provoked a spate of commentary trivializing the parents' claims and dismissing them as out of sync with mainstream America, for the parents involved these claims struck at the core of their deeply cherished values and religious beliefs.[9]

The conflict began in the fall of 1983 when several families requested that school officials offer their children alternate reading assignments in lieu of the basic Holt, Rinehart, Winston reading series that was used in schools throughout the county. Although one principal granted their request, the school board yielded to community protests and unanimously adopted a resolution requiring all students to use the Holt series under threat of school suspension. The parents remained adamant that their children would not participate in the program. They argued that the stories presented built upon one another and that after reading the entire series, a child might adopt the views of a "feminist, a humanist, a pacifist, an anti-Christian, a vegetarian, or an advocate of 'one-world government.'"[10] Although the fundamentalist parents could accede to some views so long as the school labeled them as incorrect and acknowledged that their views were the correct ones, other ideas—such as evolution and feminism—were so contrary to their beliefs that the school would have to eliminate entirely all references to these subjects. As far as these parents were concerned, mere exposure to these materials was a form of values inculcation that violated their free-exercise rights under the First Amendment.

The district court's opinion, subsequently reversed on appeal, attempted to strike a balance between the interests of the school district in developing literacy skills and the interests of the parents and children to remain free from the burdens placed on their religious beliefs. The court ruled that the parents could teach their children reading at home, subject to state testing. In this way, the students could forgo the course without forgoing the course requirements. To the parents and their supporters, this Solomonic decision was nothing less than a symbol of parental rights. To their detractors, it posed a grave threat to public education. By the time the case reached the appeals court, six amicus curiae briefs arguing for reversal had been filed. The court heeded the warnings contained in the briefs but, unable to reach consensus on a rationale, it reversed in three separate opinions, the first two emphasizing education for democratic citizenship and the third driven by court precedent and judicial restraint.

Chief Judge Pierce Lively, speaking for the court, unequivocally rejected the parents' argument that mere exposure to the materials would place a burden on their children's religious beliefs. The school had made no attempt to indoctrinate them with any specific value or religion. The opinion recognized the role that public schools play in inculcating values that are fundamental to democratic government, including tolerance of diverse political and religious views. But it qualified that tolerance as civil and not religious. Individuals need not accept other religions as equal to one's own but need merely recognize that in a pluralist society "we must 'live and let live.'"[11] For Judge Lively, the *Mozert* parents failed to meet that threshold. And unlike the Amish, for whom it was not possible to reconcile their religious requirements and the needs of their agrarian community with the goals of public education, here the parents wanted their children to acquire the full range of skills required for life in modern society while remaining insulated from certain ideas that their parents found offensive.

In the second opinion, Judge Cornelia Kennedy focused on the underlying concerns that justified the school board's imposing uniformity on all students. Included among these was an interest in preparing students for citizenship and self-government through the development of critical thinking skills. This turned the parents' fear of indoctrination on its head, embracing as a civic good what they considered a potential harm. In doing so, the opinion essentially espoused the progressive view that education in a democracy must give students the opportunity to form independently their own ideas and judgments on "complex and controversial social and moral issues."[12]

The third opinion, by Judge Danny Boggs, was clearly conflicted. On the one hand, he was most sympathetic to the concerns raised by the parents. He challenged the state's interest in "critical reading" and the argument that accommodation would have proven administratively disruptive. He even recognized that the program placed a burden on the parents' exercise of their religious beliefs. But Supreme Court precedent and judicial restraint prevented this "common sense" burden from rising to the level of a constitutional violation. In the end, the school board was entitled to say, "my way or the highway."[13] Nonetheless, the implication was clear that although the court could not mandate opting-out as a legal remedy, the approach would have provided a valid political compromise between the cultural community of Christian parents and the political community represented by the school board.

In contrast to *Yoder,* the Supreme Court denied the parents' request for a hearing, ending the *Mozert* story at the appeals court level. The Court was not ready to make the giant leap from the Amish to Christian fundamentalists. As the appeals court undeniably recognized, the two cases were significantly different. The Amish embraced only partial citizenship in civil society, which justified a limited state interest in educating their children in basic literacy and computational skills. Nor did they stand firm on any particular view of biblical interpretation as it related to the school curriculum. The *Mozert* parents, on the other hand, were unwilling to tolerate certain views and unflinchingly demanded that school officials recognize their worldview as correct.

But not only were their practical concerns and educational goals for their children distinguishable from those of the Amish. So was their potential impact as a group on the larger society. *Mozert* was decided on a far more politically charged landscape than *Yoder.* In contrast to the insularity and historically apolitical posture of the Amish, Christian fundamentalists were rapidly mobilizing and utilizing the political process to challenge the status quo. If the Court had harbored any glimmer of intent to extend *Yoder* beyond its narrow facts, the political activism of religious conservative parents in the decade and a half between the two cases undoubtedly gave the justices serious pause. In fact, *Mozert* became the first in a series of such cases in which the justices declined the opportunity to resolve the tension between parental interests in religious accommodation and the interests of the state in preparing children to participate in the democratic process.

Yet we should not summarily dismiss *Mozert* for its failure to provide binding precedent. Despite its limited jurisdiction, the "mere exposure" standard articulated in Judge Lively's opinion subsequently has defined scholarly debate over parental autonomy and religious values. Together with and in juxtaposition to *Yoder,* all three appeals court opinions have attracted considerable attention not only for their legal rationales but also for what they reveal about the conflicts lying beneath the surface of contemporary schooling. Both *Mozert* and *Yoder* strike at the heart of values inculcation, the political purposes of the common school, and the tension between cultural pluralism and assimilation. The similarities and distinctions between the two cases have provided an ideal context for examining the potential and limits of education for democratic citizenship, the ambiguities within education's liberal underpinnings, and the implications for policy reform.

EDUCATION IN A LIBERAL DEMOCRACY

For the past two decades, political theorists have drawn on the various opinions in *Yoder* and *Mozert* in an attempt to work through the inherent tension between commonality and diversity. Inevitably, the discussion gets caught in a tangled web of interconnected principles drawn from America's liberal roots in the eighteenth-century Enlightenment and nourished by the spirit of twentieth-century progressivism. Prominent among these are the principles of autonomy, neutrality, rationality, and tolerance. Each presents paradoxes that continue to engage political philosophers and legal scholars in vituperous debate over the meaning of education in a liberal democracy and the respective roles of parents and the state in that process. Implicit in that debate is an unspoken distinction between common education and common schooling.

For purposes of analysis, I will use as a baseline for discussion a form of liberalism based in an almost unyielding commitment to core political virtues, particularly autonomy and rational deliberation.[14] Here the political is given salience over the cultural. According to this view, political education is the mechanism for leading children to appreciate and evaluate ways of life that are contrary to those of their families. And rather than teach children to behave in accordance with authority, schools should develop in them the attitudes and skills to think critically about authority so that they can fulfill the democratic ideal of shared political sovereignty among citizens. In recent years, various scholars, writing in a more minimalist liberal mode, have juxtaposed the *Yoder* and *Mozert* opinions against such arguments. They and others have refuted, in varying degrees, comprehensive interpretations of liberal commitments, such as Mill's ideal of individuality or Kant's value of autonomy, and have shifted the focus to the political values shared by reasonable people. In developing a variant broadly defined as "political liberalism," they have left a winding trail of insights. The arguments they advance are not monolithic, at times resting in sharp disagreement with each other. Nevertheless, taken together, they selectively reveal the truths, myths, and speculations surrounding the liberal virtues and how they relate to parental dissent, religious accommodation, and the notion of the common school.[15]

First, consider the principle of autonomy. This raises two critical questions. What exactly do we mean by an autonomous individual and specifically the autonomous child? And what is the appropriate degree and type of critical reflection that fosters an acceptable level of autonomy? These questions are difficult to answer, in part because there is something internally inconsistent about the claim for autonomy. Despite its philosophical grounding in individuality and the promise of freedom, autonomy can in fact lead to homogenization and the negation of differences. This contradiction comes into bold relief when we consider autonomy as an aim of liberal education, which necessarily involves systematically introducing children to the public symbolic forms that constitute a particular culture.

The bare notion of autonomy conjures up images of the rootless child untouched by choices made by others. The educational process, however, touches children deeply through specific visions of the good life. These visions typically reaffirm those valued by the larger secular culture, but they may also negate the vision fostered by the family. Education exerts a powerful indoctrinative force. The scope and direction of that force are largely a function of district policy, school practice, and teacher discretion. In effect, this process potentially can undermine children's autonomy by forcing them to choose a life contrary to that of their parents and community. To acknowledge this reality is to reject the notion that education is an activity that expresses or nurtures a person's autonomy. But there is an equally troubling aspect to this that draws from child development and not democratic education. To be autonomous is not to be "freefloating" but to engage in a dialogue between reflectiveness and embeddedness. Children need to establish a stable worldview early in life as a precondition to this internal dialogue.[16]

The discussion of autonomy inevitably evokes the principle of neutrality. To the liberal mind, political decisions must not represent any one specific vision of the good life. But as seen in the case of autonomy, neutrality is nonneutral, stemming as it does from partisan assumptions. This issue bears significance to schooling, where attendance is compulsory, the curriculum represents contemporary favored positions on myriad social issues beyond the core political commitments, and financial constraints limit the ability of families to realistically seek private alternatives. The curriculum in the broadest sense—both what is included and what is excluded—is clearly value laden, from textbooks and other materials, to methods of teaching (didactic or participatory) and learning (individual or collaborative), to grading policies (letters, numbers, or anecdotal reports), extracurricular activities, and the historical figures profiled as role models.

The decided subjectivity within neutrality bears on the related discussion of critical thinking or rational deliberation. Conventional wisdom tells us that public schools teach children to think critically in the sense of reaching independent conclusions. But that wisdom again is based on the mistaken belief that schooling is neutral. This becomes more understandable when placed in historical perspective. John Coons refers to the "neutrality legend" of the common school, which, he reminds us, was borne out of "nativist folklore" in an attempt to free immigrant children from the shackles of their culture and religion.[17] Although school officials might like to think they develop in children the critical thinking skills to form their own opinions, the curriculum unavoidably leads them to those opinions espoused by the educational establishment, the school, and its teachers.

The notion that critical thinking skills are crucial to democratic participation is intuitively appealing. It is unfair and misguided, however, to assume that all religiously inclined parents who challenge certain instructional programs oppose rational deliberation. Like most parents, many merely want their children to reach conclusions similar to their own, especially on value-laden questions. Does critical thinking demand that the decision reached "independently" of the teacher be free of parental influence? If so, the implication is that there is one conclusion that the school finds preferable, which in turn suggests a state-imposed orthodoxy. An outcome preference of this nature not only violates the neutrality principle but even hints at totalitarianism.

The ability to deliberate critically among a range of good lives is encompassed in what is referred to as the "examined life." But as William Galston unequivocally counters, liberal freedom also entails the right to live an "unexamined life." This is not to deny that a life guided by unquestioned authority may very well be incompatible with individual freedom. Galston makes that concession. But it is questionable whether the state can incorporate the examined life into a system of public schooling without endorsing a particular conception of the good life that is "unrelated to the functional needs of its sociopolitical institutions and at odds with the deep beliefs of many of its citizens."[18] For example, many religious conservative parents, as well as other traditionalists, firmly believe that children must be taught to obey authority without question. Is the state justified in undermining this parental preference in child rearing? Is it not possible for children to obey authority unquestioningly in their personal lives and yet acquire the necessary skills and attitudes to critically examine governmental policies and practices? To hold otherwise gives credence to Stephen Carter's observation that contemporary culture conveys a message that "people who take their religion seriously . . . [are] scary . . . [and] maybe irrational."[19]

As Martha Nussbaum wisely points out, a religious search for the good is a liberty "most deserving of protecting by a liberal state."[20]

From the child's perspective, the liberal insistence on the examined life overlooks the child's need for cultural coherence. Children need a consistent moral code and values base connecting the school with their family and cultural community. The child psychiatrist Robert Coles tells us that "children try to understand not only what is happening to them but why; and in doing that, they call upon the religious life they have experienced, the spiritual values they have received, as well as other sources of potential explanation."[21] Children need more than education for civic competence. They need a moral and sentimental education, the type typically provided by such small social units as the family, the church, and the community.[22] These constituent parts of civil society not only help the child achieve an integrated sense of self but further the ends of democracy and maintain a stable civic order.

This leads into the discussion of tolerance. On the one hand, by presenting a wide range of life choices, it is conceivable that schools could make children skeptical of their family's values. This was the fear expressed by the parents in *Mozert*. On the other hand, children have the right to an education that includes an understanding of ethical diversity, which the *Mozert* parents strongly and unambiguously opposed. Children need exposure to diversity in some measure in order to learn the basic civic virtue of tolerance, which is essential to the success of democratic education in a society that values pluralism. But similar to other liberal virtues, tolerance is often misunderstood and overstated. In theory it promises too much, while in practice it delivers too little.

A theory of tolerance that is wedded to the promotion of individual autonomy seems to apply only to those worldviews that value autonomy. The question naturally arises whether we should tolerate the intolerant. But are those who follow a totalistic or ascetic religion necessarily intolerant? That depends on how we define tolerance. I suggest that a less robust definition may prove more suitable to the ends of liberal democracy. From this vantage point, one need not place equal value on all beliefs and ideas nor afford them equal concern and respect. Undoubtedly we all would prefer that our views were widely respected. Yet such a requirement asks too much of those who "self-consciously" tolerate opposing views or visions of the good life.[23] Then again, neither should tolerance permit indifference toward one another's views. That would ask too little. We must also avoid confusing respect for one another's views with the mutual respect that we owe each other as individuals regardless of race, ethnicity, gender, religion, or any other marker. Individuals can demonstrate such mutual respect without demonstrating equal regard for each other's beliefs. In the context of curricular challenges brought by religious conservatives, tolerance must be a two-way street between minority and majority values and beliefs, where the bottom line is set at mutuality and noncoercion and neither side is required to adopt the other's convictions as one's own.

This brings to mind the *Mozert* parents who objected to the very concept of religious diversity and further demanded that school officials affirm at least some of their beliefs as truth. As I will demonstrate, religious tolerance is a core political commitment that cannot give way to contrary beliefs. But we should not assume that all religious parents who challenge the curriculum are as extreme or as removed from the mainstream as the parents in *Mozert.* Many can peacefully live within a regime that neither lays claim to any comprehensive truth, such as one grounded in autonomy or rationality, nor marginalizes their religiously based view of the truth. Some challenge educational programs not because they are reflexively intolerant toward diverse views but merely because they fear, as did the Amish in *Yoder,* that an improperly mediated presentation may lead their children to act in conformity with those beliefs and ultimately strip them of their moral bearings.

BALANCING COMMON AND DIVERSE VALUES

The notion of tolerance as "mutual forbearance despite our differences" makes possible a constitutional consensus in a general sense and, more specifically, sets the stage for more peaceful coexistence in the realm of education. But it also collides head-on with the homogenizing political purposes of the common school as it was originally envisioned and as it continues to function in contemporary society. So how do we resolve this dilemma?

Looking at it from the view of a new social landscape and changing demographics, I suggest that we consider shifting from the rigid, and frankly anachronistic, concept of the common school to the more flexible and accommodating notion of common education.[24] The one seeks to homogenize students by imparting a fixed set of values through a system of neighborhood schools funded partially by the state and controlled by local government. This "one size fits all" approach historically has shown little if any regard for differences in family values or divergent perspectives on educational practice. The other aims to impart a common core of political principles, virtues, and understandings while recognizing differences at the broad margins. The focus on common education supports contemporary initiatives that allow families greater choice, and therefore voice, in the education of their children. It also comports with the arguments advanced by minimalist liberals who make a strong case, some more qualifiedly than others, for greater accommodation of diverse views.

Whether this shift is achieved through public school choice, such as districtwide schools or magnet schools, through loosely regulated charter schools run by community groups with public funds, or through a voucher program that may or may not include religiously affiliated schools is the subject of a much larger and contentious debate. For purposes of this discussion, I simply suggest that repositioning the more narrow discussion of accommodation from the common school framework to one of common education not only moves the discussion forward but also places it in step with more general trends in school reform.

But that claim is legitimate only if the notion of common education, as compared with common schooling, can more effectively reconcile society's conflicting demands of commonality and diversity, which takes the discussion back to where it began. In the name of commonality, education must develop shared values, principles, and political commitments to promote stability, coherence, and justice for free and equal citizenship. In the name of diversity, it must recognize legitimate demands of pluralism and encourage understanding and tolerance.[25] In the abstract, this sounds perfectly reasonable and possible. But when put into operation, the question inevitably arises: how do we identify and define our shared values and political commitments in a meaningful way?

Within the common school setting, partial opting out is the mechanism typically used to accommodate parents whose values clash with those reflected in the curriculum. But accommodation, particularly as applied to the common school, is a normative term. The assumption is that the dominant values of the school represent those of the local political majority. Anyone who disagrees is considered deviant. This masks the reality of local school politics. At times schools speak more directly for the educational establishment and/or a visible and vocal minority within the community than for the numerical majority, who, consciously or unconsciously, defer to the professionals or do not participate in local decision making for a variety of reasons.

But common values ideally should emerge from joint deliberation on policy choices. This process helps establish the shared identities and self-definition that enable community members to engage in yet further debate and discussion. The farther away we move from the conventional common school toward common education, the closer we approach this ideal based in an institutionalized model of shared values and purposes rather than grudgingly granted exemptions. The more real this sense of community becomes, the more robust and pervasive its values.

For values to be meaningful, they must infuse the entire curriculum. And they should be "ontologically deep"—that is, they should constitute the "dominant forms of being" of those involved in the educational enterprise.[26] I recognize that any attempt to identify a core of shared values inevitably runs the risk of being criticized as merely constructing, in an almost illusory way, an abstract, feel-good "bag of virtues." Nevertheless, as a practical matter, in order to balance the interests in diversity against the fundamental purposes of democratic education, we must first identify a bottom line of essential commonalities. Idiosyncratic views cannot fall below that line. If there exists no ascertainable set of such common commitments that bind us together as a nation, then the whole republican project falls apart.

A listing of these common commitments might include a mix of virtues, social values, and political principles. On the virtue side we might include such incontestable moral values or character traits as honesty, integrity, responsibility, delayed gratification, self-control, and respect for authority. Concern for the environment might serve as an example of a shared social value. Political principles are those more fundamental social values that are commonly imparted through what we call civic education. Included among these are justice and fairness, freedom of conscience and belief, freedom of expression, political and religious tolerance, and equality in the sense of equal dignity for all. These shared political commitments draw from several sources, including our common history and folklore and more specifically from legal norms established in the federal Constitution as interpreted by the Supreme Court, from federal statutes with supporting administrative regulations, and from federal executive orders. Taken together, these legal pronouncements represent a statement of national consensus.

The Supreme Court itself has relied on positive sources of law in defining, for example, the nation's commitment to the principle of racial equality. The clearest case in point is *Bob Jones University v. United States,* in which the Court upheld a federal policy that denied tax-exempt status to a private religiously affiliated university and a high school on the grounds that their racially discriminatory policies did not render them institutions organized for "charitable" purposes under the federal tax law. In reaching its decision, the Court drew upon a quarter-century history beginning with *Brown v. Board of Education* and including an "unbroken line of cases" and "myriad Acts of Congress and

Executive Orders" to establish that "racial discrimination in education violates a most fundamental public policy."[27]

This is not to deny that definitional attempts at shared values inevitably present potential stumbling blocks, particularly when we try to apply abstract principles to changing social norms. The equality principle provides a good illustration of this problem. Historically exalted as a moral precept, equality has evolved in recent decades into an antidiscrimination principle transcending culture. Yet even in the case of race, there is still widespread disagreement over the distinction between formal and substantive equality and what that means for public policy. The ongoing debate over affirmative action and preferential treatment is a clear reminder that we have never achieved consensus on the operational details. This is so even though, as the justices suggested at oral argument in the *Bob Jones University* case, racial equality stands unique in our political commitments in our having fought a war to bring it to reality.

The national consensus on equality for women is even more complex and less clearly defined. The most basic and generally accepted principle is that women should not be discriminated against—that is, that they deserve equal treatment with men, at least in the public sphere, such as employment, housing, and places of public accommodation. But gender equality, unlike racial equality, also raises controversial issues of role models and lifestyle choices, which bear on privacy as well as religious concerns. Gender equality, in fact, evokes exceptionally heated debate from within the organized conservative religious network as well as within Islamic communities. For Muslims in particular, tolerance implies "a right to cultural reproduction."[28] Disagreement over gender roles has arisen in the context of the curriculum and the role models presented in textbooks. The *Mozert* parents, for example, objected to a reading exercise depicting a boy making toast while a girl reads to him. In their view, the story "denigrates the differences between the sexes" affirmed in the Bible.

There is even less evidence of national consensus over homosexual rights. This became evident in the events preceding and following the adoption, by popular referendum, of an amendment to the Colorado state constitution prohibiting local and state governments from granting protected status on the basis of homosexual, lesbian, or bisexual orientation. The controversy eventually came full circle when the Supreme Court ruled that the amendment violated the Equal Protection Clause of the Fourteenth Amendment. It should be noted, however, that the Court avoided making any sweeping pronouncements on homosexual rights and instead grounded its decision in political process.[29]

It thus becomes clear that even within our core commitments there are sharp disagreements. Yet despite these disagreements, all discussion of contested cultural norms should not be considered off-limits in schools that are publicly funded, provided the subject is presented within the bounds of age-appropriateness, no one particular position is endorsed, and all views are presented evenhandedly, including those grounded in religious beliefs. Without this dialogue among the students' "primary moral languages," the common culture will become too thin, a phenomenon now apparent in the drive to avoid controversy by producing textbooks that are morally bland. Such dialogue is also critical for students to understand views with which they disagree.

Neither would the concept of common education accede to parental views that directly challenge such core values as racial equality or religious tolerance. The *Mozert* case raised such an issue. There the parents objected to a passage describing "a belief in the dignity and worth of human beings" as a central idea of the Renaissance. They claimed that such a belief was incompatible with their religious convictions. They clearly did not appreciate the fact that government funded schools must teach such public values as religious tolerance, which demands an understanding of diverse ways of life and respect for human dignity, both of which are essential to democratic citizenship.[30] There lies the bottom line below which diversity cannot be accommodated.

CONCLUSION

For well over a century, Americans have demonstrated an almost unabiding faith in the common school as the symbol and practical engine for preserving the ideal of education for democratic citizenship. In recent years, legal challenges brought particularly by religious dissenters have shaken that faith and opened to question the basic assumptions underlying the common school project and its continued vitality in promoting the democratic ideal. These lawsuits have brought to the forefront of philosophical discussion and policy debate the difficulties that mass compulsory schooling now faces in balancing our common and increasingly diverse values. When examined "outside the box," however, these conflicts also suggest that a common education in core political commitments is not necessarily dependent upon common schooling but may in fact flourish in a system that allows parents educational options that more clearly affirm their values and their views on educational practice. From here we can begin to envision an alternative model of education that develops in children the fundamental understandings and commitments necessary for democratic participation while accommodating, within reasonable limits of tolerance and administrative efficiency, the diversity in values now found throughout the U.S. population. The details of this model must be worked out, over time, on the slowly evolving template of school choice.

NOTES

1. See Charles Leslie Glenn, *The Myth of the Common School* (Amherst: University of Massachusetts Press, 1988), p. 10.

2. *Wisconsin v. Yoder*, 406 U.S. 205 (1972); *Mozert v. Hawkins County Board of Education*, 827 F.2d 1058 (6th Cir. 1987), *cert. denied*, 484 U.S. 1066 (1988).

3. William Bentley Ball, *Mere Creatures of the State? A View from the Courtroom* (Notre Dame, Ind.: Crisis, 1994), p. 61.

4. *Brown v. Board of Education*, 346 U.S. 483, 493 (1954).

5. *Brief for Petitioner, Wisconsin v. Yoder*, no. 70-110, United States Supreme Court, October term, 1971, p. 18.

6. Martha Minow, "Pluralisms," *Connecticut Law Review* 21 (1989), at 969.

7. *Yoder*, 406 U.S. at 232, 235–36.

8. Ibid., 245 n.3, 245–46.

9. For a sympathetic case study, see Stephen Bates, *Battleground: One Mother's Crusade, the Religious Right, and the Struggle for Control of Our Classrooms* (New York: Poseidon, 1993).

10. *Mozert*, 647 F.Supp. 1194, 1199 (E.D. Tenn. 1986).

11. *Mozert*, at 1066 (quoting *West Virginia Board of Education v. Barnette*, 319 U.S. 624, 633 (1938)(opinion of Chief Judge Pierce Lively).

12. Ibid., 1071 (opinion of Judge Cornelia Kennedy).

13. Ibid., 1074 (opinion of Judge Danny Boggs).

14. Amy Gutmann's book *Democratic Education* (Princeton: Princeton University Press, 1987) is emblematic of a position that is very close to being comprehensive, although her more recent writings have inched away from that position, at least in theory if not in fact. See Amy Gutmann and Dennis Thompson, *Democracy and Disagreement* (Cambridge: Belknap/Harvard University Press, 1996).

15. See, e.g., Stephen Macedo, *Diversity and Distrust* (Cambridge: Harvard University Press, 2000); John Rawls, *Political Liberalism* (New York: Columbia University Press, 1993); William Galston, *Liberal Purposes* (New York: Cambridge University Press, 1991).

16. Deborah Fitzmaurice, "Liberal Neutrality, Traditional Minorities, and Education," in John Horton, ed., *Liberalism, Multiculturalism, and Toleration* (New York: St. Martin's, 1993), 68.

17. John E. Coons, "Intellectual Liberty and the Schools," *Journal of Law, Ethics, and Public Policy* (1985), at 522.

18. Galston, *Liberal Purposes*, p. 254.

19. Stephen L. Carter, *The Culture of Disbelief* (New York: Basic, 1993), p. 24.

20. Martha C. Nussbaum, "A Plea for Difficulty," in Joshua Cohen, Michael Howard, and

Martha Nussbaum, eds., *Is Multiculturalism Bad for Women?* (Princeton: Princeton University Press, 1999), 107.

21. Robert Coles, *The Spiritual Life of Children* (Boston: Houghton Mifflin, 1990), p. 100.

22. Shelley Burt, "In Defense of *Yoder:* Parental Authority and the Public Schools," in Ian Shapiro and Russell Hardin, eds., *Nomos* (New York: New York University Press, 1996), 428.

23. Sanford Levinson, "Some Reflections on Multiculturalism, 'Equal Concern and Respect,' and the Establishment Clause of the First Amendment," *University of Richmond Law Review* 27 (1993), at 1019.

24. The distinction between education and schooling is borrowed from Eamonn Callan, *Creating Citizens: Political Education and Liberal Democracy* (Oxford: Oxford University Press, 1997), pp. 163, 165–66.

25. Terence H. McLaughlin, "Liberalism, Education, and the Common School," *Journal of Philosophy of Education* 29, no. 2 (1995), at 239.

26. Pierre Schlag, *Laying Down the Law: Mysticism, Fetishism, and the American Legal Mind* (New York: New York University Press, 1996), p. 51.

27. *Bob Jones University v. United States,* 461 U.S. 574, 593 (1983).

28. Michael Walzer, *On Tolerance* (New Haven: Yale University Press, 1997), p. 65.

29. *Romer v. Evans,* 517 U.S. 620, 633 (1996).

30. Gutmann and Thompson, *Democracy and Disagreement,* pp. 63–68.

Chapter 10 Once More into the Breach: Reflections on Jefferson, Madison, and the Religion Problem

Jack N. Rakove

When Alexis de Tocqueville arrived in America in 1831, Thomas Jefferson had been dead five years, but James Madison was still alive—physically feeble at eighty years of age, but mentally as acute as ever. It is a great regret that Tocqueville did not visit Madison at Montpelier. When Tocqueville described "The Federal Constitution" in chapter 8 of *Democracy in America* (published in 1835, the year before Madison's death), he relied on *The Federalist,* which Madison had written with Alexander Hamilton nearly half a century earlier.[1] And, of course, in their common concern with the phenomenon of majoritarian government, the two men would have quickly discovered a basis for sustained philosophical reflection. It would have been a terrific conversation, and if Tocqueville could have explained to Madison the sources of his own concerns about the nature of democratic society, he might have inspired the great architect of the Constitution to consider questions he never fully explored in his own writings.

For if obvious lines of intellectual affinity connect these two theorists of popular government, there is nevertheless at least one sense in which the young visitor saw more deeply than the aged statesman.

Madison may have been the founding father of republican constitutionalism, but Tocqueville articulated a concept of civil society that Madison never really developed. The difference is evident in a simple comparison of their respective great works on America. *The Federalist* is a treatise on government; we read it for its thoughts on the advantages of union, the intricacies of federalism, and the design of institutions. But *Democracy in America* really is about civil society; we turn to it for its observations about democratic culture, the sources of sociability and loneliness in a democratic people, the limited and pragmatic ambitions of its great men, the mediating role of town governments and village churches. Even though Madison's best-known essay, *Federalist* 10, provided a proof-text for the first modern theorists of pluralism, its observations about factions and interests in politics seem abstract and formulaic when set against the insights that Tocqueville bequeathed to social theory.[2]

This disparity reminds us how much American society had changed—exploded, really—in the decades between the adoption of the Constitution and the age of Jackson. And that reminder in turn cautions us about the difficulty of drawing useful lessons from the still quite agrarian world that the authors of the Constitution inhabited. It was vastly different not only from ours, of course, but even from the one Madison lived long enough to witness.[3]

Yet Madison and Jefferson did possess coherent and well-articulated views about at least one realm of belief and behavior that recognizably falls under the modern rubric of civil society. Their thoughts on the religion problem, as it might be called, continue to occupy an important place in our ongoing wrangling over questions of church and state, especially as they relate to the issues this book addresses. No discussion of the sticky quandary posed by the double helix of the Religion Clause, which simultaneously proscribes any practice smacking of "establishment" while defending citizens in the "free exercise" of their rights of conscience, can long avoid some invocation of the authority of the two Virginians. In part, of course, this reflects their authorship of key texts that express their distinctive conception of the separation of church and state: the Virginia Statute for Religious Freedom and the Religion Clause of the First Amendment, along with the supporting briefs supplied in query 17 of Jefferson's *Notes on the State of Virginia* and his letter to the Danbury Baptists, or in Madison's *Memorial and Remonstrance Against Religious Assessments* and the "Detached Memoranda" of his retirement.[4] Whether the issue is school prayer or school choice or the rights of religious groups at the university they founded to receive funds from the pooled funds for student activities, the ghosts of Jefferson and Madison ride still in our politics and jurisprudence.[5]

Why they continue to do so is not quite as obvious as it might seem at first glance. Of course, Jefferson survives as our leading philosopher of equality (though it might be better here to speak of a trinity with Abraham Lincoln and Martin Luther King), and Madison's reputation as our preeminent constitutional theorist has never stood higher. That they were bona fide great men (warts and all) may alone suffice to explain their lingering hold on our discourse. Yet it has also been well established that their thinking on the religion question did not wholly typify the accepted opinion of their day. Whether one compares the variety of practices in the early state constitutions with the religious indifference of the Constitution and the prohibitions of the First Amendment, or considers the interweaving of religious and secular themes in nineteenth-century education and culture more generally, it seems evident that the positions taken by the two Virginians occupied a fairly advanced and less than representative point on a broader spectrum of public opinion that had strongly accommodationist elements.[6]

Even so, considerations of prestige and authority give their pronouncements on the religion question an almost transcendent importance. Because so much seems to ride on enlisting their authority on one side or another of our current debates, these appeals cannot take the form of merely academic or antiquarian inquiries. For strict separationists, the deep principles that Jefferson and Madison invoked when they wrote most eloquently about matters of religion demonstrate that they really did prefer bright-line, high-wall policies that would consistently minimize and avoid the possibility of slippery-slope entanglement. On the other side of the question, any evidence that Jefferson and Madison might have been inconsistent or sometimes tolerated deviations from high principle suggests that sound considerations of contemporary public policy need not be held hostage to an absolutist constitutional rigidity. In this view, the real principle is best observed in its breach, by asking why modern Americans cannot pursue the pragmatic accommodations required to meet urgent concerns without risking a revival of the religious maelstrom of post-Reformation Europe.

There is, in my view, an asymmetry in these two distinct interpretations of the Madison-Jefferson legacy. One position strives to understand why the religion question loomed so large in their thinking, and why they seemed to espouse such radical views at a time when many, perhaps most, of their countrymen would have accepted more moderate positions that can be correlated with modern notions of accommodation. The other position involves looking at exceptions that arguably lie toward the margins of the larger question: congressional chaplains, or a treaty provision to build a church for the Kaskaskia Indians, or the proclamation of a fast day during the War of 1812. Intriguing as these particular actions might be as chinks in the proverbial high wall of separation, none involves an area of policy or regulation as substantial, vital, and potentially entangling as public support for religious schools of the kind that proposals for school vouchers would represent. Whether exceptions occurring at the margins, or in gray areas where the government is not truly legislating for its citizens, establish an adequate precedent to sustain policies relating to as essential an activity of the modern state as education is a reasonable question.

To make a case for appreciating why the deeper principles sustaining high-wall separation should outweigh exceptions at the margin in recovering the historical dimensions of Madison's and Jefferson's thinking about the religion problem is manifestly not to say that their views offer the definitive solution to our own debates. Such a position would suppose that the current meaning of the Constitution was largely fixed by the intentions and understandings prevailing at the moment of its adoption, and moreover, that the ideas of these two men fairly capture the dominant understanding at the time. Both of these claims are, to put it mildly, highly controvertible.[7] Furthermore, one does not have to be a rabid cynic to suspect that here, as on other issues, most of us tend to argue instrumentally, favoring those interpretations of the Constitution that support outcomes we prefer for other reasons, rather than grounding our political positions on an impartial reading of the Constitution. Given the indeterminacy of constitutional language, there will nearly always be latitude enough to sustain a range of plausible and often contradictory interpretations. Despite the absolutist quality of the "no law" proscription of the First Amendment, the range of meanings that can be ascribed to the operative phrases "establishment of religion" or "free exercise thereof" will always give proponents of nonpreferential accommodation the linguistic wiggle room needed to make constitutionally plausible arguments in favor of school choice.

Yet it is equally evident that Madison and Jefferson have a hold on our formulation of the problem, and before proceeding, it is worth asking why. Two further reasons immediately suggest themselves. First, it might well be true that there really is something to be learned from our political ancestors, not because they were patriarchs or because their opinions are legally authoritative, but simply because they thought deeply and powerfully about the matters in question. Second, the ongoing debate no longer permits us to pretend that their thoughts do not matter. Their wisdom and authority have been invoked too often to be forgotten; Jefferson, Madison, and their generation are ineluctably part of our debate, because partisans on all sides have already invoked them. And because they have been deployed in this way, we are obliged to try to understand why they espoused the positions they did, not only to give them their due but also to force us to be honest about why we think their views still matter.

Today we think of religious associations as only one element of that larger construct we know as civil society—an important element, to be sure, with some distinctive claims, yet still only one form of association among many. In the eighteenth century, however, the sphere of religion might well have qualified as the most important element in whatever latent conception of civil society existed. To understand, therefore, why Jefferson and Madison gave it such importance, it might be useful to begin by briefly sketching why other elements of such a conception commanded less concern.

What conceptions of civil society were available to the founders of the American republic, and how large a role did such conceptions play in their political and constitutional thinking? To suggest that the constitutional disputants of the 1780s said relatively little about the nature of American civil society is not to say that ideas about civil society formed no part of their general intellectual inheritance. If John Locke and Adam Smith can both be described as founding theorists of a modern concept of civil society, their American readers must have absorbed critical elements of their theories. Locke's doctrine of resistance presupposes that the property we privately possess—in our faculties and rights as well as in the fruits of our labor—justifies overthrowing governments that have grown tyrannical in the abuse of their legitimate powers. Smith's *Wealth of Nations*—published in the *annus mirabilis* of 1776, when Americans carried their reading of Locke to their own logical conclusion—"lies at the heart of all modern theories of civil society," John Ehrenberg concludes. Its "attack on mercantilism . . . anticipated the modern conception of civil society as a market-organized sphere of private advantage that stands apart from the state."[8] Smith's earlier philosophical work *The Theory of Moral Sentiments* presented another dimension of civil society as it explored the nature and sources of the feelings of sympathy that enable one person to attempt to enter the moral world of another. So did the eighteenth-century fascination with the rise of gentility, politeness, and refinement as the distinguishing marks of a society consciously celebrating the pleasures of good manners, elevated conversation, and conspicuous consumption—all manifestations of the rise of a commercial culture.[9]

More broadly still, the eighteenth-century Anglo-American obsession with the defense of liberty presupposed the existence of an autonomous realm of private behavior in which the authority of the state could intrude only when its decisions and actions were undertaken with due respect for the rule of law.[10] So, too, Americans could readily understand that they and their countrymen "at home" in Britain enjoyed the blessings of a civil society still struggling to be born in the absolutist states of continental Europe—a distinction perhaps best captured in William Hogarth's famous depiction of a French monk slobbering over an enormous joint of English roast beef, while the self-portrayed artist sits in the distance, awaiting the arrest that Hogarth actually incurred as a putative spy sketching the fortifications at Calais.[11]

Each of these considerations contributes something to a reconstruction of the conceptions of civil society available to eighteenth-century Americans, but they will not help us very much on the concerns that most interest us. Although they establish that Americans possessed a more than rudimentary conception of the elements of civil society, they say almost nothing about citizenship, or education, or religion, much less the relation among them. This is rather less than the usable past Americans love to seek.

But the American colonists had good reasons not to think too seriously about the nature of civil society. They lived, after all, in a culture in which political power was highly decentralized, where most of the rules that ordered daily life were adopted and adapted by town meetings, county courts, and juries that evidently played a far more active role in governance than their latter-day counterparts. The authority of the British Empire never penetrated very deeply into the American countryside; it was a thin template, resting lightly and unobtrusively on a people who rarely encountered Crown agents. In eighteenth-century America, most politics was provincial, while most governance was local. Provincial legislatures occasionally passed general-purpose statutes, but most of their legislative activity involved responding to petitions and requests emanating from local communities.[12] Where power was decentralized in this way, where not even a glimmer of bureaucracy existed, law tended to follow customary practice and community consensus, and thus to be responsive to values, attitudes, and habits formed within the locus of civil society.

What was problematic, in other words, was not the domain of civil society but the existence of the state. This was the eighteenth-century foreshadowing of the phenomenon that so amazed Tocqueville later. "Nothing is more striking to a European traveler in the United States than the absence of what we term the government, or the administration," he observed. "Written laws exist in America, and one sees the daily execution of them; but although everything moves regularly, the mover can nowhere be discovered." A state seemed to exist, somewhere; its laws were enacted and executed, somehow; but "the hand that directs the social machine is invisible."[13] Simply put, the problem of the Revolutionary and post-Revolutionary era was not to create or protect a civil society that, if primitive, was altogether healthy. It was rather to constitute a state and delineate the authority of its institutions—a state consisting (anomalously, by conventional standards) of two (or really three) levels of government, each purporting to govern, and in turn to represent, one people who had two (or really three) political identities: members of local communities, citizens of individual states, and initiates in that grand mystical fellowship constituting "We the People of the United States." Given the difficulty of making sense of the complicated governing entities that the Revolution had created, it is no wonder that Americans might be more preoccupied with describing the boundaries of governments and institutions than with exploring the elements of civil society.

Yet in at least two critical respects, the events of the Revolution did give a powerful and creative impetus to American thinking about the nature of civil society. One set of issues revolved around what the historian Richard D. Brown has called "the idea of an informed citizenry," a problem that, in its broadest terms, subsumes education, the press, and new notions of maternal duty under a common rubric.[14] And the second, of course, was concerned with the religion question, that long-simmering, occasionally festering, and sometimes downright disputatious problem that the break with Britain allowed to be examined afresh.

As Brown tells his nuanced story, the notion that citizens actually should be informed about public affairs was one of those radical concepts that began to take hold in Anglo-American political culture as a consequence of the turmoil of the seventeenth century. Its acceptance, however, was far from complete, nor was there any consensus about just how informed citizens should be or how much information they could usefully absorb. Memories of the chaos and tumult of the seventeenth century offered the ruling class of Georgian Britain ample reasons not to allow the ranks of the informed to grow too numerous. In Britain the most ardent advocates of freedom of the press were likely to be found at the outer margins of political life, among those radical whigs who worried that the rise of ministerial government after 1720 was sapping the principles of constitutional government established by the Glorious Revolution of 1688–89.

At midcentury, Brown observes, "the idea of an informed citizenry remained inconsequential in the American colonies as well as in Britain," but the eruption of the great imperial controversy that developed after 1765 gave new urgency to the idea that a people intent on protecting its fundamental rights needed to be literate, educated, and informed.[15] Americans already enjoyed a reasonably vigorous press, and they were proving themselves more sympathetic readers of radical whig ideas than their countrymen in Britain. From 1765 on, colonial political leaders actively used the press and other organs of transmission—including the information network of coffeehouses, taverns, clubs, and churches—to disseminate their briefs and pleas for the people to mobilize in defense of their rights.[16] A true "public sphere" of substantial proportions, safely insulated from the regulation or repression of government, clearly existed. Its effectiveness was measured by the remarkable mobilization of an aroused public that greeted the passage of the Coercive Acts of 1774 as the occasion for escalating resistance into a full-blown revolutionary crisis. The success of Thomas Paine's *Common Sense* further testified to the emergence of this expansive public sphere, not only through its reputed sales but also because the popular argot in which Paine consciously wrote signaled that his intended audience was not limited to the genteel classes to whom other pamphleteers addressed their learned arguments.[17]

The American decision for independence added a further dimension to the concept of the informed citizen. With independence, Americans began writing new constitutions of government to replace the old colonial regime, and these constitutions took an avowedly republican cast. Republican governments, it was well known, rested on the virtue of their citizens: their public-spiritedness, their willingness to subordinate private interest to public good, their capacity to monitor their rulers for signs of tyrannical ambition, their knowledge of the essential rights government existed to protect. A republican government required a republican society. Although Americans could enjoy some confidence that they already possessed the right stuff to be republicans—especially through the broad ownership of property—history cautioned against taking the survival of republican governments and manners for granted.[18] In fact, there was ample and growing evidence that Americans of all classes were pursuing their happiness in a self-interested, utility-maximizing way, speculating in lands, for example, or simply squatting on them in the hope of making doubtful title good, and conjuring all kinds of schemes for improvement in a society visibly poised to break across the Appalachians into the interior.[19]

But this evidence only reinforced the normative convictions that the commitment to republican government entailed. Americans had to be made into republican citizens, citizenship required education, and education might require a mix of old and new institutions and practices.[20] As always, the family could be regarded as the traditional primary institution for transmitting ideas and values from one generation to the next.[21] That traditional reliance, however, might also point the way toward a new and significantly enlarged appreciation of the role that mothers would play in nurturing not only the sons who would become republican citizens, but also the daughters who would love them—the departure now described as the invention of "republican motherhood."[22] It would also entail a renewed and increasingly libertarian commitment to the role of the press as a "palladium" or "bulwark" of liberty, and, after 1789, an appreciation that a well administered postal system could serve essential public functions.[23] And, of course, it also meant that formal institutions of education—not only colleges, but schools as well—should acquire duties beyond the preparation of a ministry qualified to preach Scripture and a laity qualified to read it.

This project of creating an informed citizenry, Brown concludes, embodied a dualist approach. The first emphasized the importance of "liberating the channels of information by assuring the right to free speech and press and freedom of assembly and petition." The movement toward disestablishment of religion also furthered this end "by releasing religious energy in order to encourage virtue." This approach was consistent with the radical whig beliefs to which Americans had previously subscribed. The second approach broke new ground. It proposed "using the state in a positive way to support the institutions required by an informed citizenry—schools, colleges and universities, libraries, and learned societies," and this, Brown notes, "represented a new departure."[24] In the different but equally visionary ideas expressed simultaneously by John Adams (in the Massachusetts constitution of 1780) and Thomas Jefferson (in his 1779 Bill for the More General Diffusion of Knowledge), the two most "ancient" American commonwealths would venture where no society had previously gone before, attempting to use specific means of education to inculcate knowledge in the citizenry—that is, the mass of the free population—while simultaneously working to cultivate natural leaders in a society lacking the formal aristocracy from which traditional society had drawn its rulers.

Between aspiration and implementation, however, there was a catch. The commitment to public education espoused in Jefferson's bill or Adams's Massachusetts constitution or Article 41 of the North Carolina constitution of 1776 or Article III of the compact section of the Northwest Ordinance represented the concerns and desires of a political elite.[25] But the implementation of those aspirations in governments that proved highly responsive to the wishes of the citizenry was another matter. The American state that emerged from the Revolution found itself constrained by the circumstances of its birth. The enormous burdens that had to be borne to carry the Revolution to victory deepened the antitax ideology that was already apparent in American political culture. Schemes of public education generally foundered upon the rock of popular resistance to taxation and the reluctance of the propertied classes to sustain the costs of educating the poor; as a result, the American commitment to education typically relied more upon voluntarism and the support of local communities than upon any system for providing adequate public support on a statewide basis. The results were predictably uneven, demonstrating how far Americans still had to go before the principle of publicly supported education for the entire population would become a hallmark of American democratic ideology.[26]

Understanding the limitations of eighteenth-century ideas both of education and of the role and capacity of the state (or states) should caution all of us about the difficulty of drawing easy inferences about the relevance of Founding-era ideals to our contemporary concerns. Glimmers of the modern concept of public education might well be seen in key documents of the period. But the notion of education as a fundamental right of citizenship was not yet available, nor would it have occurred to American parents to think that formal education would provide the stepping-stone to the social mobility of their children. Most children were still expected to learn their occupations from their parents, boys working aside their fathers in the fields, daughters acquiring the domestic arts from their mothers. If a craft or a trade was to be learned, then a lad should be apprenticed to an artisan or merchant or captain. True, an awareness of the value and utility of acquiring an education did become a key element in the ideology of opportunity and improvement that became so conspicuous an element of American culture after 1800, and schools quickly proliferated throughout the towns and into the countryside. Yet even then, the manner in which education was conducted should give us pause. Many of the poorly paid male striplings whom schools preferred to hire came to teaching as part of their own individual bids to escape the tedium of farm or store. As Joyce Appleby nicely encapsulates the situation, "Young men and women turned to teaching to support a bid for independence, churning annually through primary schools, where farmers' children went for a few months for four or five years to learn the fundamentals of reading, writing, and 'summing.'" Once they had taught themselves, they would find it easier to obtain employment in a commercial economy where literacy and numeracy were valued—but they did all this in the name less of civic ideology than of individual opportunity.[27] Education may thus have been far more valuable in promoting the careers of teachers than those of their students.

Similarly, the modest role that the state played in directing social policy makes it difficult to translate the concerns of the revolutionary and early republican eras into a modern understanding of the responsibilities of government. Today we assume as a matter of course that citizens and other residents of the United States are entitled to a host of services and benefits from government, and that many of these benefits—including, arguably, the right to education—are to be distributed in conformity with the equal protection norms of the Fourteenth Amendment. No such conception of the distributive responsibilities of government was available in the late eighteenth or early nineteenth centuries, nor was the egalitarian norm yet the dominant ideal. Individuals had an equal right to petition government for redress of grievances and the like, but that did not oblige government to treat all petitions equally. In the United States, as in Britain, much of the social policy of government took the form of granting legal privileges (such as incorporation) to clusters of individuals, enabling them to undertake some activity of public benefit (constructing transportation infrastructure, most notably) from which they would also derive legitimate private benefits. In a general sense, the public chartering of private academies and colleges in the early decades of the nineteenth century was based on the same conception of the role of the state. But there remains a significant difference between that conception, on the one hand, and the ideology of mass public education, on the other. Again, the reluctance or inability of politically responsive state legislatures to impose tax burdens on their constituents was one of the most conspicuous aspects of post-Revolutionary political economy, and this pervasive attitude exposes a fundamental fault line in the very conception of the role of the state.

Thus far our discussion of Founding-era conceptions of civil society has all but neglected the one realm that arguably deserves the strictest scrutiny: the state of religious belief and behavior in a society that Richard Hofstadter once described as "a concentrated repository of the Protestant ethic," combining as it did a middle-class morality with an ascetic sensibility refined in the crucible of the Great Awakening.[28] Intrigued as we may be by the culture of refinement and consumption, the sociability of the coffeehouse and tavern, or the ideal of an informed citizenry, it is difficult to deny the primacy of religion as the most salient aspect of American civil society. In part this is because "the contagion of liberty" that the Revolution released made the relation between church and state more problematic than it had been previously, reinforcing the pressures for disestablishment arising from sectarian dissenters with the liberal political ideas associated with Jefferson and Madison.[29] In part, too, this is because the recruitment of a multidenominational population and the difficulties these denominations faced in keeping pace with population growth and geographic expansion left conventional religious institutions hard pressed to serve the needs of American society. And perhaps most important, an emphasis on the primacy of religion is deserved because we also know how this challenge was eventually met and mastered. In the decades following the Revolution, the process that Nathan Hatch has called "the democratization of American Christianity" quickly gathered force, in turn generating what Jon Butler has described as "the antebellum spiritual hothouse."[30] Old denominations were being reformed; new sects, even new creeds, were being invented; everywhere there was deep spiritual ferment and competition for believers, driven both by the supply-side entrepreneurship of sectarian leaders and the demand-side yearnings of would-be congregants. Evangelicals who had previously been regarded as disruptive pests in many sectors of southern society were now gaining converts and adherents by the tens of thousands; Methodism was being transformed from a small scale dissenting movement into its dominant position as the largest and most dynamic of America's proliferating and prolific Protestant denominations.[31]

Yet amid all this evidence of resurgent religiosity, we also hear the rather different voice of those two Enlightened liberals whose own religious convictions remain elusive, the Sage of Monticello and the Father of the Constitution. To approach the problem of the place of religion in the civil society of the Founding era from their vantage point is (again) manifestly not to assert that their views are the most authoritative or representative, much less that they are legally binding. It merely suggests that the importance we ascribe to their beliefs and opinions should rest on something more than their iconic stature and prestige or the rhetorical advantage we gain by selective quotation and "law office history." It should instead depend on coming to grips with the deeper logic and power of their arguments, and this in turn entails understanding why both believed that republican liberty required and would be best served by securing the maximum degree of separation possible, even while tolerating, reluctantly, some deviation at the ambiguous margins of politics.

If their approach to the religion problem can be described as constituting an expression of a theory of civil society (even if merely latent or implicit), then that theory could be said to address at least these four questions:

1. the relation between the rationale for freedom of conscience and their conception of the individual as a subjective actor possessing a core realm of personality into which the authority of the state could not intrude;
2. the relation between the state's authority to support or regulate religion and the basic conception of limited government;
3. the role to be played by religion in inculcating the proper attitudes and behaviors expected of republican citizens; and
4. the relation between the free marketplace of religious opinions and the pluralist restraints on the dangers of majoritarian misrule.

Under each of these headings, Jefferson and Madison seemed to reach conclusions that arguably carried their thinking well beyond the boundaries of the conventional notions of their era—which may help explain why their positions, however controvertible, have never seemed so compelling as they do now.

If the conclusions they drew were radical, however, their philosophical point of departure lay closer to the best wisdom of the day. There can be no doubt that Jefferson and Madison grounded their commitment to freedom of conscience on the foundation laid by John Locke in his *Letter Concerning Toleration*. Jefferson's notes on his reading of the *Letter* provide an important link in the documentation illuminating the opening round of his campaign for disestablishment in Virginia in the fall of 1776.[32] As for Madison, the letters he wrote on religious questions to his college friend William Bradford after his return to Virginia in 1772 indicate how thoroughly he had absorbed the enlightened lessons he had learned at Princeton.[33] For both men, this commitment was a deeply intellectual one that originated in their education: a product of their reading and instruction, and the fact that they lived the life of the mind. But this commitment was not merely academic, for both men sought to forward it in action at the first available opportunity.

Locke's defense of toleration hinges on the recognition that the belief that is the essence of religious faith is an internal state of mind that the magistrate has neither the right to regulate nor the capacity to compel. The power of the magistrate "consists only in outward force," Locke observed, "but true and saving religion consists in the inward persuasion of the mind, without which nothing can be acceptable to God."[34] Outward conformity to religious practices might be enforced, but belief itself—most notably, the saving faith that is the essence of Christianity—is always a matter of inner conviction and persuasion that each individual must resolve for himself. Freedom of conscience is thus an inalienable natural right because it represents a property or faculty of mind that we constantly exercise and can never truly forfeit. But Locke's theory of toleration remained just that: a theory which presupposed that certain beliefs about religion entailed behavioral consequences that the state could not safely afford to tolerate. Loyalty to a foreign prince (the pope) entailed by adherence to Catholicism was one; outright atheism another (because without a belief in the rewards and penalties of an afterlife, individuals would defy the law whenever opportunity offered to do so undetected).

Jefferson and Madison did not venture beyond the philosophical foundation laid down by Locke, but they consciously and explicitly extended its political applications. Madison, the younger man, had the opportunity to act first when, as a delegate to the provincial convention in the spring of 1776, he gained approval for his amendment to the Virginia Declaration of Rights, broadening its promise "that all men should enjoy the fullest toleration" to a more expansive recognition "that all men are equally entitled to enjoy the free exercise of religion, according to the dictates of conscience."[35] Jefferson, in his own prospective (and quite distinctive) draft of a declaration of rights, had included a simpler statement affirming that "all persons shall have full and free liberty of religious opinion; nor shall any be compelled to frequent or maintain any religious institution." When he resigned his seat in Congress to enter the new House of Burgesses in the fall of 1776, he made disestablishment and broad recognition of free exercise his first cause. In his reading notes on the *Letter Concerning Toleration,* evidently prepared concurrently with these efforts, Jefferson added a wonderfully revealing comment to his summary of Locke's position: "It was a great thing to go so far (as he [Locke] himself sais of the parl[iament] who framed the act of tolern.) but where he stopped short, we may go on."[36] To "go on" meant recognizing that there was no compelling reason for the state either to support religion or to regulate its exercise—short of overt acts that also violate otherwise valid laws of society.

The distinction between toleration and free exercise marks a first step in defining the relation between the religion question and the problem of civil society, especially when we consider its significance for a general theory of constitutional rights. Freedom of conscience differs in several critical respects from the other rights that documents like the Virginia Declaration of 1776 sought to recognize (if not fully codify). With its foundation in the Lockean psychology of belief, it recognizes a core element of personality over which the state can exercise no legitimate authority whatever. In doing so, it also insists upon an equality of faculties among individuals that we would be hard pressed to extend to other realms. Considerations of gender and property, for example, certainly affect the quantum of political and legal rights that citizens can exercise; but all adults are presumed competent to judge religious truth. The commitment to freedom of conscience thus inverts the condescension that often accompanied conventional arguments for religious establishment; it denies the upper-class prejudice that the active inculcation of religious beliefs by sanctioned churches and the state was necessary primarily to imbue in the brutish lower orders the discipline and deference they would otherwise lack.[37] Most important, freedom of conscience becomes the quintessential and paradigmatic liberal right. It goes further than most of the common-law rights simultaneously recognized in the various Revolutionary-era bills of rights. Those rights—even those relating to search and seizure—do not suppose that our activities lie completely beyond the purview of public authority. They suppose only that when the state acts, it must be able to demonstrate its basis for doing so, and then must conform to some set of established norms in carrying out its lawful duties. Our homes may be our castles, but a deputy armed with a warrant has every right to search our property. Even in the realm of freedom of speech, significant qualifications of individual autonomy existed in theories of libel and sedition, not to mention the modern ambiguities introduced by the proliferation of new media. But in the realm of freedom of conscience, Jefferson and Madison were prepared to carve an absolute preserve within which the state could not interfere with the autonomy of the individual. Anyone looking for the constitutional source of a right to privacy more specific than Justice Douglas's ill-advised metaphor of "penumbras, formed by emanations" from the Bill of Rights need search no further than the concept of free exercise as it was stated in its most expansive terms.

The corollary to this conception of a realm of rightful thought and behavior immune from public regulation was a new definition of limited government. When Jefferson and Madison first made common cause (and personal acquaintance) in pursuit of their solution to the religion problem in 1776, the prevailing idea of limited government was associated with the concept of the balanced constitution, as famously celebrated by Montesquieu in his description of the eighteenth-century British constitution. Limitation implied procedural and institutional restraints on the arbitrary exercise of the power of government rather than a formal delineation of the activities that government could and could not regulate. Two circumstances militated against the idea that the powers of government could in fact be subject to formal limitation. One was the principle of legislative supremacy against which the American colonists found themselves contending when they disputed Parliament's authority to legislate for them "in all cases whatsoever." The other was the absence, before 1776, of the critical conceptual innovation that set American constitutionalism on its distinctive course: that of a written constitution as supreme fundamental law, delegating powers to government and thereby (perhaps) specifying what it could and could not do. But the clearest specification of that concept came not in 1776 but a decade later, when the legislative powers vested in Congress took the form of the enumeration of Article I, Section 8, to be reinforced, with the ratification of the Tenth Amendment, with the truism reminding readers that powers not delegated to the Union were reserved to the states or the people. In 1776, however, the concept of legislative supremacy derived from the precedent of Parliament made it difficult to identify realms of behavior that the plenary lawmaking power of the state legislatures could not reach. Americans might not, in practice, have great expectations that their governments would do much; and arguments were already available—in the political economy of Adam Smith, and the anti-improvement mentality of Mandeville—to explain why governments indeed should not do much. But what area of behavior lay beyond the potential reach of legislation? Not the economy, for no one could dispute that governments could regulate markets in any of a number of ways. Not the family, for it, too, was subject to a variety of regulations and obligations. Not the community, for local governments were the real administrative agencies of the provincial governments. Not the workhouse or the poorhouse or the turnpike or canal, for all were organized as quasi-public activities needing and meriting public promotion.

To pursue a thorough, root-and-branch policy of disestablishment thus marked the first instantiation of the principle that the creation of a limited government might involve something more than the pursuit of balance and accountability. Disestablishment involved identifying an entire realm of behavior that could be safely removed from the jurisdiction of government. Nor was this a trivial concession or limitation. For any sensible observer, reflecting on the troubled history of post-Reformation Europe, would have to conclude that the state could not prudently or completely abjure its responsibility and authority to police religious matters, or even to use religious institutions as an extension of state policies. That, after all, was also part of the Lockean logic that recognized the limits of the state's power to monitor without renouncing the idea that some beliefs need not be tolerated. To say that government could simply get out of the religion business, making both matters of belief and membership in particular religious communities completely voluntary decisions, thus marked a radical step in converting the general principle of limited government into a significant reduction of the domain in which government could operate. An entire, vital realm of behavior could, in effect, be removed from the agenda of public regulation, left free to operate entirely in private, under the control not of the state but of the autonomous choices of free-thinking individuals.

Here, then, lay a second dimension in which the program of disestablishment contributed to a theory of civil society by demonstrating how the sphere of government power could be contracted. But that in turn implicated at least two further questions. If government did evacuate the religion business, might that not redound to its own disadvantage by depriving the people of moral resources they required to act as virtuous republican citizens? And was it really wise to allow unregulated denominations to compete with one another, given the terrible history of persecutions that still burned bright in the historic memory?

The common answer to the first question would in fact advise "caution," as President Washington observed in farewell, in "indulg[ing] the supposition, that morality can be maintained without religion." Washington went no further in this pursuit than to issue two proclamations for loosely observed days of thanksgiving.[38] But of course the same sentiment appears in the Massachusetts Constitution of 1780 and the Northwest Ordinance, and it was manifested, with far greater import, in the casual interweaving of religion and education in the schools of the early republic. But was this a view with which Jefferson and Madison were sympathetic, or did their historically derived fears about the excesses of religiosity outweigh their hopes for its benefits?

One of the editors of this book has recently implied that Madison, at least, was somewhat more amenable to the latter possibility than Jefferson, but this, too, is a view to be indulged with some caution.[39] One of Madison's critical papers, the memorandum on the "vices of the political system of the U. States," which framed his agenda for the Constitutional Convention, took a rather different view. Here, in the precursor to *Federalist* 10, Madison asked whether religion might operate as one of three possible restraints upon the common propensity of popular majorities to commit "unjust violations of the rights and interests of the minority, or of individuals." His answer was somewhat less than upbeat.

It is not pretended to be such on men individually considered. Will its effect be greater on them considered in an aggregate view? The conduct of every popular assembly acting on oath, the strongest of religious Ties, proves that individuals join without remorse in acts, against which their consciences would revolt if proposed to them under the like sanction, separately in their closets. When indeed Religion is kindled into enthusiasm, its force like that of other passions, is increased by the sympathy of a multitude. But enthusiasm is only a temporary state of religion, and while it lasts will hardly be seen with pleasure at the helm of Government. Besides as religion in its coolest state, is not infallible, it may become a motive to oppression as well as a restraint from injustice.[40]

It takes quite a leap of imagination to read this passage as an endorsement of the value of religion as a source of civic virtue. Religion here is only another of the "opinions," "passions," and "interests" which constituted the triple threats of mischievous factionalism whose cure Madison sought. It is true, as Joseph Viteritti further observes, that Madison believed that the vitality of religion could act as an essential source of the social pluralism required to provide a republican cure for the "mischief of faction." Indeed, Madison was more optimistic about the capacity of free-thinking Christians (and members of other faiths) to fruitfully multiply their doctrinal differences than he was about the comparable likelihood that the course of economic development would produce similar degrees of liberty-enhancing diversity. Yet Madison also understood that religion would produce these beneficent effects simply by being left to its own disputatious devices, as the faithful disagreed about the best road to salvation, the meaning of the sacraments, the proper organization of a church, and other arcane questions. And it was this understanding that sustained his confidence that the withdrawal of all public support for religion would redound to the advantage of church and state alike.

The case of Jefferson is more complicated. His aversion to priestcraft and organized religion notwithstanding, Jefferson certainly believed in the importance of cultivating a moral sense in the citizens.[41] And like Lincoln, he did not allow his own doubts about the truth of revealed religion to prevent him from appealing to the Christian sensibilities of his countrymen. That, after all, was the clear intent of the famous passage in query 18 of his *Notes on the State of Virginia*, where he reminded his countrymen of the divine justice that may deservedly befall them should they allow slavery to continue. "And can the liberties of a nation be thought secure when we have removed their only firm basis, a conviction in the minds of the people that these liberties are of the gift of God?" Jefferson asked. This query might be read narrowly to suggest that religious conviction is only instrumentally useful insofar as it promotes popular, not elite virtue. Yet so skeptically secular a reading seems unduly cynical. As Thomas Buckley has argued, Jefferson did articulate a "political theology" — but one that could operate independently of the particular beliefs of any one creed: "He was convinced that for all important purposes, religion is reducible to morality, and that the morality taught by all religious groups or churches is essentially the same." Individual churches might assert the superiority of their moral teaching, and individuals might choose their church on the basis of those claims, but these differences could be regarded, politically, as matters of indifference so long as they conduced to the same end and left the peace of the commonwealth undisturbed.[42]

Even so, there is no reason to think that either Jefferson or Madison believed that formal religious instruction should be part of any program of education at any level of instruction. They assumed that individuals would come to their religious convictions or doubts on their own, either by accepting the beliefs of their family and community or by acquiring the means to question them. In his commentary on his ill-fated bill for promoting the "general diffusion of knowledge" by creating a statewide system of public schools, Jefferson explicitly advised against "putting the Bible and Testament into the hands of the children, at an age when their judgments are not sufficiently matured for religious enquiries," preferring instead that their education for citizenship begin with history and languages.[43] The implication seems to be that the inculcation of religious knowledge is dangerous until and unless individuals have acquired the faculties to engage in "religious enquiries" which presumably involve thinking critically about the claims made by religion, perhaps the better to separate the genuine sparks of moral knowledge from the husks of quarrelsome denominationalism. Much later Madison, who had certainly absorbed a great deal of divinity in his own youth, took a similarly secular approach in his most extended commentary on education, endorsing an expansive system of public schools for Kentucky modeled on Jefferson's bill. Here, again, any reference to religious instruction, even in the form of Bible reading, is conspicuous by its absence.[44] And again, as is well known, both men labored hard in their joint efforts in founding the University of Virginia to make sure that the education it provided would be wholly secular. Better to "incur for a time at least, the imputation of irreligious tendencies, if not designs," Madison observed in 1822, than to risk the greater "difficulty" that would occur by either privileging one sectarian professorship of divinity or creating "an Arena of Theological Gladiators" by establishing "professorships of rival sects."[45]

Collaboration on the founding of the University of Virginia was the last great project that Jefferson and Madison shared in their retirement.[46] They were not similarly committed, however, to the other half of the educational scheme that Jefferson had sketched in his Bill for the More General Diffusion of Knowledge, drafted back in the late 1770s. Under its terms, the entire state was to be divided into neighborly "hundreds," with a schoolhouse to be constructed in each, where "all the free children, male and female, resident within the hundred, shall be intitled to receive tuition gratis" for three years, with further education permitted at private expense. In the preamble to this bill, Jefferson justified this scheme with a frankly republican agenda: to guard against the danger of tyranny, the mass of the citizenry had to be taught enough history to be able to recognize "ambition under all its shapes" and thus "to exert their natural powers to defeat its purposes" should tyranny ever raise its head. This bill anticipated the mass education plans of the coming century, but it differed from them in one critical respect. For the deeper guiding animus of Jefferson's bill was the education not of citizens at large but of their leaders, to be culled from the mass without regard to class but also through a ruthless winnowing that would make the rigorous testing systems of most modern industrial democracies seem tame by comparison. In Jefferson's scheme of promotion, only one student from each hundred would be graduated to the next level of multicounty grammar schools, from which in turn one-third of the students would be eliminated after the first year and all but one survivor from the remaining two-thirds after two years. "By this means twenty of the best geniuses will be raked from the rubbish annually," Jefferson observed, in another of his catchy phrases, and after six years of grammar school half of these would go on to the College of William and Mary.[47] All this was visionary, of course. After it became evident that a parsimonious legislature dominated by the planter elite would never adopt such a proposal, Jefferson turned his attention to the problem of establishing a university whose students would be largely drawn from his own social class. But neither there nor in the abandoned idea of public schools would religious instruction be allowed, much less regarded as an essential element of an education.

If religion was thus to serve as a foundation for republican citizenship and leadership, it was not because the state should take any active agency in its promotion. Jefferson and Madison could easily have assumed, even desired, that the striving for religious truth and conviction would remain an essential source of the moral compass that Americans would individually seek and ideally find—and thus, a key constitutive element of civil society. But that quest should remain a private, individual one, neither supported nor regulated by a state that had no capacity to judge which path was best. The key objection militating against this position would, of course, be that religion was too essential to the welfare of the commonwealth to be left on its own, to flourish or wither at the sufferance of its voluntary adherents. Yet this was exactly the countervailing contention to which the two Virginians refused to yield.

Here it was Madison, I think, who better grasped the unique implications and consequences that the commitment to disestablishment would have for the constitution of American civil society. In part, this was because he predicated his general solution to the overarching problem of "curing the mischief of faction" on the empirical evidence that the existing multiplicity of sects had already promoted the general security of religious liberty that he now hoped to advance in an even more principled and consistent way. As the classic formulation of *Federalist* 51 asserts: "In a free government, the security for civil rights must be the same as that for religious rights. It consists in the one case in the multiplicity of interests, and in the other, in the multiplicity of sects."[48] Such diversity (within reasonable limits) would prevent any one faction or narrowly drawn coalition from dominating government, using its power to impose policies inimical to the just rights and interests of the minority.

But while Madison regarded religion as a paradigmatic example of the benefits of diversity to liberty, he also had reason to think that protecting rights of conscience might prove easier than protecting rights of property, his other great area of concern. In the realm of religion, the recognition of freedom of conscience as a natural and constitutional right and the rigid application of the principle of disestablishment would have the joint effect of preventing government from acting at all. Left alone to dispute the best road to salvation, the proper organization of the church, the number and mystery of the sacraments, and the proper reading of Scripture, Madison could reasonably predict that American Protestants—and Catholics, should they appear in significant numbers, or even non-Christians—would fruitfully multiply their disagreements, preserving and even enlarging the number of sects required to maintain freedom of religion. By contrast, he was privately less optimistic that rights of property would benefit in the same way. In part, this was because he worried that future decades would widen the gap between the propertied and unpropertied classes without creating sufficient diversity in the rival economic interests. Equally important, Madison understood that government could not abdicate its responsibility to act in the economic realm in the same way that it could in the religious. "The regulation of these various and interfering interests" that constituted the economies of all modern society, he observed in *Federalist* 10, "forms the principal task of modern legislation, and involves the spirit of party and faction in the necessary and ordinary operations of government." And as he then went on to offer examples of the different ways in which all governments unavoidably engaged in acts of economic legislation, he demonstrated that the simple solution promised by disestablishment could never wholly apply in this other realm.[49]

It was one of the great intellectual satisfactions of Madison's twenty years of retirement that he could observe how correct his approach to the religion problem had been. Unlike Jefferson, who hoped that the progress of religious discussion would produce increasing numbers of rational deists like himself—unitarians who would read Scripture for moral truth but treat miracles and revelations as something akin to fables—and who therefore looked on the evangelical upsurge with some dismay, Madison took comfort in its confirmation of his original position. Look, he told inquiring correspondents: we'd been warned back in the 1770s and 1780s of the ills that religion would suffer if we pushed disestablishment too far, but events have proved us right and our critics wrong. "Every relaxation of the alliance between Law & religion," he wrote Edward Everett in 1823, "has been found as safe in practice as it is sound in theory. . . . And no doubt exists that there is much more of religion among us now than there ever was before the change; and particularly in the Sect which enjoyed the legal patronage [the Episcopalian, formerly Anglican Church]. This proves rather more than, that the law is necessary to the support of religion."[50] What it proved, in fact, was that religion would never fare better than when it was completely privatized, deregulated, and left open to the marketplace competition that flourished after 1800. There was no observable difference between the state of religiosity in New England, where an attenuated establishment still survived in Massachusetts and had only just been eliminated in Connecticut, and in his own state of Virginia or others.

There is a terrific, not to say delicious, irony in casting the Madisonian solution in these terms. On the religion question, Madison was a veritable Milton Friedman, skeptical of the rationale for public regulation and subsidies, confident in the capacity of consumers to choose, and justified in thinking that competition in the spiritual marketplace would reduce the transactions costs that would otherwise arise if dissatisfied truth seekers had to struggle against official monopolies to find more efficacious paths to salvation. And to judge by the results, that market-oriented approach offers the best explanation for the remarkable success of the American experiment in religious pluralism. The distinctively Protestant character of nineteenth-century American civil society should be seen, that is, as something more than a natural or foreseeable by-product of the dissenting origins of the American population. It drew its strength as well from the pronounced spur to competition that the Virginia program encouraged. Privatization (in the form of free exercise) and deregulation (in the form of disestablishment) created what was, in effect, an active market for salvation, as sects sought their own niches as they competed for adherents while anxious adherents actively compared the spiritual wares offered.

The greatest contribution the Sage of Monticello and the Father of the Constitution made to the creation of American civil society, then, was to articulate a principled basis for abjuring public regulation of religion, thereby helping to establish a completely privatized marketplace in which a variety of denominations, sects, and cults were forced to innovate and compete to gain adherents from a population whose religious convictions and allegiances were entirely voluntary.

I have suggested that the "high-wall" interpretation of Jefferson's and Madison's writings does far greater justice to the underlying consistencies and continuities in their beliefs than other attempts to identify ambiguities and exceptions that might be cited in support of various policies of accommodation. The basic point could be belabored with other arguments not developed in this essay, and supported with recourse to additional scholarly authorities.[51] Next to these and other data, the usual candidates rounded up to suggest temporizing and inconsistency on the part of Jefferson and Madison seem distinctly secondary in importance. One simply cannot equate the nod to religion suggested in the odd fast day or Indian treaty with the more extensive evidence of their deep and principled opposition to entanglement. Similarly, evidence that the two men continued to confront the practical difficulty of maintaining a rigid separation in all cases does not obviate the greater importance of understanding how early in life they came to their separationist convictions and how quickly they sought to act on them when opportunity first offered. To my mind, the effort to co-opt the two Virginians as compliant authorities for lowering the high wall or opening some portals across it represents a textbook case of missing the forest for the trees; and that is the conclusion that most historians, examining the record without an eye on our contemporary debates, would probably reach.

There are, I believe, three principal reasons why it is important to come to grips with the extent of their desire to keep church and state as separate as they possibly could. The first and most obvious is that it provides a more accurate and comprehensive account of their position than casual exercises in selective quotation would otherwise do. Second, it enables us to understand why the religion question loomed so large in their political and constitutional thinking; why it was not simply another problem to be tackled but a matter of critical importance. Third, only by coming to grips with the nature and extent of their concern about religion can we ask how, why, and whether their views should still have any significance. We might well conclude, after two centuries of our constitutional experiment, that the sources of their anxieties need no longer trouble us today, and that we can afford to lower the high wall without jeopardizing anyone's rights of conscience or creating a corrupting entanglement between church and state. Or we might look at the revival of religious enthusiasms around the world, including the United States, and conclude that a high wall still offers the best security against the misuse of public power in the cause of intolerance. In either case, our thinking will be sharpened if we struggle with the reasons why Jefferson and Madison were so eager to tackle the religion problem with a new militance.

In wrestling with this challenging legacy, we should keep two further points in mind. The first involves asking why Jefferson and Madison were so intent on finding a definitive solution to the religion problem. To answer this question, it might be useful to draw a more modern analogy. For enlightened thinkers of their stamp, the religion question occupied a position similar to that of the race question in mid-twentieth-century America. In their world, memories of the persecution of religious dissenters in the sixteenth and seventeenth centuries seemed to provide the same textbook examples of arbitrary power and injustice as came to be perceived after 1950 in the imposition of racial hierarchies under the regimes of slavery and segregation. It had become, for them, a matter of fundamental principle, brooking no compromise, in much the same way that the root-and-branch elimination of legal discrimination became the lodestar of American liberalism in the late twentieth century.

Second, and arguably more important, we might benefit from understanding that Jefferson and Madison attempted to wield the principles of free exercise and disestablishment as a sort of Ockham's Razor, minimizing at every turn the possibility that the spheres of church and state would overlap. The great advantage of such an approach, of course, is that it promises to provide an escape from the observed morass into which the modern jurisprudence of separation has fallen. If one could safely predict any one criticism that either man might make of the muddled state of current judicial doctrine, it is that its painfully drawn distinctions only confirm the wisdom, or at least the economy, of the commitment to separation they espoused. Unlike Professor Viteritti, I doubt very much that Madison or Jefferson would be troubled by a doctrine denying "religious institutions or those individuals who associate with them" the enjoyment of "public benefits that are provided by the government on a universal basis."[52] The whole tenor of their thought pointed in exactly the opposite direction. The simplest way to avoid the confusion and contention that would arise from placing government in a position where institutions and individuals expected its support in connection with activities having a strongly religious component was to prevent any such support from being given.[53]

Would Madison or Jefferson hold to these convictions if they had the same evidence on which we have to act—not only of the continued vitality of disestablished American religiosity but also of the urgent concerns that underlie the contemporary case for school choice and vouchers, made with the sometimes tacit, sometimes explicit recognition that most of the schools that stand to benefit from such a policy would have avowedly religious affiliations? Arguably, other elements in their political and social theories might incline the two Virginians—could they be transported to our own time—to modify their aversion to religious establishment in the interest of securing other legitimate ends. Jefferson, after all, was no friend to the capacity of the state to exercise monopolistic powers or grant monopolistic privileges; and many advocates of school choice can plausibly argue that the edifice of public education, resting as it does on the coercive authority of the bureaucratic state and the support of politically powerful teachers' unions, depends on the enjoyment of a quasi-monopolistic privilege. Or again, Madison's distinctive commitment to the protection of minority rights—especially the rights of religious dissenters—might incline him to accept the value of policies that would enable citizens possessing deep religious convictions to escape the tyranny of a secular humanism that is often perceived (or at least alleged) to be hostile to such beliefs. When Madison introduced the proposal that eventually became the Second Amendment, he included a provision affirming that "no person religiously scrupulous of bearing arms, shall be compelled to render military service in person"; presumably one could infer from this principle a similar right to be exempt from the conscientiously obnoxious educational activities of a militantly secular state.[54]

Of course, securing exemption from the coercive and monopolistic authority of the state is one thing; actively requiring the state to support the educational establishments of religiously imbued minorities is another (and easily distinguished) matter entirely. If the problem is posed in these terms, the best case to be made for school choice and vouchers—especially if predicated on the recognition that our private schools remain preponderantly religious in nature—would rely not on a low-wall, broadly accommodationist reading of the Religion Clauses, but rather on an expansive interpretation of the Equal Protection Clause of the Fourteenth Amendment. Such an ordering of the relevant clauses might well be possible as a matter of constitutional interpretation, and if the two Virginians were allowed to reason instrumentally, on the basis of the same empirical evidence available to us, they might well conclude that the demands of equal citizenship and the crisis of public education leave no viable alternative to a program of school choice and public vouchers. If, however, they were allowed or required to judge solely on the basis of their original convictions, it seems far more likely that their principled desire to preserve the high wall of separation would still trump the countervailing claims made in the name of free exercise or equal protection.[55] That was what the lessons of history had taught them.

But the choice, after all, is ours, not theirs, and in making it, we have to ask whether and why their views should matter to us. Answering that question may, in fact, pose a more difficult challenge than simply attempting to recover the sources of their original militance on the religion problem.

NOTES

1. Alexis de Tocqueville, *Democracy in America,* ed. Phillips Bradley (New York: Alfred Knopf, 1945), 1: 112–25.
2. See the valuable essay in intellectual history by the late Paul Bourke, "The Pluralist Reading of James Madison's Tenth Federalist," *Perspectives in American History* 10 (1975).
3. The extent of this contrast is nicely illustrated in Joyce Appleby, *Inheriting the Revolution: The First Generation of Americans* (Cambridge: Harvard University Press, 2000).
4. Merrill Peterson, ed., *Thomas Jefferson: Writings* (New York: Library of America, 1984), 346–48, 283–87, 510. For the latest round of interpretation of the Danbury letter, occasioned by an FBI analysis of its blotted lines, see the forum conducted in the *William and Mary Quarterly,* 3d ser., 56 (1999), with contributions by James H. Hutson, Robert M. O'Neil, Thomas E. Buckley, S.J., Edwin Gaustad, Isaac Kramnick, and R. Laurence Moore. Jack N. Rakove, ed., *James Madison: Writings* (New York: Library of America, 1999), 29–36, 759–66.
5. *Rosenberger v. Rector and Visitors of the University of Virginia,* 115 S. Ct. 2510 (1995). I have benefited from discussions of the current state of religion clause jurisprudence in Kathleen M. Sullivan, "Parades, Public Squares, and Voucher Payments: Problems of Government Neutrality," *Connecticut Law Review* 28 (1996); and Jesse H. Choper, "Federal Constitutional Issues," in Stephen D. Sugarman and Frank R. Kemerer, eds., *School*

Choice and Social Controversy: Politics, Policy, and Law (Washington: Brookings Institution Press, 1999).

6. On this point see Stephen Botein, "Religious Dimensions of the Early American State," in Richard Beeman et al., eds., *Beyond Confederation: Origins of the Constitution and American National Identity* (Chapel Hill: University of North Carolina Press, 1987); Peter S. Onuf, "State Politics and Republican Virtue: Religion, Education, and Morality in Early American Federalism," in Paul Finkelman and Stephen E. Gottlieb, eds., *Toward a Usable Past: Liberty Under State Constitutions* (Athens: University of Georgia Press, 1991); and Thomas James, "Rights of Conscience and State School Systems in Nineteenth-Century America," in Finkelman and Gottlieb, *Toward a Usable Past.*

7. As readers of my writings on constitutional originalism will know, I have serious doubts about both the feasibility of originalism as a method of constitutional interpretation and the normative theory on which it rests. At the same time, I think the historian's task when such issues arise is to provide the best account possible of how and why particular ideas, concerns, and debates shaped the relevant constitutional language. See Jack N. Rakove, *Original Meanings: Politics and Ideas in the Making of the Constitution* (New York: Alfred Knopf, 1996), xv and n., 3–22.

8. John Ehrenberg, *Civil Society: The Critical History of an Idea* (New York: New York University Press, 1999), 97. For a wonderful essay linking Smith and other authors of 1776 to the crisis of American independence, see Bernard Bailyn, "1776: A Year of Challenge—A World Transformed," in *Faces of Revolution: Personalities and Themes in the Struggle for American Independence* (New York: Knopf, 1990).

9. Richard L. Bushman, *The Refinement of America: Persons, Houses, Cities* (New York: Knopf, 1992).

10. Bernard Bailyn, *The Ideological Origins of the American Revolution* (enlarged ed., Cambridge: Harvard University Press, 1992); John P. Reid, *The Concept of Liberty in the Age of the American Revolution* (Chicago: University of Chicago Press, 1988).

11. Jenny Uglow, *Hogarth: A Life and a World* (New York: Farrar, Straus, Giroux, 1997), discussing Hogarth's painting *The Gate of Calais* (1749), also known as *O the Roast Beef of England.*

12. For further discussion, see Rakove, *Original Meanings,* 209–14, 297–302.

13. Tocqueville, *Democracy in America,* 1: 70.

14. Quotation from Richard D. Brown, *The Strength of a People: The Idea of an Informed Citizenry in America, 1650–1870* (Chapel Hill: University of North Carolina Press, 1996); for a shorter statement of main arguments, see Richard D. Brown, "The Idea of an Informed Citizenry in the Early Republic," in David T. Konig, ed., *Devising Liberty: Preserving and Creating Freedom in the New American Republic* (Stanford: Stanford University Press, 1995). Other essays in *Devising Liberty* would be useful to framing an inductive general account of American ideas about civil society, but in ways that go beyond the parameters of this book.

15. Ibid., 146–57.

16. Two recent books offer interesting insights into particular sites of civil society in eighteenth-century America: Peter Thompson, *Rum, Punch, and Revolution: Taverngoing and Public Life in Eighteenth-Century Philadelphia* (Philadelphia: University of Pennsyl-

vania Press, 1999); and David S. Shields, *Civil Tongues and Polite Letters in British America* (Chapel Hill: University of North Carolina Press, 1997).

17. Brown, *Strength of a People,* 64–65.

18. The advent of American republicanism and its relation to liberalism have been dominant themes in the historiography of the past generation, beginning principally with the epochal work of Gordon S. Wood, *The Creation of the American Republic, 1776–1787* (Chapel Hill: University of North Carolina Press, 1969). A useful critical introduction to the enormous literature on this subject is Daniel Rodgers, "Republicanism: The Career of a Concept," *Journal of American History* 79 (1992).

19. On these general themes, see Gordon S. Wood, *The Radicalism of the American Revolution* (New York: Knopf, 1992); Alan S. Taylor, *Liberty Men and Great Proprietors: The Revolutionary Settlement on the Maine Frontier, 1760–1820* (Chapel Hill: University of North Carolina Press, 1990); and Charles Royster, *The Fabulous History of the Dismal Swamp Company: A Story of George Washington's Times* (New York: Knopf, 1999).

20. Brown, *Strength of a People,* 66–84.

21. This, of course, was the theme of Bernard Bailyn's pathbreaking essay in educational history, *Education and the Forming of American Society: Needs and Opportunities for Study* (Chapel Hill: University of North Carolina Press, 1960).

22. See especially Linda Kerber, *Women of the Republic: Intellect and Ideology in Revolutionary America* (Chapel Hill: University of North Carolina Press, 1980).

23. Bernard Bailyn and John Hench, eds., *The Press and the American Revolution* (Worcester: American Antiquarian Society, 1980); Leonard Levy, *The Emergence of a Free Press* (New York: Oxford University Press, 1985); Richard John, *Spreading the News: The American Postal System from Franklin to Morse* (Cambridge: Harvard University Press, 1996).

24. Brown, *Strength of a People,* 83.

25. Article 41 provided "that a school or schools shall be established by the legislature, for the convenient instruction of youth, with such salaries to the masters, paid by the public, as may enable them to instruct at low prices; and, all useful learning, shall be duly encouraged and promoted in one or more universities"; quoted in Brown, *Strength of a People,* 141.

26. Brown, *Strength of a People,* 98–103.

27. Appleby, *Inheriting the Revolution,* 103–4.

28. Richard Hofstadter, *America at 1750: A Social Portrait* (New York: Knopf, 1971), 293.

29. The quotation is the title of the sixth and (originally) concluding chapter of Bailyn, *Ideological Origins.*

30. Nathan Hatch, *The Democratization of American Christianity* (New Haven: Yale University Press, 1989); Jon Butler, *Awash in a Sea of Faith: Christianizing the American People* (Cambridge: Harvard University Press, 1990), 225–88.

31. On the disruptive nature of early evangelicalism, see Christine Heyrman, *Southern Cross: The Beginnings of the Bible Belt* (New York: Knopf, 1997).

32. Notes on Locke and Shaftesbury [1776], in Julian P. Boyd, ed., *The Papers of Thomas Jefferson* (Princeton: Princeton University Press, 1950–), 1: 544–50; Thomas Buckley, S.J., "The Political Theology of Thomas Jefferson," in Merrill D. Peterson and

Robert C. Vaughan, *The Virginia Statute for Religious Freedom: Its Evolution and Consequences in American History* (New York: Cambridge University Press, 1988), 84–89.

33. Madison to William Bradford, Jan. 24 and April 1, 1774, in Rakove, *Madison: Writings,* 7; Lance Banning, "James Madison, the Statute for Religious Freedom, and the Crisis of Republican Convictions," in Peterson and Vaughan, *Virginia Statute,* 110–12, 131n9.

34. John Locke, *A Letter Concerning Toleration* (1689), excerpt in Philip Kurland and Ralph Lerner, eds., *The Founders' Constitution* (Chicago: University of Chicago Press, 1987), 5: 53.

35. For the earlier draft see Jack N. Rakove, *Declaring Rights: A Brief History with Documents* (Boston: Bedford, 1997), 84; for the amendment as proposed by Madison and subsequently approved, with revisions, by the convention, see Rakove, *Madison: Writings,* 10. It is worth noting that the final version of Article 18 did reserve a regulatory power to the magistrate when "the preservation of equal liberty and the existence of the State are manifestly endangered."

36. Boyd, *Papers of Jefferson,* 1: 363, 548.

37. Onuf, "State Politics and Republican Virtue," 99–100.

38. Farewell Address, Sept. 19, 1796, in Kurland and Lerner, *Founders' Constitution,* 1: 684; Botein, "Religious Dimensions," 323–24.

39. After alluding to Washington's support for the General Assessment bill of 1785 on the grounds that it would aid government, and not only the churches, Joseph Viteritti intimates that "Madison was also sympathetic to the republican idea that religion could serve as a positive political and social force." Joseph P. Viteritti, *Choosing Equality: School Choice, the Constitution, and Civil Society* (Washington: Brookings Institution Press, 1999), 124. Although the implication seems to be that Madison saw religion as a source of individual political virtue, the supporting analysis returns to the rather different point about the advantages of a multiplicity of sects, as formulated in *Federalist* 10 and 51. That is, whether or not particular sects, denominations, or faiths actually inculcate in their members traits and attitudes conducive to democratic citizenship, the republic as a whole benefits from their proliferation.

40. Rakove, *Madison: Writings,* 76–78; the other restraints were "a prudent regard to their own good as involved in the general and permanent good of the Community," and "respect for character." Reiterating the point for Jefferson six months later, Madison revised this last sentence to suggest that religion "has been much oftener a motive to oppression than a restraint from it." Madison to Jefferson, Oct. 24, 1787, ibid., 151.

41. For an extended treatment of this entire question, see Jean Yarbrough, *American Virtues: Thomas Jefferson on the Character of a Free People* (Lawrence: University Press of Kansas, 1998).

42. Buckley, "Political Theology," 89–90. But cf. Jefferson's letter to John Adams of Oct. 12, 1813, which seems to quote approvingly a dismissal of Jewish law as so much "wretched depravity" by way of introducing the "pure principles" of morality propounded by Jesus, which, however, would have to be extracted from "the artificial vestments in which they have been muffled by priests." Peterson, *Jefferson: Writings,* 1300–1301.

43. Jefferson, *Notes on the State of Virginia,* in Peterson, *Jefferson: Writings,* 273; for the bill, see ibid., 365–73.

44. Madison to William T. Barry, Aug. 4, 1822, in Rakove, ed., *Madison: Writings,* 790–94.

45. Madison to Edward Everett, March 19, 1823, ibid., 795.

46. Their collaboration in this project can be traced in the concluding chapters of James Morton Smith, ed., *The Republic of Letters: The Correspondence Between Thomas Jefferson and James Madison, 1776–1826* (New York: Norton, 1995), vol. 3.

47. Jefferson discussed his scheme in query 14 of the *Notes on the State of Virginia,* in Peterson, *Jefferson: Writings,* 272.

48. Rakove, *Madison: Writings,* 297.

49. *Federalist* 10, ibid., 162–63. For further discussion, see Rakove, *Original Meanings,* 310–16.

50. Madison to Edward Everett, March 19, 1823, Rakove, *Madison: Writings,* 796.

51. For example, Madison's *Memorial and Remonstrance* of 1785 really does seem to be aimed at the eighteenth-century equivalent of nonpreferentialism. The refusal of Presidents Jefferson and Madison to permit Sunday mail delivery does seem to imply a fairly rigid, high-wall view of the Establishment Clause. For further historical argumentation, see Leonard Levy, *The Establishment Clause: Religion and the First Amendment* (New York: Macmillan, 1986); Isaac Kramnick and R. Laurence Moore, *The Godless Constitution: The Case Against Religious Correctness* (New York: Norton, 1996).

52. Viteritti, *Choosing Equality,* 126.

53. Anyone naive enough to think that such a razor could indeed be successfully wielded would be advised to read Steven D. Smith, *Foreordained Failure: The Quest for a Constitutional Principle of Religious Freedom* (New York: Oxford University Press, 1995), though Smith, in his skepticism about the consequences of judicial attempts to enforce religious liberty, bares a sharp blade of his own.

54. Speech of June 8, 1789, in Rakove, *Madison: Writings,* 442.

55. For brief but intriguing further discussion, emphasizing the stringency of Madison's views while suggesting a subtle difference between his position and Jefferson's, see David P. Currie, "God and Caesar and President Madison," *Green Bag,* 2d ser., 3 (1999).

Chapter 11 Civil Society, Religion, and the Formation of Citizens

Jean Bethke Elshtain

Civil society is on the tips of our tongues nowadays whenever the question arises of how well democratic societies, whether old or new, are faring. That this is so is perhaps unsurprising. For we seem to have arrived at a point of recognition of an old truth—namely, that neither markets nor states suffice to order a decent way of life in common. So if we ask: Why civil society? Why now?—we are drawn, first, to a consideration of civil society as a concept with a long and uneven history. For the political philosopher Georg Wilhelm Friedrich Hegel, for example, civil society was a realm of competition and contract whose divisions would be healed over when the citizen entered that most universal of all ethical realms, the state.[1] In the Hegelian scheme of things, civil society is a higher realm than that of individuals and families but lower in the sociopolitical and ethical system than that more complete and perfect entity, the state.[2] This way of talking about civil society is not what those claiming the term for contemporary political debate have in mind, however. For contemporary advocates of civil society, *civil society* signifies a sphere of associational life that is "more" than families, yes, but it is also other than states or government. This is precisely one of its virtues rather than a defect or an inadequacy. The state in this latter scheme exists not to transcend civil society but, rather, to serve it.

What, exactly, is being served? A variety of plural associations, the many forms of social life that dot the landscape of well-functioning democratic cultures, from families to churches to neighborhood groups. Civil society encompasses labor organizations, professional associations, and voluntary civic associations of many kinds. Political parties are also part of this picture. This network lies outside the formal structure of state power. Observers of democracy have long recognized the importance of civil society thus understood. Some have spoken of "mediating institutions" that lie between the individual and the government or state. These mediating institutions locate each of us in a number of little estates, so to speak, which are themselves nested within wider, overlapping frameworks of sustaining and supporting institutions.

Perhaps one might think of this as a densely textured social ecology. For civil society is a realm that is neither individualist nor collectivist. It partakes of both the "I" and the "we." One aim of maintaining a robust civil society is to forestall concentrations of power at the top or at the core. A second lies in the recognition that only many small-scale civic bodies enable citizens to cultivate democratic civic virtues and to play an active role in civil life. Such participation turns on meaningful involvement in some decent form of community, by which is meant commitments and ties that locate the citizen in bonds of trust, reciprocity, and civic competence.

Embedded in the civil society framework is a recognition that our social and political worlds are enormously complex and that they emerge and take shape concretely over time in and through institutions. No social engineer can "design" a civil society. No linear model can explain one. Civil society is a repository of generations of human actions and reactions to a material and moral environment. A sturdy yet supple civil society embodies the decocted wisdom of the ages yet remains open to new insights and challenges. A civil society is a system, but it is an open system. If environmental thinkers have shown us how the cumulative effect of misuse of an environment can, at one point, be more than a natural ecology can bear, so civil society analysts argue along much the same lines. They call upon us to evaluate the ways in which depletion and misuse of civil and moral resources can have debilitating, perhaps at one point even catastrophic effects.

Thus, for example, the cumulative effect of thousands upon thousands of individual "choices" may redound to the benefit or disadvantage of a community as a whole. If I live in a culture that encourages almost unlimited consumption, perhaps no single act of my consumption will be seen as harmful in a direct way to others. But hundreds of thousands of persons choosing unwisely, in a way that encourages or even comes to require what Pope John Paul II labels as a culture of overconsumption and "super-development," promotes corrosive results over time.[3] Eventually, we may even relinquish our developed capacities—at least we hope that such capacities, through education, have developed—to choose wisely and well. For our great gift and responsibility of moral autonomy and free will may atrophy if we reduce human freedom to a selection from among a vast array of consumer choices in a world in which individual goods triumph and the notion of a common good is rejected or lost.

The increasingly atomized culture of late modernity—or so civil society advocates with a specifically ethical and religious orientation insist—pushes us in this harmful direction as human beings are cut off from the saving grace and presence of their fellow human beings. We come to see ourselves as independent in all things. Others are there for us to use, much as we make use of tools in our environment. We ignore or even refuse to acknowledge those complex interdependencies that help to sustain and even to create our own individual identities in the first place. Civil society, then, is a concrete way we have of recognizing and fostering decent and life-affirming interdependency. Our dominant religious traditions call us to love and to serve our neighbor. But we cannot do this unless we have a neighborhood; unless there are institutions that are present and strong, first and foremost churches, synagogues, and mosques; unless there are processes of moral formation through institutions, beginning with families and continuing through schools, that call us to responsibilities as well as to rights, to recognition of our own frailties as well as to action in freedom.

CIVIL SOCIETY AND THE GOOD OF PERSONS

Thinking about what civil society is reminds us that human beings are complex creatures who do not do good spontaneously most of the time. Wanting to do good, we have turned at various points to government to take over when charity did not suffice. Wanting to reap the rewards of self-discipline and hard work, we have turned to economic structures to generate jobs and prosperity. In the minds of some, unfortunately, government became not only a line of defense against social distress and unacceptable levels of injustice but the only font of ethical decency and concern. Those enamored of top-down state action disdained or despaired of civil society because it didn't seem up to the tasks they believed needed to be done and, as well, because the plural complexities of civil society challenge all top-down social engineering and totalizing efforts. Similarly, the market, many optimistically believed, should be the source of social well-being as individual opportunities and rewards ushered into an overall social benefit. The economy alone, they argued, was powerful enough to fend off efforts to locate too much power in governments. And there matters often got stalled. But we have learned in the past half-century that though families and churches and other associations of civil society have been buffeted about and even undermined by external powers of many kinds, there is no substitute for them. Without civil society, a political culture cannot sustain a decent moral and social ecology.

The evidence on this score is abundantly clear. It tells us that neither government alone, nor the economy alone, nor the two in tandem, can sustain the rich world of democratic civic life. The evidence also tells us that government and markets may even be harmful in specific ways. Rather than serving civil society, they may grow too powerful and may erode civil independence, social interdependence, and plurality. It is therefore not surprising that a growing sense of unease pervades much of the moral landscape of both developed and developing democracies. For all the wealth being generated in some sites (the United States being *primus inter pares* in this regard), there is a gnawing sense that all is not well with us. Take, for example, the fact that social science surveys indicate that U.S. citizens no longer trust either their government or one another.[4] This is debilitating as democracy presupposes an affective bond between citizens to help sustain a shared sense of participation in a way of life in common.

At our best as social beings, we trust one another; we have some confidence in our ability to work together and to face our difficulties with hope; we try to act decently in our dealings and we expect the same from others; we understand the role of government but we know that we have direct responsibility for democratic civic life; we extol the workings of a free economy but we believe that economic forces must be shaped by a moral sense. The great moral teachers have long insisted that human beings are more likely to be stirred to action and to compassion when they think concretely of fellow citizens and neighbors; when there are specific tasks they are called upon and able to do; when reciprocity is an ever-present possibility and expectation. We need social institutions—a civil society—in order to channel, to shape, and to sustain our civic dispositions. Thus it is altogether unsurprising that a body of recent work by American social scientists indicates that regular churchgoers are less likely to divorce, to abuse their children, to get caught up in cycles of violence and addiction, and more likely to serve their neighbors. Why? Because membership in an institution that instills ethical habits of the heart helps people to enact that ethic in the lives of their communities. There are many institutions that historically aided in this effort. But in all too many places at present, they are faltering, not flourishing.

Let us dig into this matter in more depth. Recall, if you will, my use of the notion of a moral and civic ecology as somewhat analogous to natural ecologies. I insisted that, even as the one can be sullied and depleted, so can the other. Civil society as a way we have to sustain and to recognize our interdependencies is based on a long tradition of moral, philosophical, and theological thought. Aristotle insisted that the proper end of human beings required membership in associations, both household and polis. Alexis de Tocqueville, whose work on *Democracy in America* is a recognized classic, contrasted the rich world of associational self-help he found when he toured America in the Jacksonian era with a worst-case scenario of what he feared might be America's fate at some future point.[5] Because Tocqueville's argument has more general bearing on thinking about civil society in the context of religion and education, it is worth pondering at length.

According to Tocqueville, democracy requires laws, constitutions, and authoritative institutions. But it also depends on what he called "habits of the heart" forged within the framework such institutions provided. He urged Americans—and all future citizens of democracy, for he saw democracy and equality as trends that would develop everywhere, at least in the West—to take to heart a possible corruption of democratic cultures over time. For democratic citizens might awaken one day and realize that something terrible had happened. Separated from the saving constraints and nurture of the overlapping associations of civil society, persons in democratic cultures might come to be more dominated by a lower and lower mean on the level of culture and, as well, might find themselves caught up in webs of control instigated from above with the express aim of muffling the disintegrative effects of atomized self-interest.

It is worth remembering that for Tocqueville, religious belief was inseparable from free public life. Why? Because our religious institutions engage in ethical formation; they teach us moral restraint, thereby releasing us for civic life and stewardship. Without strong churches and religious liberty, no flourishing civil society is possible. What religion has to offer can help to chasten the forces unleashed, in part, by what Christianity taught, namely, the moral equality of all persons. Translated into a social and political force, this striving for equality can lead to an unseemly quest for the "same" things and pit people against one another. Egalitarianism in a commercial republic such as the United States unleashes a materialistic quest. Faith communities therefore must serve not simply as a goad and a kind of adjunct feature of civic life but, rather, in their robust specificity and particularity, as a way to keep alive traditions and communal institutions that serve as a chastening force on striving ambition. Religion, in Tocqueville's words, helps to "purify, control, and restrain that exclusive taste for well-being human beings acquire in an age of equality."[6] Tocqueville here surely had in his sights the early covenantal tradition and its living remnants in America. The notion of a covenant is one that stresses the mutual accountability of persons to one another and before God. This creates and sustains "a kind of moral equality among the people," Tocqueville avers, even as it acts as a brake on the leveling and isolating tendencies of materialistic "equality."[7]

Without strong churches and religious liberty, then, the Tocquevillian would argue that no flourishing civil society is possible. Tocqueville himself would encourage us to consider where we now find ourselves. We should ponder whether American religion—by which I mean our diverse religious communities in which Protestant Christianity still predominates, though Roman Catholicism is the single most significant denomination in terms of numbers—remains strong enough to exert a complex role that is simultaneously chastening and invigorating. Here Tocqueville wasn't at all confident about our prospects. He determined that there were at least two great dangers threatening religion and, indirectly, American democratic civil society, namely, schism and indifference. Schism pits us against one another in suspicion and enmity. Indifference invites us not to care about one another at all. Tocqueville, were he to reappear in our midst, would surely point to both worries and suggest that we are in danger of losing that generous concern for others that religion as institutionally robust faith communities promotes. Moreover, believers—because they operate from some common moral basis that does not require doctrinal leveling but does demand searching for certain core norms we share—are more apt to learn how to compromise because they agree on so many important things.

CIVIL SOCIETY AND THE CRISIS OF AUTHORITY

What sustains a civil society? I propose to zero in on one theme, that of authority, as a prelude to a direct consideration of moral formation and education. Legitimate, accountable authority is implicated, at least tacitly, in every discussion of civil society. Robust yet resilient authority is required to sustain democratic institutions. Surely one reason civil society is in trouble lies in our present confusion over the meaning and function of authority in all spheres of civil and moral life. For example, there is a tendency in modernity, exemplified most tellingly, perhaps, by John Stuart Mill in his classic tract *On Liberty*, to contrast liberty with authority. Rather than posing liberty against tyranny or domination or authoritarianism, Mill sets liberty and authority up as antinomies. Mill got things entirely wrong. We require authority in order to sustain decent, other-regarding liberty. Authority derives from the notion "to authorize," to help generate and even bring into being and to hold and to secure that which is generated. Authority helps to secure and to sustain social institutions. It derives from the fact that we see people as responsible and can hold them accountable.

If we are incapable of distinguishing authority from unacceptable forms of coercion and even violence, we fall into a deep conceptual and ethical abyss. This was the argument of the political theorist Hannah Arendt in a famous essay on authority. Minus authority, claimed Arendt, we lose a sense of the past and of tradition, as "the permanence and durability" of the world seems to melt away. This loss is "tantamount to the loss of the groundwork of the world, which indeed . . . has begun to shift, to change and transform itself with ever-increasing rapidity from one shape to another, as though we were living and struggling with a Protean universe where everything at any moment can become almost anything else."[8] Arendt singles out for critical fire arguments deeply implicated in the conflation of coercion and authority. She also helps to remind us that the legitimate authoritative figure historically—whether parent, teacher, or legislator—was one who was bound by law, by tradition, and by the force of past example and experience. Being bound in particular ways guaranteed a framework for action and helped to create and to sustain particular public spaces—whether of church, polity, or other institutions of social life. Bounded freedom, constituted by authority, is the only way human beings have to guarantee creation of those spaces of public freedom—civil society—Arendt so cherished, spaces within which our action is both nurtured yet constrained.

The point of a decent civil society and polity, after all, isn't just about life but about realizing some vision of a good life. This good life plays a formative and educative role even as it depends in the first instance on formed, civically educated citizens. It inducts each generation into a way of being in the world made possible only when people submit to authority mutually and thereby hold one another accountable. Without such an authoritative framework, there is only violence or rampant antinomianism. Let us return to Tocqueville and his fears about where the age of democracy and equality might take us. He suggested that, over time, the horizon of democratic civil societies might recede as complex, authoritative traditions eroded or collapsed. The upshot would be the triumph of the cynical notion that the past had been nothing, in any case, but a story of chicanery and arbitrariness. But we err in presuming that in order to be free, we must escape binding institutions altogether, as this condition would be one not of freedom but of a kind of license in a civil universe stripped of its moral texture.

In such a world, we would grow more and more apart from one another. We would likely repudiate even the possibility of a rough and ready sharing of moral norms and aspirations of the sort that helped us to treat one another decently and to work together in the first place. Even the procedural norms of democratic governmental institutions might be called into question. Our confidence in the possibility of sustaining shared truth claims would wane. We would come to believe that all that exists is self-interested and self-serving opinion. This is indeed worrisome for, as Hannah Arendt also insisted, in her great work *The Origins of Totalitarianism,* "The ideal subject of totalitarian rule is not the convinced Nazi or the convinced Communist, but people for whom the distinction between fact and fiction . . . and the distinction between true and false . . . no longer exist."[9] Here education in and for democracy enters as crucial, for education and religion are two great formative institutions each of which has as its aim—or at least once did—the discovery and the embrace of truth and the honing of our ability to discern the truth.

DEFINING EDUCATION UP

The aims of education in and for a democratic civil society have always been rather lofty, moving much beyond questions of adaptation and functional skills to an appreciation of the moral wages of democracy itself and its deep reliance on citizens formed to, and for, civic life. Because a democratic culture is one in which freedom and responsibility go hand in hand, human beings must be taught how to sort out the important from the less important, the vital from the trivial, the worthy from the unworthy, the excellent from the mediocre, the false from the true. This is an enormous challenge, one that is undermined rather than strengthened if we accept John Locke's famous distinction, in his classic *Letter on Toleration,* between soulcraft and statecraft.

Locke insisted, as a precondition for civil government, that religion and government had to be distinguished sharply. In his civic map, religion was in one sphere (the private) and dealt with soulcraft, the forming of souls to and for the truths of religion. But statecraft was properly public and had to do with the civil realm. In the civic realm, God and religion do not figure directly anymore. Religion becomes irrelevant in a public sense. In practice in America, however, religion and politics have always been entangled, nowhere more so than in the formation of citizens as persons with developed ethical sensibilities and civic attachments. In recent decades, however, the formation of souls and formation of citizens has once again been theoretically severed in the United States by those strong separations who construe church-state separation to mean a bifurcation between religion and civil society.

But the logic of the one—church/state separation—need not extend to the other—religion and civil society. There has always been considerable overlap in practice, in part because religion and politics trench on one another's turf unavoidably. Each embraces some normative vision of what is fair or decent or just. Each offers criteria for distinguishing truth from falsehood. Each calls human beings to service to a good that goes beyond self-interest. If one falters, the other does as well. Any attempt to take the "soul" out of statecraft and the state (or civic life) out of soulcraft must fail and will harm each enterprise, inviting the possibility that politics becomes soul-less and that the formation of souls becomes privatized and stripped of any civic dimension.

To bring statecraft and soulcraft together is not to call for blatant politicization of education. That danger comes from other directions. For example, we are all aware that at present in our culture, education is increasingly defined with reference to diversity or, as it is usually put, multiculturalism. We are asked to become sensitive to group exclusivities and grievances. Too often, however, rather than making us aware of the wondrous variety of idioms and voices in a plural civic world, such concentration results in an inappropriate politicization of education and the triumph of a discourse of victimization. Of course, education is never outside a world of which politics—how human beings order a way of life in common—is a necessary feature. Education is always cast as the means whereby citizens of a particular society get their bearings and learn to live with and among one another. Education always reflects a society's view of what is excellent, worthy, and necessary, and this reflection is ongoingly refracted and reshaped as definitions, meanings, and purposes change through contestation. In this sense education is political, but this is different from being directly and blatantly politicized. Education is neither the family nor the state nor a church. It is not the primary locus of child rearing, nor an arm of governance, nor the source of knowledge about understandings of God in relation to the human person and vice versa. Schools are, in many ways, somewhat set apart, or should be: they are places of refuge, a kind of civically sacred space at their best, where young people come together and learn—among the many things they learn—how to live with and among one another by respecting distinctions and eschewing destructive divisions.

But the underlying moral impetus for civic brotherhood and sisterhood cannot come from a civic life that has been stripped of its sustaining moral markers as these are embodied in religious institutions. Religion should help us tap the "better angels of our nature," in Lincoln's memorable phrase, and it cannot do that if it is segregated to a private realm of "soulcraft" stripped of civil significance and legitimacy. When our civil society works well, it helps us to see the sturdy interplay of our basic formative institutions as they engage in the process of creating loving parents and friends, decent colleagues, fair-minded citizens. Thus those among us who seek a thoroughly secularized society, stripped of any and all public markers and reminders of religion in the view that religion must be privatized and become invisible to public life, wind up, however inadvertently, weakening our civic life.

In light of the fact that we live in a skeptical if not disillusioned era and, on the best available evidence, those most cynical about our civic prospects are the young, it is a task of critical importance to civil society that we do all that we can to form sturdy, caring, involved young people in and through the overlapping—not separated—institutions assigned that task. Here religion and education can and should walk together, not in lockstep but in the direction of a shared recognition that forming souls and forming citizens are tasks that go together. Our democratic country is dependent, as I have noted several times, on responsibility and self-limiting freedom. If we drain education of its normative, character-forming tasks, we open children up to more, not less, manipulation by such powerful forces in our culture as technology and the media; in effect, we cede responsibility to whatever constitutes a culture's overriding *Weltanschauung* at any given moment.

This can have tragic consequences. For once a world of personal responsibility with its characteristic virtues and marks of decency (justice, honor, friendship, fidelity) is ruptured or emptied, what rushes in to take its place is politics as a "technology of power," in Vaclav Havel's phrase. Responsibility, according to Havel, flows from our plurality and capacity for independent self-constitution by contrast to the conformity, uniformity, and stultifying dogmas of ideologues (whether of the left or the right) who abandon the complexities of moral development and civic ordering in favor of abstract chimeras.

Our malaise over how education is to be defined within our democracy stems in part from a culturally sanctioned abdication by adults of their responsible authority as parents and educators. What Hannah Arendt, writing in the 1960s, already referred to as a "crisis in education" has come about not because a few self-interested groups have hijacked the system. It is far more plausible to argue that education in America is in its present straits because of a general withering away of authoritative meanings and institutions and an undermining of authoritative persons (teachers, parents, politicians) as part and parcel of a general cultural drift toward antinomianism. Only the bringing together of what we too often separate, including the forces of religion and of education, can stem the tide that seems to rush in the direction of civic withdrawal and depletion and the generation of widespread cynicism about our human capacity for thinking about a good in common that we cannot know alone.

I noted above that one troubling sign of our times is growing evidence that those most cynical about our prospects, particularly politics and government, are the young, with high school students the most "turned off" of all. This is a complex phenomenon, no doubt. But I suspect that one factor in the triumph of cynicism is that young people are too often fed stories that represent U.S. history as nothing but a tale of failed promises. In an attempt to be more critical, and not to instill in our young people a simplistic and too-benign view of the past, some have gone overboard in the other direction. Because our civic story is so intertwined with narratives about American religious history, a sour sense of civic life is surely one by-product of accounts that stress only the marginalization of this sect or the maltreatment of some other, losing sight along the way of the millions of Americans whose commitments to their faith lifted them up, sustained hope and faithfulness, and helped to form them as good stewards and responsible members of their communities. Everyone knows by now that both civically and religiously, we have too often failed to live up to our promises and our premises. But the staccato repetition of the dark side of our history, if that becomes the dominant motif, fuels cynicism rather than active participation. Let us look, then, at contrasting models of how to treat the history of religion, education, and civic life in America.

Model One: The Traditional Story

Our then-five-year-old granddaughter told me her vision of the traditional story shortly before Thanksgiving Day, 1999. It went like this:

Grandma, we learned about Thanksgiving and why we have turkeys. The Pilgrims got on a boat called the *Mayflower* because the king wouldn't let them be free. They couldn't pray free. So they got on the *Mayflower* and then they sailed for a long time across the ocean to come to America. Some Pilgrims got sick and died. The Pilgrim children had to sleep on the hard wood floors on the ship. They thought they'd never get there. But they did! It was cold and they were hungry. They got to be friends with the Indians and they shared some turkeys and some corn and that's why we eat turkey and have Thanksgiving, because the Pilgrims could pray free.

This isn't a bad story, and it is essentially the one many of us were taught. It is a hopeful baseline from which to work. The story gets more complex over time. The encounter with the indigenous people is, we know, one with many layers of suspicion, violence, failed and occasionally successful attempts at communication, pathos aplenty. We are familiar with how this proceeds and how, indeed, it should proceed as education continues and a child's capacities for critical interpretation are engaged. But jump-starting the civic formation of children with a strong, decent story seems appropriate. One could not, and no responsible parent or teacher would, offer a benign version of the coming of slavery in America. But one could tell even this horrific tale in a way that emphasized the strength of the African slaves and their determination to try to hold on to their dignity even under conditions of slavery; their valiant efforts to sustain families; their cultural contributions even enslaved.

The traditional story becomes a problem if it gets reified and frozen. An example I give in my book *Democracy on Trial* is that of the teacher who turns the story of the Founding Fathers into an exercise in hagiography and the Constitution into a nigh-miraculous distillation of the essence of the wisdom of the ages, good for all times and places. If uncritical adulation triumphs, the dialogic, deliberative, and critical dimensions of civic engagement, an encounter that is always both retrospective and prospective, is lost. A traditional story of the reified sort about American religion and civic life would present it as a cheery tale of beleaguered folks seeking to "pray free"—true enough—but then go on to envelope the entirety of our religious history in a kind of roseate haze that overlooks the vituperation meted out against religious dissenters, the often violent exclusions, the organized attacks (here the Know-Nothings or the Ku Klux Klan, who were anti-Catholic and anti-Jewish as well as antiblack), the pretense that the common or public schools were solely a generous and benign effort to educate all American young people, thus sanitizing the effort and neglecting the explicit anti-immigrant, anti-Catholic thrust of the common schools, and so on. The good, the bad, and the ugly must be part of the story without any single element dominating, for that would be to distort through oversimplification. Thus there is a traditional model narrative that illuminates, another that narrows and distorts.

Model Two: The Hermeneutics
of Suspicion Ascendant

The hagiographer's mirror image is offered by the teacher who, if the American founding and the beginning of our civic story is the reference point, declares that nothing good ever came from the hand of that abstract, all-purpose villain, the "dead, white European male." The words and deeds of the Founders were nefarious, as they were hypocritical racists and patriarchalists. It follows that their creations, including the Constitution, are tainted. The key words in this negative scenario are "nothing but," for these two little words always signify a reductionistic agenda. Within the rigidities of this model, debate similarly ends or is discouraged. To express a different point of view, to say maybe there were some courageous, brilliant, good things that emerged from the hands of the complex and quite various men who made so much of our early history, is to betray one's own "false consciousness" or class or race privilege. If a hermeneutics of suspicion goes all the way down, that is surely one of the strands inviting cynicism, especially among students.

Turned against religion, a harsh hermeneutics of suspicion sees "nothing but" patriarchy, horror, and hypocrisy at work. But here, too, there is much to be gleaned and learned and appropriated for a generous civic education. For there is a version of a mode of critical interpretation that is vital and necessary in offering up a complex, nuanced, rich tapestry that affords ways for us to ask such questions as: are there resources internal to this religious tradition, or that one, that enable its adherents to criticize followers of the religions who are acting (so they say) on their religious beliefs but who are, in fact, betraying those beliefs in some fundamental way? One can ask what textual distortions, elisions, excisions, and selective use or abuse of history is required in order, for example, to draw upon the New Testament for a defense of chattel slavery even as other Christians declared slavery a sin. Looking closely at such examples, one can readily see that this is by no means a case of two equally valid interpretations between which one just opts arbitrarily. Rather, one can readily see that those who found support for race-based chattel slavery in the New Testament systematically distorted the message of Jesus of Nazareth in order to make that message fit with the institution they sought to defend. The best response to such claims is to go to the text itself and to show how such distortions occurred.

This is a complex enterprise that relies on the well-educated, robustly and ethically formed intelligence. It is far simpler to debunk cynically than to criticize intelligently. Does our education today prepare children for intelligent criticism—or push them toward cynical debunking?

Model Three: Civic and Hopeful

The civic and hopeful approach to education and formation draws upon elements from the traditional and critical interpretive models, then intermingles them with a strong civic philosophy to which a faith community brings its own beliefs that may well challenge or put pressure upon an extant civic scheme of things. Within the Christian tradition with which I am most familiar, for example, believers are called not to conform to the world but to be formed in such a way that they can transform the world: active citizenship and membership is a good. This model begins with a presupposition that each and every person is dignified and that the religious dimension is obliged to honor and to lift up that dignity. Other traditions would have their own starting points. The critical-hopeful model promotes a dialogue between faith and culture and civic life, striving to prevent the triumph of any and all philosophies that isolate us from one another, invite us to mistrust one another, or construe us as always in competition with one another. In this model, schools would play the central role in educating in hopeful civic ways; churches and synagogues and mosques in educating in hopeful faith-based ways. But each overlaps with the other, and each dimension of formation conjoins to encourage young people to develop an orientation toward notions of a common good.

THE FUTURE OF CIVIL SOCIETY

The stakes, it seems, couldn't be higher. We have entered the twenty-first century with many of our fellow citizens perplexed and deeply skeptical about the fate of all our basic institutions. The most penetrating observers of Western culture, whether in developed democracies like our own or in developing democracies, like the Czech Republic, fear that democratic civics are either withering or not developing in the first place. Thus President Havel of the Czech Republic, in a state of the republic address delivered on December 9, 1997, to that nation's parliament and senate, commented critically on the state of Czech culture. His comments are worth quoting at some length. He noted:

> I have left culture to the end not because I consider it to be some super-structural "icing on the cake," but for precisely the opposite reason. I consider it the most impor-

tant of all, something that deserves to be mentioned at the very conclusion of my remarks. I am not thinking of culture as a separate sphere of human activity. . . . I
mean culture in the broadest sense of the word—that is, the culture of human relationships, of human enterprise, of public and political life. I refer to the general level
of our culture. Culture . . . can be measured, for example, by what skinheads shout
in the bar U Zabranskych, by how many Roma have been lynched or murdered, by
how terribly some of us behave to our fellow human beings simply because they have
a different color of skin. . . . You must know that I am talking about what is usually
called a civil society. That means a society that makes room for the richest possible
self-structuring and the richest possible participation in public life. In this sense, civil
society is important for two reasons: in the first place it enables people to be themselves in all their dimensions, which includes being social creatures who desire, in
thousands of ways, to participate in the life of the community in which they live. In
the second place, it functions as a genuine guarantee of political stability. The more
developed all the organs, institutions, and instruments of civil society are, the more
resistant that society will be to political upheavals and reversals. It was no accident
that communism's most brutal attack was aimed precisely against this civil society. It
knew very well that its greatest enemy was not an individual non-Communist politi-
cian, but a society that was open, structured independently from the bottom up, and
therefore very difficult to manipulate.[10]

Havel's words conjure up the concept of subsidiarity, a powerful theoretical
framework for explaining what a civil society is and what it does that cannot be
done by other, more centralized and top-heavy institutions and forces. Subsidiarity is a direct contribution by a tradition of religious thought—Catholic
Social Thought—to our self-understanding as a democratic society. In the
modern social encyclicals, culminating with the extraordinary contributions of
Pope John Paul II, we find an affirmation that human rights should be seen not
in individualistic but in social terms. Working from the principle of subsidiarity, John Paul and others find a violation of a right order of things in assigning
to greater or higher associations what smaller associations can do.[11] The purpose of larger associations, including the state, is to help members of a body
politic and society rather than to erode or to absorb its many plural associations. Subsidiarity, then, is a theory of, and for, civil society. It keeps alive alternatives between individualism, on the one hand, and collectivism, on the other.
It helps us to understand why families, schools, churches are all vital and must
remain vibrant and healthy if a "more perfect union" is ever to be realized.

But who knows about subsidiarity, or Alexis de Tocqueville, for that matter?
No doubt parochial schools do a better job working in Tocqueville than public
schools do evoking the concept of subsidiarity (at an appropriate grade level) in

courses of civic education, to the extent that civics is even taught any longer. Perhaps what has happened is something like this: our very success as a vibrant, energetic democracy went to our heads and we began to take too much for granted that on which we depend—families, schools, religious institutions. We thought they would always be there and always be strong. So even if we weren't that engaged in one or more of these areas, others were bound to be. It turns out this was far too optimistic a view. It turns out that a democratic civil society requires the efforts of all of us.

NOTES

1. The key text by Hegel is *The Philosophy of Right,* trans. T. M. Knox (Oxford: Clarendon, 1975).
2. In this, of course, Hegel is building on an Aristotelian foundation and Aristotle's ranking of the *polis* as "the final and perfect association." See Aristotle's *Politics,* ed. and trans. Ernest Barker (New York: Oxford University Press, 1962), p. 4.
3. See especially John Paul's discussion of these themes in the encyclicals *Sollicitudo Rei Socialis* and *Centesimus Annus.*
4. For a detailed account of the state of civil society and the debate in America, consult "A Call to Civil Society: Why Democracy Needs Moral Truths. A Report to the Nation from the Council on Civil Society," available from the Institute for American Values, New York.
5. Alexis de Tocqueville, *Democracy in America,* trans. George Lawrence (New York: Harper Perennial, 1988).
6. Ibid., p. 448.
7. See Robin Lovin, "Social Contract or a Public Covenant?" in Robin Lovin, ed., *Religion and American Public Life* (New York: Paulist, 1987), p. 135.
8. Hannah Arendt, "What Is Authority?" in *Between Past and Future* (Baltimore: Penguin, 1980), p. 95.
9. Hannah Arendt, *The Origins of Totalitarianism* (New York: Harcourt Brace Jovanovich, 1973), p. 474.
10. Vaclav Havel, "The State of the Republic," *New York Review of Books,* March 5, 1998, 45–46.
11. For a helpful, theoretically rich summary of papal teaching, see Michel Schooyans, "Democracy in the Teaching of the Popes," Miscellanea 1, Proceedings of the Workshop on Democracy (Vatican City: Pontifical Academy for Social Science, 1998).

Chapter 12 Schooling and Religious Pluralism

Alan Wolfe

"The Catholic school system . . . is a no-man's-land in American education," wrote Paul Blanshard in his best-selling *American Freedom and Catholic Power* of 1949. Blanshard, briefly a Congregationalist minister before embarking on a career as a journalist and aide to New York City Mayor Fiorello La Guardia, decided to visit this terra incognita and to report back to the American people what he found. His account was not encouraging. Unlike public schools, which, Blanshard wrote, are run "democratically by elected school boards," Catholic schools are governed by a "tightly controlled hierarchy." Catholics say that they believe in academic freedom, but they define the term in such a way that "no teacher in a Catholic school is free to disagree with the hierarchy on any social or religious policy that the hierarchy cares to include in its modicum of 'eternal truths.'" Most of those teachers are nuns, who "belong to an age when women allegedly enjoyed subjection and reveled in self-abasement" and whose "unhygienic costumes and . . . medieval rules of conduct establish a barrier between themselves and the outside world." At a time when Catholics, many of whom are recent immigrants, required assimilation into U.S. society,

Blanshard found their schools devoted to "a whole philosophy of education that is alien to the American way of life." Blanshard hoped that his book, in making available to Americans the details of what happened in the exotic, foreign, and separatist land, would constitute a wakeup call to the danger that existed in their midst.[1]

In a revised edition of his book published in 1958, Blanshard devoted considerable attention to an issue easily recognizable to any student of American education at the start of the twenty-first century: the proper relation between public and private. Between the first and second editions of his book, the Catholic Church, which had long opposed federal aid to education, reversed course and began to argue for federal funds. This would not matter if there were no support in the United States for federal aid to education, but Blanshard, a liberal, believed that the experiences of the Great Depression and World War II would lead to greater federal involvement in many walks of life, schooling among them. Catholics, he pointed out, realized this too, which is why they began to lobby for federal money to support busing for their students, released time for religious instruction, and assistance for textbook purchases. Government had every reason to deny them what they sought, he believed, because the main concerns of the Catholic hierarchy were sectarian. The church wanted to keep Catholics out of public schools and to keep non-Catholics out of parochial schools. Education, he argued, ought to be the business of the whole community, not the province of any particular self-interested group.

Not all books should be judged on their predictive power, but some invite such judgment, Blanshard's among them. For the whole thrust of his analysis was that the Catholic Church, with the weight of two thousand years of tradition behind it, was incapable of responding positively to the ideals of liberty, democracy, and equality so central to the modern world. It would be difficult to find any book from the 1950s that was as wrong about its predictions as Blanshard's. (To take just one counterexample, one can still read with profit Will Herberg's *Protestant, Catholic, Jew*, which first appeared in 1955.[2]) In 1958, the year that the second edition of Blanshard's book appeared, John XXIII assumed his position as pope and immediately began the deliberations that resulted in the Second Vatican Council (1962–65). Two years after that, Americans elected John F. Kennedy, a liberal Democrat and a Catholic, as their president. The combined effects of these two developments—each seeming to reinforce the other—transformed Catholicism, both worldwide and in America, into a modern religion no longer at war with contemporary liberalism.

Between the 1960s and the present, American Catholicism has been modernized even further.[3] When Kennedy was elected president, Catholic colleges and universities were segregated by gender and were not academically distinguished; most Catholics were working-class and lived in cities and supported urban political organizations like Mayor Richard J. Daley's in Chicago; the overwhelming majority of Catholics were the children and grandchildren of immigrants from Europe, primarily Ireland, Italy, and Poland; the leading voices of the church strongly supported the Cold War; and the expression "gay Catholic" would have been taken to mean a parishioner who had a bit too much to drink. Now Catholics flock to the suburbs like ethnic groups; one hears prominent Catholic voices in support of pacifism and against the death penalty; the U.S. Catholic Bishops were the only significant force lobbying against welfare reform during the Clinton administration; pro-choice Catholics oppose the church's position on abortion; Catholic colleges and universities can be found among the elite institutions in America; huge numbers of American Catholics are immigrants from Mexico, Cuba, and the Philippines; and many of America's richest and most successful businessmen are Catholic.[4]

As a result of these rapid and deep sociological transformations, Catholic schools in America bear no resemblance to the picture painted by Blanshard. Nuns no longer can be easily recruited to teach in them, and those who do tend to be strongly independent women in secular dress who have voluntarily chosen a life dedicated to education and social justice. Suburbanized Catholics are less likely to send their children to parochial schools in any case, preferring either wealthy Catholic academies, traditional prep schools, or good suburban public schools. Contrary to what Blanshard said, Catholic schools welcome non-Catholics as students, especially inner-city African Americans. Although Catholic schools continue to emphasize a religious education, the hierarchy that Blanshard saw as controlling them has difficulty controlling much of anything. The single most important consequence of the modernization of American Catholicism is that Catholics make up their own minds about what is important to them, and the church either accommodates or withers.

Although Paul Blanshard's book received great praise from John Dewey, Albert Einstein, Bertrand Russell, and McGeorge Bundy, the entire episode seems rather embarrassing in light of the transformation of American Catholicism since the book was published.[5] Blanshard eventually softened his position without ever recanting it. Still, the irony remains: he was quick to assume that Catholics were closed-minded, but the passage of time reveals him to be the thinker so wedded to a dogma that his book reads now like little more than bigotry. His thoughts need to be kept in mind as we consider contemporary ex-

amples dealing with the presumably pernicious consequences of religious belief
for schooling in a democratic society, examples expressed in language strikingly
similar to the way Blanshard posed the issue in the years after World War II.
However much both America and its religions may have changed since the late
1940s, the attitudes of many intellectuals and policy activists toward religious
believers appear not to have changed much at all.

SCAPEGOATING THE RELIGIOUS RIGHT

When liberals of a certain sort worry about the possible pernicious consequences of religion in American public life today, their focus is less on Catholics
and more on one of the most rapidly growing religious movements in America:
fundamentalist and Evangelical Protestants. No one has written a book attacking fundamentalism with quite the fervor of Blanshard's book on Catholicism,
but from both scholarly and popular quarters comes concern that public
monies used by religious believers will result in a victory for sectarian and
undemocratic forces.

Paul Blanshard was a founder of an organization called Protestants and
Other Americans United for Separation of Church and State. Now renamed
without the exclusionary reference to Protestants, that organization, along with
the American Civil Liberties Union and People for the American Way, has
taken the lead in charging that conservative Christians are attacking American
public schools on every conceivable front. According to these organizations,
conservative Christians condemn any efforts by schools to teach about sexuality, especially when those efforts include discussions of homosexuality. They
insist on equal time for "creation science" because they know it will drive out
the teaching of evolutionary biology. They want to be able to control what students read and will use censorship to achieve that end. They support legislation
purportedly designed to protect "parental rights," but in fact meant to erode
school authority. If they withdraw their children to educate them at home, they
are attacking public schools by reducing the constituency for them. If they send
their children to public schools, they are attacking them by insisting on the
right of their children to hear school prayer or to abstain from reading texts that
violate their beliefs. In all these activities, what fuels the strength of the religious Right, its critics charge, is the same thing that, in Blanshard's analysis,
made Catholics so formidable a foe: because they do not adhere to democratic
values, they can act in disciplined ways that exaggerate their influence.

Unlike Blanshard, whose book, however flawed, was based on research into actual Catholic sources, these criticisms of the religious Right are made without much attention to the religious ideas of conservative Christians. But with the publication of Vincent Crapanzano's *Serving the Word,* we do have an account of the theological perspectives of conservative Christians from a serious social scientist. Although Crapanzano, an anthropologist, primarily concerns himself with the question of how conservative Christians make sense out of the world, he too is persuaded that they make poor democratic citizens. "One prerequisite for democracy is an openness to the position of the other," he writes. But "where we believe, as the fundamentalists do, that we have special access to *the* truth, then we have no choice but a stubborn proclamation of that truth. Such a position is absolutist." For Crapanzano, there can be neither compromise nor dialogue with fundamentalists. They approach the world with an attitude of combat. Hence politics with them will always be one-sided. "We see this, most dramatically, in the dispute over abortion, but it occurs frequently over other less dramatic issues in the United States today. I am speaking not just of school prayer, homosexuality, and the right to bear arms, but in the way these and other issues are argued by the absolutists. Theirs is simply an assertive discourse."[6]

Because they reject democratic values, conservative Christians today, like the Catholics of yesterday, are seen as threatening the liberties America holds dear. "Religious extremists are attempting to impose their beliefs and practices on everyone else by enlisting the government's support and aid. These efforts, if successful, will threaten each individual's right to worship, or not worship, as he or she pleases."[7] This warning, posted on the web page of the American Civil Liberties Union, suggests that, unlike people genuinely committed to liberal democracy, adherents to the religious Right do not recognize a distinction between private and public. They are not content, the argument runs, to practice their own religion as they see fit; instead, they have designs on everyone else. "While objectors often justify their demands by claiming to be acting only as parents concerned about their children's education," declares People for the American Way, "a deeper agenda becomes evident when demands are made that district-approved books and materials be withdrawn not just from their own children, but from all children, or that other parents' children be indoctrinated by the Right's view of education and religion."[8] Two years after the original publication of his book on the Catholic Church, Blanshard wrote another one arguing that Catholics and communists both pursued methods incompatible with democracy.[9] The same argument runs throughout the publications of groups like People for the American Way and the ACLU: conservative Christians do not play by the rules of the democratic game. "Rather than acknowledging an honest disagreement and seeking to find a workable compromise, these leaders, and often their activist followers, seem determined to make the battle a personal one, and make a point of claiming that God is on their side," People for the American Way concluded.[10]

According to their critics, there are also similarities in tactics between Catholics in the postwar period and conservative Christians now. Blanshard believed that Catholics had developed a two-pronged attack on public education. First, they tried to undermine support for public schools by "suggestions to the effect that the 'Godless' schools are extravagant and expensive." Their purpose in using this tactic was "to weaken and even to destroy a public school by drawing off the majority of the children into a parochial school." If they failed in that objective, they relied on their fall-back strategy, one of "moving the parochial school into the public-school system and forming a kind of hybrid school that is semi-public in nature. Its funds come from the public, but its controls and spirit are Catholic."[11]

Nearly identical language is used by today's critics of the religious right. It is an article of faith among these groups that a deliberate plot to weaken public confidence in public schools—carried out state by state and community by community in a systematic way—fuels the efforts of conservative Christians. According to a writer for *The Nation,* conservatives who bankroll movements for vouchers favor "dismantling the democratically controlled public education system."[12] The truth of the matter, writes Liz Galst in *The Progressive,* is that "the religious right doesn't believe in public education."[13] "Religious Right political groups," suggests People for the American Way, "are waging a long and bitter battle against public education. Their long-term goal is the enactment of a private school voucher plan, in which private and religious schools would be funded with public money."[14]

But this attack on the schools is something of a diversionary tactic, these critics continue. As befits those unwilling to play fairly, conservative Christians are really seeking not to destroy public schools but to take them over. Their motivations, according to People for the American Way, are twofold: "first, to redirect substantial public funds into private sectarian schools that can serve a core constituency of the Right; and second, to use whatever public education system that remains to impose a set of beliefs and ideas on America's next generation."[15] This same determination to take over rump schools also explains why the religious Right runs "stealth candidates" for local school boards; recognizing that public schools are here to stay, they would rather control them than ignore them. Earlier in the twentieth century, fundamentalist Protestants, like Catholics, opposed federal aid to education (primarily because, unlike Catholics, they opposed federal aid to just about everything). But sensing an opportunity, they now jump on the bandwagon for school choice. Charter schools, one form taken by advocates of school choice, seem an example of the very same kind of "hybrid schools" sought by Blanshard's Catholics. But even vouchers, which ostensibly benefit private schools, can be viewed as creating such hybrids. On the one hand, the schools that will benefit from vouchers will be private. On the other, they will have indirect public support. Then again, when public authorities insist that they follow federal law and develop policies against discrimination or in favor of free speech, they can claim to be private and constitutionally protected from government "entanglement" with religion. There is, critics believe, a kind of deliberate obfuscation of the public/private distinction going on here, exactly what one would expect from groups that do not take their obligations of open democratic citizenship seriously.

Will today's critics prove to be as wrong about the intentions and influence of conservative Protestants as Blanshard was about yesterday's Catholics? I believe that they probably will be. Already many leading conservative Christians, in the wake of their failure to remove President Clinton from office, have pronounced themselves losers in the culture war and have urged their followers to drop out of day-to-day politics.[16] One would never know, from reading the material of the ACLU or People for the American Way, that organizations like the Christian Coalition are having difficulty raising funds and sustaining membership. Nor do these materials recognize that many Christians who are conservative on religious matters are liberal on political ones, no group more so than African Americans. Nor, finally, does one find in their way of thinking much recognition that efforts to introduce creationism or to post the Ten Commandments in public places, once exposed, are often subject to local ridicule and stopped. We cannot know what the future will bring, but if the past is any indication, most religious movements, no matter how traditional their origins, moderate themselves over time. American democracy "softens" religious purism far more often that strict religious movements "harden" American democracy.

Whether or not today's critics of the religious Right correctly predict the future, there is another, more important reason to concern oneself with what they have to say. Persuaded that people with strong religious views are not as committed to the rules of the democratic game as are cosmopolitan liberals, both Blanshard and contemporary critics of the religious Right raise the question of how a liberal democratic society ought to respond to groups perceived as neither particularly liberal nor particularly democratic. Paul Blanshard, echoing his contemporary Sidney Hook's remarks about academic freedom, argued that pluralism could not be extended to those who did not share a commitment to pluralism.[17] Any group that views itself as a highly disciplined organization dedicated to the single-minded pursuit of its narrowly defined objectives cannot be allowed to go unchallenged, for it will inevitably have an advantage over groups committed to open procedures, internal dissent, and respect for its opposition. Many well-meaning Americans want to find a compromise with Catholics, Blanshard wrote, but as Crapanzano argues with respect to today's fundamentalists, compromise was "not feasible" wherever the church had a strong interest. "It should not be forgotten that in a democratic society adjustment to reactionary clerical politics can mean the surrender of basic liberties," he continued. To protect those liberties, one cannot adopt the policy of "appeasement" favored by many "idealists." Instead of falling for false pleas of tolerance and broad-mindedness, one instead has to "face unpleasant facts" and "to increase the tensions between social groups until the threat of the triumph of reactionary politics is past." From such a perspective, pluralism is best served by inoculating the body politic against foreign invaders who would destroy its immune system. "It seems clear to me that there is no alternative for champions of traditional American democracy except to build a resistance movement designed to prevent the hierarchy from imposing its social policies upon our schools, hospitals, government, and family organization."[18]

Few writers today are likely to be as explicit as Blanshard in writing off their opponents as illegitimate; People for the American Way urges its followers to organize politically against the religious Right, certainly a more responsible course of action than Blanshard's. Still, the questions remain: what does pluralism require of us? Does pluralism demand that we all play by the same rules? Or is the very meaning of pluralism a willingness to accept that people who disagree on the ends they seek can also be allowed to disagree on the means by which they seek them?

THE PLURALIST PARADOX

One of the most important theorists of pluralism in America today is the political philosopher Amy Gutmann. At first glance, she writes, pluralism would seem to be best served by allowing parents maximum choice in the education of their children. In a society in which there are many religions, Protestants would choose to send their children to Protestant schools, Catholics to Catholic schools, and so on, producing a wide variety of educational institutions. But this would be a specious pluralism, she continues. In the real world, nineteenth-century public schools, run by Protestants to further Protestant values, were furiously anti-Catholic. If those public schools had been abolished, the result would be a situation in which the schools of each religious group would have been free to transmit their biases to their children without ever having to pause and address the question of whether different religions ought to be respected. "Pluralism," Gutmann writes, "is an important political value insofar as social diversity enriches our lives by expanding our understanding of different ways of life. To reap the benefits of social diversity, children must be exposed to ways of life different from their parents and—in the course of their exposure—must embrace certain values, such as mutual respect among persons, that make social diversity both possible and desirable."[19]

The key word in this passage, repeated twice by Gutmann, is *must.* For in order to achieve the respect for diversity that all members of a liberal society ought to have, we sometimes have to insist on common standards for all. Gutmann acknowledges that this is difficult to do in a society in which people disagree over the fundamental aims of their institutions: some people believe that schools should teach freedom and others that they should teach virtue, and these aims often part company. There is, however, a more inclusive standard, which Gutmann calls "conscious social reproduction." Gutmann describes this standard as follows: "As citizens, we aspire to a set of educational practices and authorities of which the following can be said: these are the practices and authorities to which we, acting collectively as a society, have consciously agreed. It follows that a society that supports conscious social reproduction must educate all educable children to be capable of participating in collectively shaping their society."[20]

Should anyone object to the imposition of this standard as a violation of their sense of virtue and morality, there would be, in Gutmann's view, a ready response: "'The virtues and moral character we are cultivating,' the educational authorities can reply in the first instance, 'are necessary to give children the chance collectively to shape their society. The kind of character you are asking us to cultivate would deprive children of that chance, the very chance that legitimates your claim to educational authority.'"[21] There can be little doubt that Gutmann is correct to anticipate that a response such as hers may be necessary, for there are many groups in America—most, but not all of them, inspired by their religious beliefs—that would deny the importance of putting children's chances of shaping their society first. Those parents can, of course, choose to send their children to private schools that put something else first—such as respect for the truth of God's word—but if they do, we begin to approximate a situation in which each group goes its own way without teaching respect for the viewpoints of others.

What happens instead if conservative religious parents want to send their children to public schools? If pluralism means respecting different ways of life, the ideal situation would be one in which those of orthodox religious belief came to understand the worldview of liberals while liberals showed respect for those who put virtue ahead of freedom. Yet as Gutmann continues to reason her way through this issue, she comes to the conclusion that such mutual respect is impossible to achieve. "A necessary (but not sufficient) condition of conscious social reproduction," she writes, "is that citizens have the capacity to deliberate among alternative ways of life. To put this point in more 'liberal' language: a good life and a good society for self-reflective people require (respectively) individual and collective freedom of choice."[22] Because Gutmann has already acknowledged that freedom stands in tension with virtue, virtue-first people must give way to the freedom-first principle if education is going to emphasize the importance of the individual's playing a role in shaping his or her society. Gutmann's sophisticated and tightly argued position is worlds away from the liberal intolerance of Paul Blanshard. But like Blanshard, she reaches the paradoxical conclusion that to achieve the pluralist goal of encouraging respect for all, we have to insist on the nonpluralist means of having everyone subscribe to the same liberal point of view.

That these are not just abstract issues becomes clear when we consider the debates surrounding political correctness on U.S. campuses. Many universities once pursued exclusionary policies that effectively kept out Jews, women, and African Americans, and, in so doing, they created student bodies whose racial, religious, and gender homogeneity made a mockery of pluralism. Seeking to be as inclusive as they can, these universities now welcome all those groups who were once excluded. Yet representatives of some of the once-excluded groups argue that for women or African Americans to be truly accepted on campus, students and faculty who believe in their inferiority or who denigrate their accomplishments cannot take refuge behind rules protecting academic freedom, for their views really amount to a form of hateful harassment and discrimination. These debates once again raise the question of how a liberal institution like the university ought to respond to the existence of groups within it who dissent, sometimes vigorously, from liberal ideals. When the chancellor of the University of New Orleans says that "the university will not tolerate anyone's use of the classroom as a forum to promote racial disharmony," he is saying, much like Paul Blanshard said, that liberal institutions have no place for illiberal voices.[23]

Let me call the views I have been describing guided pluralism. In theory, people who subscribe to guided pluralism want a situation of equal respect and dignity for all. But in practice, they are persuaded that neither people nor educational institutions can be fully trusted to ensure that such equality will come about of its own accord. If we were to allow all groups, no matter how divergent their understandings of morality and freedom, to clash with each other directly, the result would be a Hobbesian war of all against all in which no one would emerge the winner. To protect against that outcome, pluralism, like the economy free market, requires regulation enforced by some political authority.

There is an important truth contained in the theory of guided pluralism. When worldviews clash, the result is often uncivil, on occasion even bloody. Ideological extremists have a way of bringing out the worst in each other; the language in which contemporary liberals denounce fundamentalists can easily be matched by language from fundamentalists accusing liberals of serving as agents of Satan. Yet a guided pluralism designed to contain the passions of politics cannot help but take sides in the conflict it presumably is regulating. Guided pluralism is another name for what Isaiah Berlin called positive liberty.[24] Freedom matters, but before we can really know what freedom requires of us, we must develop those capacities we have as human beings that enable us to know where our interests truly lie.[25] Yet because any theory of human development is premised on a particular view of human nature and human purpose, the very act of guiding us toward a particular end carries with it that suggestion that not all views of human nature and human purpose are equal. What begins with a commitment to the equality and dignity of all people ends—indeed, must end—with the proposition that those who adhere to conventional, traditional, or faith-based ideas of human purpose have an understanding that is too cramped and unfair to its own adherents to be accorded full equality with other, more Kantian, views of human purpose.

ROBUST PLURALISM

Crucial to the theory of guided pluralism are notions of fragility. Blanshard believed that democracy was not strong enough to withstand the tactics of a Catholic hierarchy he viewed as undemocratic, a point of view shared by others, like Sidney Hook, who were not persuaded that democrats could stand up to tough-minded and ruthless communists. Along similar lines, arguments in favor of excluding racist views from the university are premised on the notion that ethnic and racial identity, especially for those against whom discrimination has been persistent, is too fragile to withstand full-scale and direct attack. Yet are people, institutions, and political systems really as fragile as all that? The political philosopher Steven Holmes points out that totalitarian states inevitably lose wars or collapse from within, while democratic ones flourish.[26] If true of democratic foreign policy, the same ought also to be true of democratic domestic policy. A political system that successfully defeated fascism and successfully outlived communism ought to be considered strong enough to allow the active participation in public life of groups that do not share liberal or democratic values.

Guided by the notion of strong democracy, one can speak of pluralism that is robust rather than guided. Robust pluralists look at a world in which groups have radically different conceptions of the nature of the good life and conclude that they are best off competing directly with each other to win adherents to their point of view. Except for preventing or punishing violence, government ought not to step in to ensure that the struggle is fought fairly. Groups should be presumed to know what is best for themselves. If groups with radically different perspectives come together in public institutions, one group cannot insist that its terms be adhered to by the other. If instead groups prefer to form associations that reinforce their own worldview—and do so by excluding others who do not share that worldview—they ought to be permitted to do so. Robust pluralism would rather see internally homogeneous private associations clashing with each other—the situation negatively envisioned by Gutmann in which private schools associated with specific religions would be free to pass on their prejudices—than seek illusory or biased harmony enforced by the state.

The leading theorist of robust pluralism in America is Nancy Rosenblum, whose vision of what pluralism demands, outlined in her book *Membership and Morals,* speaks directly to the concerns of Blanshard, People for the American Way, Gutmann, and advocates of regulations designed to protect vulnerable individuals against racial or sexual harassment. Rosenblum directs her analysis against advocates of what she calls congruence, which she defines as the principle "that the internal life and organization of associations mirror liberal democratic principles and practices."[27] The problem is that not all private associations are congruent with liberal democracy: clubs like the Jaycees excluded women, the Boy Scouts exclude not only women but homosexuals, and African-American student organizations on some campuses want to exclude whites.

And these are relatively benign examples of illiberalism among associations. For better or worse, civil society includes such organizations as secret societies, various militia that stockpile (and, on rare occasions, use) weapons, and groups that not only seek to make abortions illegal but try to prevent women from obtaining them. In the face of these realities, what is a pluralist to do?

Rosenblum's answer is that a pluralism must accept what she calls indeterminacy. We cannot establish an outcome to which groups in civil society are expected to adhere and then insist that they guide their efforts to reach that outcome. The reason we have politics in the first place is that outcomes are not determined. Thus to say that organizations should encourage their members to be civically engaged, or to promote democratic understanding, or to value pluralism itself, closes those groups off from deciding for themselves what their purposes are. Pluralism is valuable, Rosenblum argues, because membership in organizations is valuable. The groups that people join enable them to fashion their political identity, to experience the solidarity of working with others, to overcome isolation—and to give them a voice in public policy. Rosenblum goes so far as to suggest that hate groups are just as likely to perform these functions for their members as any other group, which means that society is better off if the alienated be allowed to join them than it would be to leave them out in the cold.

Rosenblum's analysis has obvious implications for the question of religious pluralism. Many religious associations are congruent with liberal democracy, but not all of them are. When we are dealing with fundamentalist religions that seem to close their members off from participation in the wider society, Rosenblum warns, we should nonetheless recognize that they offer moral benefits to their members. Indeed, she argues, even "cults" can perform valuable functions, teaching "rehabilitation, habits of industry, and ability to earn." Associations that are not congruent with liberal democracy, without ever intending to do so, can make better citizens. "Religious associations can be hostile to consent and choice yet heighten perceptions of the voluntarism of membership. They can deprecate personal liberty yet provide a powerful experience of social experiment and elective affinity." Rosenblum therefore concludes that "active rejection of liberal virtues within associations is compatible with fostering other, positive moral dispositions. For liberals attempting to assess the morality of association and the parameters for religious associations, this is the crisis from which we cannot be spared."[28]

With Rosenblum's analysis, we come about as far from the worldview of Paul Blanshard as it is possible to go. Even if Paul Blanshard were right about the authoritarian character of the Catholic Church, liberal democracy has no business passing judgment on the internal dynamics of the groups that compose it before deciding which will further liberal democracy and which will not. Nor would Rosenblum be as quick as is Gutmann to regulate the diversity found in civil society so that it conforms to liberal standards. Gutmann considers the question of whether fundamentalist Christians ought to be allowed to establish schools that segregate by race a "hard choice" but concludes that "Christian fundamentalists are not just members of a church, they are citizens of *our* society."[29] Rosenblum, by contrast, cites a jurist who confidently proclaimed that fundamentalist religions could practice nondiscrimination without impairing their viability as religions, and suggests that that point of view is an example of a "remarkable, speculative conclusion" in which a judge "invents his own theology."[30]

Rosenblum points out that her view does not imply that government has a positive duty to support religious organizations in their quest to pursue their goals as they define them. But it does suggest that liberal democracy not only need not fear sectarian organizations but can be strengthened by taking a hands-off approach to their sectarianism. Wary of what she calls "tutorial government," Rosenblum argues for a pluralism that resists the temptation to guide people and organizations to represent their better side.[31] A truly pluralistic society would contain not only groups with different visions of the nature and purposes of human life but groups with radically different understandings of how those purposes could be achieved, including those whose understandings are at variance with the rules and procedures of liberal democracy itself.

LIVING WITH DIVERSITY

As refreshing as I find Rosenblum's version of robust pluralism, it is not without problems. One of the reasons U.S. democracy is strong is because it has been shaped and reshaped by waves of new immigrants bringing with them new entrepreneurial and political energy. Unlike what has been called the "segmented societies" of Europe, such as Belgium or Holland, Americans seek to assimilate different groups into a common culture that borrows from all of them but resembles none of them.[32] Since the 1960s this ideal of assimilation has been under attack by a wide variety of groups speaking in favor of specific identities rather than cultural assimilation. We usually associate identity politics with groups on the left: African Americans, women, and gay activists. But separatist trends can be found all across the political map. In recent years,

America has seen a resurgence of orthodox Jewry, including, for the first time in its history, a significant trend among Jews to prefer private schools to public ones.[33] Islamic immigrants often want schools of their own as well. Even conservative Christians, at least those in the academy, describe themselves as a religious minority excluded from the dominant culture of secular humanism and find themselves turning to identity politics and a postmodern criticism of hegemony as a result.[34]

An additional example of this tendency to resist assimilation into America involves the very religion that Paul Blanshard made the focus of his concerns. Despite, or because of, the great success of Catholic colleges and universities in modernizing themselves, the Vatican has called for those colleges and universities to strengthen their Catholic character, including methods—such as mandates of faith for theology professors—that seem to violate principles of academic freedom.[35] Not many theology professors at Catholic universities—or college presidents—are happy about this turn of events, but, were he alive today, no doubt Paul Blanshard would be.[36] Here is proof, he would say, that the Catholic hierarchy really is exceptional. Many colleges and universities originated as religious institutions but eventually became integrated into the culture of higher education. The leadership of the Catholic Church is determined to avoid that outcome.

I remain a strong enough advocate of assimilation to be worried about whether girls-only schools, African-American curricula, and conservative Christian academies give students the exposure to others that they ought to have. For the same reason, I believe the Vatican to be wrong in its efforts to impose greater orthodoxy on American Catholic colleges and universities if the cost of doing so results in few non-Catholic students and faculty. There is merit to Amy Gutmann's argument that people benefit from exposure to viewpoints other than those instilled by their parents. The important question is not whether such exposure should be welcomed but how it should be accomplished. A wise polity, just like a wise school, I believe, would not force assimilation explicitly but encourage it indirectly. And it would insist that it is just as important for liberal cosmopolitans to be exposed to the views of traditional religious believers as the other way around. We ought not to turn all Americans into liberal citizens because not all citizens want to be liberal. But government can insist that all citizens be treated as citizens, members of a common society with rights and obligations. (Noncitizens, as well, are subject to the laws of the society and, because they have a right to use society's institutions, including its schools, they are also subject to the authority of those institutions.) Schools are agents of society and as such fail in their mission if they treat those whom they presume to educate as fully formed when they enter, for then there would be no purpose in their attending school in the first place.

Still, if Gutmann is correct to emphasize the benefits of exposure, Rosenblum is right to remind us that there is only so much that we as a society can do to ensure the outcomes we prefer. If we really want diversity, we must live in an untidy world in which others different from us go about doing things differently from us. That is why, for all my discomfort with *Ex Corde Ecclesiae,* the Vatican's efforts to maintain the Catholic character of Catholic institutions, I recognize that what attracted me to a Catholic college in the first place was that it was not a typical, directionless, research university. In an ideal world, I would like to see all institutions be pluralist within. But if we are not to have that, we are best off having pluralism between institutions. The point is to have pluralism somewhere.

Much has changed since Paul Blanshard wrote *American Freedom and Catholic Power.* But one thing has not changed at all. America is a society of extraordinary diversity and will continue to be one for the foreseeable future. It is inherent in diversity that not all people share the same views of God, human nature, the purposes of politics, and the meaning of community. Whatever form pluralism takes, it demands of us that we do our best not to treat those with whom we differ as political enemies. Paul Blanshard never did that with Catholics, and all too few contemporary liberals do that with respect to conservative Protestants. This does not mean that we ought not to have our political disagreements and to express them strongly. But it does mean that we treat them with the respect due to fellow members of a common society.

NOTES

1. Paul Blanshard, *American Freedom and Catholic Power* (2d ed., rev. and enlarged; Boston: Beacon, 1958), pp. 83, 85, 87–88, 94, 98.
2. Will Herberg, *Protestant, Catholic, Jew: An Essay in American Religious Sociology* (Garden City, N.Y.: Doubleday, 1955).
3. For perspectives on these changes, see Charles R. Morris, *American Catholic: The Saints and Sinners Who Built America's Most Powerful Church* (New York: Times Books, 1997); Philip Gleason, *Contending with Modernity: Catholic Higher Education in the Twentieth Century* (New York: Oxford University Press, 1995); Gene Burns, *The Frontiers of Catholicism: The Politics of Ideology in a Liberal World* (Berkeley: University of California Press, 1992); and Michele Dillon, *Catholic Identity: Balancing Reason, Faith, and Power* (New York: Cambridge University Press, 1999).

4. I have written about these changes at greater length in "Liberals and Catholics," *American Prospect* 11 (January 31, 2000).

5. An analysis of Blanshard's book and its reception can be found in John T. McGreevy, "Thinking on One's Own: Catholicism in the American Intellectual Imagination, 1928–1960," *Journal of American History* 84 (June 1997).

6. Vincent Crapanzano, *Serving the Word: Literalism in America from the Pulpit to the Bench* (New York: New Press, 2000), pp. 394–95.

7. Freedom Network Page, www.aclu.org.

8. People for the American Way, *A Right Wing and a Prayer: The Religious Right and Your Public Schools,* pamphlet, p. 15.

9. Paul Blanshard, *Communism, Democracy, and American Power* (Boston: Beacon, 1951).

10. People for the American Way, *A Right Wing and a Prayer,* pp. 4–5.

11. Blanshard, *Communism, Democracy, and American Power,* pp. 124–25.

12. Barbara Miner, "Target: Public Education," *Nation* 267 (November 30, 1998): 6

13. Liz Galst, "The Right Fight," *Mother Jones,* March–April 1994, p. 59.

14. People for the American Way, *Right Wing and a Prayer,* p. 12.

15. Ibid., p. 6.

16. These include Paul Weyrich, who expresses his views at www.freecongress.org. For a similar argument, see Cal Thomas and Ed Dobson, *Blinded by Might: Can the "Religious Right" Save America?* (Grand Rapids, Mich.: Zondervan, 1999).

17. Sidney Hook, *Heresy Yes, Conspiracy No* (New York: John Day, 1953).

18. Blanshard, *Communism, Democracy, and American Power,* pp. 325, 337, 346–47.

19. Amy Gutmann, *Democratic Education* (Princeton: Princeton University Press, 1987), p. 33.

20. Ibid., pp. 38–39.

21. Ibid., p. 39.

22. Ibid., pp. 39–40.

23. Quoted in Alan Charles Kors and Harvey A. Silvergate, *The Shadow University: The Betrayal of Liberty on America's Campuses* (New York: Free Press, 1998), p. 107.

24. Isaiah Berlin, "Two Concepts of Liberty," in *Four Essays on Liberty* (Oxford: Oxford University Press, 1969).

25. Charles Taylor, "What's Wrong with Negative Liberty?" in *Philosophical Papers,* vol. 2, *Philosophy and the Human Sciences* (Cambridge: Cambridge University Press, 1985).

26. Stephen Holmes, *Passions and Constraint: On the Theory of Liberal Democracy* (Chicago: University of Chicago Press, 1995).

27. Nancy Rosenblum, *Membership and Morals: The Personal Uses of Pluralism in America* (Princeton: Princeton University Press, 1998), p. 36.

28. Ibid., pp. 104, 108.

29. Gutmann, *Democratic Education,* p. 120

30. Rosenblum, *Membership and Morals,* p. 96.

31. Ibid., p. 350.

32. Arend Lijphart, *The Politics of Accommodation: Pluralism and Democracy in the Netherlands* (Berkeley: University of California Press, 1968).

33. Peter Beinart, "Education: The Rise of Jewish Schools," *Atlantic Monthly* 284 (October 1998).

34. For one example, see George M. Marsden, *The Outrageous Idea of Christian Scholarship* (New York: Oxford University Press, 1997).

35. Draft Text of *Ex Corde Ecclesiae,* Implementation Document, by Subcommittee of U.S. Bishops' Ad Hoc Committee on the Implementation of "Ex Corde Ecclesiae," *Origins: CNS Documentary News Service* 28 (December 3, 1998).

36. See J. Donald Monan, S.J., and Edward A. Malloy, C.S.C., "Ex Corde Ecclesiae Creates an Impasse," *America,* January 30, 1999.

Chapter 13 Religion and Education: American Exceptionalism?

Charles L. Glenn

The world of K–12 schooling in the United States is regularly troubled by controversies over religion. "School wars" (as they were often called) of this sort were a primary focus of political life in Europe in the nineteenth century, but they are so no longer. How did France and Germany, Belgium and the Netherlands, and other Western democracies manage to get beyond these troubling issues? Why does public life in the United States have such difficulty accommodating the diverse religious concerns of parents?

Controversies over American education occur on two quite distinct levels. Policy specialists, education organizations, and business groups worry about the quality of public schools: do they set high enough expectations? Why is the quality so uneven? What accounts for the complacency of many students who are learning much less than their European or Asian counterparts? The policy debates also call into question whether various strategies to improve the schools could have unanticipated negative consequences. Reducing class size might have a negative effect on teacher quality. Stress on measurable outcomes might sacrifice valuable educational objectives that are not easily measured. And so it goes . . .

Few parents are troubled by these questions—though perhaps they should be—but many are deeply concerned about the disparity between what they believe is healthy and good for their children and what they believe is provided in school. Many show their concern by taking their children out of the public schools, and a rapidly growing number are schooling their children at home. Stephen Carter reported, in his 1995 Massey Lectures, that he frequently meets "people who complain that the deck is stacked against a family trying to teach what they often call 'traditional values' or 'family values.' . . . There is a widely shared perception that the institutions of the government, far from reinforcing the values many people want their children to learn, actively frustrate them."[1] It is in relation to public schools that parental disappointment and even suspicion are most acute.

Some of these discontented parents are troubled by the way the public schools seem to dismiss their own religious beliefs or moral codes. Other parents object when—perhaps in the name of "multi-culturalism"—their children are exposed to any religious beliefs or practices at all. Teachers may come under criticism for seeking to promote their own beliefs . . . or unbelief. Pupils are told that they cannot use religious themes that are meaningful to them in their homework. Too often, these conflicts between the worldviews of parents and those that are presented to their children in public school end up in court.

Why is this a problem? More is at stake in these conflicts even than ebbing support for public schools and growing interest in vouchers and home-schooling. Ironically, the public schools, which Horace Mann and other nineteenth-century reformers saw as the unifying institution of a diverse and rapidly changing society, have become an occasion of disunity. This is evident, for example, in the great difficulty that policy makers have in developing educational standards specific enough to serve as the basis for accountability. It is evident also in the inability of most public high schools to engage their students in a way that leads to academic effort and thus to the virtuous habits of application and persistence. "Across the country, whether surrounded by suburban affluence or urban poverty," Laurence Steinberg and his associates found, "students' commitment to school is at an all-time low."[2] It is tempting to attribute this disengagement—and consequent mediocre achievement—to the self-indulgence characteristic of the wider culture, but in fact by international standards American adults work unusually hard and productively at their jobs. Something else is going on in public secondary schools; they have become "shopping malls" that cater to every taste and allow students to decide whether or not they will make an effort. Public schools have become incapable of communicating that their academic mission is important. This contrasts with Linda Valli's description of the "curriculum of effort" in the Catholic high school, where "the school's emphasis on effort is assisted by an archdiocesan policy that no student fail because of ability. . . . Tracking is viewed by students as one school effort to keep them from failing courses too difficult for them. . . . Some teachers pass students if they do their homework but fail quizzes, but automatically fail students if they neglect a certain amount of homework. This focus on effort is not lost on students."[3]

The incoherence of the public high school, which makes it unable to engage students effectively in their own learning, grows in large part out of the conflicting worldviews that public schools must accommodate. Staff do not, unless by sheer and unlikely accident, share the same understanding of the nature of human life and the conditions of its flourishing, nor have parents chosen the school. In contrast, "instead of a neutrality shaped by conflicting values among school participants, private schools seek agreement about institutional purpose. Ideally families and schools are fused in a single community of values. . . . Instead of promoting individualization by the presence of boundless opportunities and the absence of restraints, private schools attempt to promote it by giving intimate personal attention." This agreement about school purpose is especially important for average students. But many teachers accept as inevitable and desirable the neutrality of the shopping mall high school. It is the price that has to be paid to accommodate the entire spectrum of adolescent values and capacities. One teacher admitted that his school had no clear commitment to learning, only a clear commitment to accommodating student diversity.[4]

Although vouchers and standards are debated by policy elites as competing methods for reform through bringing market forces to bear on stagnant schools, their resonance with parents has much more to do with the possibility of choosing a school based on a coherent worldview and a clearly articulated academic mission. Parents are (unfortunately) not up in arms about the general mediocrity of academic expectations in American schools, but many are anxious about the messages that are being communicated to their children.

It should not be surprising that religion is a source of controversy for American education. After all, the slogan of "educational neutrality" is naive when it is not disingenuous. To educate is to take a stand for a particular understanding of what life is about and how its challenges should be met. The teacher who communicates that such questions are unimportant, or that any answer to them is as good as any other, is not being neutral—he or she is expressing a viewpoint that may be as intolerantly proselytizing as any other. Americans are a highly religious people who send their children to schools organized on the basis of a local monopoly of public education. The reality that this system is secularistic—by no means neutral between the claims of religious and materialist understandings of reality—is a formula for conflict. For two generations American public schools have suffered from a sort of low-grade fever which has never become a major political crisis but cumulatively has undermined their capacity to educate with undivided conviction. Teachers are forced to teach defensively, in schools that have become incoherent.[5]

When teachers and parents come together around shared and clearly articulated goals, there is a much greater prospect than in monopoly systems that effective education will occur and that students will buy into the mission of the school. Something else happens, as well: trust and habits of cooperation are developed as adults discuss and negotiate about matters important to children. Schools that are not enmeshed in bureaucracy help to develop, in adult participants, the characteristics upon which a healthy civil society depends. It was no accident that the creation of independent schools was one of the first signs of a reviving civil society in postcommunist eastern Europe and is a matter of pressing concern in our own inner cities.[6]

How has it come about that the United States, so much less "secular" than western Europe, as measured by church attendance and surveys of religious belief, is so much more secular when it comes to educational policy? Although almost every country in Europe provides public funds to faith-based schools, this is—in principle at least—forbidden in the United States. And though the famous "wall of separation" is showing some cracks, it continues to be an absolute article of faith in American public education circles.

There are obviously two ends to this puzzling contrast. One is the rigid separation of government from religious activities (or at least from those affecting elementary and secondary schooling) in the United States; the other, the lack of such a 'bright line' in the sociologically much more secularized societies of Europe.

European nations (as well as Canada and Australia) have chosen to provide public funding to schools with an explicitly religious character, in contrast with the "strict separation" practiced in the United States. What explains this greater readiness to accommodate the religious convictions of some parents in societies that are in fact highly secularized? There are a number of reasons, no one of which alone would explain this phenomenon.

HISTORICAL ROOTS

First, there are historical commonalities and differences. The development of universal schooling in Europe, as in the United States, took place against the background of the transformation from agricultural to industrialized societies. Rootless urban workers seemed much more dangerous than peasants going through their immemorial routines. Concerned about the rapid changes in the character of their societies, elites came to believe that schooling should be extended to the entire population. "For a post-Enlightenment, nineteenth-century West, education stood out as a god and an engine of progress. Faith in its beneficial results, for states, societies, and individuals, was one of the premier tenets of the world view that emerged in the era."[7]

Accompanying the confidence in progress was an anxiety among elites about social control of the newly mobile population gathered in cities and other industrial areas. Universal schooling seemed not only an instrument of progress but also a way to tame the masses. In particular, it was hoped, schooling would disseminate a national spirit to replace regional loyalties, as the national language would replace local dialects and minority languages. Schooling under state supervision would be a way to bind together nations that were emerging from dynastic states or (in the American, Canadian, and Australian cases) from loosely linked colonies.

As "progressive," change-oriented elites sought to hasten the pace and control the direction of social change through developing systems of universal schooling, they came up inevitably against the traditional role of churches as the educators of the people. In Great Britain, Scandinavia, the Netherlands, and those areas of Germany with established Protestant churches, the solution was simple: government subsidized the official church's schools, or where these were lacking established its own with primary oversight exercised by the clergy of the state church. Little tension was felt between the educational interests of church and state; theologians like Schleiermacher in Prussia and Hofstede de Groot in the Netherlands served as government school inspectors, as did—for thirty-five years—the writer Matthew Arnold in England.[8] In the Netherlands, in Canada, in Great Britain, and in Germany, strong Catholic minorities were accommodated by providing parallel Catholic and Protestant educational systems, with the latter gradually emptied of distinctive religious character.

In predominantly Catholic countries like France and Belgium, Italy and Spain, however, conflict developed very soon between secular elites and church leaders over the control of popular schooling.[9] Blame for this conflict rests on both sides. To the progressive elites, Catholicism was, as Voltaire and other *philosophes* had insisted several generations earlier, a barrier to progress, incapable of making any positive contribution to society. For Catholic leadership, still recoiling from the persecution and the anti-Christian propaganda of the French Revolution's radical phase, no compromise was possible with liberalism and democracy. This mutual antagonism was only reinforced by political events during the course of the nineteenth century. In France, for example, the Revolution of 1848 had anticlerical dimensions and was followed by a period of Catholic support for the imposition of order by the prince-president, soon Napoleon III. Similarly, the violence of the Commune in 1871, which included the murder of the archbishop of Paris, was followed by another period of Catholic reaction, which in turn led to a phase of deliberate limitations upon the political influence of the Catholic Church. With each turn of events, control of popular schooling was a central issue. Similar (though not generally as dramatic) events occurred over the course of the century in other countries with a largely Catholic population.

The primary controversies over religion and education in western Europe were not about whether religion should be taught in state-supported schools but about the extent of government control over those schools. In Germany almost all state schools were either Catholic or Protestant until the postwar period, but there were few nonstate schools. In the Netherlands and Belgium, by contrast, the number and enrollment of nonstate schools came to exceed that of the schools operated by public authorities. The massive demonstrations over educational policy in France and Spain in 1984 were in reaction to efforts by socialist governments to gain greater control over Catholic and other nonpublic schools supported with public funds.

In the United States, however, the demand for religious schooling came to be identified with efforts of Catholic and, to a lesser extent, Protestant, immigrant groups to maintain aspects of their distinctiveness. This apparent threat to the U.S. social and political order was perceived as deeply threatening by the native Protestant majority, and they were willing to purge public schools of what had been their religious character in order to meet (though without ever satisfying) objections to them by Catholic leadership.[10] As a result, the development of American education was different in two fundamental respects from that in western Europe and even in Canada: government-operated schooling came to be nonreligious, and church-operated schooling received no public funding.

PUBLIC ACCOUNTABILITY

A second reason for the puzzling—to most Americans—European support for nonpublic schools, most of them with a religious character, is that these schools are far more integrated into the public education system than is the case in the United States. They operate within a framework of accountability and outcome standards; nowhere in Europe is it assumed that if policy makers simply "let the market rip," the result will be adequate and equitable. The requirements placed upon "free schools" (the term used in preference to "private schools") are essentially the same as those placed by government upon schools operated by municipalities, though the former are considerably freer of ordinary bureaucratic requirements.

These requirements include, in general, a national (or, in the case of Germany, a state) curriculum that specifies in some detail the subjects which must be covered and the number of hours to be devoted to each; rules about the qualifications, salaries, and working conditions of teachers; and tests that students must take at major points of transition.[11] Although testing is less frequent than in the United States, the consequences of the tests tend to be more significant; this has a definite effect on individual schools, whether operated by government or not, as well as on the seriousness with which pupils and teachers take their work.[12]

European nonpublic schools, unlike those in the United States, play by the same quality control rules as do public schools, and their teachers, unlike teachers in the United States, belong to a unified profession whether they work in public or in nonpublic schools. One result of this similarity is that there is little political challenge to the inclusion of these schools on equal terms in public funding. In particular, there is nothing like the entrenched opposition of the American teachers' unions to public funding for nonpublic schools. European teachers' unions seek instead to expand government control over nonpublic schools and in particular to impose upon them the same employment conditions as in government-operated schools.

This creates its own problems, of course. Much debate goes on about whether and to what extent nonpublic schools continue to be distinctive and thus fill a useful role in society. Groups that are opposed to religious schooling for ideological reasons suggest on the one hand that if nonpublic schools are really different from public schools, they can only exacerbate the growing divisions within society as a result of the presence of Muslim immigrants; on the other hand, if nonpublic schools are not really different, critics say, they have no reason to exist. Catch-22! But such objections have found little support, and generally all political parties support continued subsidies for nonpublic schools.

More dangerous, many supporters of religious schooling believe, is the temptation they face to conform to the model provided by public schools, especially as the ever-increasing burden of regulation and standards reduces the scope for distinctiveness. Nor is government alone to blame. Staff and governing boards of nonpublic schools may drift into conformity with prevailing norms for education, and all the more because public funding removes the necessity of defining their mission clearly to supporters within a religious community.[13]

THE COMMITMENT TO RELIGIOUS AND EDUCATIONAL FREEDOM

The loss by nonpublic schools of their distinctive character is a political as well as an educational issue in western Europe. The public funding provided to faith-based schools is understood as a basic human right and as a political accommodation of the demands of parents, not as a market mechanism to improve the quality of education. If these schools no longer correspond to what parents motivated by religious convictions want and are entitled to for their children, they fail in their mission of providing an institutional support to religious freedom.

Americans are inclined to pay little attention to the abstraction of universal "human rights" and to focus instead upon those rights protected by our Bill of Rights and by state and federal laws. Perhaps this is a result of the remarkable stability and continuity of our legal system over the past two centuries. In most other countries, however, the international covenants adopted in the wake of World War II and in revulsion against fascism are taken seriously as a protection against arbitrary government action.

The *Universal Declaration of Human Rights* (adopted in 1948) states that "parents have a prior right to choose the kind of education that shall be given to their children" (article 26, 3).[14] Of course, this goes no further that the U.S. Supreme Court's decision in *Pierce v. Society of Sisters* (268 U.S. 510 [1925]) and does not require that government subsidize the choices of parents. Similarly, the language of the *International Covenant on Economic, Social and Cultural Rights* (1966) affirms that "the States Parties to the present Covenant undertake to have respect for the liberty of parents . . . to choose for their children schools, other than those established by public authorities, which conform to such minimum educational standards as may be laid down or approved by the State and to ensure the religious and moral education of their children in conformity with their own convictions" (article 13, 3). Like the *Pierce* decision, this clause asserts a right of parents without a corresponding duty of government to ensure that parents can exercise that right. Indeed, the only duty of government implied here is to set educational standards and to ensure that non-government schools meet them. This, too, is parallel to the language in *Pierce* affirming "the power of the state reasonably to regulate all schools, to inspect, supervise, and examine them, their teachers and pupils; to require that all children of proper age attend some school, that teachers shall be of good moral character and patriotic disposition, that certain studies plainly essential to good citizenship must be taught, and that nothing be taught which is manifestly inimical to the public welfare."

By contrast, the First Protocol to the *European Convention for the Protection of Human Rights and Fundamental Freedoms* (1952) provides that "in the exercise of any functions which it assumes in relation to education and teaching, the State shall respect the right of parents to ensure such education and teaching in conformity with their own religious and philosophical convictions" (article 2). There is a subtle but significant shift evident in this language. To the extent that governments do anything about education, it suggests, they should do it in an even-handed way that does not make it more difficult for parents to provide their children with a religious than a secular education. And whereas the other covenants have largely a moral effect, compliance with the *European Convention* is monitored by the European Commission for Human Rights and enforced against member governments by the European Court in Strasbourg. It has teeth.

It seems unlikely that such language would have been adopted by the Council of Europe if it did not reflect what is already the practice in most of its member states.

POPULAR DEMAND

Despite widespread secularization, there continues to be strong demand, in a number of European countries, for faith-based schooling. This is true even of many parents who themselves profess no religious convictions. This demand seems to arise from a perception that schools with a religious character are more effective than the schools operated by government, both academically and in supporting broad educational development. Research evidence from the Netherlands supports that from the United States and Great Britain in suggesting that schools with a religiously based ethos have an advantage over schools committed to value neutrality.[15]

A nationwide study of the effectiveness of Dutch secondary schools found that both Protestant and Catholic schools produced better results on cognitive measures and also on the satisfaction of students and teachers than did government-operated schools. The author concluded that this result had to do in large part with the clarity of identity of the former, and urged that public schools seek to develop something of the same quality.[16] Another Dutch study found that "after allowing for social background, primary school career, preceding career in secondary education and present school features, the Protestant sector effect leads to relatively high achievement, giving them a considerable advantage over other students. . . . Of the Protestant school students, 51% enroll in college and university education, whereas only 40% of the public school students and 45% of the Catholic school students take this decision." The study concluded that "if private schools produce better outcomes for nearly the same price and if parents perceive this quality of schools correctly, it is a rational decision for parents to send their children to private schools, despite their own religious preferences." According to the authors, this confirmed American research showing a religious school advantage, since "our research suggests that sector effects remain when the effects of selection and self-selection due to an unequal government support of private and public schools are eliminated."[17]

To the extent that the American, British, and Dutch researchers are correct, it is not just the relative or complete autonomy of most religious schools that gives them an advantage in effectiveness (as Chubb and Moe seem to believe), but also the moral coherence that they derive from a shared ethos.[18] "Consensus on goals, high expectations for students and the like could be reflections of the cultural aspects of schools rather than their rational aspects, tied more closely to social organization and to a community of values . . . than to role compliance within a bureaucratic structure."[19]

Whether from the intuitions of parents or the research of scholars, the apparent advantage of faith-based schools poses a challenge to public schooling. One response is to seek to bring nonpublic schools under the same disadvantages as public schools by greatly increasing the regulatory and procedural burden they must bear; this was, as we have seen, the cause of massive protests by parents in France and Spain in 1984. Another response would be to free public schools to function more like nonpublic schools, as in the case of charter schools in the United States. Experiments along these lines have been common in recent years in Europe, from the Thatcher government's initiative to allow schools to "opt out" of their local school systems, to various measures in Germany and the Netherlands to increase the autonomy of public schools, to French experiments with nongeographical attendance as a way to promote parental choice.

A more daring possibility, suggested by Bryk, Lee, and Holland in the United States, would be to create a secular ideology of sufficient power to take the place of religious belief as the ethos at the heart of a school.[20] This idea resurfaces periodically in France, where, under the challenge of increased ethnic and cultural diversity, some have argued for a new definition of *laïcité* (secularity, in the sense of a humanistic worldview) that takes into account the growing diversity of French society "without surrendering to relativism from above or tribalism from below." France needs, they say, to rediscover a set of values that could without apology be taught to all students, taking into account "the situation of ethical pluralism in which contemporary France finds itself." Louis Legrand asked hopefully whether "the concept of man in the world that emerges from anthropology would not make it possible to establish a new unifying ethic, acceptable to all." A shared search for truth would replace religion as a source of meaning, and "the tolerance thus developed would be the cement of a secular and democratic society." Only through such an ethos could the "common school" *(l'école unique)* continue to exert a broadly educating influence.[21] But efforts to create a secular equivalent of religion have proved no more successful in the late twentieth century than they did in the late eighteenth (with Robespierre's Cult of Reason) or in the mid-nineteenth (with Comte's Religion of Humanity) or, indeed, in the mid-twentieth, with Dewey's proposal that a "common faith" of secular humanism be made the basis for education and social progress.[22]

No, millions of parents in secularized western Europe continue to choose schools for their children that are based on the traditional faiths. This preference seems to reflect what could be called broadly cultural concerns for which religion serves as an organizing principle. In Belgium, for example, research in the 1970s found that, quite apart from social class and income, there continued to be differences in lifestyle and in moral convictions and behavior between those who chose Catholic and those who chose public schools. Given this pattern, the growing secularization of Belgian society has not led to the decline of

Catholic "free" schools, which continue to serve the majority of school-age children in Belgium. Among parents who did not attend church but were rooted in a Catholic milieu, three out of four sent their children to a Catholic school. Billiet suggested that the Catholic milieu—including its schools—might be coming to take the place of the church for many secularized Belgians. After all, "a change in religious convictions and practices is not necessarily accompanied, on the structural level, by the abandonment of networks of social relationships, and in addition there can be a development, on the cultural level, of a sort of surrogate for churchliness."[23]

In the Netherlands, debate breaks out periodically over whether there is an excessive supply of Protestant and Catholic schooling in view of the low church attendance. One survey cited to support that position asked parents what reasons were important or unimportant in choosing a secondary school. For critics of the present system of support for confessional education, it was significant that only 12 percent of the parents said that it was very important that the school "base its education on the religion or worldview of our family." On the other hand, the "important" and "very important" responses on this item were a combined 40 percent. By comparison, 31 percent of parents found the quality of the school building important or very important. For 88 percent it was important or very important that the school "operate on the basis of ideas about the education of children that we support."[24]

What can we make of such results? Certainly not that choice is unimportant to Dutch parents, such that they could be satisfied with a single type of schooling: for seven out of eight the educational philosophy of a school is important, and it is fair to assume that this means they are not satisfied with every variety. Religious identity of a school is less significant as a motivation for making a particular choice, though 40 percent represents a large constituency.

Researchers working in the Utrecht area asked parents about their primary reason for selecting an elementary school. Of 666 sets of parents who responded to the written inquiry, 70 percent stated that school quality was the most important consideration, and for only 22 percent was the particular religious character of the school the most important. This seemed to suggest that there was an oversupply of religious schooling in the Netherlands, but this conclusion is misleading. Many parents who value schooling shaped by a particular religious tradition would nevertheless put quality even higher; indeed, it is striking that as many as 30 percent of the parents were willing to give quality the second place to another school characteristic. A more satisfactory analysis of the strength of motivation would ask what proportion of parents would accept a school at some distance from their home (in a country where children must get themselves to school). Considered in this way, the figures suggest a rather different picture: 54 percent of the parents regarded the religious character of the school as more important than the distance from home to school. It is fair to conclude, then, that for something more than half of the parents, the religious or ideological characteristics of the school were an important consideration in making a selection. For 27 percent of the parents, religious character was more important than quality, while for 44 percent it was the least important consideration.

This study provides an opportunity to compare the proportion of Dutch parents who characterized themselves as having religious convictions with the proportion with a preference for particular school choices. Of the total sample, 35 percent identified themselves as Protestant or Catholic, 50 percent expressed a preference for a Protestant or Catholic school, and 32 percent expressed a preference for a public school. If this sample is representative of the Netherlands as a whole, there is an almost exact correspondence between the proportion wanting public schools and the proportion of total elementary enrollment in such schools. These results do not suggest a fundamental mismatch between parental wishes and the availability of nonreligious public education.[25]

As in Belgium, it appears that the choice of faith-based schools in the Netherlands reflects general cultural preferences for many parents whose specifically religious views do not correspond with those of the school. In the early 1970s, a study was made of the reasons that parents chose Protestant schools. For 77 percent of the parents, the Christian character of the instruction was an important consideration, and 69 percent wanted a school that would shield children from "worldly ideas." A third important motive had to do with the atmosphere of the school: the Protestant school was seen as more concerned with the happiness and personal development of the child and less with worldly success, and teachers were seen as more approachable. This group of parents placed the primary responsibility for education on parents (69 percent) rather than on the government (21 percent) or the churches (4 percent). When asked how Protestant schools differed from public schools, far more gave answers related to atmosphere and values than to "quality" as such.[26]

In short, there seems to be broad and continuing support for faith-based schooling in western Europe, despite the extensive secularization of most European societies compared with the United States.

DIFFERENT APPROACHES TO
ACCOMMODATING RELIGION IN EDUCATION

Although we can learn a good deal by comparing the European approach to accommodating religious conviction in publicly funded education with the American refusal to make such accommodations, we should also note some differences among the European systems. Emerging as compromises from nineteenth-century struggles over the control of schooling, these arrangements include both government schools with a religious character, as in Germany and Great Britain, and equal funding for nongovernment schools, as in Belgium, France, and the Netherlands. The first alternative has come to seem less attractive than the second to those who wish faith-based schooling, because nongovernment schools have somewhat greater autonomy and scope to maintain the distinctive religious flavor of the education provided . . . and to maintain other characteristics which many parents value in the schooling of their children. Indeed, over recent decades, in Germany and in much of Canada government schools with a Protestant character have surrendered that character and become religiously neutral alternatives to Catholic schools. These, in turn, perhaps because of more formalized connections with an institutional church, have retained their identity, however attenuated it may be in practice.

Germany

In most of the states that came together to form Germany in the late nineteenth century, public schooling was overwhelmingly confessional, and this pattern continued in the predominantly Catholic states North Rhine–Westphalia, Rhineland-Palatinate, and Bavaria even after World War II.[27] During the postwar period, the predominantly Protestant states opted for nonconfessional schools, while making provision for public funding of nongovernment confessional schools. This reflects the fact that in recent decades the Protestant state churches have made much less use than has the Catholic Church of the opportunity to insist upon confessional schools. Seventy-one percent of the elementary schools in Germany were Protestant in 1911, and 56 percent were Protestant in 1932, but by 1965 only 17 percent of public elementary schools in the Federal Republic (apart from the three city-states Bremen, Hamburg, and Berlin) were Protestant, compared with 40 percent that were Catholic and 43 percent nonconfessional or other.[28] The accommodation of religious convictions in German education began to weaken during the 1960s, not least because the convictions themselves weakened through growing secularization. Protestant leaders came out in formal support of nonconfessional schools in 1958, and through the next decade many schools gave up their Protestant identity. Catholic bishops fought a rearguard action, but with declining support from parents. A referendum in 1968, for example, overwhelmingly approved an amendment to the Bavarian constitution that made all public elementary schools "Christian" or interconfessional, with some instruction on a confessional basis. Where public confessional (mostly Catholic) schools continue to exist in Germany, they are operated by local school authorities and are subject to essentially the same controls as nonconfessional public schools.

Although the role of state-sponsored confessional schooling has faded in postwar Germany, that of nongovernment independent schools, while still numerically insignificant, has grown somewhat. Article 7 of the federal constitution guarantees the rights of nongovernment education.[29] The first section, in the German tradition, states that "the entire educational system shall be under the supervision of the state." The next section asserts a limited right of parents "to decide whether [the child] shall receive religious instruction," which is offered in most schools, as provided under the third section. This is as far as the constitution goes in asserting a right of parents to make decisions about the schooling of their children. Nevertheless, some argue that to the extent that the state's own educational system does not provide the variety of forms of schooling—whether religious or pedagogical or structural—desired by parents, the state is under a constitutional obligation to provide support to independent schools to meet that demand.[30]

The fourth section of Article 7 guarantees "the right to establish nongovernment schools" but then makes them subject to government approval if they are to serve as a replacement for municipal schools. The approval "must be given" if they are equal to public schools "in their educational aims, their facilities and the professional training of their teaching staff." Another requirement is that the operation of the nongovernment school not have the effect of promoting "segregation of pupils according to the means of their parents." Finally, the "economic and legal position of the teaching staff" employed by the nongovernment school must be ensured. Thus the right to establish a nongovernment school is in fact highly circumscribed under the German constitution. While state laws in the United States may require that nongovernment schools provide an education equivalent to that available in local public schools, the schools' right of existence is not limited by considerations of social class integration or the interests of teachers, as it is in Germany.

Limitations are even more apparent in the fifth section of the German constitution, which specifies that a nongovernment elementary school will be permitted "only if the education authority finds that it serves a special pedagogical interest, or if, in the application of persons entitled to bring up children, it is to be established as an interdenominational or denominational or ideological school and a state or municipal elementary school of this type does not exist in the community." In other words, there must be an explicit educational justification for a nongovernment elementary school, and it is not sufficient to cite the quality of the instruction provided. The school must have some pedagogical, religious, or ideological specialty that is not available in the local public schools. These additional conditions applicable to elementary education (grades 1 through 4) are based on "the interest of the state in pupils from all sectors of the population receiving a common basic education."[31] As a consequence, the proportion of all pupils attending nonpublic schools is only 2 percent at the elementary level, compared with 8 percent at the secondary. Leaving it up to public-education authorities to decide whether a particular form of schooling "serves a special pedagogical interest" has had the effect of reducing significantly the diversity of German education. For example, an independent alternative school might be turned down on the grounds that no experimental justification exists because similar schools already exist elsewhere.[32]

Controversy has arisen over the extent to which public funds should subsidize the right of parents to make choices among schooling alternatives for their children. As early as 1955 the argument was made that a right guaranteed by the constitution should be secured by public funding—especially if independent schools were to be required to be equivalent to state-funded schools.[33] Initially, state education officials agreed among themselves that the language of Section 7 of the constitution guaranteeing the right to nongovernment schooling did not create an obligation to provide public funding to nongovernment schools. A Federal Administrative Court ruling in 1966 found, however, that the stringent conditions for approval of nongovernment substitute schools would be impossible to meet without subsidies.

The provision of subsidies did not put the issue to rest, however, because the ruling left it up to the *Länder* to determine how best to meet their obligation to make it possible for nongovernment schooling to survive. The actual practices varied. The Federal Constitutional Court issued a ruling in April 1987 based upon the constitutional guarantee that "everyone shall have the right to the free development of his personality" (article 2.1) that went further than ever before in asserting a right to publicly funded nongovernment education. The case was brought by several state-approved nongovernment schools in Hamburg that had been receiving a public subsidy of 25 percent of the costs of comparable public schools. The nongovernment schools pointed out that they were having difficulty surviving with this level of support and that confessional schools in Hamburg were receiving a 77 percent subsidy. The government responded that "the function of nongovernment schools consists of the widening and enrichment of the public school system through alternative offerings." Experience had shown that the greatest demand for such alternatives was for confessional schools on the one hand and for "reform-pedagogical" schools on the other. "The higher support for schools with a distinctive worldview rests in the final analysis on their reliance [upon this support], developed through many years of constant demand. Confessional schools have always played a special role in the German educational system. For this reason, but also as a matter of duty, in order to make up for the closing [by the Nazi government] of the confessional schools in 1939, Hamburg gave them a high level of support in the years after the War."[34] The court concluded that Hamburg could not treat the support of nongovernment schools as a matter of its absolute discretion, so as to make them prosper or decline as seemed best to public officials. The constitution recognized the right to operate nongovernment schools as based on the concern for human dignity, for the unfolding of personality in freedom and self-direction, for freedom of religion and conscience, for the neutrality of the government in relation to religion and worldview, and for respect of the natural rights of parents.

It was not enough, the court found, for the government simply to allow nongovernment schools to exist; it must give them the possibility to develop according to their own uniqueness. Without public support, such self-determination would not be possible. Nongovernment schools could not, at current cost levels, meet the requirements for government approval out of their own resources. To expect them to do so, the court ruled, would inevitably force them to become exclusive schools for the upper classes. But this was precisely contrary to the constitution's decree that nongovernment schools not cause economic segregation. Nongovernment schools must remain accessible for all, not in the sense that they need accept every qualified student but in the sense that economic circumstances not function as a barrier to attendance. "Only when [nongovernment schooling] is fundamentally available to all citizens without regard to their personal financial situations can the [constitutionally] protected educational freedom actually be realized and claimed on an equal basis by all parents and students. . . . This constitutional norm must thus be considered as a mandate to lawmakers to protect and promote private schools."[35] The constitutional right to the free development of personality requires, Jach argues, that the state abstain from defining a single model of maturity that all schools should strive to develop in their pupils. In particular, it should recognize that the goal of individualization does not necessarily point toward the liberal model of the free-standing individual but may rather require meaningful participation in a community. Simply to proclaim "toleration" as the fundamental principle of public schools does not satisfy the developmental need of children to form secure identities in relation to such communities. The state is thus obligated to make it possible for young citizens to have a variety of types of schooling, based upon different concepts of the meaning of "development of personality," and to support independent schools to the extent that public schooling does not include the necessary diversity.[36]

The Netherlands

The Dutch have developed a very different model of the relation between government and faith-based schools, with government directly operating only about 30 percent of the elementary and secondary schools and paying the running costs of approved schools that it does not operate. Most nonpublic schools are either Catholic or Protestant, but there are also Jewish, Muslim, and Hindu schools as well as nonreligious alternative schools of various types, all funded by the national government. The constitutional guarantee of educational freedom has been applied to ensure that most parents have access to the sort of school that they wish for their children within a reasonable distance, not so difficult in this densely populated country.

The role of religiously identifiable institutions of all kinds continues to be significant in Dutch society despite widespread secularization, which has proceeded much further than in the United States. Ninety-four percent of those surveyed in the United States in 1995 said that they believed in God; the comparable response for the Netherlands was 55 percent. In the United States, 93 percent reported that they belonged to a church, though only 34 percent had attended church in the previous week; comparable figures for the Netherlands were 44 percent and 16 percent. The major denominations—Roman Catholic, Dutch Reformed *(Hervormde),* and evangelical *(Gereformeerde)*—have all suffered major losses in recent decades, while a growing number of smaller religious groups have emerged.

Despite this extensive secularization, however, there continues to be support for institutions with a religious identity. Approximately 35 percent of Dutch parents prefer a faith-based school for their own children. The support is much stronger among the more "evangelical" *Gereformeerden*. Ninety-five percent of those who attend church regularly want denominational schools; even among the "marginal" members of this group, 87 percent want schools that have a denominational character, and 36 percent of those who have definitely left the evangelical churches still want denominational schools. On the other hand, support for separate schools (54 percent) is now lower among marginal Catholics, who a generation or two ago would have lived in an almost entirely Catholic social and institutional world.

It should perhaps be noted here that the continuing attachment to some forms of confessional structuring of life—especially that affecting youth—has been accompanied by massive changes in attitudes about a variety of issues. For example, surveys have found that there is very little animosity or suspicion between Catholics and Protestants, and that both are as positive as are the unchurched toward the rights of Muslims to say and do what they will (Catholics 68 percent positive, evangelicals 69 percent, unchurched 67 percent).[37]

Although many social agencies and more than two-thirds of schools continue to claim a religious identity, there is considerable evidence that this has been "hollowed out" by decades of dependence upon the government as well as growing secularization. For example, there has been a perceptible decline in what has been a strong tradition of volunteering, or rather a diversion of the volunteering impulse toward groups seeking to promote causes—often in the Third World—and raise funds rather than provide direct help. "As the societal middle ground continues to lose its independence," Adriaansens and Zijderveld point out, "volunteering changes its character and loses significance." The irony is that the new forms of volunteering directed toward affecting public policies themselves contribute to an ever-expanding state role and further weakening of the civil society.[38]

Alongside professionalization and the devaluing of volunteer help, the growing secularization and weakening of the denominational "pillars" has also changed the nature of the nonprofit organizations that provide social services and education. Organizations which had provided an all-encompassing religious sense of meaning within Catholic or Protestant subsocieties lost their taken-for-grantedness and became at best lifestyle choices and at worst shells stripped of all meaning.[39] Although one might expect that the Netherlands, where two-thirds of the schools have a religious identity, would be a paradise for religiously distinctive education, many Protestant and Catholic schools have become only residually religious. Some policy analysts argue that they have thereby lost their raison d'être and should simply be taken over by the state.[40] In a period of declining enrollments and school closings, determining in practice the meaning of school distinctiveness acquires considerable importance. The availability of a nearby Catholic school, for example, would permit the closing of another that is underenrolled, even though the staff of the two schools might approach Catholic teaching from very different perspectives, with one stressing liberation theology and another the traditional catechism. Such situations are by no means unheard-of; indeed, as long ago as 1933 the Dutch government decided that a group of more conservative Protestant schools deserved to be treated as a separate category from the more liberal Protestant schools, creating a right on the part of a group of parents with a sufficient number of children to have the establishment of one sort of Protestant school funded even if the other sort was available locally.[41]

More recently the question has arisen whether a "neutral" private school, one that reflects no single belief or worldview but is distinctive only in terms of pedagogy, may be considered equivalent to a public school offering the same program and (by law) committed to the same religious neutrality. Is there, in other words, a right to such a private school distinct from any issue of conscience? An advisory opinion of the Education Council (Onderwijsraad) in May 1985 found that there is such a right, because even the deliberate lack of common convictions can be seen as a "philosophical foundation."[42]

Such discussions grow directly out of the perceived need to consolidate schools for budgetary purposes, but they also reflect developments in Dutch society in recent decades. First of these is the way that weakening of traditional religious loyalties has reduced not only church attendance but also commitment to institutions based upon religious identification. This secularization has led to questions about the continuing need for confessional schooling, at least on the present scale.

The second development, related in a complex fashion to the first, is a certain loss of nerve among those upon whom confessional schooling depends to confirm its purpose, from church hierarchies to teachers. If schools are no longer distinctively Catholic or Protestant beyond their labels, public school advocates ask, how does their maintenance with public funds guarantee liberty of conscience? Given the growing ethnic diversity of Dutch society, would it not be better to abandon confessional schooling in favor of a common school that would bridge not only confessional and class differences but ethnic ones as well?

Leaders of Catholic and Protestant schooling have been working for the past twenty years to clarify the meaning of education on a Christian basis, and to help schools to work that out in the details of their daily activities. To accept Max Weber's separation between spheres of facts-without-values and values-without-facts, they argue, is fatal to creating the kinds of schools that are needed, because it suggests the possibility of adding on elements of moral teaching or character development as a supplement to the fundamental instructional mission of the school. Schools should rather integrate their entire program of instruction in subject matter and also development of character and the habits that sustain it into a single value-impregnated vision of what the school is about. A Christian school should not seek to express its religious character simply by a prayer at the beginning of the school day, or a period each week of religious instruction, or by reading from the Bible now and again. A serious engagement with what it means to be a Christian school would require that every aspect of the school be examined from that perspective.

This does not mean, they take care to point out, that a little flavoring, a little sauce of Christianity should be poured over every subject, but rather it means that in the entire teaching enterprise of the school there should be a fundamental seriousness about raising the important questions and addressing them from the perspective of a consistent framework of values and convictions. Specifically, when issues of worldview are being discussed, they should be discussed in relation to the competencies that pupils are developing in the school and not as a separate and otherworldly set of concerns. By the same token, when competencies are being developed and discussed, there should also be consideration of how and why they are being developed and for what purposes they will be used. As schools express their distinctiveness within the framework of general educational goals, this needs to be worked through in all the details of how the schools operate, of their distinctive character.

France

The Netherlands and France serve almost as ideal types of how to think about and then design school autonomy and choice. While much of Dutch public life has long been organized along denominational lines, with extensive consultation among religious and secular pressure groups at every stage of decision making, in France there is an even longer history of conflict over religious issues. The French Republic is explicitly described as secular *(laïque)* in its constitution. Roughly from 1750 to 1950, secular humanism (in an evolving form) and Catholicism competed to serve as the basis for the unity of the French people, and that competition rarely admitted the possibility of a pluralistic resolution, as in the Netherlands. It was winner take all. Whenever Catholics had the top hand, they sought to make all schools Catholic, and whenever the secular forces were in the ascendancy, they sought to make it impossible to operate Catholic schools as an alternative to government schools.

For the past several decades, however, the national government has been funding the "secular instructional program" (though not the religious instruction) in Catholic schools. In what has been described as "a situation unprecedented since the French Revolution, the public school no longer is specifically responsible for defending the political institutions of the current State." What is more, public support for funding nonpublic schools grew from 23 percent right after World War II to 46 percent in 1951 (with 42 percent opposed). Thirty-two percent of respondents favored full funding by 1974, 32 percent favored partial funding, and only 23 percent opposed any public funding of nonpublic schools.[43] A survey in 1983 found that 51 percent of those questioned were prepared to sign a petition in support of private education, compared with 28 percent who would sign one in support of a public-education monopoly. Even 30 percent of the Communist voters and 35 percent of the Socialists indicated support for private education. Two years earlier, 81 percent of the French people surveyed supported free choice of schools, with 30 percent in favor of making the government funding even more generous in order to render private education completely cost free.[44]

Under the *loi Debré,* enacted in 1959 and subsequently amended, the French government enters into contracts with more than 98 percent of the country's nonpublic schools; their teachers are salaried in full by the national government, and other educational costs are paid as well. Fifteen percent of elementary pupils and 20 percent of secondary pupils attend nonpublic schools, the great majority of them Catholic. Careful research has demonstrated that more than one-third of all pupils in France obtain at least part of their schooling in nonpublic schools, for these have become an important resource for families (many not practicing Catholics) when their children are experiencing difficulties in the public schools. It has been estimated that about half of all French families with children make use of these schools at some point or other. The sociologist Robert Ballion describes middle-class parents as aggressive consumers of education for their children.[45]

Those who sponsor schools can choose whether to accept state requirements governing curriculum and testing in exchange for staff salaries *(contrat simple),* or to accept, in addition, some government control over pedagogy and the selection of teachers, in exchange for operating expenses as well as salaries *(con-*

trat d'association). To receive support under the contrat d'association, a school must demonstrate that it meets an educational need. Schools under either form of contract are required to teach the regular public school curriculum leading up to the state examinations (which they would do in any case, because there is no other way for their pupils to obtain university admission or vocational qualifications) but are explicitly protected in maintaining their distinctive religious character and may require that the state-salaried teachers respect that character. Although the teachers in Catholic schools under contract are paid by the national government on terms which are parallel to those of public school teachers, they are required to respect Catholic moral expectations: in a 1978 case, for example, the firing of a divorced-and-remarried teacher was upheld.[46]

Suspicion has persisted that government funding of nonstate education would lead to increasing government control, with private schools carried irresistibly by a sort of escalator effect into the public system. Such an intent was expressed by anticlerical forces in 1959: "If the private sector is destined to receive State aid, it is appropriate that it be subjected to the financial, administrative and pedagogical control" of the national Ministry of Education.[47] This expectation is the background of the major political crisis over education in the early 1980s, which led to the fall of a Socialist government. The government had declared its intention of forcing private schools under contract to conform more closely to the practices of the public system, especially with respect to employment of staff, and a massive mobilization of parents rallied successfully to defend the right to maintain the distinctive character of these schools.

The experience of other Western democracies demonstrates clearly that even in a society like France whose political culture is strongly opposed to a blurring of the lines between church and state, a reasonable accommodation can be reached over public education. Sooner (as in the case of Belgium) or later (as in the case of France), the political leadership in each of these democracies has put aside the rhetoric and focused upon the practical goal of ensuring the adequacy of the schools which all children attend, while respecting the wishes of many parents for faith-based schooling.

American policy making, by contrast, seems determined to turn its back on the nonpublic schools—many of them drastically underfunded—attended by millions of children, by no means all of them from financially secure families. In a free society, well-off parents cannot, in the name of justice, be prevented from giving their children a better quality of schooling by exercising residential decisions or by spending some of their wealth for private schooling. Only through public subsidy of all schools that are of sufficient quality to meet the school-attendance obligation can the opportunity to choose among all available schools be at least partially detached from family resources. This equity issue is recognized explicitly in the German constitution and in the policies of the other Western democracies . . . but not, so far at least, in American public policy.

Subsidizing nonstate schools shows commendable respect for the religious liberty of families and concern for educational equity. It has also created a variety of problems, which would no doubt arise in the United States as well if, as seems probable, public funds were made more widely available to support faith-based schools.

One problem has to do with the regulation that grows up with public subsidies. Faith-based schools in the Netherlands, for example, are regulated by government to a far greater extent than are those in the United States; essentially, they are expected to meet all of the conditions required of the government's own schools, though with freedom to infuse the curriculum and instruction with religious perspectives.

It is well to keep in mind that government—in the United States as much as in Europe—is free to set such requirements for all schools that meet school-attendance requirements. Public funding does not have to lead to a greater degree of government interference, though in practice it usually does. The fine print of the arrangements through which public funding is provided is thus important.[48] The overregulation of nonstate schools in Europe is currently being addressed as part of the widespread efforts to reduce the overall burden of regulation and to promote the autonomy of all schools, state and nonstate alike.

Another problem arises from the effects of government funding. The additional resources provided encourage—indeed, require—the professionalization of teaching staff and their conformity to the standards set for teachers in the government's own schools. One of the results is that professionwide norms can come to be more influential than the mission of the particular school. This further source of pressure toward conformity to the public school model works against a flourishing pluralism in education.

The drift toward common secular norms makes it all the more urgent that those operating faith-based schools work at defining, elaborating, and maintaining their mission, what in France and Spain is called "distinctive character" and in the Netherlands "identity." Hiring decisions, ongoing discussion and curriculum design, and regular events that express and reaffirm this mission for all participants in the school are vital.

That is easily said, less easily done. Educators find it difficult to resist feeling that the goal of their work must be to nurture autonomous individuals who have not been affected by the values and perspectives of their teachers—naive and self-contradictory as that objective is. There is a tendency, as we have seen, to define a single model of maturity which all schools should strive to develop in their pupils—that of the autonomous individual—and to perceive approaches to education that seek to foster participation in communities and traditions as unworthy of the schools of a democratic society. The effort of some families to provide schooling for their children that reinforces their own convictions about life is seen, from this perspective, as something to be countered by educators and by the educator-state.[49]

Surely it is more appropriate in a free society for the state to extend its support to a variety of schools (of adequate quality) that provide education based upon alternative understandings of human flourishing, understandings based upon different concepts of what the German constitution protects as the "development of personality." This requires a recognition that toleration and individualization are not in necessary opposition to what parents hold to be most deeply true and important for their children.

There is one more danger often attributed to educational diversity: the possibility that social divisions of all kinds will be exacerbated if the nation's children do not attend school together. For nineteenth-century reformers, this was the primary argument for the "common school," especially in the face of massive immigration.[50]

Although warnings about social disintegration are a constant theme of opponents of various forms of parent choice of schools, there are three reasons why these warnings should not be taken too seriously. The first is that the experience of other Western democracies with publicly funded educational pluralism over the past eighty and more years does not provide any examples of social divisions as a result, despite constant predictions of disaster. France, the critics of Catholic schooling warned, would be torn apart by two conflicting groups of youth (deux jeunesses); of course, nothing of the sort has happened. Indeed, arrangements to provide equal access to religious schooling for those who wanted it was in several countries the way to bring peace after decades of conflict.

The second reason to minimize the social dangers associated with parent choice is that the attendance of faith-based schools by millions of American youngsters has not resulted in a divided society. They have turned out very much like other American youth, and a growing body of research suggests that they have more commitment to tolerance, are more involved in service projects, and have more civic knowledge and skills than students in public schools.[51]

The third reason why those concerned with social justice can support parent choice of schools with a clear conscience is that by now we know a great deal about the nuts and bolts of how to make it function in a way that provides equal access for those children whose parents have less information and fewer resources. Hundreds of thousands of pupils have taken part in school choice programs in the United States, including some that have made parent choice the universal basis for school assignments.[52] These programs have been studied extensively to ensure that their effects are benign. While many mistakes have been made along the way, we have learned from them how to design equitable school-choice programs that respect the autonomy of distinctively different schools.

Parental choice, in short, is not an untried experiment. We should not allow ourselves to be frightened by unsubstantiated predictions of disaster. Young Americans who attend schools that their parents have chosen, schools with a coherent sense of mission that is translated into the details of curriculum and school life, are likely to receive a better education than those who are assigned to lowest-common-denominator schools. Isn't it time that the United States joined all the other Western democracies that consider it the responsibility of government to support parental choice among schools as a fundamental freedom?

NOTES

1. Stephen L. Carter, *The Dissent of the Governed: A Meditation on Law, Religion, and Loyalty* (Cambridge: Harvard University Press, 1998), p. 11.
2. Laurence Steinberg, *Beyond the Classroom* (New York: Simon and Schuster Touchstone, 1997), p. 13.
3. Linda Valli, "A Curriculum of Effort: Tracking Students in a Catholic High School," in Reba Page and Linda Valli, eds., *Curriculum Differentiation* (Albany: SUNY Press, 1990), p. 63.
4. Arthur G. Powell, Eleanor Farrar, and David K. Cohen, *The Shopping Mall High School* (Boston: Houghton Mifflin, 1985), p. 199; quotation from p. 197.
5. See Charles L. Glenn, "Religion, Textbooks, and the Common School," *Public Interest*, July 1987.
6. See Charles L. Glenn, *Educational Freedom in Eastern Europe* (2d ed., Washington, D.C.: Cato Institute, 1995); Charles L. Glenn, "Free Schools and the Revival of Urban Communities," in Stanley W. Carlson-Thies and James W. Skillen, eds., *Welfare in*

America: Christian Perspectives on a Policy in Crisis (Grand Rapids, Mich.: Eerdmans, 1996).

7. Harvey J. Graff, *The Legacies of Literacy* (Bloomington: Indiana University Press, 1991), p. 261.

8. Paul Nash, Introduction to Matthew Arnold, *Culture and the State: Matthew Arnold and Continental Education* (New York: Teachers College Press, 1966).

9. For a discussion of one example, see Charles L. Glenn, "The Belgian Model of Peacemaking in Educational Policy," in *Het schoolpact van 1958: Ontstaan, grondlijnen en toepassing van een Belgische compromis* (Brussels: VUB, 1999).

10. Charles L. Glenn, *The Myth of the Common School* (Amherst: University of Massachusetts Press, 1988).

11. For details, see Charles L. Glenn, "Common Standards and Educational Diversity," in Jan De Groof, ed., *Subsidiarity and Education: Aspects of Comparative Educational Law* (Louvain, Belgium: Acco, 1984).

12. John H. Bishop, "Signaling, Incentives, and School Organization in France, the Netherlands, Britain, and the United States," in Eric A. Hanushek and Dale W. Jorgenson, eds., *Improving America's Schools: The Role of Incentives* (Washington, D.C.: National Academy Press, 1996).

13. These developments are discussed in Charles L. Glenn, *The Ambiguous Embrace: Government and Faith-based Schools and Social Agencies* (Princeton: Princeton University Press, 2000).

14. The text of education provisions of international covenants is taken from Alfred Fernandez and Siegfried Jenkner, *International Declarations and Conventions on the Right to Education and the Freedom of Education* (Frankfurt am Main: Info3-Verlag, 1995).

15. See, for example, Anthony S. Bryk, Valerie E. Lee, and Peter B. Holland, *Catholic Schools and the Common Good* (Cambridge: Harvard University Press, 1993); James S. Coleman and Thomas Hoffer, *Public and Private High Schools: The Impact of Communities* (New York: Basic, 1987); Peter Mortimore et al., *School Matters* (Berkeley: University of California Press, 1988).

16. L. Marwijk Kooy-von Baumhauer, *Scholen verschillen: Een verkennend vergelijkend onderzoek naar het intern functioneren van vijventwintig schoolgemeenschappen vwo-havo-mavo* (Groningen, The Netherlands: Wolters Noordhoff, 1984).

17. P. Van Laarhoven, B. Bakker, J. Dronkers, and H. Schijf, "Achievement in Public and Private Secondary Education in the Netherlands," *Zeitschrift für internationale erziehungs- und sozialwissenschaftliche Forschung* 4, no. 2 (1987).

18. See John E. Chubb and Terry Moe, *Politics, Markets, and America's Schools* (Washington: Brookings Institution, 1990).

19. James G. Cibulka, Timothy J. O'Brien, and Donald Zewe, *Inner-City Private Elementary Schools: A Study* (Milwaukee: Marquette University Press, 1982), p. 179.

20. Bryk, Lee, and Holland, *Catholic Schools and the Common Good.*

21. Louis Legrand, *L'École unique: quelles conditions?* (Paris: Scarabée, 1981), pp. 62, 78, 118.

22. John Dewey, "A Common Faith" (1934), in *Later Works,* vol. 9, *1933–1934,* ed. Jo Ann Boydston (Carbondale: Southern Illinois University Press, 1986).

23. Jacques Billiet, *Secularisering en verzuiling in het onderwijs: Een sociologisch onderzoek*

naar de vrije schoolkeuse als legitimatieschema en als sociaal proces (Louvain, Belgium: University Press, 1977), pp. 203–4, 209.

24. Suus van der Boef, R. Bronneman, and M. Konings, *Schoolkeuzemotieven en meningen over onderwijs* (Rijswijk, The Netherlands: Sociaal Cultureel Planbureau, 1983).

25. M. van Eck, W. M. J. M. Groot Antink, and P. W. V. Veraart, *Gewenst basisonderwijs in de tweede helft van de jaren 80 in de provincie Utrecht* (Utrecht: Tangram, 1986).

26. D. J. F. Flaman, J. de Jonge, and T. Westra, *Waroom naar de Christelijke School?* (Amsterdam: Instituut voor Toegepast Sociaalwetenschappelijk Onderzoek van de Vrije Universiteit, 1974).

27. For a detailed account, see Marjorie Lamberti, *State, Society, and the Elementary School in Imperial Germany* (New York: Oxford University Press, 1989).

28. Peter Lundgreen, *Socialgeschichte der deutschen Schule im Überblick,* vol. 2, *1918–1980* (Göttingen: Vandenhoeck and Ruprecht, 1981), p. 42.

29. Text in Siegfried Jenkner, ed., *The Right to Education and the Freedom of Education in European Constitutions* (Frankfurt am Main: Info3-Verlag, 1994).

30. Frank-Rüdiger Jach, *Schulvielfalt als Verfassungsgebot* (Berlin: Dunker and Humblot, 1991), p. 42.

31. Manfred Weiss and Cornelia Mattern, "The Situation and Development of the Private School System in Germany," in Hasso von Recum and Manfred Weiss, eds., *Social Change and Educational Planning in West Germany* (Frankfurt am Main: Deutsches Institut für internationale Pädagogische Forschung, 1991), p. 54.

32. Jach, *Schulvielfalt als Verfassungsgebot,* p. 51.

33. Hans Heckel, quoted by Johann Peter Vogel, "Bildungspolitische Perspektiven," *Freie Schule II. Öffentliche Verantwortung und freie Initiative* (Stuttgart: Arbeitsgemeinschaft Freier Schulen, 1972), p. 38.

34. Bundesverfassungsgericht, *In den Verfahren zur verfassungsrechtlichen Prüfung der . . . Privatschulgesetzes der Freien und Hansestadt Hamburg,* April 8, 1987, p. 12.

35. Bundesverfassungsgericht, *In den Verfahren,* pp. 30–32.

36. Jach, *Schulvielfalt als Verfassungsgebot,* pp. 64–65, 81.

37. J. W. Becker and R. Vink, *Secularisatie in Nederland, 1966–1991: De verandering van opvattingen en enkele gedragingen* (Rijswijk, The Netherlands: Sociaal en Cultureel Planbureau, 1994), p. 27, table 2.1; p. 30, table 2.4; pp. 147–48, table 5.13; p. 149, table 5.15.

38. H. P. M. Adriaansens and A. C. Zijderveld, *Vrijwillig initiatief en de verzorgingsstaat,* (Deventer, The Netherlands: Van Loghum Slaterus, 1981), pp. 10, 74.

39. Adriaansens and Zijderveld, *Vrijwillig initiatief,* p. 124.

40. A. P. M. Van Schoten and H. Wansink, *De nieuwe schoolstrijd: Knelpunten en conflicten in de hedendaagse onderwijspolitiek* (Utrecht: Bohn, Scheltema, and Holkema, 1984).

41. J. Koppejan, "Ontstaan en groei van het reformatorisch onderwijs," in M. Golverdingen, et al., eds. *Belijden en opvoeden: Gedachten over de christelijke school vanuit een reformatorische visie* (Houten, The Netherlands: Den Hertog, 1989), p. 96.

42. L. A. Struik, "De openbare school en de 'algemeen bijzondere' school," *Schoolbestuur* 5, no. 8 (September, 1985).

43. Gabriel Langouet and Alain Leger, *Public ou privé: Trajectoires et réussites scolaires* (Paris: Publidix, 1991), pp. 159–60.

44. Gérard Leclerc, *La bataille de l'école: 15 siècles d'histoire, 3 ans de combat* (Paris: Denoel, 1985), p. 196n103.

45. Langouet and Leger, *Public ou privé,* p. 48; Robert Ballion, *Les consommateurs d'école* (Paris: Stock, 1982).

46. Yves Madiot, "Le juge et la laïcité," in *Pouvoirs,* no. 75, *La laïcité* (1995): 76.

47. Leclerc, *La bataille de l'école,* pp. 72–73.

48. Glenn, *Ambiguous Embrace.*

49. See, for example, Amy Gutmann, *Democratic Education* (Princeton: Princeton University Press, 1987), or, more recently, James G. Dwyer, *Religious Schools v. Children's Rights* (Ithaca, N.Y.: Cornell University Press, 1998).

50. Glenn, *Myth of the Common School.*

51. Several as-yet-unpublished studies to this effect were presented at the March 2000 conference on Charter Schools, Vouchers, and Public Education at the Kennedy School, Harvard.

52. Charles L. Glenn, "Controlled Choice in Massachusetts Public Schools," *Public Interest* 103 (April 1991).

Chapter 14 Risking Choice, Redressing Inequality

Joseph P. Viteritti

Gunnar Myrdal called it the "Great American Dilemma." He described the dilemma as a moral one, manifested by the nation's failure to reconcile the democratic "American creed" of liberty, equality, justice, and fair opportunity with what was referred to in 1944 as "the Negro problem."[1] Although the term is no longer in fashion, the problem is still very much with us. Racial inequality remains the most glaring blemish on the face of American democracy. At its core is an inequality in education defined by race, an inequality that persists in both opportunity and achievement. Not only is education the most crucial social variable for promoting meaningful citizenship in a modern age; all the others that matter—wealth, occupation, social standing, and skill—are to some degree a function of education.

My objective in this essay is to assess how school choice might help to alleviate the problem of inequality and to explain why I believe trying choice is worth the conceivable risk. Because we can never fully anticipate the consequences of what the sociologist Robert Merton dubbed "purposive social action," any fundamental change in public policy involves a certain measure of risk.[2] The bigger the change, the greater the risk. As many of the critics understand it, the risks that charters and vouchers might impose on civil society are considerable, some would say intolerable. Choice could encourage political, cultural, racial, and religious fragmentation; and if implemented irresponsibly, choice could aggravate the problems of educational and social inequality rather than diminish them. On the other hand, one might argue, as I will, that there are serious risks involved, both measurable and immeasurable, in letting things remain as they are. But of course, nobody wants to leave things the way they are. The question is how to make them better, or more specifically, whether school choice is likely to do so.

ASSESSING RISK

Even though the black-white test-score gap that had reached its peak in 1971 seemed to be narrowing in the 1980s, the gulf remained dangerously wide at the end of the twentieth century.[3] When Steven and Abigail Thernstrom completed their cyclopedic study in 1997 reconsidering the racial dilemma that Myrdal had brought to the attention of the nation fifty-odd years earlier, their report on education was especially discouraging. They found that the average black twelfth-grader in the United States reads with the same proficiency as the average white eighth-grader.[4] A study released a year later by the U.S. Department of Education indicated that the educational status of Hispanic Americans was even worse: the high school dropout rate among Hispanics was twice that of blacks and more than three times that of whites.[5]

It is difficult to exaggerate the significance of educational disparities among the races. Social science research has found that educational achievement is correlated to a wide array of social indicators, including earning capacity, physical health, crime rates, and family structure.[6] More to the point of this book is the correlation between education and civic participation. For more than five decades, behavioral evidence in political science has consistently shown that education is the most reliable predictor of civic involvement, whether involvement is measured in terms of group membership, voter turnout, donations to political campaigns, or the act of making demands upon government and political leaders.

In one recent survey Nie, Junn, and Stehlik-Barry distinguish between two dimensions of democratic citizenship, both of which are related to education: "political engagement" measures the capacity of individuals to pursue their interests through governmental channels, "democratic enlightenment" concerns their appreciation and acceptance of democratic norms.[7] One is about a person's ability to be an effective citizen who gets what he wants from government, the other about his ability to be a good citizen with an aptitude to embrace values such as tolerance, deliberation, and compromise. With the passage of the Voting Rights Act in 1965, Congress eliminated many of the egregious legal impediments that stood in the way of political equality since the Civil War. Once-common practices like poll taxes, literacy tests, and white primaries are now things of the past; but the full benefits of democratic citizenship will not be realized for all Americans until we succeed in eliminating the learning gap between the races.

Ten years after Myrdal completed his two-volume treatise on race, the U.S. Supreme Court took its turn explaining the central role that education plays in advancing the American promise of equality, declaring that all people have the right to a decent education. Although the landmark *Brown* decision of 1954 specifically addressed the problem of racial segregation in southern schools, the vision of educational opportunity articulated by Chief Justice Earl Warren was broader in scope, encompassing every aspect of life, recognizing that educational equality is a prerequisite for economic, social, and civic equality:

> Today education is perhaps the most important function of state and local governments. Compulsory school attendance laws and the great expenditures for education both demonstrate our recognition of the importance of education to our democratic society. . . . It is the very foundation of good citizenship. Today it is the principal instrument in awakening the child to cultural values, in preparing him for later professional training, and in helping him to adjust normally to his environment. In these days, it is doubtful that any child may reasonably be expected to succeed in life if he is denied the opportunity of an education. Such an opportunity, where the state has undertaken to provide it, is a right that must be made available to all on equal terms.[8]

Since the landmark decision was handed down nearly a half-century ago, the federal government has gone to great lengths, legally and financially, to deliver on its promise, but to limited avail. Judicial intervention was successful at eliminating the legal segregation of the races in the South, no mean accomplishment in a society constructed around the principle of apartheid. Later attempts by the courts, however, to promote racial integration throughout the nation proved to be a spectacular failure.[9] Most American school children today attend class with other children who look very much like themselves.

School profiles are a function of residential patterns. Busing plans designed to overcome residential segregation were not very successful in achieving racial balance. Most of the burden of busing fell on minority children, and in recent years minority parents have grown frustrated with it. In a national survey conducted in 1998 by Public Agenda, 80 percent of the black parents polled said that they preferred to have schools place more of a priority on raising academic standards than on achieving racial integration.[10] Federal initiatives have not done well on that count, either. After billions of dollars invested in compensatory education programs begun under the auspices of the Title I Program, there is little evidence of sustained improvement in the academic performance of the poor children who were targeted.[11]

In the same Public Agenda study cited above, a majority of black parents surveyed voiced support for school vouchers. This is remarkable for a number of reasons. While black and white attitudes seemed to converge on key educational priorities—raising academic standards, ensuring safety, maintaining order, teaching the three R's—they differed dramatically on the issue of choice, with only 36 percent of the whites voicing approval for vouchers. These results replicate the findings of numerous other surveys. Poll after poll shows that the strongest support for school vouchers is found among low-income minority parents who live in large urban areas. The strongest opposition is found among white parents who live in the suburbs. There are two interrelated explanations for the wide disagreement between the races, one perhaps more obvious than the other.

Minority parents perceive vouchers as a passport for escaping from failing inner-city public schools. Their support for choice is an expression of dissatisfaction with the educational opportunities that are typically available for their children. White suburban parents, who are generally more satisfied with the quality of their public schools, do not share the same sense of urgency to implement change. In a more subtle way, most of these suburban parents have actually exercised a form of choice that is not available to their less fortunate counterparts who live in the city. The advantages of class and race provide them with the residential mobility to choose to live in communities where the public schools perform at a level that is at least acceptable. When people with children select a neighborhood or town to live in, they are implicitly also selecting a school.[12]

Other middle- and upper-class families are even more fortunate, enjoying both residential mobility and the economic means to pay tuition for gaining access to private schools. Viewed in the context of current realities, the paramount policy question to resolve is not whether to have choice but whether choice should be extended to a broader class of people. Would providing choice to the poor pose any greater risk to civil society than a system that gives some measure of choice to almost everyone but the poor? Perhaps the answer to that question depends upon whom you ask. Certainly, it is not outlandish to argue that the exercise of choice by the middle class has contributed to racial, ethnic, and cultural separation among students. As the middle class abandons inner-city schools, a disproportionate number of the students left behind are black and Hispanic. It is also arguable, however, that denying choice to the poor has intensified the isolation of poor and minority students because it leaves them with no alternative but to stay where they are.

Let us consider some alternatives. One possibility, busing for racial balance, has already been discussed. Not only have parents of every race grown weary of substituting transportation for education, there is an extensive research literature suggesting that forced integration through busing contributes to white flight and exacerbates racial isolation.[13] Short of requiring people to live in racially integrated communities or prohibiting middle-class parents from sending their children to private school, the effective alternatives open to government authorities are limited.

Offering vouchers to economically disadvantaged families is an alternative that has not been given a chance, except for the limited experiments in Milwaukee, Cleveland, and Florida. We already know that many poor and minority parents want vouchers. They appear less taken with the civic anxieties that worry many social analysts. But then it must seem altogether silly for parents living in racially isolated communities with inferior schools to hear middle-class professionals brood over the threat of social fragmentation, especially when the impending danger would supposedly be presented by giving poor people educational privileges usually taken for granted by the same social analysts.

What is it that poor people expect to gain from school choice? Maybe it is just a desire to have what everybody else has. That's understandable; and it also happens to be fair. Then again, there could be more to it than parental envy. Minority parents tend to express about the same level of support for charter schools as their white counterparts do. It is the voucher question that sets them apart, and the implications are noteworthy. Charter schools are a form of public school choice. Vouchers give parents access to private and parochial schools. Because most of the nonpublic schools that populate inner-city neighborhoods where minority families live are Catholic parochial schools, there appears to be a particular attraction to these institutions. No doubt part of the attraction is proximity. Catholic schools are mainly an urban phenomenon. So if you live in the city, they are neighborhood schools that do not require long bus rides to attend. Yet there must be something that minority parents expect to get from these parochial schools that they do not get in their local public schools. Why bother, if not?

We do not need to speculate about this. Parents who participate in voucher programs have been asked why they choose the schools they choose. Their responses are consistent and definitive. Parents usually identify four key factors: high academic standards, safety, community, and values.[14] Those with children in parochial schools openly admit that they specifically like the religious values that are conveyed through the curriculum. When asked, after some time, to compare the parochial school experience with that of their previous public school, they consistently give higher marks to the parochial school. For most there is little doubt that the advantages involved in offering choice to the poor (meaning themselves) outweigh the potential risks. But do these parents really know what they are talking about? Is there any real advantage that their children derive from attending parochial schools?

COLEMAN'S WAGER

I am constantly amused by it. The same man who in 1975 was nearly censured by his professional colleagues—the term *peer* is hardly appropriate here—and cast out of the American Sociological Association keeps showing up at professional conferences long after his death. He haunts us. We can't stop discussing him. There is virtually no significant topic in educational research that has not benefited from the provocative insights of James Coleman. He keeps prodding us along, forcing us to look beyond the narrow boundaries of our own scholarship. In 1975 the disciplinary reprimand was stirred up when he warned the nation that school busing causes white flight. After having been a prominent advocate of busing for racial balance, he changed his mind. He had the audacity to reverse his position on a favored policy when new evidence indicated that the policy was counterproductive.

In 1982 Coleman changed his mind again. Almost twenty years earlier Coleman had overseen the most massive social science study in national history when, at the request of the U.S. commissioner of education, he examined "the lack of equal educational opportunities for individuals by reason of race, color or national origin."[15] Among the most startling findings to emerge from the controversial Coleman Report of 1964 was that family background is a more significant determinant of student achievement than what goes on in school.[16]

Coleman abandoned the "schools don't matter" thesis later when he completed another national survey that compared public, private, and parochial schools. His 1982 study showed that private schools produce more positive cognitive outcomes, even after controlling for the family background of students. Among the more intriguing of Coleman's discoveries was the specific effect that Catholic schools had in reducing the performance gap between students of different racial and social backgrounds. Coleman was so impressed by the findings that he recommended the implementation of government-funded tuition vouchers for minority students who could not afford to attend private schools, as a strategy for addressing the persistent problem of educational inequality.

The new Coleman Report sparked a considerable amount of dissension within the scholarly community. Many researchers challenged the methodological rigor of Coleman's survey and refused to accept the finding that private schools, particularly Catholic parochial schools, outperform public schools—debates which continue to rage today. Similar methodological disagreements characterized evaluations of the voucher experiments that were implemented in Milwaukee and Cleveland.[17] Some assessments indicated that the poor and minority children who participated in the voucher programs registered small but significant gains in academic achievement over short periods of time; other assessments found no significant gains. In the meantime, while social scientists quibble over methodological details, the parents of former public school children who actually attend private schools through the voucher experiments are attesting that their children are better off than before. Who are we to believe?

The most consistent evidence to emerge over recent years, derived from larger data bases than the voucher experiments allow, concerns graduation rates rather than test scores. It shows that even after controlling for economic and social influences, minority students who attend Catholic high schools are more likely to graduate, go on to college, and earn a degree. This is not exactly the same as claiming that Catholic schools are superior to public schools, but it demonstrates a real "Catholic school effect" so far as a certain target population is concerned.[18] Perhaps the point is best made by citing the work of one of the most skeptical critics. Professor Henry Levin of Teachers College does not accept the general proposition that Catholic schools outperform public schools. In a comprehensive review of the existing literature he concedes that at best it can be claimed that minority students who attend Catholic high schools are more likely to graduate and to score slightly better across the grades on standardized tests.[19]

Now we may be on to something. We have already discussed the significance of a high school diploma as a means to improve the life chances of a young man or woman growing up in adverse social circumstances. If we could raise the probability that such a student is more likely to graduate from high school and attend college, we would advance the movement toward social equality immeasurably. Of course while such evidence suggests that school choice may make good sense from a public-policy perspective, it does not necessarily explain the demand for it on the part of poor parents. Most are not privy to such precious information, and those who do clamor for choice usually do so long before their children get to high school.

In truth, the evidence does not need to be so compelling. Picture yourself the mother or father of a child attending a chronically failing inner-city public school. The incentive to pull your child out of the situation is obvious; the choice regarding an alternative is less clear. If Coleman's assertion and the claims made by the more optimistic evaluators of the voucher experiments are correct, the modest to moderate academic advantage attained by placing your child in a parochial school is probably enough to warrant the switch. It may not be sufficient for the social analyst bent on radical reform, but for the parent of the child who is in a miserably failing school that can be both physically unsafe and academically unsound, the change makes sense. Research on parental behavior indicates that while poor parents may not know much about the educational alternatives available, they know enough to make informed decisions that will improve the opportunities of their children.[20]

Let us assume for a moment that the more negative assessments of the voucher experiments are correct: that the academic achievement of students who attend public and parochial (or private schools) is about the same. This may also be sufficient to justify advancing choice. Even if the probability of finding a desirable placement were the same in the parochial and public sectors, choice would at least expand the range of options for a population of urban residents who are desperately in need of more options. The mother in search of a reasonable educational opportunity for her child does not need evidence that all schools in the nonpublic sector are superior to all schools in the public sector. She just needs to find one school that is appropriate for her child, and the more schools she has to choose from, the more likely it is that she will find what she is looking for. If we are to believe the surveys, most of the parents who opt out of public schools accept Coleman's proposition as true and expect that the odds are better that they will get what they want in a parochial school.

We must dig deeper. Let us now take as a given that there may be something to Coleman's claim. What is it about inner-city Catholic schools that allows them to overcome, or at least mitigate, the effects of economic and social hardship on the academic achievement of minority students? Coleman's answer takes us back to the central theme of this book, and its implications are vast. Most of us know that Coleman attributes the success of Catholic schools to their unusual abundance of "social capital."[21] Coleman explains how the sense of community built around a core set of religious values helps establish a network of social relationships within these schools characterized by mutuality and trust; he describes a supportive environment that is instrumental in helping students to overcome other disadvantages and disincentives to perform well academically. While Coleman's assertions about the interpersonal dynamics of parochial schools are not uncontested, they have been corroborated by other research.[22] His observations about the value structure and sense of community found in Catholic schools are consistent with the reports of many parents whose children participate in the voucher experiments.

Although Coleman believed that the religiosity of parochial schools was crucial in explaining their social cohesiveness, one does not have to come away from his work with the presumption that faith-based values are essential to creating a community within a school. There are many successful schools within the private and public sectors that have formed cohesive communities without the benefit of religion. Religion aside, however, it is more difficult to cultivate a functional community in a typical public school.

One important factor that facilitates the process of community building within parochial, private, and a relatively small number of public schools stems from their being voluntary associations; to use the vernacular of school reformers, they are schools of choice. People come together in these institutions—including parents, students, teachers, and administrators—because they share certain core values or priorities that are identified with the institution. It is this common allegiance constructed around an institutional ethos that facilitates community building. These natural associations of joiners that evolve on the basis of choice are the antithesis of the organizational arrangement found in the traditional public school, where membership is assigned. There employees and clients are brought together by bureaucratic accident and then are expected to form a functional community. The obstacles can be, and usually are, insurmountable.

This is why so much hope is invested in charter schools. Charter schools are public schools of choice that function outside the bureaucratic and political jurisdiction of the local school district, more akin to civic associations than to government agencies.[23] The commonality around which they form may vary: a pedagogical philosophy such as the Core Knowledge curriculum of E. D. Hirsch or Robert Slavin's Success for All; an orientation toward an occupation or profession like public service, medicine, or science; or the desire to accommodate the needs of a particular clientele like a racial or cultural group, or a population with specific learning needs like the deaf or visually impaired. Because many charter schools are beginning to open in urban communities, attendance does not require a long commute. This is the promise of charter schools, according to their proponents: promoting choice, enriching instruction, enhancing capacity, extending local options, cultivating communities of learning animated by a clear mission.

What charter schools cannot offer their clients is religion. As public schools they are not permitted to teach religion or convey religious values. This is what the First Amendment requires, but for some parents the constitutional prohibition may represent a significant compromise. For many years choice proponents have argued that vouchers, in violation of the Establishment Clause, provide parents with a public incentive to practice a religion. The assumption has been that poor parents are so desperate to find decent schools for their children that they are willing to tolerate the religion that comes along with the parochial school education, even though they might not be inclined toward that religion. Now we know that these assumptions are not altogether valid.

Yes, these urban parents are motivated by the desire for a better education, and many children who are not Catholic wind up in the Catholic schools that dominate the private school market in their communities. But many of these parents—some Catholic, others not—also tell us that they are attracted by the religious aspect of the curriculum in these same schools. On some level the parents seem to understand the interrelation between religious values, community building, and academic achievement that Coleman tried, not altogether successfully, to explain to his professional colleagues. Yet they also place an independent value on religion that is not generally appreciated by social scientists. Many partisans to the choice debate have not come to terms with the unique role that religion plays in the black community. In order to explore this we need, at least temporarily, to go beyond Coleman.

TOCQUEVILLE IN THE CITY

By every measure, Tocqueville remains the most insightful student of American civil society.[24] It was he who told us about our unique capacity to join together in voluntary associations and who recognized, more than any foreign observer before, our unusual devotion to equality. It was he who taught us that civic association is a sound foundation for building a young democracy, not just by preparing us to be good citizens but also by furnishing us with mediating institutions that buffer our private lives from government authority. It was he who informed us that our churches were our most potent community institutions and who warned us about the "negro problem" that Myrdal would investigate one hundred years later. Ironically, as the first volume of *Democracy in America* was being published in 1835, the seeds of the common school movement were being planted, and education was in the process of being transformed from a civic activity conducted as a private matter to a governmental function overseen by a public bureaucracy.

We wonder how Tocqueville would have responded to the present-day discussion on the decline of civil society, whether he would have agreed with the more gloomy reports. He would likely have joined in the more general consensus about America's failure to achieve its vision of equality, and would have agreed that the most conspicuous sign of that failure revolves around race. He probably would have been encouraged by the news that our churches remain our most viable civic institutions. As the Frenchman might ponder, so much has changed, so much remains the same. But could even Tocqueville have imagined, during his long journey across the young agrarian nation, that a century and a half later his most prescient observations on the vigor and vulnerability of American democracy would be so pronounced in our once great cities?

Americans exhibit the highest rate of church attendance in the world. From the most positive to the most negative commentaries on the contemporary scene, there is wide agreement that "church affiliated groups are the backbone of civil society in America."[25] Nowhere is church attendance more vigorous or religion more valued than in the black community, followed very closely by the Hispanic.[26] As Eric Lincoln and Lawrence Mamiya explain in their definitive book on the subject, "The Black Church has no challenger as the cultural womb of the black community."[27]

This finding is affirmed in the seminal work on civic voluntarism by Verba, Schlozman, and Brady. Their study, chock full of empirical data, reaches further than any analysis extant to explain how various social factors interact to enhance civic participation, defined broadly to include such activities as voting, election campaigns, financial contributions, informal local activity, contacts with government officials, demonstrations, protests, and service on local governing bodies. Like others before, Verba and his colleagues give special attention to the role of religion in civil society, not just to confirm its significance but to draw a more piercing conclusion concerning its leveling effect on the American polity. In comments that are of particular relevance to minority communities, they explain: "Only religious institutions provide a counterbalance to this cumulative resource process. They play an unusual role in the American participatory system by providing opportunities for the development of civic skills to those who would otherwise be resource poor."[28]

One characteristic that sets religious institutions apart from other voluntary organizations is their democratic structure. Whereas other groups are stratified on the basis of class, race, and ethnicity, churches tend to be more egalitarian in their governance. The Protestant churches to which a disproportionately high number of blacks belong are especially organized so that all of their members can play a meaningful leadership role. This gives everyone a chance to develop participatory skills. Black churches also tend to be more politically oriented than other churches, largely because local churches provide the most natural route through which members can channel their political energy. Thus the contribution of the church to the political socialization of the poor is extraordinary. As Verba and his team conclude, "Religious institutions play a much more important role in potentially enriching the stockpile of participatory factors for those who are otherwise disadvantaged."[29]

It is a historic phenomenon that reaches back to the plantation days of the old South, when the church meeting was the only place where slaves could congregate outside their quarters free from the supervision of their masters.[30] The power of the black church was boldly reinforced during the civil rights movement of the 1950s, when clergymen like Martin Luther King Jr. tweaked the conscience of the nation to demand an end to racial discrimination.[31] Today the church remains an engine for social progress, mounting programs to fight delinquency, offering services to the elderly, helping to build affordable housing, and assisting in setting up health clinics.[32] Some of the more entrepreneurial pastors, like the Reverend Floyd Flake in New York, have even been instrumental in launching small businesses in their communities.

Now, as always, the black church is more than a religious institution. As the political scientist John DiIulio emphasizes, in urban neighborhoods that have few institutions with large reserves of social capital, ministers have been able to convert their "spiritual capital" into social capital, leveraging the dividends to promote meaningful change.[33] The pity of this miraculous story is that so powerful an institution, perhaps the richest resource in the midst of deprivation, has been virtually excluded from the important job of educating young people.

In recent years many ministers have started their own schools in response to the pattern of educational neglect that has been commonly associated with public schools in their communities. Most are Christian academies, but an increasing number are Muslim in orientation. A survey completed by the Institute for Independent Education in Washington, D.C., counts nearly four hundred black independent schools throughout the nation, some affiliated with local ministries and some not.[34] These religious and independent schools share a common problem inherent in their mission to educate poor children whose families are looking for an alternative to failing public schools but lack the personal resources to pay the tuition. The reach and effectiveness of these institutions are stifled by a system of school funding that pours millions of dollars into chronically failing public institutions while denying support for students to attend educational institutions connected to the heart and the soul of functioning communities.

The state of educational distress is a well documented phenomenon in urban scholarship. Less attention has been given to understanding how decades of ill-conceived educational policy have had a debilitating effect on the civic vitality of inner-city communities. I am not referring here just to the marked connection between educational achievement and participation in public life. The damage imposed by government decision makers was more subtle and unknowing, often implemented in the name of higher-order ideals: educational opportunity on the one hand, religious freedom on the other.

From the perspective of black civil society, aggressive policies implemented in the name of school integration were at least as damaging as the condition of de facto segregation it was designed to correct. Not only did busing fail to integrate urban schools and intensify racial isolation. The policy was based on the dangerous precept that children needed to leave their home communities to receive a decent education. Generation upon generation of Americans have viewed their neighborhood schools as a central forum for civic life in their communities. After being subjected to years of de jure segregation in the South, the inhabitants of depressed urban communities were treated to a judicially imposed requirement that unwittingly undermined their neighborhood schools in the North.

Nor were we offering them any viable local alternative in the private sector. Government decision makers, guided by a strict philosophy of church-state separation, took care to prevent that, too.[35] But at considerable cost. Rather than build on the strength of the most vital local institution, one with an obvious role to play in the academic, civic, and moral development of the younger population, policy makers disqualified local churches from participation in the educational enterprise.

Toward the end of his career Coleman wrote another essay in which he reviewed the results of some new research. It showed that across denominations religious schools replicate the "Catholic school effect": they had a similar capacity to build functional communities, produce social capital, and advance academic achievement.[36] It makes sense. If Catholic schools could do this in inner-city communities, then there is all the reason to believe that schools affiliated with local black churches could do the same. We do not have strong data to support that claim yet, but many of the parents who have children in low-performing public schools are probably willing to take a chance and accept the risk.

These are not the same risks that preoccupy social scientists when they consider the choice option for other people's children. For the parents in question the risks are more personal, involving the movement of their children from a bad, sometimes horrendous, situation to an untested one. But for these parents facing the unknown, the measure of risk can be calculated by assessing just how undesirable the present situation is. That is the essence of choice. Those who reside in the gravest of circumstances usually have the least to risk by making a change; and, of course, those parents who are disinclined will not be required to pursue options they find unattractive.

For the usual participants to the choice debate, the risks may appear substantial, but they are not personal. They hail back to the original question that prompted this essay: whether choice will promote social fragmentation, or, to be more precise, whether choice for the poor will intensify the fragmentation that already exists. In the end the response to this question must turn on one's understanding of how we might integrate our least fortunate citizens into the mainstream of American life.

Choice does matter. It is a question, however, not just of what choices are to be made but, more important, of who makes the choices. In the past, policy alternatives have been determined by those whose stake in the issue is intellectual rather than immediate, and the outcome has not been favorable for those whose children are most at risk. We need to alter the terms of the discussion so that there is a better fit between the risks involved and the power to decide. We need to let poor people make their own choices about the future of their children. The act of choosing, the ability to determine where one's child attends school, is a form of civic involvement that builds individual social capital. It is a manifestation of economic and political empowerment that should be shared by all people.[37]

FUTURE PROSPECTS

Speculation is a dangerous but irresistible temptation that befalls social analysts, and I do not intend to pass up the chance here to indulge myself before closing. What does a world inhabited by charter schools and vouchers hold? How much change is in the offing? Will it all be for the better or for the worse?

That all depends upon what we allow to happen. If vouchers are limited to low-income children and targeted primarily to those who attend failing schools, then their greatest impact is likely to be felt in urban areas where there is a large population of poor children attending failing schools. Even if no limit were placed on the number of charter schools that come into existence or on where they might appear, charter schools still can be expected to cluster in the same urban areas where parents are searching for educational alternatives. Most suburban parents who are satisfied with their local schools are likely to keep their children where they are.

It will be interesting to see whether charter schools present a challenge for inner-city Catholic schools that historically have provided a refuge for less fortunate students fleeing low-performing public schools. The simultaneous implementation of charters and vouchers in poor communities will certainly allow scholars to determine more definitively how much of the attraction that parochial schools hold is religious in nature. Ideally, if both charters and parochial institutions thrive, the competition will provide public schools with an incentive to improve, to the benefit of the overall quality of urban education.

If the charter school movement advances without the provision of vouchers, as is generally the case today, then poor people will be given an all but irresistible incentive to choose them over their nonpublic competitors. Private institutions that cater to the upper classes who can afford the tuition will not be adversely affected. Cities where poor people congregate will experience an unprecedented decline in parochial schools, and the people who live in them will have fewer opportunities to acquire a religious education.

More important, the potential role that black ministries can play in developing future generations of leaders in their communities will remain diminished. Education and religion will stay separate, at least for the poor. Perhaps the only people who will fully appreciate the loss are those who had the most to gain from playing the option. Nonetheless, it will become increasingly difficult within these communities and without for political representatives to ignore demands from constituents for educational alternatives. Once the prospect for choosing is put before parents by the growing number of public and private experiments sweeping across the nation, there is no turning back.

But what about those extremist political types who prey on urban neighborhoods, who may use charters and vouchers to advance a separatist agenda or promote an undemocratic ideology? What about the radical Right that operates in other regions of the country? Isn't it they who represent the real threat to American civil society insofar as school choice is concerned?

The most straightforward response one can render in the face of such concerns—and they are legitimate—is to remind those who raise them that political extremists represent a small minority of activists on the American political scene. They do not enjoy wide support from the larger population. Those groups, whether they come from the Left or the Right, should not be allowed to run charter schools; nor should they be granted authority by the states to operate private schools, let alone take advantage of publicly supported vouchers to abet their causes. No doubt some impostors may slip under the screen of public vigilance. But it is not these fringe groups that represent the most significant threat to American democracy.

The Great Dilemma of American democracy remains inequality. To the extent that choice can offer some relief, it is well worth the risk.

NOTES

1. Gunnar Myrdal, *An American Dilemma: The Negro Problem and American Democracy,* vol. 1 (New York: Harper and Row, 1944), p. lxx.
2. Robert Merton, "The Unanticipated Consequences of Purposive Social Action," *American Sociological Review* 1 (1936).
3. Christopher Jencks and Meredith Phillips, "The Black-White Test Score Gap: An Introduction," in Christopher Jencks and Meredith Phillips, eds., *The Black-White Test Score Gap* (Washington, D.C.: Brookings Institution Press, 1998).
4. Stephen Thernstrom and Abigail Thernstrom, *America in Black and White: One Nation Indivisible* (New York: Simon and Shuster, 1997), p. 19.
5. United States Department of Education, No More Excuses: The Final Report of the Hispanic Dropout Project, 1998.
6. See Jencks and Phillips, *Black-White Test Score Gap;* Susan E. Mayer and Paul E. Peterson, eds., *Earning and Learning: How Schools Matter* (Washington, D.C.: Brookings Institution Press, 1999).
7. Norman H. Nie, Jane Junn, and Kenneth Stehlik-Barry, *Education and Democratic Citizenship in America* (Chicago: University of Chicago Press, 1996).
8. Brown v. Board of Education, 347, U.S. 483, 493 (1954).
9. For opposing perspectives that reach similar conclusions see David Armor, *Forced Justice: School Desegregation and the Law* (New York: Oxford University Press, 1995); and

Gary Orfield and Susan E. Eaton, *Dismantling Desegregation: The Quiet Reversal of Brown v. Board of Education* (New York: New Press, 1997).

10. Public Agenda, *Time to Move On: African American and White Parents Set an Agenda for Public Schools* (New York: Public Agenda, 1998). See also Christine H. Rossell, "The Convergence of Black-White Attitudes on School Desegregation Issues During the Four Decade Evolution of the Plans," *William and Mary Law Review* 36 (1995).

11. See Tyce Palmaffy, "Title I: Despite the Best Intentions," in Marci Kanstoroom and Chester E. Finn, eds., *New Directions: Federal Education Policy in the Twenty-First Century* (Washington, D.C.: Thomas B. Fordham Foundation, 1999); Stanley Pogrow, "Title I: Wrong Help at the Wrong Time," in Kanstoroom and Finn, *New Directions;* David J. Hoff, "Chapter I Aid Failed to Close Learning Gap," *Education Week,* April 2, 1997.

12. National Center for Education Statistics, "National Household Education Survey," *The Condition of Education, 1997* (Washington, D.C.: U.S. Government Printing Office, U.S. Department of Education, 1997).

13. James S. Coleman, Sara D. Kelly, and John A. Moore, *Trends in School Segregation, 1968–1973* (Washington, D.C.: Urban Institute, 1975); Armor, *Forced Justice,* p. 170; Christine H. Rossell and David Armor, "The Effectiveness of School Desegregation Plans, 1968–1991," *American Politics Quarterly* 24 (July 1996).

14. See Joseph P. Viteritti, *Choosing Equality: School Choice, the Constitution and Civil Society* (Washington, D.C.: Brookings Institution Press, 1999), pp. 92–116.

15. *Civil Rights Act of 1964,* 42 U.S.C. 2000c-1, sec. 402.

16. James S. Coleman, et al., Equality of Educational Opportunity (Washington, D.C.: Office of Education, National Center for Education Statistics, 1964).

17. See Viteritti, *Choosing Equality,* pp. 92–116.

18. Derek Neal, "The Effects of Catholic Schooling on Educational Achievement," *Journal of Labor Economics* 15 (1997); William N. Evans and Robert M. Schwab, "Finishing High School and Starting College: Do Catholic Schools Make a Difference?" *Quarterly Journal of Economics* 110 (November 1995); William Sander and Anthony C. Kroutman, "Catholic Schools, Dropout Rates, and Educational Attainment," *Economic Inquiry* 33 (1995); Timothy Z. Keith and Ellis B. Page, "Do Catholic Schools Really Improve Minority Achievement?" *American Educational Research Journal* 22 (1985).

19. Henry M. Levin, "Educational Vouchers: Effectiveness, Choice, and Costs," *Journal of Policy Analysis and Management* 17 (1998).

20. Mark Schneider et al., "Shopping for Schools: In the Land of the Blind, The One Eyed Parent May Be Enough," *American Journal of Political Science* 42 (1998).

21. James S. Coleman and Thomas Hoffer, *Public, Catholic, and Private Schools: The Importance of Community* (New York: Basic, 1987).

22. Anthony S. Bryk, Valerie E. Lee, and Peter B. Holland, *Catholic Schools and the Common Good* (Cambridge: Harvard University Press, 1993); Andrew M. Greeley, *Catholic High Schools and Minority Students* (New Brunswick, N.J.: Transaction, 1982).

23. Viteritti, *Choosing Equality,* pp. 64–76; Chester E. Finn, Bruno E. Manno, and Greg Vanourek, *Charter Schools in Action: Renewing Public Education* (Princeton: Princeton University Press, 2000).

24. See the excellent symposium on "Democracy in the World: Tocqueville Reconsidered," *Journal of Democracy* 11 (January 2000).

25. William A. Galston and Peter Levine, "America's Civic Condition: A Glance at the Evidence," in E. J. Dionne, ed., *Community Works: The Renewal of Civil Society in America* (Washington, D.C.: Brookings Institution, 1998), p. 33.

26. Robert Booth Fowler, Allen D. Hertzke, and Laura R. Olsen, *Religion and Politics in America: Faith, Culture, and Strategic Choices* (Boulder, Colo.: Westview, 1999), pp. 157–58.

27. C. Eric Lincoln and Lawrence H. Mamiya, *The Black Church in the African American Experience* (Durham: Duke University Press), p. 8.

28. Sidney Verba, Kay Lehman Schlozman, and Henry E. Brady, *Voice and Equality: Civic Voluntarism in American Politics* (Cambridge: Harvard University Press, 1995), p. 18.

29. Ibid., p. 519.

30. See Eugene D. Genovese, *Roll Jordan Roll: The World the Slaves Made* (New York: Vintage, 1974). pp. 232–84.

31. See Taylor Branch, *Parting the Waters: America in the King Years, 1954–1963* (New York: Simon and Schuster, 1988); David Garrow, *Bearing the Cross: Martin Luther King and the Southern Christian Leadership Conference* (New York: Morrow, 1986).

32. Andrew Billingsly, "The Social Relevance of the Contemporary Black Church," *National Journal of Sociology* 8 (1994); Robert D. Carle and Louis A. DeCarlo, eds., *Signs of Hope: Ministries of Renewal* (Valley Forge, Pa.: Judson, 1997).

33. John J. DiIulio, "The Lord's Work: The Church and Civil Society," in Dionne, *Community Works*. See also John J. DiIulio, "Black Churches and the Inner City Poor," in Christopher H. Foreman, ed., *The African American Predicament* (Washington, D.C.: Brookings Institution Press, 1999).

34. Joan Davis Ratternay, *On the Road to Success: Students at Independent Neighborhood Schools* (rev. ed., Washington, D.C.: Institute for Independent Education, 1996). See also Gail Foster, "Black Independent Schools," in Diane Ravitch and Joseph P. Viteritti, eds., *City Schools: Lessons from New York* (Baltimore: Johns Hopkins University Press, 2000).

35. For a review of the constitutional issues, see Viteritti, *Choosing Equality*, pp. 117–44.

36. James S. Coleman, "Changes in Family and Implications for the Common School," *University of Chicago Legal Forum* (1991).

37. Mark Schneider et al., "Institutional Arrangements and the Creation of Social Capital: The Effects of Public School Choice," *American Political Science Review* 91 (1997).

Contributors

Diane Ravitch is a research professor of education in the School of Education at New York University and holds the Hermann and George R. Brown Chair in Education Policy at the Brookings Institution. She served as assistant secretary in the U.S. Department of Education from 1991 to 1993. Her most recent book is *Left Back: A Century of Failed School Reform* (2000). She is also the author of *National Standards in American Education* (1995), *The Schools We Deserve* (1985), *The Troubled Crusade: American Education, 1945–1980* (1983), *The Revisionists Revised* (1978), and *The Great School Wars: New York City, 1805–1973* (1974); coauthor of *What Do Our 17-Year-Olds Know?* (1987); editor of *The American Reader* (1991); and coeditor of *The Democracy Reader* (1992). She is a member of the National Academy of Education, the Society of American Historians, and the American Academy of Arts and Sciences.

Joseph P. Viteritti is a research professor of public policy in the Robert F. Wagner School of Public Service at New York University. He has served as a senior adviser to the heads of the New York, Boston, and San Francisco public school systems. He is the author of *Choosing Equality: School Choice, the Constitution, and Civil Society* (1999), *Across the River: Politics and Education in the City* (1983), *Bureaucracy and Social Justice* (1979), and *Police, Politics, and Pluralism in New York City* (1973). His legal scholarship has appeared in *Annual Survey of American Law* (2001), *Harvard*

Journal of Law and Public Policy (1998), *Virginia Journal of Social Policy and the Law* (1997), *Yale Law and Policy Review* (1996), *Fordham Urban Law Journal* (1995), and *Cornell Journal of Law and Public Policy* (1994).

Professors Ravitch and Viteritti are cochairpersons of the Program on Education and Civil Society at New York University. They have previously coedited *New Schools for a New Century: The Redesign of Urban Education* (1997), and *City Schools: Lessons from New York* (2000).

William Damon is director of the Center on Adolescence and professor of education at Stanford University. His books include *The Youth Charter: How Communities Can Work Together to Raise Standards for All Our Children* (1997), *Greater Expectations* (1995), *Some Do Care: Contemporary Lives of Moral Commitment* (1992), *The Moral Child* (1990), and *Self-Understanding in Childhood and Adolescence* (1988).

Jean Bethke Elshtain is the Laura Spelman Rockefeller Professor of Social and Political Ethics at the University of Chicago. Her publications include *Who Are We? Critical Reflections and Hopeful Possibilities* (2000), *New Wine in Old Bottles: Politics and Ethical Discourse* (1998), *Real Politics: Political Theory and Everyday Life* (1997), *Augustine and the Limits of Politics* (1996), *Democracy on Trial* (1995), and *Public Man, Private Woman: Women in Social and Political Thought* (1992).

Nathan Glazer is professor emeritus of education and sociology at Harvard University. He is the author of *We Are All Multiculturalists Now* (1997), *Ethnic Dilemmas, 1964–1982* (1983), and *Affirmative Discrimination* (1975); and coauthor of *Beyond the Melting Pot* (1963) and *The Lonely Crowd* (1950).

Charles L. Glenn is professor and chairman of administration, planning and policy studies in the School of Education at Boston University. His publications include *The Ambiguous Embrace: Faith-Based Schools and Social Agencies* (2000), *Educational Freedom in Eastern Europe* (1995), *Choice of Schools in Six Nations* (1989), and *The Myth of the Common School* (1988).

Gerald Grant is the Hannah Hammond Professor of Education and Sociology at Syracuse University. He is the author of *The World We Created at Hamilton High* (1988) and *The Politics of the Coleman Report* (1972). He is coauthor of *Teaching in America: The Slow Revolution* (1999), which won the Stone Prize awarded by Harvard University Press, and *The Perpetual Dream* (1978), which won the Borden Award of the American Council on Education.

Mark Holmes is professor emeritus at the Ontario Institute for Studies in Education at the University of Toronto. His books include *Making the School an Effective Community* (1989), *Educational Policy for the Pluralist Democracy: The Common School, Choice, and Diversity* (1992), and *The Reformation of Canada's Schools* (1998).

Norman Nie is research professor of political science and director of the Institute for the Quantitative Study of Society at Stanford University. He is coauthor of *Education and Democratic Citizenship in America* (1997) and *The Changing American Voter* (1976), both of which won the Woodrow Wilson Award; *Participation in America* (1972), which won the Gladys Kammaner Award; and *Participation and Political Equality* (1978). D. Sunshine Hillygus is a Ph.D. candidate in the Department of Political Science at Stanford University and a research assistant for the Stanford Institute for the Quantitative Study of Society (SIQSS).

Warren A. Nord is director of the Program in the Humanities and Human Values at the University of North Carolina, where he teaches in the Department of Philosophy. He is the author of *Religion and American Education: Rethinking a National Dilemma* (1995), and coauthor of *Taking Religion Seriously Across the Curriculum* (1998).

Robert D. Putnam is the Peter and Isabel Malkin Professor of Public Policy and former dean of the Kennedy School of Government at Harvard. He is currently president of the American Political Science Association. His publications include *Bowling Alone: Civic Disengagement in America* (2000) and *Making Democracy Work: Civic Traditions in Modern Italy* (1993).

Jack N. Rakove is the W. R. Coe Professor of History and American Studies and professor of political science at Stanford University. He is the author of *Original Meanings: Politics and Ideas in the Making of the Constitution* (1997), which won the Pulitzer Prize in history, *Declaring Rights* (1997), *James Madison and the Creation of the American Republic* (1990), and *The Beginnings of National Politics: An Interpretive History of the Continental Congress* (1979).

Rosemary C. Salomone is professor of law at St. John's University School of Law, where she has been director of the Center for Law and Policy. She is also a fellow of the Open Society Institute. Her publications include *Visions of Schooling: Conscience, Community, and Common Education* (2000) and *Equal Education Under Law: Legal Rights and Federal Policy in the Post-Brown Era* (1986).

Alan Wolfe is professor of political science and sociology, and director of the Boise Center for Religion and American Public Life at Boston College. Among his books are *Moral Freedom: The Search for Virtue in the World of Choice* (2001), *One Nation After All* (1998), *Marginalized in the Middle* (1998), and *Whose Keeper? Social Science and Moral Obligation* (1989).

Index